Teaching for Quality Learning at University

SRHE and Open University Press Imprint

Current titles include:

Teaching for Quality Learning at University

What the Student Does

4th edition

John Biggs and Catherine Tang

Society for Research into Higher Education
& Open University Press

Open University Press
McGraw-Hill Education
McGraw-Hill House
Shoppenhangers Road
Maidenhead
Berkshire
England
SL6 2QL

email: enquiries@openup.co.uk
world wide web: www.openup.co.uk

and Two Penn Plaza, New York, NY 10121-2289, USA

First edition published 1999
Second edition published 2003
Third edition published 2007
This edition published 2011

A catalogue record of this book is available from the British Library

ISBN 13: 978-0-33-524275-7
ISBN 10: 0-33-524275-8

Library of Congress Cataloging-in-Publication Data
CIP data applied for

Typeset by RefineCatch Limited, Bungay, Suffolk
Printed in the UK by Bell and Bain Ltd, Glasgow

Fictitious names of companies, products, people, characters and/or data
that may be used herein (in case studies or in examples) are not intended to
represent any real individual, company, product or event.

FSC
www.fsc.org

MIX
Paper from
responsible sources
FSC® C007785

The McGraw·Hill Companies

Learning takes place through the active behavior of the student: it is what *he* does that he learns, not what the teacher does.

Ralph W. Tyler (1949)

If students are to learn desired outcomes in a reasonably effective manner, then the teacher's fundamental task is to get students to engage in learning activities that are likely to result in their achieving those outcomes. . . . It is helpful to remember that what the student does is actually more important in determining what is learned than what the teacher does.

Thomas J. Shuell (1986)

Constructive Alignment . . . is one of the most influential ideas in higher education.

Warren Houghton (2004)

Contents

Boxes

Figures

Tables

Tasks

Foreword to original edition

The book is an exceptional introduction to some difficult ideas. It is full of downright good advice for every academic who wants to do something practical to improve his or her students' learning. So much of what we read on this subject is either a recycling of sensible advice topped by a thin layer of second-hand theory, or a dense treatise suitable for graduate students with a taste for the tougher courses. Not many writers are able to take the reader along the middle road, where theory applied with a delicate touch enables us to transform our practice. What is unique about Biggs is his way with words, his outspoken fluency, his precision, his depth of knowledge, his inventiveness, or rather how he blends all these things together. Like all good teachers, he engages us from the start, and he never talks down to us. He achieves unity between his objectives, his teaching methods and his assessment; and thus, to adapt his own phrase, he entraps the reader in a web of consistency that optimizes his or her own learning.

Perhaps not everyone will agree with Biggs's treatment of the academic differences between phenomenography and constructivism. I'm not sure I do myself. But does it matter? The author himself takes a pragmatic approach. In the daunting task that faces lecturers in responding to the pressures of mass higher education, reduced public funding, and students who are paying more for their education, the bottom line of engineering better learning outcomes matters more than nice theoretical distinctions.

Readers of the present book will especially enjoy its marvellous treatment of student assessment (particularly Chapters 3, 8 and 9).* Biggs's most outstanding single contribution to education has been the creation of the Structure of the Observed Learning Outcome (SOLO) taxonomy. Rather than read about the extraordinary practical utility of this device in secondary sources, get it from the original here. From assessing clinical decision making by medical students to classifying the outcomes of essays in history, SOLO remains the assessment apparatus of choice.

---

* This material is covered in Chapters 10, 11 and 12 in the present edition.

There are very few writers on the subject of university teaching who can engage a reader so personally, express doubts so clearly, relate research findings so eloquently to personal experience and open our eyes to the wonder around us. John Biggs is a rare thing: an author who has the humility born of generosity and intelligence to show us how he is still learning himself.

Paul Ramsden
Brisbane

Preface to fourth edition

Since the third edition of *Teaching for Quality Learning at University*, we have been consulting on the implementation of constructive alignment in Australia, Hong Kong, Ireland and Malaysia. This fourth edition draws on this experience, allowing us to say even more here about the practicalities of implementation and the evaluation of constructive alignment at work.

Also since the third edition, there has been an increasing interest in outcomes-based education as a means of coping with the expansion of post-secondary education, which in Europe has come about as a result of the Bologna Process. We are not concerned here with the managerial aspects of benchmarking across institutions that Bologna requires, but we are concerned with the quality of teaching and learning that some might say is challenged by this expansion. One of the virtues of constructive alignment in this context is that it makes quite explicit the standards needed if the intended learning outcomes are to be achieved and maintained, and it helps teachers design the teaching and learning activities that are most helpful in bringing students to achieve those outcomes. It also allows teachers to give credit for open-ended higher order outcomes, and for desirable but unintended outcomes. This is important in the present context for the criticism is often made that outcomes-based teaching is concerned only with closed skills and competencies, which is assuredly not what university education is about – and it is not what constructive alignment is about. In the last few years our experience has been more and more about implementation in and beyond the classroom to implementation institution-wide – and in the case of Malaysia, the beginning steps to implementation nationwide.

We are grateful to several anonymous reviewers of the last edition for their comments and suggestions. We have accommodated many of these where we could, but not all. For example we were asked to address such matters as students' age and ethnicity, their personal development, their levels of literacy and numeracy, even to address specific learning disabilities. These are important issues, especially now that 60 per cent of school leavers comprise the intake into university, and when, as in Australia, universities are forced to rely on international students as a major source of their income. However, in the space available here, our focus must remain on the design of a teaching and learning *system*, not on the student as a 'person'. We will say however that constructive alignment as a design for teaching is a great deal more flexible than other designs, and through reflective practice, and with the help of the writing of others on these matters, teachers can adjust teaching and assessment to allow for such differences in their own teaching context.

Given, too, the practical nature of this book, which is aimed directly at practising teachers, staff developers and administrators, we have not attempted a comprehensive update of general research into student learning, except where studies directly address the point under discussion. As before, we provide two or three tasks in every chapter. Doing those tasks as you, the reader, progress will without doubt enhance your understanding of constructive alignment, but you may prefer to tackle them if and when you are seriously attempting to implement constructive alignment in your own teaching. In that case, the tasks are virtually a 'how-to' manual. We also provide URLs for some excellent material that is 'up there' waiting to be accessed.

A note on terminology. Many different terms are used to refer to degree programmes and the unit courses making up those programmes. Bachelor's degree programmes we refer to as 'programmes', which some refer to as 'courses'. The units of study that make up programmes we call 'courses', which others refer to as 'units', modules' or 'subjects'.

Design of this book

This book is addressed to teachers, to staff developers and to administrators. Individual teachers will need to generate the solutions to the teaching problems they encounter in their classrooms. Those solutions will not be found in learning a whole new bag of teaching tricks, any one of which may or may not be useful for your particular circumstances. Solutions are likely to be found in reflecting on your teaching problems, and deriving your own ways of handling them within your departmental context (see Chapters 3 and 13). But before you can do that, you need a framework with which to structure your reflections. Constructive alignment provides such a framework, anchoring teaching decisions all the time to aiding students in achieving the intended learning outcomes and assessing how well they do so.

Staff developers, for their part, will continue to work with individuals in generic stand-alone workshops. However, in keeping with the idea that the responsibility for teaching lies not on how well individual teachers perform but on the departmental and institutional infrastructure, staff developers need especially to work with departments on their teaching programmes, and with administration to get the institutional policies and procedures right on teaching-related matters.

University administrators need to have policies and procedures in place that support innovative, and particularly outcomes-based, teaching. This would include such things as abolishing norm-referenced assessment requirements, and ensuring that the ubiquitous teaching evaluation questionnaires do not assume, as typically they do, that lecturing is the default teaching method. How the institution may be reflective is addressed in Chapter 13, together with the closely related theme of quality enhancement of teaching.

All three of teachers, staff developers and administrators need to immerse themselves in the 'scholarship of teaching' (Boyer 1990). Academics have always been teachers, but the first priority of the majority is to keep up with developments in their content discipline and to contribute to them through research. Developing teaching expertise usually takes second place: a set of priorities dictated as much by institutional structures and reward systems as by individual choice. But there is another body of knowledge, apart from their content areas, that academics also have a responsibility to address. This is the scholarship of teaching and learning, or SoTL as it is called: the body of knowledge that underwrites good teaching, much of which is addressed in this book.

Part 1: Effective teaching and learning for today's universities

In Chapter 1, we look at how universities have changed in the short course of this century, and how an outcomes-based approach to teaching and learning seems well suited to the changing context. Chapter 2 presents some of the research on student learning that helps in designing more effective teaching. Students can use effective (deep) and ineffective (surface) approaches to their learning, so that effective teaching maximizes the former and minimizes the latter. Chapter 3 sets the stage for effective teaching by looking at what 'motivating' students might mean and what the climate for teaching might be like: this requires that teachers reflect on what they are doing, why they are doing it and if it can be done more effectively. Chapter 4 describes contexts for effective teaching and learning that apply to all modes of teaching. Chapter 5 delves into the nature of what we teach, describing the natures of declarative and functioning knowledge and how we need to articulate levels of understanding these forms of knowledge. Chapter 6 describes how constructive alignment came about and explains how it fits into the outcomes-based model of teaching and learning.

Part 2: Designing constructively aligned outcomes-based teaching and learning

Part 2 describes how a constructively aligned system of outcomes-based teaching may be designed. Chapter 7 looks at intended learning outcomes at three levels: graduate outcomes, programme outcomes and course outcomes, focusing on declarative or functioning knowledge as appropriate. Chapters 8 and 9 go into the design of teaching/learning activities for declarative and functioning outcomes respectively. Principles of assessment are discussed in Chapter 10, and assessment for declarative and functioning outcomes in the next two chapters.

Part 3: Constructive alignment in action

Having discussed the theory and design of constructively aligned teaching, Chapter 13 discusses questions of how best to implement constructive alignment at various levels: course and department, faculty and school, the whole institution, and beyond, looking at the implications for policy and support at the various levels. We then summarize what the research says about the effectiveness of constructively aligned teaching. In Chapter 14, we present several examples of implementing constructive alignment at various levels, with particular emphasis on a variety of courses, whose designers have been willing to share their work with us. Perhaps Part 3 will convince any readers who might have lingering doubts that constructive alignment is not pie in the sky but eminently manageable, workable and effective.

John Biggs, Catherine Tang
Hobart, Tasmania

Acknowledgements

As was stated in the acknowledgements in the first three editions, there are many ideas in this book that came about through interacting with friends and colleagues over the years. These are not repeated here.

For this edition, we thank Professor Paul Lam, Professor Lilian Vrijmoed and Cheung Hokling of the City University of Hong Kong, Dr Eva Wong of the Hong Kong Baptist University, and Professor Mohd. Majid Konting and Mr Zulhazmi from the Centre for Learning and Teaching of Higher Education Leadership Academy (AKEPT), Ministry of Higher Education, Malaysia, for their various modes of assistance. We would also like to thank Denise Chalmers and Paul Ramsden who have been directly helpful in providing stimulation, ideas and content for this edition. We are also grateful to those teachers who have allowed us to include their courses and other teaching materials as examples of constructive alignment in practice, and who names are acknowledged in the text as they appear.

Finally, we must thank Katy Hamilton, Louise Caswell, Shona Mullen and Catriona Watson of McGraw-Hill/Open University Press who have seen us through this edition, patiently and helpfully.

John Biggs, Catherine Tang

The outcomes we intend readers to achieve

When you have read this book you should be able to:

1 develop a personal theory of teaching that enables you to reflect upon and improve your own teaching;
2 explain to a colleague what 'constructive alignment' is about and its application to designing a curriculum;
3 write a set of no more than five or six *intended learning outcomes*, each containing a key 'learning verb', for a semester-long course you are teaching;
4 reflect on your current teaching using the constructive alignment framework and devise:

- *teaching/learning activities* that address your course intended learning outcomes and that activate those key verbs;
- *assessment tasks* that likewise address those key verbs;
- *rubrics* or criteria for assessment that enable judgements to be made as to how well those outcomes have been addressed.

5 develop quality enhancement processes for your own teaching;
6 reflect on the quality assurance and enhancement processes within your institution and suggest improvement of these processes to further support the implementation of constructively aligned teaching.

Part 1

Effective teaching and learning for today's universities

1

The changing scene in university teaching

Since 2000 there have been dramatic changes in the nature of higher education. It is not just that participation rates are higher than ever, bringing much greater diversity in the student population, but that these and other factors have altered the main mission of higher education and modes of delivery. One consequence is that the major thrust in teaching is more on professional and vocational programmes and concerns about teaching effectiveness. The 'Robert and Susan problem' illustrates how increased student diversity challenges teaching. Susan is academically committed and will learn well, virtually whatever the teaching; Robert is at university simply to obtain a good job, he is not academically inclined, and he represents the student who would not have been at university years ago. We argue that teaching that requires active engagement by students decreases the gap between Susan and Robert. Just so, today's universities need to address the quality of teaching and learning. The Bologna Process requires member countries of the European Union to put in place national qualification frameworks to define learning outcomes at various degree levels, with quality assurance systems. Similar concerns in universities worldwide have led increasingly to the adoption of one form or another of outcomes-based teaching learning (OBTL). The form of OBTL outlined and exemplified in this book is constructive alignment. This book outlines the theory and implementation of constructively aligned OBTL, with hands-on tasks and detailed examples.

The nature of the change worldwide

The university sector in countries worldwide continues to change at an increasingly hectic rate. In a 2009 report to UNESCO, Altbach et al. (2009) review trends in higher education and come to the conclusion that:

> Arguably, the developments of the recent past are at least as dramatic as those in the 19th century when the research university evolved, first in

Germany and then elsewhere, and fundamentally redesigned the nature of the university worldwide. The academic changes of the late 20th and early 21st centuries are more extensive in that they are truly global and affect many more institutions and populations.

(Altbach et al. 2009: 3)

The UNESCO Report deals with all aspects of higher education, but here we are concerned only with those aspects that bear upon teaching and learning. These would include increasing participation rates, or 'massification', and inevitably with that an overall lowering of academic standards as universities and student populations become yet more diversified (Altbach et al. 2009). In the 1990s the participation rate was around 15%; now it is over 40% in many countries, and some politicians are signalling a target of up to 60%. The brightest and most committed students still go to university, as they have in the past, but so do proportionately more students of rather different academic bent. Thus, for financial, academic and vocational reasons, more professionally or vocationally oriented programmes are required and more institutions that serve different needs and constituencies from the traditional academic ones. But even within the same university, the range of ability within classes is now considerable, which presents teaching-related problems to staff.

As participation rates increase, institutions are relying more and more on student fees. This means that students demand high profile programmes that are well taught and will enhance their employment prospects. Some, using the logic that education is a commodity to be bought, feel that having paid for a degree they are entitled to be awarded one. The pressures on staff are complex and in some cases have had the effect of encouraging lower standards. Such downward pressures, in some celebrated cases, have also emanated from administration, because of the funding implications of failing students. A twist in this issue in universities in western countries is that international students have become a highly significant source of funding, thus introducing another pressure-point on the maintenance of standards (Burke and Jopson 2005).

These pressures and the changing nature of the institution have brought about increased concern with the quality assurance – or, as we would rather have it, the quality enhancement – of teaching and learning. But first let us look at the question of diversity within the classroom.

Student diversity

One major source of diversity is the massive worldwide movement of international students, mostly from the Asian and African continents to universities in the West, to provide an important source of income to those receiving universities. While international students undoubtedly have specials needs with regard to provision for language and social support, problems of learning in a second language, of homesickness, of cultural isolation, these are areas that need to be addressed by other supportive specialists and structures, not necessarily by their classroom teachers. Ethnic diversity in the classroom undoubtedly raises issues of teaching and learning but, as was argued in previous editions of this book, teaching that engages students' learning activities appropriately minimizes differences of ethnicity between students as far as learning itself is concerned. This problem is somewhat related to that of the differences between Susan and Robert discussed below; in both cases, actively engaging students in their learning becomes the issue.

Another source of diversity, then, is the academic orientation and commitment of students. Maintaining standards when the commitment and range of ability of students are so varied presents an interesting teaching challenge that in previous editions we have called the 'Robert and Susan problem'.

Let us look at two students attending a lecture. Susan is academically committed; she is bright, interested in her studies and wants to do well. She has clear academic or career plans and what she learns is important to her. When she learns, she goes about it in an 'academic' way. She comes to the lecture with sound, relevant background knowledge, possibly some questions she wants answering. In the lecture, she finds an answer to a preformed question; it forms the keystone for a particular arch of knowledge she is constructing. Or it may not be the answer she is looking for and she speculates, wondering why it isn't. In either event, she reflects on the personal significance of what she is learning. Students like Susan virtually teach themselves; they do not need much help from us. Academics like the Susans – indeed, they were once Susans themselves – so they tend to assume that she represents how most students learn, and they teach accordingly.

Now take Robert. He is at university not out of a driving curiosity about a particular subject, or a burning ambition to excel in a particular profession, but to obtain a qualification for a decent job. A few years ago, prior to the Bologna Process say (see below), he would never have considered going to university. He is less committed than Susan, possibly not as bright, academically speaking. He has little background of relevant knowledge. He comes to lectures with no or few questions. He wants only to put in sufficient effort to pass and obtain that meal ticket. Robert hears the lecturer say the same words as Susan is hearing but he doesn't see a keystone, just another brick to be recorded in his lecture notes. He believes that if he can record enough of these bricks and can remember them on cue, he'll keep out of trouble come exam time.

Students like Robert are in higher proportions in today's classes. They need help if they are to reach acceptable levels of achievement. To say that Robert is 'unmotivated' may be true, but it is unhelpful. All it means is that he is not responding to the methods that work for Susan, the likes of whom were sufficiently visible in most classes in the good old days to satisfy us that our teaching *did* work. But, of course, it was the students who were doing the work and getting the results, not our teaching.

The challenge we face as teachers is to teach so that Robert learns more in the manner of Susan. Figure 1.1 suggests that the present differences between Robert and Susan (point A) may be lessened by appropriate teaching (point B). Three factors are operating:

High level engagement

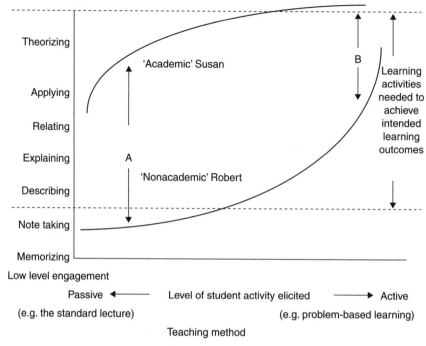

Figure 1.1 Student orientation, teaching method and level of engagement

- the students' levels of engagement in relation to the level of learning activity required to achieve the intended learning outcomes (ranging from 'describing' to 'theorizing', as between the dashed lines in Figure 1.1;
- the degree of learning-related activity that a teaching method is likely to stimulate;
- the academic orientation of the students.

Point A is towards the 'passive' end of the teaching method continuum, where there is a large gap between Susan's and Robert's levels of engagement. A lecture would be an example of such passive teaching and we get the picture just described: Susan working at a high level of engagement within the target range of learning activities (relating, applying and theorizing from time to time), Robert taking notes and memorizing, activities that are below the target range of activities. If you compare this with Figure 2.1 (on p. 29), you will see that Susan is using a 'deep' approach, comprising learning activities appropriate to the outcomes, while Robert is using a 'surface' approach, meaning that he is operating below the cognitive level required.

At point B, towards the 'active' end of the teaching method continuum, the gap between Susan and Robert is not so wide. Robert is actually using many of the learning activities needed to achieve the intended learning outcomes. Problem-based learning would be an example of an active teaching method, because it requires students to question, to speculate, to generate solutions, so that Robert is encouraged to use the higher order cognitive activities that Susan uses spontaneously. The teaching has narrowed the gap between their ways of going about learning and between their respective performances. This is because the teaching environment requires the students to go through learning activities that are designed to help them achieve the intended outcomes.

Of course, there are limits to what students can do that are beyond the teacher's control – a student's ability is one – but ability after a certain level isn't the only determinant of performance or even the major one. There are other things that are within our control, and capitalizing on them is what good teaching is all about. Although Figure 1.1 is a hypothetical graph, it helps us to define good teaching, as follows:

Good teaching is getting most students to use the level of cognitive processes needed to achieve the intended outcomes that the more academic students use spontaneously.

Good teaching is unlikely to close the gap between the Susans and the Roberts of this world completely, but it should certainly narrow it. How that can be done is one of the major issues we address in this book.

The Bologna Process

In the twentieth century, standards, procedures, staffing, degree structures and academic freedom varied enormously across European universities. In some countries, courses and even staff appointment had to be approved by parliament. With the creation of the European Union in 1993, greatly increased movement between countries for employment and for further study meant that something had to be done to make transfer across educational institutions possible and equitable. Ministers of education from 27 countries met in Bologna in 1999, and given also the backdrop of globalization, the Bologna Process was set in motion. The following details were obtained from the official website (Bologna Process 2010).

Today, 47 European countries are committed to the Process, which aims to create a European Higher Education Area (EHEA) based on international cooperation and academic exchange in order to

- facilitate mobility of students, graduates and higher education staff;
- prepare students for their future careers and for life as active citizens in democratic societies, and to support their personal development;
- offer broad access to high-quality higher education.

Countries are currently setting up national qualifications frameworks that are compatible with the overarching framework of qualifications for the European Higher Education Area. The qualifications frameworks define learning outcomes for each of bachelor, master and doctorate levels, describing what learners should know, understand and be able to do on the basis of a given qualification. If a degree is commenced in one university and completed in another there must be assurance as to the quality and equivalence of the degrees so that credit transfers are equitable. Accordingly, there is common agreement as to quality assurance and recognition of foreign degrees and other higher education qualifications.

The Process also includes areas of broader societal relevance, such as the links between higher education, research and innovation; equitable participation and lifelong learning and links to higher education systems outside Europe. Regular meetings of European ministers of education determine priorities and set up working groups to make recommendations. Coming priorities include: equitable access and completion, lifelong learning, employability, student-centred learning and the teaching mission of higher education, research and innovation, international openness, mobility between institutions, and others. Lifelong learning is seen as a central issue, involving greater focus on: recognition of prior learning, including non-formal and informal learning; student-centred flexible modes of delivery and wider access to higher education.

To achieve these aims, each country will operate a quality assurance agency to which are referred all the policies, ongoing review processes and actions that are designed to ensure that institutions, programmes and qualifications meet and maintain specified standards of education, scholarship and infrastructure. Institutions and stakeholders in higher education are thereby provided with some sort of assurance that quality and accountability are being achieved. Enhancement and improvement of higher education systems, institutions and programmes are also concerns.

The Bologna Process is clearly a major step towards improving teaching and learning on a massive scale, across the whole of Europe no less, but there are dangers. Benchmarking and credit transfer may threaten one of the important characteristics of the university: the pursuit of excellence. Ideally, departments should build on their strengths so that they become renowned for their research and teaching in a specific area of the discipline. Credit transfers, however, may work on the equivalence not only of standards but also of curriculum, so the net effect is likely not to differentiate universities but to homogenize their offerings. Care must be taken that credit transfers do not 'dumb down' institutions to the standards of the weakest. Many stakeholders are aware of this problem, claiming that market forces will force universities to continue to offer better quality, and/or different, programmes than the opposition. Another way, implied by Altbach et al. (2009), relying more on government deliberation than on market forces, would be to set up sectors of universities, the equivalent perhaps of Ivy League, state and private universities, with credit transfers permissible within, but not across, sectors.

While Bologna is essentially a transnational managerial process, it has strong implications for teaching at the institutional and individual classroom levels. Although Bologna does not explicitly prescribe an outcomes-based approach to teaching and learning (a search through the Bologna documents for 'outcomes-based' did not yield any results), the emphasis on student-centred learning, and on learning outcomes at bachelor, masters and doctoral levels, certainly suggests one, as does the emphasis on lifelong learning, which is a common graduate outcome. Huet et al. (2009) point out that this will involve a paradigm shift towards a more learner-centred approach, especially in many southern European countries where the teaching model is teacher centred, and to achieve this an effective use of learning outcomes requires knowledge of 'the pedagogy of teaching and learning and [of] the concept of constructive alignment' (p. 276). They advocate the use of 'curriculum maps' to facilitate alignment between learning outcomes, learning activities and assessment tasks. The design and implementation of constructive alignment is the theme of this book, and we turn specifically to the use of such maps in Chapter 7.

Putting Bologna together with other developments in western and some Asian countries, then, we may conclude that there is a strong move towards a more student-centred approach to teaching and learning, marked especially by designing curricula in terms of the outcomes students are meant to achieve at different levels.

Let us spell this approach out in more detail.

Improving teaching: towards learning outcomes

In meeting these demands for improved teaching for a broader range of students, many universities are funding staff development centres, or centres for teaching and learning, on a larger scale than previously; they are recognizing research into teaching one's content area as legitimate research. But perhaps the most important ways of improving teaching are:

1 recognizing that good teaching is as much a function of institution-wide infrastructure as it is a gift with which some lucky academics are born. Thus, policies and procedures that encourage good teaching and assessment across the whole institution need to be put in place.
2 shifting the focus from the teacher to the learner, and specifically, to define what *learning outcomes* students are meant to achieve when teachers address the topics they are meant to teach.

These two points are mutually supportive. The point about focusing on learning outcomes was first made explicit on a systemic basis in the Dearing Report (1997) in the United Kingdom. Today probably most UK universities describe course and programme outcomes in terms of the outcomes students are intended to attain, although how far these filter through into fully blown outcomes-based teaching and learning varies between institutions. In other countries, including Australia, New Zealand, South Africa and North America, individual universities are moving towards outcomes-based teaching and learning (OBTL). In Hong Kong, the move is system-wide. The then Chairman of the University Grants Committee (UGC), Alice Lam, wrote:

'The UGC's goal in promoting outcome-based approaches is simple and straightforward – improvement and enhancement in student learning and teaching quality' (Letter to Hong Kong universities, May 15, 2006).

Today all eight universities in Hong Kong are moving at their own pace to outcomes-based approaches to student learning (OBASL), as the UGC puts it – we say more about the Hong Kong situation in Chapter 14, as it is one in which we have been directly involved. Currently, Malaysia is moving nationally to implement OBTL in over 1000 post-secondary institutions (Biggs and Tang, in press). The Bologna Process, involving 47 countries in the European Union, is an even larger scale attempt to improve teaching, again with an emphasis on learning outcomes.

Outcomes-based teaching and learning (OBTL)

In outcomes-based teaching and learning (OBTL) we state what we intend the general outcomes a graduate of a university should achieve, and following from that, we derive the content-based programme and specific course level outcomes. Graduate outcomes recall the older notion of teaching goals, but placing them in a more systematic context. In a wide ranging survey of nearly 3000 university teachers, Angelo and Cross (1993) identified six goal clusters that teachers might address:

1 higher order thinking skills
2 basic academic success skills
3 discipline-specific knowledge and skills
4 liberal arts and academic values
5 work and career development
6 personal development.

This work was done nearly twenty years ago when institutions did not spell out mission statements to the extent that most do today. Graduate outcomes, also called 'graduate attributes', are outcomes of the total university experience, such as creativity, independent problem solving, professional skills, critical thinking, communication skills, teamwork, as well as lifelong learning. Graduate outcomes are conceived in mainly two different ways: as *generic*, comprising context-free qualities or attributes of individuals, as if graduates would be 'creative' whatever they do; or as *embedded*, that is, as abilities or ways of handling issues that are context dependent, so that creativity is only intended to apply in a graduate's content area. We take the embedded view here, as developed in Chapter 7. The generic view of graduate attributes claims that graduates would be creative, or think critically, whatever content they were dealing with. This is not the way it works. These context-free claims reify the attribute, making it a personality characteristic so that its acquisition becomes a matter of personality change. Such claims are exaggerated to serve a different agenda, justifying the criticism by Hussey and Smith (2002) that outcomes 'have been misappropriated and adopted widely . . . to facilitate the managerial process'. We see the purpose of

OBTL not to serve a managerial agenda, but as stated by Hong Kong's UGC: the 'improvement and enhancement in student learning and teaching quality'.

Graduate outcomes guide the design of the intended learning outcomes for the programme and its constituent courses. In this way, both higher order thinking and basic academic skills are written into the intended learning outcomes of the programme, and then of the courses making up the programme, rather than leaving it to the individual teacher to decide. The question of designing outcomes at university, programme and course levels is explained in Chapter 7.

A course outcome statement tells us how we would recognize if or how well students have learned what it is intended they should learn and be able to do. This is different from the usual teacher-based curriculum, which simply lists the topics for teachers to 'cover'. That is, an outcome statement tells us what students should be able to do after teaching, and how well they should do it, when they were unable, or only partially able, to do it before teaching. Good teachers have always had some idea of that – that is one reason why they are good teachers. In outcomes-based teaching and learning, we are simply making that as explicit as we can – always allowing for unintended but desirable outcomes. Teachers and critics often overlook that students may also learn outcomes that hadn't been foreseen but which are eminently desirable. Our assessment strategies should allow for these unexpected or unintended outcomes, as discussed in Chapter 10.

In OBTL, assessment is carried out by seeing how well a student's performance compares to the criteria in the outcome statement; that is, assessment is criterion referenced. Students are not assessed according to how their performances compare with each other and then graded according to a predetermined distribution such as the bell curve (these issues are discussed in Chapter 10). Ideally, in OBTL an assessment task requires the student to perform the intended outcome itself – which is often not easily achieved by giving students questions to which they write answers in an invigilated exam room.

Constructive alignment, the theme of this book and its previous editions, differs from other forms of outcomes-based teaching and learning in that teaching is also addressed, in order to increase the likelihood of most students achieving those outcomes. In constructive alignment we systematically align the teaching/learning activities, as well as the assessment tasks, to the intended learning outcomes. This is done by requiring the students to engage the *learning activities* required in the outcomes. Talking about the topic, as in traditional teaching, rarely does that directly as lecturing requires the students minimally to listen and to take notes. Only the really academic students, the Susans, go further and question, interpret or reflect. It is getting Robert to engage these learning activities that brings him closer to Susan's way of learning (see Figure 1.1)

All this might sound difficult, time consuming and way too idealistic. That is not what an increasingly large number of university teachers are finding. This book will explain the background and lead you through all the stages of implementing constructive alignment, but using the outcomes-based terminology that is now current.

Task 1.1 The changing scene at your own institution

Reflect on your own institution, identify any changes that you are aware of which have affected your decision made or actions taken related to teaching and learning as a teacher/staff developer/administrator.

Changes at your institution:

_____

_____

_____

Your decisions/actions related to teaching and learning based on the changes:

_____

_____

_____

When you have finished this book, revisit these decision/actions and see if you would have acted differently.

Summary and conclusions

The nature of the change worldwide

Since 2000 there has been a dramatic change in the nature of higher education. Participation rates have greatly increased, which has created much diversity both among the nature of programmes offered and in the student population. Classrooms must cater for a diverse range of students, all demanding the quality teaching they believe they have paid for and should be receiving. As a result, universities are much more concerned with improving teaching and maintaining quality assurance of teaching than hitherto. It is inevitable that universities will specialize, as one way of coping with diversity, but the real problem of diversity lies within universities and within classrooms.

Student diversity

Ethnic diversity is greatly expanded especially in western universities with increasing numbers of international students studying abroad. While this calls for much non-academic support in terms of learning in a second language, social adjustment and counselling, the pedagogical issues are somewhat similar to those met when dealing with diversity of academic commitment. 'Academic' Susan hardly needs teaching: she is motivated, knowledgeable and actively learning even while sitting quietly in a lecture. 'Non-academic' Robert, who previously would not be at university, is unsure of his goals, is doing subjects that don't really interest him and sits passively in class. There is a large gap between Susan's performance and Robert's. However, if teaching actively engages Robert in appropriate learning activities, the gap between him and Susan will decrease. Coping with academic diversity in the universities of the twenty-first century becomes largely a matter of improving teaching and learning.

The Bologna Process

The Bologna Process is an ambitious attempt to improve teaching across 47 countries Europe-wide. It requires member countries to define learning outcomes for all degrees, to establish national degree frameworks and quality assurance mechanisms, and to address wider social issues such as promoting lifelong learning as a university outcome. While the Bologna Process was originally intended to facilitate credit transfers between institutions in different countries equitably, it has become a reflection of what is happening worldwide – or some might argue that what is happening worldwide is a reflection of Bologna. All these changes point to an increasing use of outcomes-based teaching and learning.

Improving teaching: towards learning outcomes

A major feature of the change in universities is a fresh orientation to the responsibility of teaching, so that teaching is seen not so much as the responsibility of individual teachers as of the entire institution, with policies, staff development and quality assurance of teaching being put in place. In line with this, there has been a concern with anchoring performance in learning outcomes. Outcomes-based teaching and learning is in place in many universities in several countries, with some whole countries requiring teaching to become outcomes based.

Outcomes-based teaching and learning (OBTL)

Graduate outcomes, also called 'graduate attributes', are outcomes of the total university experience. They include such things as creativity, problem solving, professional skills, communication skills, teamwork, and lifelong learning, which should be contextualized in the programmes and courses students undertake. Graduate outcomes thus guide the design of programmes and courses. In OBTL, the concern is not so much a matter of what topics to teach, but what outcomes students are supposed to have achieved after having been taught. Defining those intended learning outcomes becomes the important issue, and assessment is criterion-referenced to see how well the outcomes have been attained. Constructive alignment goes one step further than most outcomes-based approaches in that, as well as assessment tasks, teaching and learning activities are also aligned to the outcomes, in order that students are helped to achieve those outcomes more effectively. How all this is achieved is the subject of this book.

Further reading

On trends in higher education

Altbach, P.G., Reisberg, L. and Rumbley, L.E. (2009) *Trends in Global Higher Education: Tracking an Academic Revolution.* Report for the UNESCO 2009 World Conference on Higher Education.

The UNESCO Report deals with all aspects of higher education apart from teaching and learning: globalization, access and equity, quality assurance and accountability, finance, the academic profession, the student experience, information and communication technology, distance education, research, links to industry and future trends. It is a comprehensive and up-to-date survey that provides excellent background for putting this chapter in context.

Dearing, R. (1997) *Higher Education in the Learning Society*, Report of the National Committee of Inquiry into Higher Education (Dearing Report). Norwich: HMSO.

The first major thrust towards outcomes-based education in the UK.

Bologna Process (2010) http://www.ond.vlaanderen.be/hogeronderwijs/bologna/ (accessed 2 February 2011).

This is the official website of the Bologna Process and it gives the history of the project, current developments, priorities and meetings and associated documents.

Gonzalez, J. and Wagenaar, R. (eds) (2008) *Universities' Contribution to the Bologna Process: An Introduction*, 2nd edn. Bilbao, Spain: Universidad Deusto.

http://www.tuning.unideusto.org/tuningeu/index.php?option=com_frontpage& Itemid=1 (accessed 2 February 2011).

A publication of the Tuning Project, which was set up to allow credit transfers between universities in the Bologna Process. However, as they explain, 'The name *Tuning* was chosen for the project to reflect the idea that universities do not look for uniformity in their degree programmes or any sort of unified, prescriptive or definitive European curricula but simply for points of reference, convergence and common understanding.' The Project distinguishes between generic competences and subject-specific competences and is producing booklets for major subject areas.

Dealing with diversity

Buckridge, M. and Guest, R. (2007) A conversation about pedagogical responses to increased diversity in university classrooms, *Higher Education Research and Development*, 26: 133–46.

Margaret, a staff developer, and Ross, an economics teacher, hold a dialogue about dealing with the increasingly large number of Roberts sitting alongside the Susans in our classes. Is it fair to Susan to divert resources from her in order to deal with Robert? Is it fair to Robert if you don't? Is it really possible to obtain the optimum from each student in the same overcrowded class? Read, and draw your own conclusions.

http://www.deakin.edu.au/itl/pd/tl-modules/teaching-approach/diversity/ (accessed 2 February 2011).

'Dealing with diversity at Deakin' is an interactive module given by the Institute for Teaching and Learning at Deakin University. This website presents eight topics on diversity among university students.

Shaw, G. (ed) (2005) *Tertiary Teaching: Dealing with Diversity.* Darwin, Australia: Charles Darwin University Press and The Centre for Learning Research, Charles Darwin University.

2

Teaching according to how students learn

How effectively we teach depends, first, on what we think teaching is. Three levels of thinking about teaching are distinguished. The first two are 'blame' models, the first blaming the learner, the second the teacher. The third model integrates learning and teaching, seeing effective teaching as encouraging students to use the learning activities most likely to achieve the outcomes intended. To do this requires some knowledge of how students learn. Students may use learning activities that are of lower cognitive level than are needed to achieve the outcomes, resulting in a *surface* approach to learning; or they can use high level activities appropriate to achieving the intended outcomes, resulting in a *deep* approach to learning. Good teaching is that which supports the appropriate learning activities and discourages inappropriate ones.

Levels of thinking about teaching

All teachers have some theory of what teaching is, even if they are not explicitly aware of that theory. Teachers' theories deeply affect the kind of learning environment they create in their classrooms (Trigwell and Prosser 1991; Gow and Kember 1993). Three common theories of teaching exist, which teachers tend to hold at different points in their teaching career. In fact, these levels describe a sequence in the development of teachers' thinking and practice: a route map towards reflective teaching, if you like. The level at which a teacher operates depends on what is the focus of teaching.

But before discussing different theories of teaching and learning, what are your theories (Task 2.1)?

Task 2.1 What are your theories of teaching and learning?

Learning is _____

_____

_____

_____

_____

Teaching is _____

_____

_____

_____

_____

When you have finished this chapter, you will revisit these statements.

Now let's see what others think.

Level 1. Focus: what the student is

Teachers at Level 1 focus on the differences between students, as most beginning teachers do: there are good students, like Susan, and poor students, like Robert. Level 1 teachers see their responsibility as knowing their content well, and expounding it clearly. Thereafter, it's up to the student to attend lectures, to listen carefully, to take notes, to read the recommended readings, and to make sure it's taken on board and unloaded on cue. Susan does – good student; Robert doesn't – poor student.

At Level 1, teaching is in effect held constant – it is transmitting information, usually by lecturing – so differences in learning are attributed to differences between students in ability, motivation, what sort of school they went to, A level results, cultural background and so on. Ability is usually believed to be the most important factor in determining students' performance, assessment being the instrument for sorting the more able from the less able students after teaching is over. Many common but counterproductive practices spring from this belief, one being that teaching is not an educative activity so much as a *selective* one, the purpose being to separate the good learners from the poor learners. This belief bedevils much common assessment practice, as we discuss in Chapter 10. The curriculum in Level 1 teaching becomes a list of items of content that, once expounded from the podium, has been 'covered'.

How the students receive and deal with that content, and what their depth of understanding of it might be, are not specifically addressed.

Level 1 is founded on a *quantitative* way of thinking about learning and teaching (Cole 1990), which manifests itself most obviously in assessment practices, such as 'marking', that is, counting the number of correct points, or rating aspects of students' performances on arbitrary scales. We examine this model, its manifestations and its consequences, in Chapter 10.

The view of university teaching as transmitting information is so widely accepted that teaching and assessment the world over are based on it. Teaching rooms and media are specifically designed for one-way delivery. A teacher is the knowledgeable expert, the sage on the stage, who expounds the information the students are to absorb and to report back accurately. How well students do these things depends, in this view, on their ability, on their motivation, and even on their ethnicity, as Asian students are frequently but unfairly and inaccurately stereotyped as 'rote-learners' (Biggs 1996a).

Explaining the variability in student learning on students' characteristics is a *blame-the-student* theory of teaching. When students don't learn (that is, when teaching breaks down), it is due to something the students are lacking, as exemplified in the following comments:

> *How can I be expected to teach that lot with those A level results? They wouldn't even have been admitted 10 years ago.*

> *They lack any motivation at all.*

> *These students lack suitable study skills. But that's not my problem, they'll have to go to the counselling service.*

In themselves, these statements may well be true: school leaving results might be poor, students nowadays may be less academically oriented. As we saw in Chapter 1, that is precisely the *challenge* for teachers to teach well, not their excuse for poor teaching.

Blame-the-student is a comfortable theory of teaching. If students don't learn, it's not because there is anything wrong with the teaching, it's because they are incapable, unmotivated, foreign or the possessors of some other nonacademic defect which is not the teacher's responsibility to correct. Level 1 teaching is totally unreflective. It doesn't occur to the teacher to ask the key generative question: 'What else could I be doing that might make them learn more effectively?' And until they do ask that, their teaching is unlikely to change.

Level 2. Focus: what the teacher does

Teachers at Level 2 focus on what teachers do. This view of teaching is still based on transmission, but transmitting concepts and understandings, not just information (Prosser and Trigwell 1999). The responsibility for 'getting it across' now rests to a significant extent on what the teacher does. The possibility is entertained that there may be more effective ways of teaching than what one is currently doing, which is a major advance. Learning is seen as more a function of what the teacher is doing than a function of what sort of student one has to deal with.

The teacher who operates at Level 2 works at obtaining an armoury of teaching skills. The material to be 'got across' includes complex understandings, which requires much more than chalk and talk. Consider the following:

> *I'll settle them down with some music, then an introductory spiel: where we were last week, what we're going to do today. Then a video clip followed by a buzz session. The questions they're to address will be on the OH. I'll then fire six questions at them to be answered individually. Yes, four at the back row, finger pointing, that'll stir that lot up. Then I speak to the answers for about seven minutes, working in those two jokes I looked up. Wrap up, warning them there's an exam question hidden in today's session (moans of 'Now he tells us!' yuk, yuk). Mention what's coming up for next week, and meantime they're to read Chapter 10 of Bronowski.*

Plenty of variation in technique here, probably – almost certainly – a good student response, but the focus of this description is entirely teacher-centred. It's about what *I* the teacher am doing, not on what *they* the students are learning.

Traditional approaches to staff development for teachers often work on what the teacher does, as do 'how to' courses and books that provide tips for teachers and prescriptive advice on getting it across more effectively, advice such as:

* Establish clear procedural rules at the outset, such as signals for silence.
* Ensure clarity. Project the voice, use clear visual aids.
* Eye contact with students while talking.
* Don't interrupt a large lecture with handouts as chaos is likely.

This is certainly useful advice, but it is concerned with *management*, not with facilitating learning. Good management is important, but it is a means of setting the stage on which good learning may occur; it is not as an end in itself.

Level 2 is also a deficit model, the 'blame' this time being on the teacher. It is a view of teaching often held by university administrators, because it provides a rationale for making personnel decisions. Good teachers are those who have lots of teaching competencies. Does Dr Jones 'have' the appropriate competencies for tertiary level teaching? If not, he had better show evidence that he has by the time his contract comes up for renewal. However, teaching competencies may have little to do with teaching effectiveness. A competency, such as constructing a reliable multiple-choice test, is useful only if it is appropriate to one's teaching purposes to *use* a multiple-choice test. Likewise, managing educational technology, or questioning skills, or any of the other competencies tertiary teachers should 'have', should not be isolated from the context in which they are being used. Knowing what to do is important only if you know why, when and how you should do it. The focus should not be on the skill itself, but on whether its deployment has the desired effect on student learning.

Which brings us to the third level of teaching.

Level 3. Focus: what the student does

Teachers at Level 3 focus on what the student does and how that relates to teaching. Level 3 is a student-centred model of teaching; the purpose of teaching is to support learning. No longer is it possible to say: 'I taught them, but they didn't learn.' Expert teaching includes mastery over a variety of teaching techniques, but unless learning takes place, they are irrelevant. The focus in Level 3 is on what the student does and on how well the intended outcomes are achieved.

This implies a view of teaching that is not just about facts, concepts and principles to be covered and understood, but which also requires us to be clear about:

1 what it is the students are to learn and what are the intended or desirable outcomes of their learning;
2 what it means for students to 'understand' content in the way that is stipulated in the intended learning outcomes;
3 what kind of teaching/learning activities are required to achieve those stipulated levels of understanding.

Levels 1 and 2 did not address these questions. The first question requires that we specify what we intend students to be able to do after we have taught a topic. It's just not good enough for us to talk about it or teach with an impressive array of visual aids: the whole point, how well the students have learned, has been ignored. The second question requires that the level of understanding that students are to achieve is stipulated, and the third that the teaching/learning activities are specifically attuned to helping students achieve those levels of understanding. Then follow the key questions:

- How do you define those levels of understanding as outcome statements?
- What do students have to do to reach the level specified?
- What do you have to do to find out if the outcomes have been reached at the appropriate level or not?

Defining levels of understanding is basic to clarifying our intended outcomes, the subject of Chapters 5 and 7, and examples are given in Chapter 6. Getting students to understand at the level required is a matter of getting them to undertake the appropriate learning activities, which is a matter dealt with in Chapters 8 and 9. This is where a Level 3 student-centred theory of teaching departs from the other models. It's not what *we* do but what *students* do that's the important thing. Finally, we need to check that their levels of understanding and of performance are what we intended. This is dealt with in Chapters 10, 11 and 12, on the theory and practice of assessment.

How do students learn?

Learning has been the subject of research by psychologists for well over a century, but remarkably little has *directly* resulted in improved teaching. The reason is that until recently psychologists were more concerned with developing the One Grand Theory of Learning that covered all learning, rather than with studying the contexts in which people learned, such as schools and universities (Biggs 1993a). Over a century ago, William James warned:

> I say moreover that you make a great, a very great, mistake if you think that psychology, being the science of the mind's laws, is something from which you can deduce definite programmes and schemes and methods of instruction. . . . Teaching must *agree* with the psychology but need not necessarily be the only kind of teaching that would so agree . . .
>
> (James 1899/1962: 3)

B.F. Skinner tried to introduce a whole technology of teaching from behaviourism (Skinner 1968), his apparently successful teaching machines being one celebrated example. Teaching machines were however not so much an application of psychology but an analogy based on pigeons pecking targets, and, not surprisingly, worked best for low level rote learning. The notion of the One Grand Theory that explains all is now dead, but the belief that psychology can improve educational practice is still very much alive. However, the nature of that relationship between psychology and education has been interpreted differently in North America and in Europe. In North America, the tendency is to apply psychological theory, derived in controlled laboratory research, to education top-down, as seen particularly in theories of intelligence (e.g. Sternberg 1988; Gardner 1999) and motivation (Pintrich and Schunk 2002; see also Chapter 3 below). In Europe and Australia, on the other hand, the focus has been to study learning bottom-up by observing students learning in context. These studies gave rise to the field of study designated as 'student learning' research.

Both perspectives have their uses and address different issues. As a generalization, the psychological foundation to American research on teaching and learning tends to put the focus on the person and 'within-the-skin' factors, such as intelligence, learning styles (see below) and motivation, while the European focus is on contextual factors, of which teaching is clearly the most important in our context.

Student learning research originated in Sweden, with Marton and Säljö's (1976a, 1976b) studies of surface and deep approaches to learning. They gave students a text to read and told them they would be asked questions afterwards. Students responded in two different ways. The first group learned in anticipation of the questions, concentrating anxiously on the facts and details that might be asked. They 'skated along the surface of the text', as Marton and Säljö put it, using a *surface* approach to learning. These students remembered a list of disjointed facts; they did not comprehend the underlying theme the author was addressing. The second group on the other hand set out to understand the meaning of what the author was trying to say. They went below the surface of the text to interpret that meaning, using a *deep* approach. They saw the big picture and how the facts and details made the author's case.

Note that the terms 'deep' and 'surface' as used here describe ways of learning a particular task, they do *not* describe characteristics of students. We can say that Robert might typically use a surface approach, but the issue – and the point of this book – is to set up ways of getting him to go deep.

The Marton and Säljö studies struck a chord with ongoing work in other countries; in particular that of Entwistle in the United Kingdom (e.g. Entwistle and Ramsden 1983) and of Biggs in Australia (e.g. 1979, 1987a). Entwistle was working from the psychology of individual differences, Biggs from cognitive psychology, and Marton and Säljö from what they later called phenomenography. However, all had a common focus: studying learning in an institutional context.

This work generates strong implications for teaching, as we explore in this chapter.

Constructivism and phenomenography

In reflecting on our teaching and interpreting our teaching decisions, we need a theory. Level 3 theories of teaching, which we looked at earlier in this chapter, are based on two main theories: constructivism and phenomenography. Which one you use may not matter too much, as long as your theory is consistent, understandable and works for you. We prefer constructivism as our framework for thinking about teaching because it emphasizes what students have to do to construct knowledge, which in turn suggests the sorts of learning activities that teachers need to encourage in order to lead students to achieve the desired outcomes.

Constructivism has a long history in cognitive psychology, going back at least to Piaget (1950). Today, it takes on several forms: individual, social, cognitive, postmodern (Steffe and Gale 1995). All forms emphasize that the learners construct knowledge with their own activities, and that they interpret concepts and principles in terms of the 'schemata' that they have already developed. Teaching is not a matter of transmitting but of engaging students in active learning, building their knowledge in terms of what they already understand: 'Constructivism does not claim to have made earth-shaking inventions in the area of education; it merely claims to provide a solid conceptual basis for some of the things that, until now, inspired teachers had to do without theoretical foundation' (von Glasersfeld 1995: 4).

'Phenomenography' was a term resurrected by Marton (1981) to refer to the theory that grew out of his studies with Säljö on approaches to learning and has developed since then (Marton and Booth 1997). Originally used by Sonnemann (1954) in clinical psychology, phenomenography in the student learning context refers to the idea that the learner's perspective determines what is learned, not necessarily what the teacher intends should be learned. Thus, in outcomes-based teaching and learning, it is important that students clearly understand the learning outcomes they are meant to achieve, and accordingly they are written from the student's perspective. The learning outcomes say what they, the students, have to do in order to achieve them, not what the teachers have to do. In the phenomenographic approach itself, however, the emphasis is not on defining learning outcomes, but on changing the learner's perspective, or the way the learner sees the world and on how learners represent knowledge (Prosser and Trigwell 1999). Teaching here starts from the student's experience. Phenomenographic studies have shown how students' ideas of a particular concept or principle develop from simple to complex and that teachers need to see the object of instruction from the student's perspective and lead them to higher order levels of understanding. One way of doing this is by using variation in presenting information and perspectives (Marton and Booth 1997; Prosser and Trigwell 1999).

Both constructivism and phenomenography agree that effective learning changes the way we see the world. The acquisition of information in itself does not bring about such a change, but the way we *structure* that information and think with it does. Thus, education is about *conceptual change*, not just the acquisition of information.

Such conceptual change takes place when:

1 it is clear to both teachers and students what the intended outcomes of learning are, where all can see where they are supposed to be going. Outcomes-based teaching and learning requires this of teachers, whereas teaching in the form of 'covering a topic' does not. This is not to say that there will not be unintended but desirable outcomes, such outcomes are of course very welcome. How we handle these is discussed in Chapter 10.

2 students experience a felt need to achieve the outcome. The art of good teaching is to communicate that need where it is initially lacking. 'Motivation' is not something that students must first possess; motivation is as much a product of good teaching as its prerequisite. This question is addressed in the next chapter.

3 students feel free to focus on the task, not on watching their backs. Attempts to create a felt need to learn by the use of ill-conceived and urgent assessments create anxiety and are counterproductive. The game changes, becoming a matter of dealing with the test, not with engaging with the task deeply.

4 students work collaboratively and in dialogue with others, both peers and teachers. Good dialogue elicits those activities that shape, elaborate and deepen understanding.

These four points contain a wealth of implication for the design of teaching and for personal reflection about what one is really trying to do, as we examine in the following chapter.

Surface and deep approaches to learning

The surface and deep approaches usefully describe how Robert and Susan typically go about their learning and studying – up to the point when teaching begins. Our aim is to teach so that Robert learns more in the manner of Susan.

Surface approach

The surface approach arises from an intention to get the task out of the way with minimum trouble, while appearing to meet course requirements. Low cognitive level activities are therefore used, when higher level activities are required to do the task properly. The concept of the surface approach may be applied to any area, not only to learning. The terms 'cutting corners' and 'sweeping under the carpet' convey the idea: the job appears to have been done properly when it hasn't.

Applied to academic learning, examples include rote learning selected content instead of understanding it, padding an essay, listing points instead of addressing an argument, quoting secondary references as if they were primary ones; the list is endless. A common misconception is that memorization in itself indicates a surface approach (Webb 1997). However, verbatim recall is sometimes entirely appropriate, such as learning lines for a play, acquiring vocabulary or learning formulae. An example of memorizing playing a part in a deep approach occurs in the examination context, in what Tang (1991) called 'deep memorizing'. The student intends to understand in depth but also needs to be able to recall details on cue, but those details are interconnected so that correct recall of the part can give access the whole. Entwistle and Entwistle (2003) report an interesting development of this in their concept of a 'knowledge object'. After a period of intensive revision, some students experience a holistic visual image of the content they are learning. They feel 'outside' the object and almost like an artist painting a picture, adding a detail here, altering something there. They can then use the object to guide their exam answers. Here rote memorizing and understanding play off each other, so that understanding is fixed and supported with relevant detail that can be remembered on cue, as is needed in exams.

Memorization becomes a surface approach when it is used to *replace* understanding, to give the impression that an appropriate level of understanding has occurred when it has not. When Robert takes notes, and selectively quotes them back, he is under-engaging in terms of what is properly required. That is a surface approach. The problem is that it works when teaching, and particularly assessment, allow it to.

> I hate to say it, but what you have got to do is to have a list of 'facts'; you write down ten important points and memorize those, then you'll do all right in the test. . . . If you can give a bit of factual information – so and

so did that, and concluded that – for two sides of writing, then you'll get a good mark.

(a psychology undergraduate, quoted in Ramsden 1984: 144)

If the teacher of this student thought that an adequate understanding of psychology could be manifested by selectively memorizing, there would be no problem. But it is unlikely that the teacher did think that – we should hope not, anyway. Rather, an inappropriate assessment task *allowed* the students to get a good mark on the basis of memorizing facts. As it happened, this particular student later graduated with first class honours. The problem lies therefore not in the student, but in the assessment task. This teacher was not being reflective while the student was highly reflective: he'd outconned the teacher.

Thus, do not think that Robert is irredeemably cursed with a surface approach if he only lists unrelated bullet points as his understanding of an article. Teaching and assessment methods often encourage a surface approach, because they are not aligned to the aims of teaching the subject, as in the case of the psychology teacher we just saw. The presence of a surface approach is thus a signal that something is out of kilter in our teaching or in our assessment methods. It is therefore something we can hope to address.

In using the surface approach, students focus on what Marton calls the 'signs' of learning; the words used, isolated facts, items treated independently of each other. This prevents students from seeing what the signs signify, the meaning and structure of what is taught. Simply, they cannot see the wood for the trees. Emotionally, learning becomes a drag, a task to be got out of the way. Hence the presence of negative feelings about the learning task: anxiety, cynicism, boredom. Exhilaration or enjoyment of the task is not part of the surface approach.

Factors that encourage students to adopt such an approach include:

1 *From the student's side*:

- an intention only to achieve a minimal pass. Such may arise from a 'meal ticket' view of university or from a requirement to take a subject irrelevant to the student's programme;
- non-academic priorities exceeding academic ones;
- insufficient time; too high a workload;
- misunderstanding requirements, such as thinking that factual recall is adequate;
- a cynical view of the subject topic and/or of the teaching context itself;
- high anxiety;
- a genuine inability to understand particular content at a deep level.

2 *From the teacher's side*:

- teaching piecemeal by bullet lists, not bringing out the intrinsic structure of the topic or subject. (We hasten to add that some bullet lists, like these two here, for instance, are OK: see Chapter 4);

- assessing for independent facts, which is almost inevitably the case when using short answer and multiple-choice tests;
- teaching, and especially assessing, in a way that encourages cynicism: for example, 'I hate teaching this section, and you're going to hate learning it, but we've got to cover it';
- providing insufficient time to engage the tasks; emphasizing coverage at the expense of depth;
- creating undue anxiety or low expectations of success: 'Anyone who can't understand this isn't fit to be at university'.

The student factors (1) are not entirely separate from the teacher factors (2). Most of the student factors are affected by teaching. Is insufficient time to engage properly a matter of poor student planning or of poor teacher judgement? Much student cynicism is a reaction to teaching busy-work and of assessing trivia. Even the last student factor, inability to understand at a deep level, refers to the task at hand and that may be a matter of poor teacher judgement concerning curriculum content as much as the student's abilities. But there are limits. Even under the best teaching some students will still maintain a surface approach. Unfortunately, it is easier to create a surface approach than it is to support a deep approach (Trigwell and Prosser 1991).

An important step in improving teaching, then, is to avoid those factors that encourage a surface approach.

Deep approach

The deep approach arises from a felt need to engage the task appropriately and meaningfully, so the student tries to use the most appropriate cognitive activities for handling it. To Susan, who is interested in mathematics and wants to master the subject, cutting corners is pointless.

When students feel this need-to-know, they automatically try to focus on underlying meanings, on main ideas, themes, principles or successful applications. This requires a sound foundation of relevant prior knowledge, so students needing to know will naturally try to learn the details, as well as making sure they understand the big picture. In fact, the big picture is not understandable without the details. When using the deep approach in handling a task, students have positive feelings: interest, a sense of importance, challenge, exhilaration. Learning is a pleasure. Students come with questions they want answered, and when the answers are unexpected, that is even better.

Factors that encourage students to adopt such an approach include:

1 *From the student's side*:

- an intention to engage the task meaningfully and appropriately. Such an intention may arise from an intrinsic curiosity or from a determination to do well;
- appropriate background knowledge and a well-structured knowledge base;

- the ability to focus at a high conceptual level, working from first principles;
- a genuine preference for working conceptually rather than with unrelated detail.

2 *From the teacher's side*:

- teaching in such a way as to explicitly bring out the structure of the topic or subject;
- teaching to elicit an active response from students, e.g. by questioning, presenting problems for them to solve, rather than teaching to expound information;
- teaching by building on what students already know;
- confronting and eradicating students' misconceptions;
- assessing for structure rather than for independent facts;
- teaching and assessing in a way that encourages a positive learning atmosphere, so students can make mistakes and learn from them;
- emphasizing depth of learning, rather than breadth of coverage;
- in general, and most importantly, using teaching and assessment methods that support the explicit aims and intended outcomes of the course.

Again, the student factors (1) are not independent of the teacher factors (2). Encouraging the need-to-know, instilling curiosity, building on students' prior knowledge are all things that teachers can attempt to do; and, conversely, are things that poor teaching can too easily discourage. There are many things the teacher can do to encourage deep learning, as will be a lot clearer by the end of this book.

Desirable student learning depends both on student-based factors – ability, appropriate prior knowledge, clearly accessible new knowledge – and on the teaching context, which includes teacher responsibility, informed decision making and good management. But the bottom line is that teachers have to work with what material they have. Whereas lectures and tutorials might have worked in the good old days when highly selected students tended to bring their deep approaches with them, they may not work so well today. We need to create a teaching context where the Roberts of this world can go deep too.

Another and more important step in improving teaching is to focus on those factors that encourage a deep approach.

What is the difference between learning approaches and learning styles?

Some people speak of students' approaches to learning as if they were learning styles that students use consistently, whatever the task or the teaching (Schmeck 1988; Sternberg and Zhang 2001). Others speak of approaches as entirely determined by context, as if students walk into a learning situation without any preference for their way of going about learning (Marton and Säljö 1976a). These interpretations reflect the American and the European perspectives (p. 21).

We take a middle position. Students do have predilections or preferences for this or that approach, but those predilections may or may not be realized in practice, depending on the teaching context. We are dealing with an *interaction* between personal and contextual factors, not unlike the interaction between heredity and environment. Both factors apply, but which predominates depends on particular situations. Have another look at Figure 1.1 (p. 6). At point A, under passive teaching, student factors make the difference, but at point B, under active teaching, the differences between students lessen. Practically speaking, however, it is more helpful to see approaches to learning as something we as teachers can hope to change, rather than as styles about which we can do little. For an analysis of the differences between learning styles and learning approaches see Sternberg and Zhang (2001).

Scores on such questionnaires as the *Approaches and Study Skills Inventory for Students* (ASSIST) (Tait et al. 1998) or the *Study Process Questionnaire* (SPQ) (Biggs et al. 2001), are most usefully seen as outcomes of teaching rather than as measuring differences between students. Responses to these questionnaires tell us something about the quality of the teaching environment, precisely because students' predilections tend to adapt to the expected requirements of different teaching environments.

Teaching and approaches to learning

To achieve most intended learning outcomes a range of verbs, from high to low cognitive level, needs to be activated. The highest would refer to such activities as reflecting and theorizing, the lowest to memorizing and recalling, while in between are various levels of activity. When using a deep approach, students use the full range of desired learning activities; they learn terminology, they memorize formulae, but move from there to applying these formulae to new examples. When using a surface approach, there is a shortfall; students handle all tasks, low and high, with low level verbs ('two pages of writing, etc.'). The teaching challenge is to prevent this shortfall from occurring, or to correct it where it has occurred (see Figure 2.1).

The conclusion to be drawn is simple but powerful: the surface approach is to be discouraged, the deep approach to be encouraged, which is a good working definition of good teaching. Preventing students from using a surface approach by discouraging the use of low level and inappropriate learning activities is the main thrust of the following chapter, while supporting the full range of appropriate learning activities, thus encouraging a deep approach, is what the remainder of the book is about.

Now try Task 2.2 (p. 30) to see how your teaching has helped shape your students' approaches to learning.

Cognitive level of learning activities

Figure 2.1 Desired and actual level of engagement, approaches to learning and enhancing teaching

Summary and conclusions

Levels of thinking about teaching

We distinguish three common theories of teaching, depending on what is seen as the main determinant of learning: (1) what students are, (2) what teachers do and (3) what students do. These define 'levels' of thinking about teaching. At Level 1, the teacher's role is to display information, the students' to absorb it. If students don't have the ability or motivation to do that correctly, that is their problem. At Level 2, the teacher's role is to explain concepts and principles, as well as to present information. For this they need various skills, techniques, and competencies. Here the focus is on what the teacher does, rather than on what the student is, and to that extent is more reflective and sophisticated. At Level 3, the focus is on what the students do: are they engaging those learning activities most likely to lead to the intended outcomes?

Task 2.2 Does your teaching encourage surface or deep approaches to learning?

Good teaching *encourages* a deep approach, and *discourages* a surface approach, to learning.

Reflect on your teaching so far. Identify aspects of your teaching that have (maybe unintentionally)

a encouraged a surface approach to learning:

_____

_____

_____

b encouraged a deep approach to learning:

_____

_____

_____

What future actions would you take to encourage a deep approach to learning in your students?

_____

_____

_____

Before we end this chapter, please complete Task 2.3.

Task 2.3 Follow-up to Task 2.1

In Task 2.1, you stated your theories of teaching and learning. Now that you have finished this chapter, we ask you to review those theories and answer the following question.

Have your theories of teaching and learning changed now that you have seen others' views? If yes, what is(are) the change(s) and why?

_____

_____

_____

If not, what sort of teaching/learning context would best help them? How can I know that they have achieved the intended outcomes satisfactorily?

_____

_____

_____

How do students learn?

It is only in comparatively recent years that researchers into learning have studied learning as it takes place in institutions, by students. There is now a body of theory called 'student learning research' which directly relates to practice, constructivism and phenomenography being the two most influential. Both emphasize that meaning is created by the learner, but constructivism focuses particularly on the nature of the learning activities the student uses and on this account in our view leads more readily to designing contexts for enhancing learning.

Surface and deep approaches to learning

Learning activities that are too low a level to achieve the intended learning outcomes are referred to as comprising a 'surface' approach to learning, for example memorizing to give the impression of understanding. Activities that are appropriate to achieving the outcomes are referred to as a 'deep' approach. At university, intended outcomes would be high level, requiring students to reflect, hypothesize, apply and so on. Surface and deep approaches to learning are not personality traits, as is sometimes thought, but are most usefully thought of as reactions to the teaching environment.

Teaching and approaches to learning

Good teaching supports those activities that lead to a deep approach to learning and to the attainment of the intended learning outcomes. How to design such teaching, and how to assess in order to see how well the outcomes have been achieved, are what the rest of this book is about. That is to accentuate the positive. But we also need to eliminate the negative. There is much in what the teacher does or says that can encourage inappropriate, surface approaches to learning. These are of course to be discouraged. To do that is to set the stage for effective teaching; and that is the subject of the following chapter.

Further reading

Between levels 2 and 3?

Bain, K. (2004) *What the Best College Teachers Do*. Cambridge, MA: Harvard University Press.
Biggs, J.B. (1993b) From theory to practice: a cognitive systems approach, *Higher Education Research and Development*, 12: 73–86.

Bain and Biggs offer two contrasting but complementary views on teaching. Bain's book is based on a study of the philosophies of exceptional teachers and what they did in the classroom, an exceptional teacher being one who 'transforms lives, changes everything, and messes with . . . student's heads' (p. 10). Biggs takes the view that the plot is about what students do, not what teachers do, and that to enhance student learning across the board it is the responsibility of the institution to support student learning with appropriate policies and infrastructure. That is, the issue is teach*ing*, not teach*ers*. Exceptional individual teachers have always transformed lives and will continue to do so, but ordinary teachers, the large majority, will affect more lives, especially if they teach badly: this is where the systems approach can help in supporting all teachers not just exceptional ones. Bain and Biggs are talking about different aspects of teaching – but ordinary teachers may well be inspired by reading about what their gifted colleagues do so effectively.

Constructivism and phenomenography

Marton, F. and Booth, S.A. (1997) *Learning and Awareness*. Hillsdale, NJ: Lawrence Erlbaum.
Perkins, D. (1999) The many faces of constructivism, *Educational Leadership*, 57, 3: 6–11.
Steffe, L. and Gale, J. (eds) (1995) *Constructivism in Education*. Hillsdale, NJ: Lawrence Erlbaum.
von Glasersfeld, E. (1995) *Radical Constructivism: A Way of Knowing and Learning*. Washington, DC: The Falmer Press.

These books present the major theories behind current student learning research and applications to teaching. Marton and Booth discuss learning from the phenomenographic standpoint; while much of the discussion is philosophical, the title of the last chapter, which outlines the phenomenographic approach to teaching, is 'A pedagogy of awareness'. Steffe and Gale and von Glasersfeld examine the constructivist position generally and how it applies to education. Perkins gives an excellent overview for teachers. The constructivist approach is that which guides the rest of the present book.

On applying student learning research to teaching

Dart, B. and Boulton-Lewis, G. (eds) (1998) *Teaching and Learning in Higher Education*. Camberwell, Victoria: Australian Council for Educational Research.
Entwistle, N. (2009) *Teaching for Understanding at University: Deep Approaches and Distinctive Ways of Thinking*. Basingstoke: Palgrave Macmillan.

Prosser, M. and Trigwell, K. (1999) *Understanding Learning and Teaching: The Experience in Higher Education.* Buckingham: Open University Press.

Ramsden, P. (2003) *Learning to Teach in Higher Education.* London: Routledge.

Sternberg, R.J. and Zhang L.F. (eds) (2001) *Perspectives on Thinking, Learning, and Cognitive Styles.* Mahwah, NJ: Lawrence Erlbaum.

Dart and Boulton-Lewis contains a collection of papers that address a range of teaching issues within the general student learning paradigm, including teachers' beliefs, creative writing, handling individual differences, collaborative learning and educational measurement. Entwistle reviews the recent student learning research comprehensively, with particular emphasis on the nature of knowledge and understanding (and to which we return in Chapter 5). Prosser and Trigwell demonstrate the implications for teaching arising from the phenomenographic framework and is in a sense a parallel to the present book, which operates from constructivism. Ramsden's approach is his own, but derives much from phenomenography, Chapters 1 to 7 giving rather more detail on the history and development of the student learning paradigm than is given here and how it may be applied to teaching. In Sternberg and Zhang most contributors argue that learning/cognitive styles are relevant to teaching, except Biggs, who argues that accommodating teaching to different learning styles is too complex to be practicable, and that surface and deep learning approaches are not styles to which teaching should accommodate, but are outcomes of teaching.

3

Setting the stage for effective teaching

Effective teaching requires that we eliminate those aspects of our teaching that encourage surface approaches to learning; and that we set the stage properly so that students will more readily use deep approaches to learning. This involves getting students to realize that appropriate task engagement is a good and impelling idea (otherwise known as 'motivation'), and that we establish the kind of climate that will optimize appropriate interactions with our students. An important aspect to effective teaching is reflective practice, using transformative reflection, which involves teachers reflecting on their current teaching through the lens of a sound theory of teaching and learning in order to create an improved teaching environment that adapts to changing conditions.

Getting students involved in learning: motivation

There is no such thing as an unmotivated student: all students not in a coma want to do *something*. Our task is to maximize the chances that what they want to do is to achieve the intended learning outcomes, and any unintended but desirable outcomes. Unfortunately, there are many aspects of teaching that actually discourage students from doing that: we need to identify and minimize these as far as we can.

The best sort of motivation arises from intrinsic interest, fascination, call it what you will, but, unfortunately, that occurs well down the track, when the student already knows a lot about the topic and, like Susan, is already involved in it. Our problem as teachers is getting students to engage in learning before they have reached that stage. Unfortunately, students like Robert resort to surface learning strategies to avoid becoming involved. It doesn't help to say that Robert is 'unmotivated'. Of course he is: that's the problem.

Teachers who have a Level 1 theory of teaching see motivation as a substance that students possess in varying quantities, the Susans having lots, the Roberts having little or none – and that's the way it is. But surely we can do *something* to encourage Robert to engage? Yes, we can. Two factors make students (or anyone, come to that) want to learn something:

1 It has to be important; it must have some *value* to the learner.
2 The learner needs to *expect success* when engaging the learning task.

Nobody wants to do something they see as worthless. Neither do they want to do something, however valued, if they believe they have no chance of succeeding. In both cases, doing the task will be seen as a waste of time.

This commonsense theory of why students do or do not want to learn is called the *expectancy-value* theory of motivation, which says that if anyone is to engage in an activity, he or she needs both to value the outcome and to expect success in achieving it (Feather 1982). Both the high value and the expectancy of success need to be present; if either one is zero, then no motivated activity occurs.

What makes a task worth doing?

Let us look first at the value term in the expectancy-value formula. How can we enhance the value of the task to the students? The general answer is clear enough: make their work important to them. Work can be important in various ways, each one producing a familiar category of motivation:

- what the outcome produces (*extrinsic* motivation);
- what other people value (*social* motivation);
- the opportunity for ego enhancement (*achievement* motivation);
- the process of doing it (*intrinsic* motivation).

Extrinsic motivation occurs when students perform the task because of the value or importance they attach to what the outcome brings, either something positive following success, such as a material reward, or something negative, such as a punishment, that would follow failure or non-engagement.

The quality of learning is usually low under extrinsic conditions. The student's attention is not so much on the task as on its consequences. Extrinsic motivation is a standing invitation to students to adopt a surface approach: indeed, the motive component of a surface approach is extrinsic, including a fear of failure (Biggs 1987a). Negative reinforcement is worse than positive, because if the learning is not successful, punishment is implicated, which introduces a range of side issues such as anxiety, anger, shame, desire for revenge, none of which is very helpful in getting the job done.

Social motivation occurs when students learn in order to please people whose opinions are important to them. If the processes of studying, or the fruits of a good education, are valued by other people important to the student, education may take on an intrinsic importance to the student. This is evident in some families, particularly Asian families, who have a high regard for education. Children with this family background are likely to accept that education is a good thing, to be pursued without question.

We can usually trace the beginning of our interest in something to someone who exhibited that interest to us. We want to be like them. This process is called 'modelling', where the models are admired and readily identified with. University teachers are in a good position to be seen as models, especially in the one-to-one situation of dissertation supervision. At the undergraduate level, in today's crowded universities, students are rather less likely to have the opportunity to engage closely with an academic but it can happen, especially if the academic publicly displays great enthusiasm for the subject.

Achievement motivation is about achieving in order to enhance the ego, such as competing against other students and beating them. They feel good about themselves. This can often lead to high achievement, and tends even to be associated with deep learning (Biggs 1987a), but the aims of deep learning and of achievement motivation ultimately diverge. The deep approach is concerned with handling the task as appropriately as possible, the achieving approach with handling it in order to obtain the highest grades possible. High grades and appropriate learning should mean the same, but in poorly designed assessment tasks the strategic student can obtain high grades using inappropriate, low level learning, as did Ramsden's student (pp. 24–5).

Achievement motivation in the raw is not a pretty sight. It kills collaborative learning. Other students become competitors, not colleagues, and so steps are taken to disadvantage others: key references are hidden or mutilated, hints are not shared, misleading advice is given. Achievement motivation needs competitive conditions in which to work, and while that suits the minority of students who are positively motivated by competition, it actually damages the learning of those who perceive competition as threatening. Achievement motivation, like anxiety, changes the priorities of students, because content mastery plays second fiddle either to winning or to avoiding the appearance of losing, for example by doing only very easy tasks or, paradoxically, too hard tasks that the student can fail with honour. More students are turned off and work less well under competitive conditions than those who are turned on and work better. Although competition is often touted as the way the 'real' world works, it does not follow that universities should make learning competitive for the general run of students, as happens when using norm-referenced assessments such as 'grading on the curve'.

Intrinsic motivation is the academic ideal but is the rarer for that. Students like Susan learn because they are interested in the task or activity itself. They do mathematics for the intellectual pleasure of problem solving and exercising their skill, independently of any rewards that might be involved. The point is to travel rather than to arrive. Intrinsic motivation drives deep learning and the best academic work.

Intrinsic motivation increases with continuing successful engagement with a specific task. Susan does not turn up at university to study mathematics without having experienced previous success in mathematics. The fact that many students may not have had much previous formal engagement in a subject does not, however, mean they will not develop intrinsic interest in it. Interest in subjects such as psychology or sociology, which may not have been studied previously, arises from curiosity and informal experience or from career plans. If the student sees the area as personally important, intrinsic interest will follow.

The question is, how do we motivate the Roberts, who have no definite career plans, no perception yet of personal importance of the area or even curiosity about related topics?

Involving students who are not yet intrinsically motivated

Rephrase the question: if a student doesn't yet see the task as important, how can we help make it so?

Let us look first at extrinsic motivation, as when the teacher sees assessment as the answer. A common cry is that students will not spend time learning a topic if they think it is not going to be assessed. Very well, some say, see that the topic *is* assessed. But this is an excellent way of devaluing it. The subtext says: 'The only value of this topic is that I have decided to test you on it!'

In an aligned system of teaching, this does not happen. The reason that the topic is being assessed is because it was important enough to be overtly included in the intended outcomes. The fact that it is there establishes its value. Assessing outside the curriculum, or at a lower cognitive level than the curriculum demands, results in irrelevant or counterproductive tasks that students will resent or turn to their advantage, as did the student who wrote 'who said what on two sides of paper'.

The effects of assessment also depend on the kind of climate that has been created. One teacher informed his senior undergraduate class: 'You're going to hate the next couple of weeks; I know I am. I see absolutely no point in this form of linguistic analysis, but there it is, it's in the syllabus and we've got to cover it.' Amazingly, one student reported she had found the topic to be the most interesting part of the course, and was designing a dissertation proposal around it! Susan can cope with this kind of thing; she has her own reasons for valuing the topic. But Robert, who has nothing but the teacher's word for it, will indeed see the topic as valueless, hence not worth learning, except for the most cynical of reasons.

Using social motivation is a good strategy. Teachers who love their subject, and show it, can be inspirational. The fact that here is someone who does perceive great value in it will cause students to be curious, to seek some of that value.

The key to motivation, then, is to ensure that academic activities are meaningful and worthwhile. This is made very clear in problem-based learning, where real-life problems become the context in which students learn academic content and professional skills. When faced with a patient with a suspected broken leg and whom the students have to help, learning all the necessary knowledge leading to the diagnosis and treatment of the patient is manifestly a worthwhile activity for a medical student. Problem-based learning is usually undertaken enthusiastically: we explore this teaching strategy further in Chapter 9.

What makes students expect to succeed or to fail?

Let us examine the following true incident:

> When we got to the Psych I lectures, the Stats lecturer said 'Anyone who can't follow this isn't fit to be at University.' That was the first message I got. I *was* having difficulty with Stats and so I thought, maybe he's right, maybe university isn't for me. I liked the rest of Psych but couldn't handle the Stats and had to withdraw.
>
> Next year, funny thing, I did Maths I and we came to probability theory, much the same stuff that I'd bombed out in last year. But the lecturer there said 'Probability is quite hard really. You'll need to work at it. You're welcome to come to me for help if you really need it . . .'
>
> It was like a blinding light. It wasn't *me* after all! This stuff really was *hard*, but if I tried it might just work. That year I got a Credit in that part of the subject.
>
> (a mature student, quoted in Biggs and Moore 1993: 272)

This student had initially been led to believe she had no chance of success. Her first teacher attributed lack of success to lack of ability, she perceived she was not succeeding, so she naturally concluded she didn't have the ability needed. As this was something beyond her control, she concluded she had no chance of ever succeeding. Her second teacher attributed success instead to effort, which is something the student could control. With that came the liberating realization that what was initially certain failure could now be possible success. So she persevered and succeeded. The reasons for that transformation are very instructive in the matter of motivating students.

A history of successful engagement with content that is personally meaningful allows the student both to build up the knowledge base needed for deep learning and, motivationally, to develop the expectations that give confidence in future success. These expectations create feelings of what psychologists call 'self-efficacy', or more simply, of 'ownership': 'I can do this; this is my thing.'

Expectations of success are instilled on the basis of previous success, but only if the conditions that are believed to lead to success remain unchanged. If a student believes that a particular success was due to factors that might change and that are uncontrollable, such as luck or dependence on a particular teacher, belief in future success is diminished.

Westerners differ significantly from the Chinese in their attributions for success and failure. Westerners tend to see success as being attributable more to ability than to effort, while ethnic Chinese see effort as more important. This is possibly one reason why Chinese students do so well in international comparisons of attainment (Watkins and Biggs 1996).

Take methods of assessing students. Norm-referenced assessment is based on grading students against each other, for example by ranking, or 'following the curve'. Students see this sort of assessment as competitive; to get a high grade you have to beat other students. This puts a premium on the importance of relative ability as determining the outcome. In criterion-referenced assessment, where students are assessed on how well they meet preset criteria, they see that to get a high grade they have to know the intended outcomes and learn how to get there, with a premium on attributions involving effort, study skill and know-how. In norm-referenced assessment success depends on the abilities of other students, over which there is no control, while in criterion-referenced assessment, the ball is in the student's court.

Teacher feedback has powerful effects on students' expectations of success, as the story on learning statistics makes very clear. The psychology teacher's comment pre-empted student control, while the mathematics teacher made students see that success was up to them. Feedback as to progress also encourages beliefs in future success, which again is easier with criterion-referenced assessment: 'This is what you did, the criteria tell you what you might have done, so that this is how to get a better result.'

But how can norm-referenced feedback, such as 'You are below average on this', help students to learn? What does Robert do with *that* information? This is not to say that some students don't want to be told where they stand in relation to their peers, but that information has little to do with teaching and learning. It is nice to be told that you're cleverer than most other students, but not very helpful for learning how to improve your performance. To be told, directly or indirectly, that you're dumber than most of the others is simply destructive.

To instil expectations of failure, as did our psychology lecturer with consummate skill, is easy to do. This is classic blame-the-student stuff: attributing failure to lack of ability or to some other trait that lies fixed within the student. A valuable act of self-reflection as a teacher is to monitor what you say, how you say it, and what comments you write in students' assignments. What does the subtext of your comments say about future success or failure?

Task 3.1 asks you to think of the messages you send your students that might leave them feeling hopeful or hopeless about future success.

Teachers might worry less about motivating students and more about teaching better. That, in a nutshell, is the message of this section. 'Motivation' is dealt with in two ways. The first is to avoid doing those things that devalue academic tasks by encouraging cynicism and debilitating anxiety or sending messages to students that they have no chance of success. The second is to teach in such a way that students build up a good knowledge base, achieve success in problems that are significant and build up a feeling of 'ownership' of their learning; motivation follows good learning as night follows day. It is a matter of getting the causes and the effects right.

The next step in setting the stage for effective teaching is establishing a productive classroom climate.

The teaching/learning climate

Teachers create a certain learning climate through formal and informal interactions with students, which establishes how we and our students feel about learning. This naturally has strong effects on students' learning.

Task 3.1 What messages of success and failure do you convey to your students?

When students succeed, do you convey the hopeful message that their success will continue: 'You're good at this, aren't you?' Or the hopeless message: 'You had it lucky that time.'

When students fail, do you convey the hopeful message that they can succeed in future: 'This is hard, but with a bit more effort you'll get it right.' Or the hopeless message: 'I guess you just don't have what it takes.'

Think back on some recent communications to students – such as comments in class, body language, handling questions, writing comments on assignments, describing what it takes to succeed, descriptions of tasks, readings and so on. Do you think you convey hopeful, or hopeless, messages? Write down a couple of telling examples:

1 _____

_____

_____

2 _____

_____

_____

Theory X and Theory Y climates

Douglas McGregor (1960) was a management psychologist who distinguished between two organizational climates: Theory X and Theory Y. The 'theory' referred to assumptions about human trustworthiness. Managers operating on Theory X assume that workers cannot be trusted, those operating on Theory Y assume that they can and that you get better results when you do – an idea that has little traction in these neo-conservative times.

Nevertheless, Theories X and Y transfer readily to the classroom. Teachers operating on Theory X assume that students don't want to learn, they will cheat if given the slightest opportunity and so must not be allowed to make any significant decisions about their learning. They need to be told what to do and what to study, attendances need to be checked every lecture, invigilated examinations must make up most of the final grade, self- and peer-assessments are quite out of the question, deadlines and regulations need to be spelled out with sanctions imposed for failing to meet them.

This way of thinking leads very quickly to a learning climate based on anxiety: put the fear of God in them, *then* they'll shape up! Theory X is essentially a blame-the-student model of teaching, and with that goes all the other baggage associated with the Level 1 theory of teaching.

Teachers operating on Theory Y assume that students do their best work when given freedom and space to use their own judgement, that while bureaucratization of the classroom and of the institution may be necessary to run a tight ship, too much will be counterproductive for good learning. Consequently, Theory Y driven teachers take the opposite view on such matters as take-home assessment tasks, self- and peer-assessment, class attendance, allowing students freedom to make their own decisions and so on. You give the benefit of the doubt. Sure, some students may be more likely to cheat when assessed on projects than on invigilated exams, but Theory Y teachers would argue that the educational benefits outweigh that risk. The aim of teaching is to support student learning, not to beat student deviousness.

These are pure cases. An all-Theory-X environment would be intolerable for students, while all-Theory-Y would be near impossible to run efficiently. Elements of both exist in the learning climates we create, but in our individual philosophies, we tend to lean more towards one theory or the other. We should create the sort of learning climate that we believe strikes the right balance for optimal learning, given our theory of teaching, the conditions under which we work, and the nature of the subject we are teaching and of our students.

The extent to which we lean more towards Theory X or more towards Theory Y translates into action at virtually all levels of student–teacher interaction. For example, when one non-Cantonese-speaking teacher told colleagues at the University of Hong Kong, where English is the official language medium of instruction, that he allowed students to use Cantonese in group discussions, because group interaction was then much livelier, he was met with: 'But they could be discussing the Happy Valley race results for all you know!' True, they could have been. They could also have been engaged in fruitful learning.

It is a question of balancing trust, risk and value. Theory X operates on low trust, producing low-risk but low-value outcomes. You don't trust students so you assess them under high-security, invigilated conditions with little risk of cheating but what is produced under these conditions may not be relevant to the most important intended outcomes (pp. 227–9). Theory Y operates on high trust, producing high-value outcomes but with the risk that some outcomes may be the result of cheating. The following quotation from a part-time student who was a teacher illustrates the balance between risk and value with great self-insight:

> The biggest point I have learned from this course is my biggest flaw as a teacher, that is, I did not trust my students to be able to behave themselves . . . [or to be] . . . capable of being responsible for their own learning. . . . I made numerous rules in class for them to follow so as to make sure that they 'behaved', did all the preparations and planning for them, giving them mountains of homework and short tests to make sure

that they revise for their lessons and so on – all rooted from my lack of trust in them! And I dared to blame them for being so passive and dependent when all along I helped to encourage them to be so!

(part-time BEd student, University of Hong Kong)

How classroom climate affects learning

Theory X restricts the range of potentially useful ways of learning, particularly self-directed learning, as the last quotation illustrates. Theory X also generates negative feelings, which distract from proper task engagement, directly encouraging a surface approach. Theory X generates two counter-productive emotions in particular: anxiety and cynicism.

Anxiety, produced for example by intimidation, sarcasm, threats of failure or heavy use of sanctions, simply creates an intense need to get out of the situation. The student's behaviour is therefore directed towards that end, rather than towards proper task engagement. Anxiety makes a mess of a student's priorities.

Cynicism works in a more coldly cognitive way. Perceptions that the teacher is degrading the task or belittling students encourages students to be cynical and, with that, to take a deliberate decision not to engage the task honestly. If the teacher doesn't take the task seriously, why should the student? There are many ways in which teachers convey cynicism:

- Showing lack of interest or dislike of a topic ('You'll hate this, but we've got to cover it').
- Playing games with students when they can't play back, such as setting facetious distracters in multiple-choice test items.
- Making fun of students' responses in class with sarcastic or put-down remarks.
- Applying Theory X by numbers, for example drawing a line after the 2000th word in a 2000 word-limit essay and marking only to that point. But if a student does exceed the limit, it may have been in order to make the argument more clearly. Messages conveyed by marking to the 2000th word include: nit picking is what it's all about, this teacher is a control freak, so do not bother to make a case, just list points within the word limit.
- Discounting grades or marks for being late or some other offence. This practice conveys the message that meeting a deadline is more important than trying to create a product of quality. It also makes genuine criterion referencing impossible. Issues of learning should not be confused with issues of discipline (see Box 10.3, pp. 211–12).
- Setting busy-work: insisting on trivia, making quality performance secondary to bureaucratic demands or to personal convenience.
- Displaying authoritarianism: refusing to accept student criticisms or suggestions as to content or teaching method, being 'too busy' to attend to reasonable student requests.

A particular source of both anxiety and cynicism is time stress brought out by an obsession with coverage: too many topics, each taught with equal emphasis.

Students become grossly overloaded and deep engagement with any topic is pre-empted. There are many reasons that students are subjected to time stress:

- lack of coordination between teachers in setting assignment deadlines;
- lack of knowledge or even concern about the students' perspective on the workload;
- shared teaching and particularly shared assessment, where each teacher thinks their own contribution is the most important;
- generally, a lack of care and forethought in designing the curriculum initially, such as duplication of topics across courses. As we shall see in Chapter 6, OBTL provides the opportunity of reviewing course outcomes in the context of intended programme outcomes that obviates these problems.

Deep engagement in a task takes time. If you don't provide the time, you won't get deep engagement:

> The greatest enemy of understanding is coverage – I can't repeat that often enough. If you're determined to cover a lot of things, you are guaranteeing that most kids will not understand, because they haven't had time enough to go into things in depth, to figure out what the requisite understanding is, and be able to perform that understanding in different situations.
>
> (Gardner 1993: 24)

Climate and direction: summary

Let us bring the two sections on motivation and climate together. A Theory Y climate is a necessary but not a sufficient condition for the cultivation of positive motivation. The teacher must further demonstrate that the task is worthwhile and that it is attainable.

Expectations of success and failure depend critically on what students are most likely to attribute their success and failure to. How these attributions are built up is partly cultural, partly upbringing and partly what goes on in the classroom. Communicating the message that failure is due to factors that aren't going to go away and that aren't controllable (such as low ability), is to instil an expectation of future failure. Attributing failure to factors that can be changed, such as lack of the appropriate skills (these can be taught) or to insufficient effort (this can be increased next time), help remove the crippling incapacity that failure may induce. Likewise, attributions of success to a special interest, or competence, are likely to increase feelings of ownership and hence positive motivation. Attributing success to luck, or to help from someone else, is likely to decrease feelings of ownership.

Finally, a Theory Y climate does not necessarily mean a disorganized teaching/learning environment. An organized setting, with clear goals and feedback on progress, is important for motivating students and to the development of deep approaches (Hattie and Watkins 1988; Entwistle et al. 1989).

Task 3.2 What sort of classroom climate are you creating for your students?

Put a cross on the continuum at a point that best represents what you currently do in your teaching regarding:

	Strict	Negotiable
Classroom management	_____
Meeting assignment deadlines	_____
Checking attendance	_____
Giving invigilated examination	_____
Not allowing students to assess their own work	_____
Not allowing students to take risk	_____
You assuming control of all teaching and assessment matters	_____

Now consider the positions of the crosses. If they are more skewed towards the 'Strict' end, you may be creating a more Theory X classroom climate. If the crosses are more skewed towards the 'Negotiable' end, then your classroom is more a Theory Y one.

So what sort of classroom climate are you creating for your students?

Is your classroom climate conducive to a deep approach to learning? If not, what actions would you take to change the classroom climate that would help your students achieve the intended learning outcomes through adopting a deep learning approach?

Your reflection:

_____

_____

_____

Knowing where you are going, and feedback telling you how well you are progressing, heightens expectations of success.

Driving in a thick fog is highly unpleasant. So is learning in one.

So what sort of classroom climate are you creating for your students? Task 3.2 is an exercise to help you identify your classroom climate. But what is more important is how you could improve it to facilitate a more desirable learning approach.

Reflective teaching

Wise and effective teaching is not, however, simply a matter of applying general principles of teaching according to rule; they need adapting to each teacher's own personal strengths and teaching context. A characteristic of award-winning university teachers is their willingness to collect student feedback on their teaching, in order to see where their teaching might be improved (Dunkin and Precians 1992). Expert teachers continually reflect on how they might teach even better.

Let us imagine that Susan and Robert graduated as teachers 20 years ago. Susan now is a teacher with 20 years' experience; Robert is a teacher with one year's experience repeated 19 times. Susan is a reflective teacher: each significant experience, particularly of failure, has been a learning experience, so she gets better and better. Robert is a reactive teacher. He goes through the same motions year after year and when things go wrong he tends to blame the students, the administration or government intervention. If it worked last year, but didn't work this year, how can it be his teaching that is the problem?

The kind of thinking displayed by Susan, but not by Robert, is known as 'reflective practice'. Donald Schön (1983) coined the term 'the reflective practitioner', pointing out that effective professionals, such as architects or medicos, need to reflect when faced with new problems or with difficulties which they have not been specifically trained to handle, and work out how to go forward. It is the same with university teachers (Brockbank and McGill 1998). A particularly inspiring and personal account of reflective practice in university teaching is given by Cowan (2002).

'Reflection' is, however, a misleading word. *Transformative reflection* is better. When you stand in front of a mirror what you see is your reflection, what you *are*. Transformative reflection is rather like the mirror in Snow White: it tells you what you *might be*. This mirror uses theory to enable the transformation from the unsatisfactory what-is to the more effective what-might-be.

Theory makes us aware that there is a problem and it helps to generate a solution to that problem. University teachers have the theory relating to their discipline at their fingertips, but many do not have explicit and well-structured theories relating to *teaching* their discipline. Reflecting on your teaching, and seeing what is wrong and how it may be improved, requires an explicit theory of teaching. As noted earlier, all teachers have some kind of implicit theory of teaching, but we need something more upfront, a consciously worked-out theory that generates answers to teaching problems. The initial jolt that says 'there's a problem here' has to be defined in such a way that the problem becomes soluble. 'My stuff isn't getting across' doesn't define a soluble problem. 'The students are only giving me back what I said in my lectures' does. The last statement is based on the theory that when students only give back what is in the lectures, something is wrong. A good theory would suggest that that something resides in the teaching, not an inherent defect residing in the students. It might be that the assessment procedures are letting students get away with repeating the lectures. So we need to present them with assessment tasks where this will not work. Transformative reflection, then, is a multi-stage process of: reflect–plan–apply–evaluate (did it work?).

To recognize and then to solve problems in teaching involves reflecting on what is happening, using a framework that gives you an angle on what is going on in your teaching and that helps you to plan an improvement. Such a framework is presented in the next chapter. When readers' theories of teaching will have been elaborated with the contents of this book, the issue of transformative reflective practice may profitably be revisited, which we shall do in Chapter 13.

The scholarship of teaching and learning (SoTL)

In 1990, Boyer (1990) introduced the notion that *scholarship* should apply just as much to teaching as it does to research. Scholarship in this context means that teachers should keep themselves up to date with knowledge about teaching, and apply that knowledge reflectively to their own teaching. More recently, Boyer's concept has been expanded to include learning, so that we now speak of the scholarship of teaching and learning (SoTL), and indeed there is now a flourishing International Society for the Scholarship of Teaching and Learning, and a journal (see end of this chapter). The scholarship of teaching and learning should be used by teachers individually, and by institutions, as the frame within which all teaching- and learning-related decisions are made. We discuss the institutional implications in Chapter 13. Now let us see how teachers may incorporate SoTL into their thinking about teaching and as a basis for transformative reflection.

Using a phenomenographic approach, Trigwell et al. (2000) interviewed 20 teachers in an Australian university and found five categories of describing the scholarship of teaching, ranging from basic to a level where transformative reflection is at its most effective:

A The scholarship of teaching is about knowing the literature on teaching by collecting and reading that literature.

B Scholarship of teaching is about improving teaching by collecting and reading the literature on teaching.

C Scholarship of teaching is about improving student learning by investigating the learning of one's own students and one's own teaching.

D Scholarship of teaching is about improving one's own students' learning by knowing and relating the literature on teaching and learning to discipline-specific literature and knowledge.

E The scholarship of teaching is about improving student learning within the discipline generally, by collecting and communicating results of one's own work on teaching and learning within the discipline.

(Trigwell et al. 2000: 159)

The first two categories are at Level 2, reading about teaching only and then applying that knowledge to teaching, while the last three are at Level 3 (pp. 18–20), which focuses on the relationship between teaching and student learning. The last three categories involve reflection for the first time, using theory to see how one can improve student learning through one's own teaching. Category C focuses on student learning generally, Category D relates such reflection to include subject-specific knowledge, and Category E generalizes that to become research, with a responsibility to make one's work known generally.

We may distinguish different foci for reflection: on teaching alone or on how teaching relates to student learning; on learning in general or on discipline-specific as well as general implications; and on the use of formal theory gained from the literature as opposed to teachers' own informal theories of teaching.

We are concerned in this book with a formal theory of student learning, that of constructive alignment as discussed in Chapter 6 and in following chapters, and using this theory as a basis for transformative reflection. We recognize the importance of discipline-specific applications, but in a book such as this we cannot address all content areas except that in the final chapter, Chapter 14, we describe examples of how constructive alignment has been applied reflectively by teachers from a wide range of content areas.

The point about reflective practice, however, is that it enables teachers to apply general principles to their own particular context including their discipline area. An excellent example follows.

An example of transformative reflection

Stuart Tyler had problems teaching oedema associated with cardiac failure to nursing students (see Box 3.1).

Now let us meet Stewart Taylor. Both Stuart and Stewart had problems teaching oedema associated with cardiac failure; both thought that the problem needed realistic three-dimensional videos, using motion, to model the process rather than lecturing and illustrating with still, two-dimensional diagrams. Both found the videos made little difference to student performance. Stewart concluded that he'd done his best; he'd used the most suitable

---

Box 3.1 An example of transformative reflection in nursing studies

Problem: 90 per cent of nursing students experience difficulty in understanding the topic: oedema associated with cardiac failure.

Hypothesis: A visual approach is more suited to the subject and to students' learning styles.

Solution: Develop 'a multisensorial approach from which there could be no escape'. It has to have visual appeal and movement: hence *multimedia*, an animated slide show.

Result: Only a 'slight' improvement in students' understanding.

Reflection: 'I had wasted my time'

But then Tyler read the first edition of this book and learned:

1 Don't blame the students.
2 Don't blame the teacher.
3 Don't blame the teaching tool.
4 Do blame the lack of alignment.
5 Do blame the lack of aligned assessment.

On further reflection: 'The multimedia program was worthwhile . . . what it lacked was alignment and assessment.'

Students now:

1 Complete an assessable worksheet at home (marked and assessed by peers).
2 Complete a similar worksheet in class (again marked by peers).

Result: Pass rates in clinical studies increased from 80 per cent to 99.5 per cent.

Adapted from: Tyler (2001)

---

educational technology according to all the good books but it turned out not to be worth the extra hassle. He went back to lecturing with diagrams. Stuart, by way of contrast, reflected: 'It didn't work, and it should have worked. *Why* didn't it?' He had a theory, which, when he thought about it, told him that there was lack of alignment between his existing assessment task and his desired outcome. He made an aligned assessment sheet a teaching/learning activity – and failure rates dropped to near zero.

Here constructive alignment was used as the theory to effect the transformation from a teaching/learning activity that was not working to a working one. Stuart's case illustrates a very important point. Constructive alignment

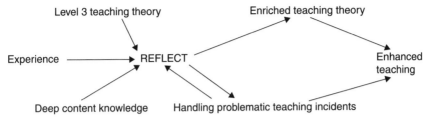

Figure 3.1 Theory and transformative reflective practice in teaching

isn't just a method or a model to be implemented: *It provides a conceptual framework for reflecting on the questions that need to be answered at crucial stages of teaching in general.* Those questions are:

1 What do I want my students to learn?
2 What is the best way in my circumstances and within available resources of getting them to learn it?
3 How can I know when or how well they have learned it?

These components, of curriculum, teaching method and assessment, are present in *any* teaching. What the constructive alignment framework does is invite us to question what we are doing as teachers at those crucial points and to rethink other ways of carrying them out, as did Stuart. These are the questions we shall be addressing in this book. But to ask those questions and rethink answers to them as the application of transformative reflection requires a theory. Figure 3.1 illustrates the steps in transformative reflection, here worded for the individual teacher, but which apply equally well *mutatis mutandis* to deans, deputy vice-chancellors and their respective creature committees.

A reflective teacher starts with three important components:

1 *Experience.* You cannot reflect on a blank slate. When you come across a difficult or challenging situation, the first question is: 'Have I come across anything like this in my past experience? If so, what did I do then? Did it work?' A further set of questions: 'What resources did I need then? What are at my disposal now?'
2 *Deep content knowledge.* You cannot teach effectively if you don't know your subject content very well indeed. So well, for example, that you can see instantly whether an unexpected answer a student confronts you with is original or misconceived (see Billy and the Creamed Wheat in Box 9.3, p. 173), or that you can see – on the run – powerful but simpler ways of expressing an idea.
3 *A Level 3 theory of teaching.* You can reflect with any theory. If you were a Level 1 teacher you might say: 'It didn't work because those students are just so *thick*. I suppose I could talk more slowly.' As a Level 2 teacher you might say (with Stewart): 'Well, the video didn't work. I'll do what I know I can do: lecture well.' As a Level 3 teacher you say (with Stuart): 'Why aren't they learning? How can I get them to be relevantly active?' *That* is

the sort of theory we want here, one that focuses on what the student does. This is a cyclical process; you keep looking at what they do, what they achieve and link that with what you are doing. You get to know your students as learners very well.

The next stage is to reflect on the teaching incident, using all three points, plus the specifics of this particular incident. There are several outcomes:

1 *Your teaching is enhanced*, eventually. You may need several goes at the problem.
2 *Your experience is enriched*. Each go at the problem adds to your store of experiences.
3 *Your teaching theory is enriched*. Using the theory in action makes you realize what aspects of the theory work and what do not.

This, then, is how transformative reflection enhances the quality of what it is we are doing. Task 3.3 asks you to reflect on a critical incident of your teaching or assessment and see how your response to the situation is related to your theory of teaching and learning as identified in Task 2.1. We will repeat this task later in Chapter 13.

Task 3.3 Reflection on a critical teaching/assessment incident

Reflect on a critical incident in your teaching – a situation in which you thought that your teaching or assessment had not gone quite how you would have liked it to have gone.

The incident:

_____

_____

_____

Consider the following questions.

a What was the problem? What went wrong? What was the evidence for the problem?

_____

_____

_____

b What was (were) the cause(s) of the problem?

_____

_____

_____

c How did you deal with the problem then?

_____

_____

d How did your solution to the problem relate to your theory of teaching and learning?

_____

_____

_____

Improving your teaching through action research

Let us return to the idea of improving your teaching using the four stage process of transformative reflection, reflect–plan–apply–evaluate, in conjunction with some of the ideas introduced in this and the previous chapter as the theoretical mirror that helps the transformation. An established and systematic way of doing this is *action research* (Kember and Kelly 1993) or *action learning* as it is sometimes called. Action research involves changing aspects of your teaching systematically, using whatever on-the-ground evidence that you can obtain that enables you to judge if the changes are in the right direction. Are your students now learning better than they used to? If so, good. If not, adjust your teaching next time in light of your theory of teaching. We thus return in a more systematic way to the continuing cycle of reflect–plan–apply–evaluate. This cycle may be repeated continually for things are never exactly right. Action research systematizes what reflective practitioners do all the time: they self-monitor their decisions and decide if they can do it better, and check to see if it really is an improvement. If not, they then repeat the cycle.

The target of action research is the teaching of the individual teacher herself or himself. The 'learning' in action learning refers not only to student learning, or even to learning about teaching, but to learning about oneself as a teacher and learning how to use transformative reflection to become a better teacher. Learning new techniques for teaching is like the fish that provides a meal today; transformative reflective practice is the net that provides meals for the rest of your life.

Now for an example of action research to find out, say, the extent to which you might be encouraging surface approaches in your teaching. Box 3.2 summarizes the aspects of your personal teaching that might lead to surface approaches.

The list comes under the two headings: motivation and learning climate, although they interrelate to some extent. Some of these things listed here as leading to surface learning – and therefore to be removed – you might think to be necessary, such as deducting marks for late submissions of assignments.

Box 3.2 Aspects of teaching likely to lead to surface approaches

Motivation

1 Conveying low evaluations of tasks, cynicism:

- Playing games with students at a disadvantage, especially in the context of assessment ('funny' multiple-choice alternatives; busy-work).
- Displaying personal dislike of content being taught.
- Assessing in a trivial way: low level tasks requiring memorizing only, marking only to the word limit, discounting grades for non-academic or disciplinary reasons, assessments not based on content taught.
- Emphasizing rules and regulations beyond their functional utility. *Subtext*: Rules are more important than learning.
- Not practising what is preached. *Subtext*: It's not worth me doing but you lot have to do it.

2 Conveying expectations of a low probability of success:

- Oral and written comments suggesting failure is due to lack of ability, success due to luck or other factors outside the student's control; not suggesting how a poor result might be remedied.
- Norm- rather than criterion-referenced assessment.
- Lack of clear direction, no feedback, no milestones of progress.

The learning climate

3 Aspects suggesting Theory X:

- Negative reinforcement, use of anxiety to 'motivate'.
- Blame-the-student explanations of student behaviour.
- Time stress: failure to consider or appreciate student workload, no time available to students for reflection.
- Students given little input in decisions that affect them.
- Anxiety: engendered by harsh sanctions, bullying, sarcasm, lack of consideration of students' perspective, work/time pressure.
- Cynicism: engendered by students feeling that you are not playing straight with them, that you don't actually believe what you are telling them.

While this is a common solution to the problem of late submission, it can get out of hand, as Box 10.3 (p. 211) tells us.

If you are committed to Level 3, you need to structure a predominantly Theory Y learning climate, with student learning as the top priority. This means using such features as time for reflection, trying to eliminate anxiety and cynicism and adopting the principles and practices of constructive alignment. We are dealing with a package: individual components that don't fit our constructively aligned package have to go. Deducting marks for managerial reasons is not on. Late submissions will have to be handled another way.

The first set of decisions, then, is to remove those aspects of your teaching that are actually encouraging surface approaches in students. Information on this or on other aspects of your teaching may be obtained from four possible sources:

1 your own reflections on your teaching
2 your students
3 a colleague in the role of 'critical friend'
4 a staff developer who can offer informed advice.

Much can be achieved by transformative reflection. We can reflect on the suitability of our intended learning outcomes and on what alternative teaching/ learning activities and assessment tasks we might best use. The constructive alignment framework is intended to encourage exactly that sort of reflection. The *Approaches to Teaching Inventory* (Prosser and Trigwell 1999; see also Chapter 13) is a very useful instrument for clarifying your conceptions (views) of teaching and how consistent your practices are with those conceptions.

Task 3.1 (p. 40) is a reflective task based on this chapter, the messages you convey to your students. Think about it and see what you conclude about the feedback you give your students.

It is hard for us to see what is wrong with some aspects of our teaching. We need somebody to tell us some things. We are likely to be blind to the more personal aspects of our teaching. What we intend as humour might come across as sarcasm; attempts at being friendly as patronizing. Both are fertile breeding grounds for anxiety and cynicism.

Our students are the most direct source of this kind of information: it is, after all, their perceptions that structure the intention to use a surface approach. This is quite a different issue from the usual student feedback questionnaire, which is about how you teach particular courses. Obtaining student feedback in the present context is best done anonymously, provided you are capable of putting up with the jibes of the faceless facetious or the negativism of the unnamed disgruntled. You can use an open question: 'What aspects of my teaching do you like most? What would you like to see changed?' A positive note is better than: 'What do you see wrong with my teaching?' You might as well walk around with a 'Kick me' sign on your backside.

Another perspective on teaching may be provided by our colleagues. A 'buddy system' or peer review (pp. 298–300) is useful, in which two teachers in the same department – and who trust each other – visit each other's classes as critical friends. They will need a common framework and a common set of assumptions about what is good teaching to do this well.

Yet another perspective is provided by the teaching and learning development centre, if your university has one. Staff developers have the expertise to

---

Task 3.4 What are the major problems in your own teaching that you would like to solve?

Take a semester- or year-long course that you are currently teaching and that presents you with particular difficulties or problems that you want to solve (e.g. teaching large classes, motivating students, lecturing successfully, dissatisfied with current assessment methods, covering the syllabus, getting students to understand, etc.). What are the *three most worrying* problems in teaching that course, which you would realistically hope to minimize by reading this book?

1 _____

_____

_____

2 _____

_____

3 _____

_____

_____

In the following chapters, bear this course in mind, even if the material being addressed is not particularly problematic. At the end, you have the chance to revisit these problems.

---

act as critical friend and to provide important insights on all stages of teaching where your own perspective might be limited.

Some problems may be located in your own personal style of teaching, which is what we are concerned with here. Task 3.4 asks you to list what at this stage you see to be major problems in your teaching that you'd like to solve.

We return to how action research may help you evaluate and transform your teaching in Chapter 13, where you will also have a chance to revisit this task.

Summary and conclusions

Getting students involved in learning: motivation

Motivation has two meanings: it refers to initiating learning, and to maintaining engagement during learning. To initiate learning, students need to see the cost-benefits: that engaging in learning has evident value and that engagement is likely to realize that value. Value accrues to a task for a variety of reasons: *extrinsic*, where the consequences either bring something we want, or avoid something we don't want; *social*, where the value comes from what other important people think; *achievement*, where the value is ego enhancement; *intrinsic*, where we don't even think to ask where the value comes from: it's the journey, not the destination. Teachers can make use of these values to bring about positive results. Extrinsic reinforcement in the form of rewards and punishments needs to be used carefully, punishment can be quite counterproductive. Likewise, competition may turn on some of the Susans but none of the Roberts. Teachers can act as enthusiastic role models – and if they want to motivate their students intrinsically, they should teach constructively.

The teaching/learning climate

The quality of the relationship set up between teacher and students, or within an institution, is referred to as its 'climate', the way the students feel about it. A Theory X climate is based on the assumption that students cannot be trusted, a Theory Y climate on the assumption that they can. If Level 1 and Level 3 theories of teaching describe two cognitive views of teaching, Theory X and Theory Y climates are their affective counterparts. The tight formal structures of a Theory X climate, with sanctions for non-compliance, result in anxiety and cynicism; both lead to surface learning. A Theory Y climate allows students freedom to make their own learning-related choices, which, as we shall see, is important if students are to become independent lifelong learners.

Reflective teaching

Improving teaching under these conditions is not a matter of simply learning a swag of teaching competencies. Teaching is personal, the context in which each teacher works being different. What is effective for this teacher, for that subject, at this level, for those students, may not apply to other teachers, working under their own conditions. Individuals have to work out their own solutions. This requires *transformative reflection*, a theory of teaching to reflect with and a context of experiences as the object of reflection. This process may be structured in action research, in which possible solutions are carefully monitored to gauge their success.

Improving your teaching

The two big questions for any individual teacher are: what do I believe in, a Theory X or a Theory Y climate? What am I doing, unwittingly, that might be creating the opposite climate to what I want? Teachers trying to implement aligned teaching must answer the first question with Theory Y. Information on the second question may come from one's own transformative reflections, from the students, from informed advice such as that of a colleague or of a staff developer. Each source provides a different perspective, but reliance on your own reflections isn't likely to be a productive source of information on those aspects of your teaching of which you are unaware. These can be supplemented with questionnaires, observations and interviews, their focus on aspects of teaching discussed in this chapter. The factors that are likely to lead to poor motivation and surface learning are summarized in Box 3.2.

Further reading

Biggs, J. and Moore, P. (1993) *The Process of Learning*. Sydney: Prentice-Hall Australia.
Feather, N. (ed.) (1982) *Expectations and Actions*. Hillsdale, NJ: Lawrence Erlbaum.
McGregor, D. (1960) *The Human Side of Enterprise*. New York: McGraw-Hill.
Pintrich, P.R. and Schunk, D.H. (2002) *Motivation in Education: Theory, Research, and Applications*. Upper Saddle River, NJ: Merrill-Prentice Hall.

Further reading for this chapter is a tough one. There is plenty of theoretical material on motivation, such as Feather's collection, but readers who don't know this literature already might have difficulty in transforming it into classroom action. Most of the recent literature on climate is addressed to business persons and is hairy-chested achievement motivation stuff, not Level 3 oriented at all. The exception is McGregor's original work on Theory X and Theory Y, which is well worth reading, but it needs translating into the university context. The general principles of both foci of this chapter are given a more in-depth treatment in Biggs and Moore. Pintrich and Schunk is an excellent summary of American research on the psychology of motivation and how it might translate into the classroom. A major distinction in that literature is between mastery goals, where the student aims to do as well as possible, and performance goals, where the student aims to achieve on external indicators of success such as grades. The parallel with deep and achieving approaches to learning is clear, but the deliberately-to-be-avoided surface approach is left out of consideration. Here is another example where parallel theories exist; we have focused on the one that works best for us.

On the scholarship of teaching and learning

Boyer, E.L. (1990) *Scholarship Reconsidered: Priorities for the Professoriate*. Princeton, NJ: Carnegie Foundation for the Advancement of Teaching.

Boyer's book kick-started the idea that university teaching is itself founded in scholarship, just as much as the content disciplines are. This idea has expanded and is fostered by the International Society for the Scholarship of Teaching and Learning, which holds annual conference and has its own journal. Website: http://www.issotl. org/SOTL.html (accessed 2 February 2011).

Carnegie Academy for the Scholarship of Teaching and Learning (CASTL) Campus Program with the American Association of Higher Education (AAHE). http://www.sotl.ilstu.edu/ (accessed 2 February 2011).

The Journal of the Scholarship of Teaching and Learning. http://www.iupui.edu/~josotl/

Google 'Scholarship of teaching and learning' or 'SoTL' and you'll get all you'll ever need to know about contacts, conferences and journals.

4

Contexts for effective teaching and learning

While particular teaching/learning activities (TLAs) need to be aligned to the target verbs in the intended learning outcomes (ILOs) they are to facilitate, there are also general criteria all TLAs should meet, whatever verbs they address. We look at these general criteria in this chapter. All teaching/learning activities set for students should be seen as having value and as readily performable. Students should be required to build on what they already know, to be relevantly active, to receive formative feedback and to be engaged in monitoring and reflecting on their own learning. A potential teaching/learning activity should meet these general criteria before it is aligned to the particular ILOs it is to facilitate. We close with a look at the context of e-learning.

Characteristics of rich teaching/learning contexts

In Chapter 1, good teaching was defined as 'getting most students to use the level of cognitive processes needed to achieve the intended outcomes that the more academic students use spontaneously'. Traditional teaching methods – lecture, tutorial and independent study – do not in themselves necessarily require students to use these high-level cognitive processes; Susan uses them but she does anyway, no thanks to the teaching. These teaching methods do not intrinsically provide support for appropriate levels of learning; they leave Robert floundering with a pile of lecture notes, a lot of trees but no wood. The challenge for teaching, then, is to select teaching activities that will encourage Robert to use learning activities that Susan already uses of her own accord.

There is no such thing as one 'best' all-purpose teaching method: what is 'best' depends on what outcomes are being addressed and, at a practical level, on what are the available resources. However, some general characteristics of good teaching/learning contexts emerge from the literature, and that are common to the achievement of a range of intended learning outcomes. In a heroic review of the literature on 'what works' in improving learning outcomes,

Hattie (2009a) synthesized over 800 meta-analyses, involving 50,000+ studies and about 250+ million students, from early childhood through to adult education, as measured by 'effect size' (a statistical manipulation that gives the strength of a factor and that is comparable across all studies). Table 4.1 gives the effect sizes that are applicable to higher education in order.

As almost everything has some positive effect on learning (that is, an effect size greater than 0.00), Hattie suggests focusing only on those effects greater than the average of all effects (0.40), that is, those effects above the dotted line in Table 4.1. The greatest single effect is when students self-assess. The

Table 4.1 What works best in higher education

Factor	Effect size
Student: Self-report grades	1.44
Teaching: Providing formative evaluation to lecturers	0.90
Teaching: Teacher clarity	0.75
Teaching: Reciprocal teaching	0.74
Teaching: Feedback	0.73
Teaching: Spaced vs. mass practice	0.71
Teaching: Metacognitive strategies	0.69
Curricula: Creativity programmes	0.65
Teaching: Self-verbalization/self-questioning	0.64
Teacher: Professional development	0.62
Teaching: Problem solving teaching	0.61
Teaching: Not labelling students	0.61
Teaching: Cooperative vs. individualistic learning	0.59
Teaching: Study skills	0.59
Teaching: Mastery learning	0.58
Teaching: Worked examples	0.57
Teaching: Goals – difficulty	0.56
Teaching: Peer tutoring	0.55
Teaching: Cooperative vs. competitive learning	0.54
Small group learning	0.49
Student concentration/persistence/ engagement	0.48
Teaching quality	0.44
Teaching: Cooperative learning	0.41
Teaching: Time on task	0.38
Teaching: Computer-assisted instruction	0.37

Source: Adapted from Hattie (2009a)

next strongest effect is formative feedback to teachers about how well they have been teaching and when they have not been teaching well; there is a 'trickle-down' effect to student learning, as Hattie puts it. There follows a list of factors, some of which are about what the teacher does, but more important is how that affects what the student does.

It is interesting that time spent teaching and computer assisted instruction fail to make the 0.40 effect size, which means these are relatively minor compared to other factors. But this obviously depends on the context. Very little time spent in teaching is likely to have quite deleterious effects on student learning, but more time than usual has a minor effect, which is as it should be if students are being taught to take control over their own learning. Likewise, using computer-assisted instruction in general may have a small effect but in distance learning, logistics make it very useful, but there again it depends on how it is being used (see pp. 70–73). In interpreting all of these factors, then, we have to bear in mind that all are relative to the context of teaching and the intended outcomes.

Hattie sums up by calling this 'visible learning', which is:

> . . . teachers seeing learning through the eyes of students, and students seeing teaching as the key to their ongoing learning. The remarkable feature of the evidence is that the biggest effects on student learning occur when teachers become learners of their own teaching, and when students become their own teachers. When students become their own teachers they exhibit the self-regulatory attributes that seem most desirable for learners (self-monitoring, self-evaluation, self-assessment, self-teaching). Thus, it is visible teaching and learning by teachers and students that makes the difference.
>
> (Hattie 2009a: 271)

Combining Table 4.1 with other work, we may distinguish seven characteristics of good learning contexts. They are those that provide:

1 metacognitive control, reflective learning
2 relevant learner activity
3 formative feedback
4 appropriate motivation
5 a base of interconnected knowledge
6 social learning
7 teaching quality.

Metacognitive control, reflective learning

Giving the student control over their own learning, 'visible learning', as Hattie calls it, is what good teaching is about. The items in Table 4.1, self-report grades, reciprocal teaching, teaching students metacognitive strategies and study skills, all address this.

In Chapter 3 we discussed reflective practice and transformative reflection, whereby teachers monitored their own practice and used their theory of teaching to see how they could teach better. The same thing applies to learning itself. When self-monitoring, learners keep a watching brief over their learning: how am I doing? Am I making mistakes here? Any pattern in my errors? If so, what is it and how can I avoid it in future? Is there any way I can approach this more effectively than I am now?

These are the sorts of questions that good learners ask themselves, like good practitioners of any sort. Formal, top-down ways of teaching discourage self-questioning. If the teacher always assesses how well the student is doing and never allows the student to self-assess, the student lets it go at that and consequently doesn't see the need for, or acquire the skills of, reflection. Indeed, the longer many undergraduate students stay at university – the Susans excepted – the less deep and the more surface oriented they tend to become. This has been observed in several countries: Australia (Watkins and Hattie 1985; Biggs 1987a), the UK (Entwistle and Ramsden 1983), and Hong Kong (Gow and Kember 1990). It seems that Robert's learning as it becomes institutionalized becomes unreflective, performed by rule of thumb and with minimum effort. All the decisions, especially about assessment, have been made for him in formal top-down teaching.

Where the teacher expounds the material and assesses it at the end, the teacher is in effect the masterbuilder for constructing the student's knowledge base, the student an apprentice bricklayer only. The student is left in a passive role both in receiving information and in monitoring what has been learned. They come to believe – or rather, they have the belief they acquired in school confirmed – that keeping track of their learning is the teacher's job, not their own. They are unlikely to become very good independent or lifelong learners.

Learning to 'monitor the construction site' involves study skills and self-management, including self-assessment, that are so important for addressing an attribute such as lifelong learning. These are dealt with in Chapter 9 under the heading of reflective learning.

E-portfolios have great potential for helping students become more meta-cognitive about their learning (Barrett 2007). They are being used at the City University of Hong Kong to help students reflect upon and integrate their learning within a specific course and across courses, including non-curricular learning experiences (Cheung et al. 2009). However, students need scaffolding to help them understand what reflection is and how to use it in order to improve their learning, otherwise they simply dump experiences and incidents in their portfolio and basically leave them there. Cheung et al. found that one important way was for students to reflect on their learning goals and how they sought to attain them. Such reflection was scaffolded by their learning context, which was outcomes based and constructively aligned. On broader learning experiences, such as an overseas excursion, reflection was encouraged by using narrative: students telling each other their stories and what they had learned. The City University experiment is ongoing.

Relevant learner activity

Being active while learning is better than being inactive. Activity is good in itself: it heightens physiological arousal in the brain, which makes performance more efficient. Physical exertion has quite dramatic effects on mental performance. Typically, four minutes of brisk exercise, such as running or pedalling on a bicycle, improves performance in such tasks as mental arithmetic. Longer periods, however, see performance worsen in the unfit, but continuing to improve in the fit (e.g. Tomporowski and Ellis 1986). Getting the adrenalin to flow increases alertness. This is one very good reason for breaking up long periods of lecturing with interspersed activities. Even just stopping the class and doing stretching exercises does more for students' learning than the teacher droning on.

In one study, students were required to learn from text in increasingly active ways: reading silently, underlining important words, writing out the key sentences containing those words, rewriting sentences in one's own words, to the most active, teaching somebody else the material. There was a strong correlation between extent of activity and efficiency of learning (Wittrock 1977).

Better still is when the activity addresses specific intended learning outcomes. Excursions are generally regarded as useful extensions to in-class learning, but their best use is when the activities in the excursion are aligned to the intended outcomes of the excursion. MacKenzie and White (1982) devised an excursion on coastal geography in which each of the intended outcomes was linked to quite dramatic actions, such as chewing mangrove leaves, wading through a muddy swamp, jumping across rock platforms and so on. Performance on a written test on what they had observed and learned three months later was near perfect. Spiegel describes a similar approach of 'adventure learning' to legal studies (see Box 4.1).

Box 4.1 Adventure learning in the School of Law

Nadja Siegel, lecturer in law at Queensland University, is the winner of the law section of the Australian University Teaching Awards. Through adventure learning she tries to develop in students the skills they will need to apply professionally. . . . She creates activities with an element of risk – physical, social or emotional – so that the experience is more real. Crossing a river using blocks as rafts, with one team missing equipment, forces them into deciding whether to adopt a competitive or cooperative approach. But she says adventure learning is not just games. '[Y]ou really need to be aware of how you're using the activity and be able to direct the students' experiences to the focus of their learning . . .'

Source: *The Australian Higher Education*, 26 November 1997

Such activities need not only to be energetic and memorable in themselves, but also aligned to an academic outcome. If discovering the role of salt in the ecology of mangrove swamps is an intended learning outcome, chewing mangrove leaves for their salt content is a teaching/learning activity directly addressing that outcome. If managing a team is an intended learning outcome, showing initiative in obtaining cooperation in building a raft is a relevant teaching/learning activity.

We learn through activating different sense modalities: hearing, touch, sight, speech, smell and taste. The more one modality reinforces another, the more effective the learning. It is like trying to access a book in a library. If all you know is the author, or the title, or the publisher or the year of publication, you could be in for a long search, but the more those 'ors' become 'ands', the faster and more precise the search becomes. Just so in accessing or remembering what has been learned. The more teaching/learning activities tie down the topic to be learned to multiple sensory modes, the better the learning.

Table 4.2 puts this very neatly. Don't take the percentages mentioned there too literally, but the messages are clear, simple and basically right. Some sensory modalities are more effective for learning than others; the more they overlap, the better; and best of all, you learn through teaching, which requires all the previous activities.

It is well worth remembering when designing teaching/learning activities that peer teaching is a particularly powerful way of learning for the teacher.

It may help to conceptualize this by realizing that the outcomes of learning are stored in three memory systems (Tulving 1985):

- *Procedural* memory: remembering how to do things. Actions are learned.
- *Episodic* memory: remembering where you learned things. Images are learned.
- *Semantic* memory: remembering meanings, frequently from statements about things. Verbal statements of knowledge are learned.

Table 4.2 Most people learn . . .

10%	of what they read
20%	of what they hear
30%	of what they see
50%	of what they see and hear
70%	of what they talk over with others
80%	of what they use and do in real life
95%	of what they teach someone else

Source. Attributed to William Glasser; quoted by *Association for Supervision & Curriculum Development Guide 1988*

When we learn something, each system is involved; we learn what we *did*, *where* it was and how to *describe* what it was. However, they are not equally easily accessed. Actions are easiest to remember (do we ever forget how to ride a bicycle?) and semantics, what was actually said, are hardest. That sequence probably reflects the sequence of psychological development: first actions, then images, then semantics. Be that as it may, recalling the context or the actions can often bring back the semantics. If you can *picture* where you learned it and what you were doing, you are more likely to recall what it was that you learned. It's like accessing the book in the library. Thus even learning straight verbal, or declarative, knowledge (see the next chapter) is best done in association with a rich store of images and actions. The adventure learning studies do exactly that.

Lecture theatres admittedly offer less scope for activity than wilderness areas, but as we see in Chapter 8, students can be kept relevantly active in the classroom and rather more so than they usually are.

Formative feedback

Arguably the most powerful enhancement to learning is feedback during learning. This is also called formative assessment, which is not to be confused with summative assessment. The purposes and effects of these two forms of assessment are so different it is a pity the word 'assessment' is used for both. Formative assessment is provided *during* learning, telling students how well they are doing and what might need improving; summative *after* learning, informing how well students have learned what they were supposed to have learned. In one project we were involved in, teachers regarded the comments they wrote on final assessment tasks as 'formative', despite the fact that the course was over. To avoid such problems, we use the term formative feedback, not formative assessment.

There are many misconceptions about feedback. Despite the claims of the best teachers, they typically do not provide feedback (Hattie 2009b). Hattie suggests that the nature of feedback is not just teachers giving information to students about their performance. Teachers need to be open to feedback from students as to where they are and where they have got it wrong. Feedback is an interactive two-way process, not just teachers writing brief comments on assignments – or on exam answers that the students never see anyway.

So important is formative feedback that the effectiveness of any particular teaching/learning activity can be judged by how well it allows students to provide feedback to teachers and from teachers to students as they learn. In a large lecture, neither teachers nor students receive much if any feedback. Interactive class teaching works so well precisely because it is interactive and ongoing, providing both parties with contemporary information about how well learning is proceeding.

Effective feedback requires that students have a baseline knowledge of where they are, and knowledge of where they are supposed to be heading.

This is where knowledge of the intended outcomes of their learning is so important in promoting metacognitive self-monitoring. Feedback is meant to bridge that gap between where they are and where they should be. Feedback can be provided by the teacher, by other students and by the students themselves, each such source giving a different aspect to the feedback.

An important part of feedback is *using error constructively*. Errors are important learning opportunities, but feedback is essential if students are to learn from error. In the course of learning, students inevitably create misconceptions that need to be corrected so that any misunderstandings can be set right, literally in the formative stage. To do this requires a Theory Y climate, where students will feel free to admit error. If they think that the information will be used summatively or that they will be judged on the result, they will be defensive about admitting to any error. In that case, an opportunity for learning has been lost. This must make one cautious about using formative test results in the final grade.

In a tutorial or group session where the tutor is censorious or sarcastic students will keep quiet, preferring not to make themselves vulnerable. This is independent of any particular teaching method. In an otherwise fine problem-based learning (PBL) course at a particular university, one tutor completely wrecked the process. The aim in PBL is for students to pose questions and to follow through with plausible answers to a given problem. This they do by reference to theory, case histories, past experience, similar cases and so on, by asking questions and testing possible answers in discussion. But in this particular case, the tutor replied to every question put to her with an all-knowing sneer: 'That's for me to know and for you to find out!' So the students in this group gave up asking questions and problem-based learning acquired a bad name. So did the tutor.

Some teachers feel awkward about drawing attention to students' errors. In wanting to create a Theory Y climate, where students can feel free to explore possibilities and ask far-out questions, these teachers are reluctant to publicly correct students' errors.

This is the dilemma teachers have to face: do I correct mistakes and risk discouraging students from expressing their understandings in public? Or do I let them go uncorrected in the interests of maintaining a productive working atmosphere? Not to correct seems to be abdicating an important teaching function: misconceptions are allowed to pass unquestioned and uncorrected. One technique is to smile encouragingly, with 'Yes, not bad. Can anyone else elaborate on that?' This signals that there is a problem, that we are part-way there, that it is a collective job to achieve a better outcome and that individuals are not to be blamed for not having a perfect answer first time round. It's a matter of the interpersonal chemistry, the rapport, that a teacher can create. With good rapport, public correction is cheerfully accepted and appreciated.

Japanese teachers do exactly this in what Hess and Azuma (1991) call 'sticky probing', which westerners might see as a little drastic. A single problem is discussed for hours by students, with teacher adjudicating, until a consensus acceptable to teacher and students is reached. The focus of the probing is a particular student's error, with the student the focus of public correction. Japanese students don't appear to see this as a punishment for making a mistake; they understand that learning is a collective activity and that learning from mistakes is part and parcel of learning.

Using error constructively to provide feedback involves two challenges:

- requiring students to expose their erroneous thinking without risk of ridicule, loss of face or low grades;
- correcting them nicely so that they feel positive about being corrected and not ashamed or resentful.

This is a personal matter that every teacher needs to resolve in a way with which each can feel comfortable.

Appropriate motivation

When we discussed motivation in Chapter 3, three major points emerged:

1 The task provided – the teaching/learning activity itself – must be *valued* by the student and not seen as busy-work or trivial. In constructively aligned teaching and learning, where as we shall see the teaching/learning activity is designed to facilitate achieving the outcomes, students will value the learning activities more than in unaligned teaching, because what the student is asked to do is patently in service of achieving the intended outcomes of the course.

2 The student must have a reasonable *probability of success* in achieving the task. Again, this is patently the case in constructive alignment – if an outcome is *intended,* then presumably the teacher has set a task that is achievable. Nevertheless, in their informal interactions with students and in their comments on student performances, teachers may convey messages to students that they have little hope of succeeding; for example, by attributing a poor performance to lack of ability rather than to lack of persistence. Probability of success nevertheless needs to be considered in light of Hattie's finding that learning is improved when teachers set relatively difficult learning goals, as opposed to a bland 'do your best'. Goals need to be attainable but challenging, and students need to be aware of the criteria, or rubrics, by which success will be determined.

3 A Theory Y climate is best for quality learning. Learners learn best when they feel free to move, are trusted and are able to make decisions and take responsibility for their own learning – *consistent with* clear policies and procedures and with an organized environment for learning. 'Consistent with' is the rub. Different teachers, and especially administrators, will disagree about the right balance between a Theory Y climate and an organized environment. Many teaching/learning activities and assessment tasks that address higher level outcomes require an extent

of student involvement and a lack of constraints on space and time that colleagues, heads of department or boards of examiners may well regard as unacceptably messy: not in the interests of running a tight ship.

A base of interconnected knowledge

The teaching context could be regarded as a construction site on which students build on what they already know. Sound knowledge is based on *interconnections*. Everything that has been written so far in this book about understanding, deep learning, the growth and development of knowledge and intrinsic motivation reiterates this. Sound understanding is itself the realization that what is separated in ignorance is connected in knowing. Cognitive growth lies not just in knowing more, but in *restructuring* what is already known in order to connect old with new knowledge.

Building on the known

The physics professor is greeting the new intake of freshers, still glowing from their A level successes:

'Now, do you remember the physics you were taught in sixth form?'
Two hundred heads nod enthusiastically.
'Well, forget it. You're here to learn *real* physics, not the simplicities you were taught in school!'

This true exchange is a good example of how not to teach. Teaching builds on the known, it must not reject it – proceed from the known to the unknown, as the old saying has it. In deep learning, new learning connects with old, so teaching should emphasize the interconnectedness of topics. It helps to make the connections explicit ('Last week we . . . Today, I am taking that further'), to choose familiar examples first, to ask students to build on their own experiences when discussing a principle or topic, to draw and explain parallels while teaching, to use cross-references in presenting material, to present topics by showing where they connect to other topics.

Teaching connectedness is easier in an outcomes-based than in a topic-based curriculum. With only five or six learning outcomes, instead of a dozen or so topics, dealing with an intended learning outcome will inevitably draw on a wider range of relevant material than teaching topic by topic.

Maximizing structure

The connections we were talking about above are drawn horizontally, but the most powerful connections are drawn vertically or hierarchically. That is, we should help students to *reconceptualize* so that what are seen as differences at a subordinate level become related at a superordinate level. In the next chapter we look at 'threshold concepts', which are superordinating concepts that in each subject area allow the student to reconceptualize so they see the subject in a new light. Thus, concepts that seem irreconcilably different to students may frequently be seen as different instances of the same higher order principle. The students see differences between the instances because they are focusing at a lower order node. In teaching, we should see that the students understand what the nodes in the structure are. Teaching using bullet lists, for example, is useful only when the points listed are at the same level or node in the structure. If they are not, the bullet list hides the real conceptual structure.

New information should not be just dumped on the learner, in rambling lessons, in poorly constructed texts or as bullet lists. Good teaching always contains a structure, hidden away, but there to be found. Teaching from lists is like sawing up the trunk and branches of a tree, stacking them in a neat pile, and saying: 'There! See the tree?'

The chances of students coming to grasp the structure can be maximized in many ways. In some circumstances, it is appropriate to present the structure upfront. An 'advance organizer' is a preview of a lecture that mentions the main topics to be dealt with and the overriding conceptual structure to which they may be related (Ausubel 1968). The student then has a conceptual framework from the start: as material is introduced, it can be fitted into place. For example, a diagram based on expectancy-value theory could be used as such an organizer to a lesson on motivation.

A 'grabber', on the other hand, relies not on structure for its effect but on its emotional impact. Starting a class with a cartoon, an interesting slide or video clip elicits interest in the topics to follow. Whereas the advance organizer is *conceptual*, the grabber is *affective*, appealing to shock or to humour. Both have their place but work on different principles – our interest here is in the structure of the material, not in its shock value.

Some teachers fall into the trap of talking down to students with an in-your-face conceptual structure, all answers and no questions. Lessons that are too well structured encourage students simply to take on board the given structure and memorize that, thereby establishing one of the lowest of the forms of understanding mentioned by Entwistle and Entwistle (1997; see p. 85). In the end, the student must *always* do the structuring – it's what the student does that is important. The challenge for teachers is to strike the right balance between, on the one hand, presenting students with chaos and, on the other, presenting them with cut-and-dried conclusions where all the interesting conceptual work has been done. As discussed later, the question of how much structure to present, given your students and their existing knowledge base, may be gauged from using formative feedback while they are learning – questions, trial runs, even the inter-ocular test (look them in the eyes for signs of life).

Social learning

Social learning refers to situations where students learn off each other, either by peer tutoring or in discussion groups of various kinds. Social learning of various kinds is well represented in Table 4.1: peer tutoring, cooperative learning over both competitive and individualistic learning, and small group learning all emerge as effective ways of facilitating student learning. Such learning has effects that may not be so readily attained in teacher-directed learning: it is broadening, it gives opportunities for heightening self-awareness, and students like it. The reasons are manifold, but include the recognition that other people just like me see things differently from the way I do. I am thus encouraged to reflect on my own learning and interpretations ('Have I got this right after all?' 'Where would I change my view?') so that my perspective and understanding of a topic become broadened and I gain insights into my own learning by comparing it to the way others are learning and to the conclusions they draw from the same data. There are various teaching/learning situations that involve social learning, and in Chapter 9 we will be considering these, together with the outcomes each different type is likely to produce.

Teaching quality

Finally, we come to what the teacher does. It should come as no surprise that the quality of teaching matters – where would we all be if it didn't? Two broad aspects of teacher quality come up. The first is about the way teachers interact with students in various teaching methods, and the second is about the structural or curricular aspects of teaching.

The sort of teaching that engages student learning and encourages student metacognition and self management has already been discussed. There is no one teaching method that does this to the exclusion of others – Table 4.1 has several that encourage student self-management: teaching metacognitive strategies such as student self-assessment, peer tutoring, study skills, reciprocal teaching, for example – but it is rather a case of the *way* almost any interaction between teacher and student, and student and student, is handled. That 'way' is summed up in what Hattie calls 'visible learning' (Hattie 2009a).

Structural aspects of teaching include variety and pacing. If students are to learn complex ideas, they will need varied presentations, where the same concepts are addressed from different angles, using different examples. They also need the learning sessions to be well paced. Spaced sessions are much more effective than massed; more frequent short periods of learning should be scheduled rather than learning at length in a single session (see Table 4.1). In one Hong Kong teacher training (!) institution, one subject was 'taught' in lectures lasting for three hours straight (but that was a few years ago, under different management, we should add). Teaching creativity is another curricular feature high on the list of effective teaching practices. We return to the issue of teaching for creativity in Chapter 9.

Finally, staff development for teachers and transformative reflection had positive effects on student learning. We return to these important issues later.

E-learning

> E-learning tools and fashions date quickly. Back at around the turn of the century, large projects were in progress to revolutionise education through electronic media . . . There was something of a gold rush to repurpose learning materials and launch large-scale, content-led, broadly self-study distance-learning programmes. Today the focus is returning to what makes good teaching, and thus encourages successful learning, whatever media are being used.
>
> (Brenton 2009: 97)

Brenton's point is well taken. In order to emphasize that e-learning is about learning, not about using gee-whiz gadgetry, he points out that e-learning is learning that happens when students engage with technology, not something teachers 'deliver'. Originally, information technology was based on the Level 1 transmission view of teaching, that there's an awful lot of information students need to know and the net is an ideal place to get it from. Then a Level 2 version came along, which is also what Brenton is reacting against: all sorts of bells and whistles that were fun to play with but seemed to be ends in themselves rather than carefully structured supports for student learning. Beetham and Sharpe (2007) take the discussion to Level 3, where they emphasize that pedagogy comes before technology. As digital technology dominates students' behaviour in everyday life, that technology can be used to enhance the dialogue between teacher and learner as new ways of engaging students in learning become available.

The first use of e-learning for accessing huge sources of information is important and understood, but students need to be taught how to use search engines strategically and selectively. This aspect of e-learning is very convenient, hence its use in distance learning and mixed mode teaching on campus learning. 'Lectopia' is a system, developed at the University of Western Australia and used throughout Australian universities, whereby lectures are recorded and posted on the net. Lectures can be downloaded at any time on computers, iPods or mobile phones, thus allowing students whose work commitments clash with scheduled lectures to listen to them at their convenience. However, care must be taken to see that Lectopia does not reinforce the idea that the main function of university teaching is lecturing: the transfer of information, without the interactive learning that – one hopes – took place in the lecture (see Chapter 8).

E-learning opens up a whole new domain for student activity, of which replaying lectures and downloading gigabytes of information is only a fraction of its potential usefulness. BlackBoard and WebCT, apart from being used as a management platform for all teaching on and off campus, also have supports for interactive teaching/learning activities and for different types of assessment, as we discuss in Chapter 12. The use of these platforms for interactive teaching, on and off campus, can be a boon for teachers and students alike with respect to large classes.

Interactive e-learning dissolves the boundaries of time and space, allowing many different kinds of interaction between people:

1 *Synchronous and asynchronous use.* Synchronous use is when a teacher or learning package interact with the student in the same time frame. This is the case when teacher and student are online at the same time, as in tele- or video-conferencing. Students attending a PowerPoint lecture is also a synchronous use. With asynchronous use, participants make their communication in their own time, such as happens when using email or a bulletin board. For example, the teacher may post questions on the board and the students respond with answers or comments, as is convenient to them, prior to the stated deadline. Asynchronous use is particularly valuable in off-campus teaching, so that individuals with full-time jobs can enter their learning space at evenings or weekends, or whenever best suits them.

2 *Individual and social use.* We normally think of online teaching as involving a lonely individual at a keyboard responding asynchronously to a distant information source. This is only one, limited, use. When used synchronously, student and teacher may converse one to one or one to many, and students may interact with each other at the same time. The social advantages can be enhanced by having pairs or even larger numbers at the same keyboard so that they may discuss their comments, questions or responses before sending them. These groupings can be used synchronously or asynchronously.

The combinations of individual and group, and synchronous and asynchronous use, are many. Each combination has its own advantages and disadvantages; as always, it depends entirely on what and how you want your students to learn. A disadvantage of asynchronous online discussion is that that those who place their views first can frustrate others who wanted to make the same points. This might be obviated by requiring students to post to a closed address, which would then be opened on a specified date. It helps considerably if groups can meet face to face first, so that when online discussion begins, people can put a face to the name and feel that they are genuinely conversing.

Personal digital assistants (PDAs) can be used in the classroom, as did Mazur for instant responding to multiple-choice-type questions (pp. 139–140), but the most recent versions have telephone, still, video and internet-accessing options, which make them incredibly flexible as learning and assessment tools. Teacher–student and student–student communication can be maintained outside the classroom in workplace or other learning situations in real or in virtual time.

Bulletin boards, either with PDA or computer, can be used to consolidate and elaborate material. Students can, in their own time – that is, asynchronously – post comments about a reading or lecture, which can lead to conversations about the content, different interpretations, elaborations and corrections. This can provide a tremendous amount of feedback both to the teacher and to the students themselves. An example of enlightened bulletin board use with teachers attending a postgraduate educational psychology course is given by Chan (2001), who integrated computer-supported collaborative learning with regular teaching. The students were asked to post their learning notes and responses to questions on a bulletin board and to comment on the notes and responses of others. The distinctive feature of her use of the bulletin board was the way she posted reflective prompts, such as:

- Is there anything interesting or useful you have learned?
- What are some things that are difficult to understand?
- How did reading these notes help you think about X and Y?
- Have the comments on your ideas made you rethink the issue?

Students did not have to address each as an assignment question, but as reminders to guide their thinking. Students were also asked about their conceptions of teaching and learning at the beginning and at the end of the course; the difference became a measure of the growth of their complexity of thinking about teaching and learning.

Chan found that the frequency of contribution to the bulletin board in itself was unrelated to a gain in complexity of thinking, but when the comments were divided into those that were derived collaboratively or were simply posted as individual contributions, those who entered into collaborative engagement gained most in complexity of thinking. This replicates a finding that face-to-face collaborative learning leads to better structured assignments than individually written ones (Tang 1998).

Knowledge Forum is a powerful program for encouraging collaborative knowledge construction (Scardamalia et al. 1994; Scardamalia and Bereiter 2006; Chan and van Aalst 2008). Knowledge Forum involves students contributing to a bulletin board by generating their own problems, posing their own questions and commenting on each other's work, rather like Chan's usage. The computer helps search all comments written by a student at different periods, which can then be rated in terms of the quality of the comments. The software comes with a program called Analytical Toolkit that can generate quantitative indices, such as how much each student has written, how much the individual has read others' notes, how often their comments are revised or elaborated, how one student's notes relate to others' notes, who is writing to whom, and so on. However, the program cannot recognize the quality of the comments written and so analyses still need to be done by teachers. The main difference between Knowledge Forum and other discussion platforms is that Knowledge Forum includes thinking prompts and other devices to help students reflect deeply as they contribute and it provides formative feedback on students' ideas as they are posted on the platform continually. One can also make a summative statement about students' growth and learning outputs at the end of the course.

Virtual environments, many available commercially on CD-ROM, provide interesting interactive environments for students to explore. For example, 'Virtual Dig' can take archaeology students through excavating a site; they can alter factors such as time of dig, method, whether to screen dirt for relics and so on. There are many science laboratory virtual environments where students can try expensive or dangerous experiments at a fraction of real cost and with no likelihood of something going badly wrong.

Computer-mediated conferencing (CMC) is a general term for teaching online with an 'e-moderator', who is in effect a tutor who 'chairs' asynchronous sessions with distance learning students (Salmon 2003). Salmon suggests a five-stage model for CMC:

1 access and motivation: making sure all participants can go online, keeping them motivated over the inevitable blips and providing technical support;
2 online socialization: getting to know each other and building a group sense;
3 information exchange: helping participants with searching, downloading and organizing the relevant information;
4 knowledge construction: participants become authors, sharing views and contributions. There are many ways of organizing this phase, with individual, dyad and group work, depending on the purpose;
5 development: participants now become responsible for their own learning, using self-critical and reflective strategies, developing where they want to go.

There is a view popular with politicians, among others, that online teaching is the answer to large classes. This view assumes a Level 1 theory of teaching as a one-way transmission: that teaching is merely providing information. But as we have seen, effective teaching involves engaging students in relevant activity, so there are obvious limits to the numbers that can be handled appropriately. The difference between a teacher responding interactively to 30 students online and 300 is obvious. Salmon's five stages of online teaching should put paid to that view. As student enrolments in a course increase, it becomes correspondingly necessary to engage online teaching assistants or e-moderators who are both computer wise and content expert.

Three changes needed in the way we usually think about teaching

The work in this chapter involves important changes in the way we normally think about teaching. First, we, as teachers, need to stop thinking about what to say in the next lecture that we have to give, or what to do in the tutorial we have to design. It is only when we have first clarified our intended learning outcomes that we should start thinking about the teaching/learning activities we might most appropriately use. This will probably not mean giving lectures. Many academics start from the assumption that their major activity is to give a 'lecture', which is after all what the timetable says they should be doing. University planners and architects accordingly designate these rooms 'lecture theatres', equipping them with stage and spotlight, as if skilled performers are to provide some pleasant entertainment there. What goes on is only rarely carried out by people skilled in the performing arts and only sometimes is it entertaining.

The assumption that the lecture method, and its satellite the tutorial, should be the defaults that academics use in discharging their teaching duties needs examining. The lecture and tutorial do have their uses, but they are limited in what they can effectively achieve. There are more effective ways of using the space in those large 'lecture' theatres. It helps to think of lectures and tutorials as *situations*, in which a range of teaching/learning activities can take place, rather than as prescriptions for a way of teaching.

The second change in thinking is to shift the focus from what the teacher does to what the student should best be doing. Teaching is, if you like, a service activity; we teach so that students may learn and what they learn depends on how they go about learning. That sounds like a Sybil Fawlty statement of the bleeding obvious, but all too frequently the messages from administration downwards are that teaching is only about what teachers do. We actually have a two-sided ledger sheet: (a) what the teacher is doing, and (b) what at the same time the students are doing. Attaining the intended outcomes depends rather more on (b) than on (a). It's a pity that in English we have two separate words for 'teaching' and 'learning'. Some languages, such as Russian, have one word for both so that you can't then say: 'I taught them but they didn't learn.' One feature of constructive alignment is that it brings teaching and learning closer together, even if in English we don't have a single word for it.

The third change is that we need to stop assuming that learning is only taking place when it is located inside a teacher-directed classroom. If you want your students to be lifelong learners – which the mission statement of your institution almost certainly requires – some learning should be taking place outside a formal teacher-directed environment. Remember that earlier in this chapter it was found that the most effective all-purpose teaching method is teaching students to be metacognitive, learning to manage their learning by themselves.

In sum, designating teaching sessions as 'lectures' and 'tutorials' should be seen not as prescribing what teachers have to do, but as situations in which a variety of teaching/learning activities can take place. Indeed, more often than not, the learning activities relevant to achieving the most important learning outcomes are best situated *outside* the classroom, not inside.

In Part 2 of this book we will be elaborating on these points in the context of designing a constructively aligned system of teaching, while in Chapter 6 we examine the theory of constructive alignment and how it came into being.

A checklist for your teaching context

Task 4.1 The teaching and learning context you have created

Reflect on a critical incident in your teaching, it could be a classroom teaching session, an out-of-class teaching session, an incident related to assessment of student performance, or even an informal interaction with students on matters related to teaching and learning. Evaluate the incident in light of its effectiveness in relation to the characteristics of an effective teaching and learning context. Provide evidence to substantiate your evaluation.

1 Enabling students to take control and be reflective in their learning.

_____

_____

_____

2 Providing relevant learner activities.

_____

_____

3 Providing formative feedback on your students' learning progress.

_____

_____

_____

4 Providing appropriate motivation.

_____

_____

_____

5 Constructing a base of interconnected knowledge.

_____

_____

_____

6 Providing opportunity for social learning.

_____

_____

_____

Your reflection:

Is the context within which this particular incident occurred effective in relation to learning? If you were to conduct a similar teaching incident again, would you do it differently to create a more effective context for your students' learning? If yes, what changes would you make?

_____

_____

_____

Summary and conclusions

In this chapter, we have been looking at the general characteristic of all teaching contexts, whether outcomes based or not, that have been found in the research literature. Largely on the basis of meta-analyses based on a very large number of studies, we came across seven such characteristics. When designing teaching/learning activities that align to our particular intended learning outcomes, then we should see that they conform to these characteristics where possible.

Metacognitive control, reflective learning

Good teaching is that which helps students take control of their learning. This happens best 'when teachers see learning through the eyes of their student, and students see themselves as their own teachers' (Hattie 2009a). There are many teaching practices that assist in this process, from peer teaching to training students to use metacognitive learning strategies. Students taking control of their learning is what lifelong learning is about, a matter we return to in Chapter 9.

Relevant learner activity

Knowledge is constructed through learner activity and interaction. Activity has two main roles. The fact of being generally active in and of itself provides general alertness and efficiency. Second, and more specifically, activity specifically keyed to the intended learning outcomes, using different sensory modes of learning to provide multiple access to what has been learned, is a very powerful way of learning.

Formative feedback

Formative feedback is essential for good learning: teaching is good or poor depending on how readily students receive feedback on how they are doing. For feedback to be effective, students need to be clearly aware of what they are supposed to be learning, and, as they are unlikely to be perfect first time, they need information as to where their deficiencies lie; any misconceptions students may have need to be confronted and corrected. Teachers, other students and students themselves can be useful sources of feedback, depending on the intended learning outcome.

Appropriate motivation

Motivation provides concentration, engagement and persistence in learning, and that is provided when tasks are valued by students and are attainable, but not too easily. Goals need to be set that require complex engagement but students need to be clearly aware of the goals and the criteria for success. The general context needs to be Theory Y so that students can take more responsibility for their learning, but some colleagues and more administrators may see this differently.

Constructing a base of interconnected knowledge

A powerful knowledge base is complex in structure and error free, built on accessible interconnections. Creating such a base involves: building on the known, making use of students' existing knowledge and emphasizing structural interconnections between topics. These points should infuse teaching, whatever the particular teaching activity.

Social learning

Social learning refers to situations where students learn from each other, either by peer tutoring or in discussion groups of various kinds, and has main effects that may not be attained so readily in teacher-directed learning. Students like it and more readily engage in learning, while the learning produced is more broadly based, and students have opportunities for increasing awareness of what they learn and how they learn it as compared to their peers.

Teaching quality

Quality teaching produces quality learning, hence the importance of staff development and reflective practice. Quality teaching has two aspects: what the teacher does when interacting with students, and how the curriculum is structured and organized. A number of teaching methods encourage student metacognition, but no particular method is as important as the way the teacher interacts with the student, whatever the method. The curriculum should be organized so that topics are taught in varied ways, and spaced over time.

E-learning

Educational technology offers a range of teaching/learning activities addressing a wide range of learning outcomes. E-learning can mimic standard classroom teaching but essentially and most importantly it offers possibilities of engaging learners in ways that are not possible in the classroom, such as computer-mediated conferencing and Knowledge Forum. Both may operate in real time or asynchronously, the latter allowing students to go online at their own convenience and to post contributions after serious reflection. E-learning may be seen to obviate some problems of large class teaching, but the fact remains that effective online interaction with students still demands teacher time; more students online means more teacher time.

Three changes needed in the way we usually think about teaching

We need to question three assumptions:

1 that lectures and tutorials are the default teaching methods: rather they are types of *situation* in which different teaching/learning activities can be organized, depending on the learning outcomes that are intended.
2 that the focus should be on what teachers are doing: in the 'lecture', or any teaching/learning situation, it is more important to focus on what the students are doing.
3 that relevant learning occurs only when inside the classroom with a teacher orchestrating the proceedings.

Further reading

On good teaching/learning contexts and principles of good teaching

Gibbs, G. (2006) On giving feedback to students. http://www.brookes.ac.uk/services/ocsd/firstwords/fw21.html (accessed 2 February 2011).

Hattie, J. (2009a) *Visible Learning: A Synthesis of 800+ Meta-analyses on Achievement.* London: Routledge.

Hattie, J. (2009b) The Black Box of tertiary assessment: an impending revolution, in L.H. Meyer, S. Davidson, H. Anderson, R. Fletcher, P.M. Johnston and M. Rees (eds) *Tertiary Assessment and Higher Education Student Outcomes: Policy, Practice and Research.* Wellington, New Zealand: Ako Aotearoa, pp. 259–75. An abridged version is downloadable at: http://akoaotearoa.ac.nz/download/ng/file/group-4/n3469-the-black-box-of-tertiary-assessment—john-hattiepdf.pdf (accessed 2 February 2011).

Petty, G. (2006) *Evidence-based Teaching.* Cheltenham: Nelson Thornes.
Ramsden, P. (2003) *Learning to Teach in Higher Education.* London: Routledge.

Hattie's book goes into much more detail on factors producing good student learning and on his concept of visible learning. His book chapter is a summary of this work and is downloadable as indicated. Petty's book shows how to put into practice the teaching methods with the biggest effect sizes in Hattie's work: feedback, interactive teaching, graphic organizers and various examples of group work are among the best. Gibbs's paper describes many ways in which feedback can be provided. Ramsden deals with six key principles of effective teaching.

More on e-portfolios

Barrett, H.C. (2007) Researching electronic portfolios and learner engagement: the REFLECT Initiative, *Journal of Adolescent and Adult Literacy,* 50,6: 436–49. Downloaded from: http://www.taskstream.com/reflect/whitepaper.pdf (accessed 2 February 2011).
And a range of examples: http://electronicportfolios.com/portfolios/bookmarks.html#hied (accessed 2 February 2011).

On e-learning and teaching

Beetham, H. and Sharpe, R. (2007) *Rethinking Pedagogy for a Digital Age: Designing and Delivering E-learning.* London: Routledge.
Hughes, J. (2008) Letting in the Trojan mouse: using an e-portfolio to rethink pedagogy. http://www.ascilite.org.au/conferences/melbourne08/procs/hughes.pdf (accessed 2 February 2011).
Laurillard, D. (2002) *Rethinking University Teaching.* London: Routledge Falmer. See references to adaptive and productive media.
Salmon, G. (2003) *E-moderating: The Key to Online Teaching and Learning.* London: Kogan Page.

Beetham and Sharpe take the view that use of e-learning needs to be embedded in a theory of learning on the one hand and the facts of students' digital sophistication on the other, thus opening out, as they put it, pedagogies that need rethinking. Likewise, Hughes asserts that 'letting in the Trojan mouse' is 'catastrophic' in its implications for the way we think about teaching and learning. Laurillard shows how technology can be used with conversations between student, teacher and machine to advance high level and creative thinking. Salmon gives solid practical advice for using computer-mediated conferencing, an interactive technique developed from the Open University for teaching distance learning students.

The University of Tasmania has a useful website for several aspects of e-learning: www.utas.edu.au/tl/improving/peerreview/ (accessed 2 February 2011).

Some useful educational development centres websites

University of South Australia: http://www.unisa.edu.au/teachinglearning/default.asp (accessed 2 February 2011).

University of Texas: http://www.utexas.edu/academic/cte/PeerObserve.html (accessed 2 February 2011).

The Higher Education Academy website www.heacademy.ac.uk/ is a goldmine on all aspects of university teaching, and in particular because it has Subject Centres, which deal with a large range of content areas. We shall be returning to this website in the following chapters.

And teaching and learning centres worldwide: http://learningandteaching.dal .ca/ids.html (accessed 2 February 2011). This URL provides very useful links to centres in most western countries. You can navigate to most topics dealt with here and in other chapters on university teaching that will discuss the topic in the context and vocabulary of your own country.

5

Knowledge and understanding

Constructive alignment is a design for teaching, but before we move on to that in the next chapter, we should have a look at the nature of what it is that is to be taught. We distinguish two main kinds of knowledge, declarative and functioning (there are many more kinds but for present purposes this distinction is the most important). Declarative knowledge is knowledge about things, expressed in verbal or other symbolic form; functioning knowledge is knowledge that informs action by the learner. In the past, and to a lesser extent today, universities emphasized declarative knowledge even when preparing students for the professions. Threshold concepts are those that, when properly understood, bring about changes in the learner's perspective of a subject and consequently changes in behaviour; these concepts need to be given careful attention in the design of degree programmes as their acquisition can be 'troublesome.' When students 'really' understand a concept – as opposed to giving verbal definitions and paraphrases of it, important as these are in their place – they behave differently, being able to carry out 'performances of understanding'. Such performances are important in designing course and programme outcomes. We also need to be specific in defining what we mean by different levels of understanding. The SOLO taxonomy classifies learning outcomes in terms of their structural quality, which makes it useful for defining levels of understanding, which in turn may be used for specifying such levels when writing learning outcomes.

Kinds of knowledge

When discussing the sorts of knowledge that are taught at university the distinction between *declarative* knowledge and *functioning* knowledge is important.

Declarative knowledge refers to knowing about things, but because it is expressed in symbol systems, usually verbal, it is also called propositional knowledge or content knowledge. Declarative knowledge is public knowledge, subject to rules of evidence that make it verifiable, replicable and logically consistent; it is in libraries and textbooks and on the Internet; it is what teachers 'declare' in lectures. The learner's role is to receive the content by what Ausubel (1968) called *reception* learning, where the learner's role is to internalize that pre-existing knowledge meaningfully. Students' understanding of it is usually tested declaratively, by getting them to declare it back, in their own words and using their own examples. Examples of declarative knowledge are: knowing that William the Conqueror invaded England in 1066, what Freud said, knowing what the terms of an equation refer to, knowing what kinds of cloud formation can be distinguished, knowing that Shakespeare married Anne Hathaway, and so on.

Functioning knowledge is knowledge that informs action, where the performance is underpinned by understanding. The learner does not only receive pre-existing knowledge but is actively involved in putting knowledge to work; if declarative knowledge is steered internally to the learner, as it were, functioning knowledge travels externally. Functioning knowledge is what professionals are concerned with; they use theory to inform their decisions on what to do in their professional context, be it solving problems, designing buildings, planning teaching or performing surgery. Functioning knowledge requires a solid foundation of declarative knowledge, but that is not to say that the declarative knowledge must be in place first. In problem-based learning, for example, functioning knowledge and theoretical or declarative knowledge are constructed simultaneously, as we discuss later in Chapter 9.

The important point for now is that this distinction tells us what our curricula might address. Originally, universities and their teachers were repositories of knowledge and learners were there to obtain some of that knowledge, and so teaching methods were correspondingly expository. While universities today are increasingly concerned with professional education, in some institutions exclusively so, curricula in many universities remain overwhelmingly declarative. One study from the University of Texas found that university teachers spent 88% of their teaching time in lecturing students (cited by Bok 2006), yet students are supposed to be educated so that they can interact thoughtfully with professional problems; to use functioning knowledge, in other words. Unfortunately, often it is only the foundation declarative knowledge that is taught, leaving it to the students after they graduate to learn how to put it to work.

Take for example the place of psychology in teacher education. The reason for teaching psychology is that teachers should know something about such topics as human learning and motivation, child development, the nature of intelligence, and so on, not for the good of their souls, but so they may *teach better*. However, until recently, these topics were taught as declarative knowledge and the students were assessed on their topic knowledge, not on how well they applied their topic knowledge to their teaching. With the exception of courses using problem-based learning, the *application* of the theoretical content to teaching or to any other professional practice was left up to the student, when 'out there, in the real world'. It was this realization that prompted the use of portfolio assessment that led, as discussed in the next chapter, to the formulation of constructive alignment.

This is a problem not only for teacher education. The theory component in professional programmes in general is often treated as an end in itself, not as a means of learning to perform in a more informed and effective way. Indeed, Leinhardt et al. (1995) referred to 'university' knowledge and 'professional' knowledge as having little in common. While some courses in a degree programme, and some topics in probably all courses, need to be taught and assessed declaratively, as topics students should 'know about' in their own right, there are many examples where the desired outcomes of learning would involve functioning knowledge, such as in applying theory to specific contexts, especially but not exclusively in professional contexts. Accordingly, such knowledge needs to be assessed in terms of how students' learning is manifested in practice, in their ability to perform more effectively. As discussed below, Entwistle and Entwistle (1997) found that the forms of understanding encouraged by university accreditation and assessment procedures are not those that are professionally relevant. The rhetoric is right, but, in practice, universities tend to focus on declarative knowledge, which students often see as irrelevant and hence worthy of only a surface approach to learning it.

The problem is lack of alignment between intended learning outcomes and the means of teaching and assessing them. Graduates need to face new problems and to interact with them, reflectively and thoughtfully. The first step in designing degree programmes and their constituent courses, then, is to decide the kinds of knowledge, declarative or functioning, that each outcome for a course should be addressing. There will be a mixture in most courses, with increasing emphasis on functioning knowledge in higher years especially of professional programmes. We need to see that we get the balance right.

Threshold concepts and troublesome knowledge

A threshold concept is like a portal, opening up a new and previously inaccessible way of thinking about something (Meyer and Land 2003). When the student goes through the gateway, a perspective of the subject is opened up that illuminates a new landscape, a level of understanding that had not been there previously. The problem is that such concepts are often troublesome to learn; the gateway is too narrow for some. It is important that teachers identify those threshold concepts and address them, which is an excellent collegial exercise for the programme committee. It is these threshold concepts that, when grasped, lead students into deep approaches to learning the subject.

We need to distinguish *threshold* concepts from *core* concepts, which are also necessary to understand a subject. Core concepts do not however lead to a dramatic shift to a new level of understanding. For example, the concept of *gravity* – the idea that any two bodies attract one another with a force that is proportional to the product of their masses and inversely proportional to the distance between them – represents a threshold concept, whereas the concept of a *centre of gravity* does not, although the latter is a core concept in many of the applied sciences (Meyer and Land 2003). The idea applies even to a homely subject like cooking, which is fundamentally a process of using heat. Understanding the implications of the threshold concepts of heat transfer and temperature gradient can transform both the cook's understanding and basic procedures, for example, how best to add liquids of different temperatures, such as adding cold milk to hot coffee, or choosing the appropriate thickness and constituency of cooking utensils for different jobs: cooking then becomes more than following the recipe.

Threshold concepts are often superordinate concepts that relate previously disparate ideas, and that give students a broader view of the subject. The ideas of intrinsic and extrinsic motivation, for example, are core concepts in educational psychology, whereas expectancy-value theory is a threshold concept, as, once grasped, it changes the learner's perception of a range of ideas in motivational theory and its application. Intrinsic and extrinsic motivation are originally seen as 'opposite' forms of motivation, each having different effects on learning; one is associated with poor learning, the other with high quality learning. Two different phenomena? Not so: each is incorporated within expectancy-value theory. The different effects are not because they are different forms of motivation, but because the individual reads the value component differently: in one case the task itself is valued, in the other the task is only a means of acquiring something else that is valued.

Each subject has its own threshold concepts. It is an important exercise for teachers to share their ideas of what are threshold concepts and design programmes, courses and teaching activities accordingly. Sometimes threshold concepts are difficult for students because they seem counter-intuitive at first, or the opposite of what they thought they had been taught, thus comprising what has been termed 'troublesome knowledge' (Perkins 2006). Davies and Mangan (2007), in discussing the idea of threshold concepts in teaching economics, suggest that teachers within the department should use these in discussing better ways of teaching the subject, as threshold concepts can transform lecturers' ways of thinking about the nature of knowledge in their subject area and, in so doing, also affect their ideas about teaching and learning.

Performances of understanding

Ask any teacher what they want of their students and they will say they don't want their students just to memorize, they want them to *understand.* The trouble is that 'understand' can mean very different things, from the trivial to the complex.

Does the teaching objective, 'The student will understand expectancy-value theory', mean that the student is able to:

1 write a textbook definition of expectancy-value theory?
2 explain how it works in the student's own words?
3 watch a video of a teacher–student interaction and be able to predict what is likely to happen to the student's motivation afterwards? Or

4 reflect on the student's own teaching to illustrate that a problem that had occurred could be accounted for and rectified in terms of expectancy-value theory?

All these outcome statements are examples of 'understanding' at some level or other. What is the appropriate statement for a given course? The teacher needs to decide that and then to pin down the required level of understanding in the intended learning outcomes for the course. We deal with that process in Chapter 7.

Entwistle and Entwistle (1997) conducted a series of studies on what students meant by 'understanding' and then asked them how they attempt to understand when preparing for examinations. The students described the experience of understanding as *satisfying*; it was good to have the feeling that you understood at last. It also felt *complete*, a whole, as previously unrelated things were suddenly integrated. The experience was irreversible; what is now understood cannot be 'de-understood'. Students thought a good practical test of understanding was being able to explain to someone else or to be able to adapt and to use what had been understood. These are pretty good definitions of sound understandings that probably fit most teachers' requirements: you want students to interrelate topics, to adapt and use the knowledge so understood, to explain it to others and to feel satisfied and good about it.

Unfortunately, when it came to the examinations, these indicators of understanding evaporated. Students attempted instead to understand in ways that they thought would meet assessment requirements. Understanding then took on much less desirable forms. Entwistle and Entwistle (1997) distinguished five:

1 reproduces content from lecture notes without any clear structure;
2 reproduces the content within the structure used by the lecturer;
3 develops own structure, but only to generate answers to anticipated examination questions;
4 adjusts structures from strategic reading of different sources to represent personal understanding, but also to control examination requirements;
5 develops an individual conception of the discipline from wide reading and reflection.

Only the last form of understanding, described by a small minority of students, is anything like the students' own pre-examination definitions. All other forms, 1 to 4, focus on meeting examination requirements. The examinations actually prevented students from achieving their own personal understandings of the content, which the Entwistles understandably found 'worrying'. Many of these students were in their final year, just prior to professional practice, yet the assessment system pre-empted the very level of understanding that would be professionally relevant. Worrying indeed.

To use our learning in order to negotiate with the world and to see it differently involves understanding of a high order. It is the kind of understanding that is referred to in the rhetoric of university teaching, yet seems hard to impart. One important procedure is that referred to by Davies and Mangan (2007): make sure that the teachers in a programme have agreed on what are the key threshold concepts and pay them special attention in teaching. It is when these concepts are understood that students 'really' understand, see the subject differently and *act differently* in contexts involving that threshold concept and its associated core concepts. These informed actions arising from deep understanding are called *performances of understanding* (Gardner 1993; Wiske 1998). This distinction between performances of understanding and verbal declarations of understanding are crucial when it comes to writing the intended learning outcomes of a course, as we see in Chapter 7.

The difference between meeting the requirements of institutional learning and 'real' understanding is illustrated in Gunstone and White's (1981) demonstrations with Physics I students. In one demonstration, two balls, one heavy and one light, were held in the air in front of the students. They were asked to predict, if the balls were released simultaneously, which one would hit the ground first and why. Some predicted that the heavy one would 'because heavy things have a bigger force' or 'gravity is stronger nearer the earth' (both are true but irrelevant). These students had 'understood' gravity well enough to pass HSC (A level) physics, but few understood well enough to answer a simple real-life question about gravity. They could correctly solve problems using the formula for *g* – which does not contain a term for the mass of the object falling – while still reacting in the belief that heavy objects fall faster. They didn't *really* understand gravity in the performative sense – and why should they if their teaching and assessment didn't require them to? These physics students hadn't changed their commonsense conceptions of gravity, but had placed alongside them a set of statements and formulae about physical phenomena that would see them through the exams. To really understand physics or mathematics, history or accountancy is to *think like* a physicist, a mathematician, a historian or an accountant; and that shows in how you behave. Once you really understand a sector of knowledge, it changes that part of the world; you don't behave towards that domain in the same way again.

Gunstone and White's physics students were good at verbally declaring their knowledge, for example explaining what gravity is about, or what the three laws of motion are. But is this why we are teaching these topics? Is it for acquaintance, so that students know something about the topic and can answer the sorts of stock questions that typify examination papers? In that case, a verbal understanding will suffice. Or is it to change the way (sooner or later) students can understand and control reality? If that is the case, then a performative level of understanding is implicated.

Levels of understanding

So far we have been talking about the end point of our teaching as 'real' understanding. However, understanding develops gradually, becoming more structured and articulated as it develops. Undergraduates will not attain the level of precision and complexity of the subject expert, but we want none to retain the plausible misunderstandings that marked Gunstone and White's physics students' understanding of gravity.

We thus need to define understanding in ways that do justice to the topics and content we teach, as appropriate to the year level taught. The task is to define what is acceptable for each stage of the degree programme, given a student's specialization and degree pattern. That is a highly specific matter that only the teacher and subject expert can decide, but a general framework for structuring levels of understanding helps teachers to make those decisions and it also provides a basis for discussing levels across different years and subject areas. Once an appropriate level of understanding the basic structural framework is achieved, adapting it to particular course intended learning outcomes is straightforward.

The SOLO taxonomy is based on the study of outcomes in a variety of academic content areas (Biggs and Collis 1982). As students learn, the outcomes of their learning display similar stages of increasing structural complexity. There are two main changes: *quantitative*, as the amount of detail in the student's response increases; and *qualitative*, as that detail becomes integrated into a structural pattern. The quantitative stages of learning occur first, then learning changes qualitatively.

SOLO, which stands for **s**tructure of the **o**bserved **l**earning **o**utcome, provides a systematic way of describing how a learner's performance grows in complexity when mastering many academic tasks. It can be used to define course intended learning outcomes, which describe where students *should* be operating, and for evaluating learning outcomes so that we can know at what level individual students actually *are* operating.

Task 5.1 tests your level of understanding of a threshold concept in student learning.

Task 5.1 Where you stand on the levels of understanding

Take *approaches to learning*, a topic with which you are now familiar. In a few sentences, outline your response to the following questions:

1 *What are approaches to learning?*
2 *How can knowledge of approaches to learning enhance university teaching?*

Stop reading any further until you have completed the task.

Your response to the questions:

_____

_____

_____

_____

Now turn to Box 5.1 and try to evaluate your own response against the suggested example response.

Box 5.1 SOLO levels in approaches to learning question and why

The following levels of response could be observed (but, it is to be hoped, the first three responses are not):

1 *Prestructural*

'Teaching is a matter of getting students to approach their learning.'

This response could have been written by somebody with understanding at the individual word level, but little understanding of what was discussed in Chapter 2. Prestructural responses simply miss the point or, like this one, use tautology to cover lack of knowledge or understanding. These responses can be quite sophisticated, such as the kind of elaborate tautology that politicians use to avoid answering questions, but, academically, they show little evidence of relevant learning.

2 *Unistructural*

'Approaches to learning are of two kinds: surface, which is inappropriate for the task at hand, and deep, which is appropriate. Teachers need to take this into account.'

This is unistructural because it meets only one part of the task, defining what approaches to learning are in terms of just one aspect, appropriateness. It misses other important attributes, for example that they are ways of describing students' learning activities and what might influence them, while the reference to teaching adds nothing. Unistructural responses deal with terminology, getting on track but little more.

3 *Multistructural*

'Approaches to learning are of two kinds: surface, which is inappropriate for the task at hand, and deep, which is appropriate. Students using a surface approach try to fool us into believing that they understand by rote learning stuff and quoting it back to us, sometimes in great detail. Students using a deep approach try to get at the underlying meaning of their learning tasks. Teaching is about getting students to learn appropriately, not getting by with shortcuts. We should therefore teach for meaning and understanding, which means encouraging them to adopt a deep approach.'

We couldn't agree more. The first part is quite detailed (but could be more so); the second part is also what good teaching is about. So what is the problem with this answer? The problem is that this response does not address the key issue, which is, *how* can knowledge of approaches enhance teaching, not *that* they can enhance teaching. This is what Bereiter and Scardamalia (1987) call 'knowledge-telling': snowing the reader with a bunch of facts, but not structuring them as required – and don't be misled by the odd connective like 'therefore'. Here, the students see the trees but not the wood. Seeing trees is a necessary preliminary to adequate understanding, but it should not be interpreted as comprehending the wood.

4 *Relational*

'*Approaches to learning are of two kinds: . . .*' then as for the multistructural response with the additional: *The approaches come about partly because of student characteristics, but also because students react differently to their teaching environment in ways that lead them into surface or deep learning. The teaching environment is a system, a resolution of all the factors present, such as curriculum, assessment, teaching methods and students' own characteristics. If there is imbalance in the environment, for example a test that allows students to respond in a way that does not do justice to the curriculum, or a classroom climate that scares the hell out of them, the resolution is in favour of a surface approach. What this means is that we should be consistent.*'

And so on. The multistructural response could be repeated verbatim but following that we have an explanation that ties the detail together. The two concepts, approaches and teaching, have been integrated by the concept of a system; examples have been given, and the structure could easily be used to generate practical steps. The trees have become the wood, a qualitative change in learning and understanding has occurred. It is no longer a matter of listing facts and details. This is the first level at which 'understanding' in an academically relevant sense may appropriately be used.

5 *Extended abstract*

Teaching is certainly a system, and a surface approach is an example of what happens when the system is unbalanced. When I see examples of surface approaches, when I had thought things had been going well, I would need to stop and reflect, using my theory of teaching to find out what is wrong and then I would work out ways of fixing the problem. I would need to assess the different aspects of teaching – the teaching/learning activities I had been using, the assessment methods, the classroom climate even – to obtain feedback on how things were going. I would see this as ongoing, like a piece of action research designed to suit my particular circumstances.

The essence of the extended abstract response is that it goes beyond what has been given, whereas the relational response stays with the given. The coherent whole is conceptualized at a higher level of abstraction and is applied to new and broader domains. Thus, this teacher thought that she was doing all the right things but this wasn't so. She needed to use transformative reflection to work her way through to a new resolution to her problem. An extended abstract response on approaches to learning would be a 'breakthrough' response, giving a perspective that changes what we think about them and their relationship to teaching. The trouble is that today's extended abstract is tomorrow's threshold concept at relational level. Marton and Säljö's original study of surface and deep approaches was such a breakthrough; linking approaches to learning to systems theory was another, but now both are conventional wisdom.

The examples illustrate the five levels of the taxonomy. Uni- and multistructural levels see understanding as a quantitative increase in what is grasped. These responses were deliberately constructed to show that the higher level contains the lower level, plus a bit more. The 'bit more' in the case of multistructural incorporates the unistructural, then there is more of the same – a purely quantitative increase. The 'bit more' at relational level structures all those multistructural bits and pieces thereby involving a qualitative change, a conceptual restructuring of the components, by seeing that the systems property integrates the components. The next shift to extended abstract takes the argument into a new dimension. SOLO describes a hierarchy, where each partial construction becomes the foundation on which further learning is built.

This distinction between knowing more and restructuring parallels two major curriculum aims: to *increase knowledge* (quantitative: unistructural becoming increasingly multistructural); and to *deepen understanding* (qualitative: relational, then extended abstract). Teaching and assessment that focus only on the quantitative aspects of learning will miss the more important higher level aspects. Quantitative, Level 1, theories of teaching and learning address the first aim only, increasing knowledge. Any deepening of understanding is left to the Susans with their spontaneous deep learning activities. The challenge for us is to highlight the qualitative aim in the intended outcomes of a course and support it by both teaching and assessment methods. Then Robert's understanding is likely to be deepened too.

Using SOLO to design particular intended learning outcome statements is helped considerably by using verbs that parallel the SOLO taxonomy. A visual representation is given in Figure 5.1, with some verbs typical of each level.

The verbs in the staircase are general, indicating what the students need to be able to do to indicate achievement at the level in question. Tables 7.1 and 7.2 in Chapter 7 provide a useful pool of verbs to be used when writing intended learning outcomes.

SOLO is very useful in pinning down the levels of understanding we would intend our students to achieve when teaching a course. The verbs are crucial in doing. In the next chapter we look at how constructive alignment came

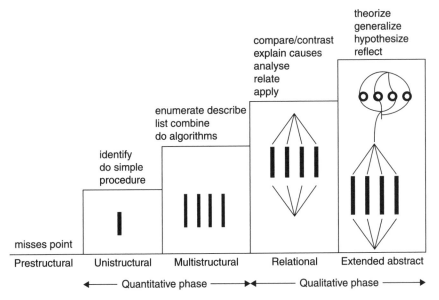

theorize
generalize
hypothesize
reflect

compare/contrast
explain causes
analyse
relate
apply

enumerate describe
list combine
do algorithms

identify
do simple
procedure

misses point

| Prestructural | Unistructural | Multistructural | Relational | Extended abstract |

← Quantitative phase →◄ Qualitative phase →

Figure 5.1 A hierarchy of verbs that may be used to form intended learning outcomes

about, and how the outcome verbs played their part in guiding teaching and assessment. In Part 2, starting from Chapter 7, we then turn to the practical question of designing and writing learning outcomes for courses and programmes.

Before leaving the present chapter, complete Tasks 5.2 and 5.3.

Task 5.2 On kinds of knowledge and levels of understanding

Take a subject you are teaching.

Identify the following that you have included in your teaching:

Kind of knowledge Declarative/ Functioning	*Levels of understanding associated with the kind of knowledge*

Task 5.3 Threshold concept and core concepts in your subject

Identify a *threshold concept* and its related *core concepts* that you have included in a subject you teach.

1 Explain why the threshold concept is threshold rather than core.

_____

_____

2 What level of understanding or performance do you intend your students to achieve in relation to the threshold and core concepts

Threshold concept: _____

_____

Core concepts: _____

_____

3 Explain how the threshold concept and the core concepts have been taught.

Threshold concept: _____

_____

Core concepts: _____

_____

We will revisit this task in Chapter 9, Task 9.4.

Summary and conclusions

Kinds of knowledge

Declarative knowledge refers to knowing about things and is 'declared' in the spoken and written word. Functioning knowledge is knowledge based on the academic declarative knowledge base that is put to work. These distinctions are important in sorting out whether students need to understand, as in 'know about', or understand, as in 'put to empowered use'. Universities have traditionally emphasized declarative knowledge, as appropriate to their original purpose as being repositories of knowledge that students came to share. Today, universities have a much more proactive role in professional preparation, and so we need to rethink the kind of knowledge we should be teaching, and with that, the ways in which different kinds of knowledge are best taught. However, declarative and functioning knowledge are complementary. Functioning knowledge depends on a deep understanding of theory and its application.

Threshold concepts

Whatever kinds of knowledge are being taught, there are some key concepts in a discipline that, once understood properly, change the students' understanding of a whole area, sometimes dramatically. These threshold concepts, as they are called, bring students to stand at the threshold, as it were, of new, broad-based understanding. They need to be isolated and emphasized in teaching. They are, however, sometimes troublesome to teach because they make a break with the way the students have been looking at the content. It is important that teachers in a programme discuss and agree what the threshold concepts are and how they should be taught.

Performances of understanding

When an area is 'really' understood, it changes the way students see the world and hence how they behave towards it within the content area in question. Thus, a deep understanding of declarative knowledge has functioning elements in that those who do understand perform differently in what are called performances of understanding. Each topic has its own performances, and it is important that teachers know what these are and build them into their teaching.

Levels of understanding

In designing learning outcomes, we need to specify the *level* of understanding intended. The SOLO taxonomy classifies learning outcomes in terms of their structural quality, which makes it useful for defining levels of understanding to be incorporated into learning outcomes.

Further reading

On kinds of knowledge

Anderson, J.R. (1976) *Language, Memory, and Thought.* Hillsdale, NJ: Erlbaum.
Ryle, G. (1949) *The Concept of Mind.* Chicago: Chicago University Press.

The distinction between declarative and what we are calling functioning knowledge was probably first made by the philosopher Gilbert Ryle, with his 'knowing-that' and 'knowing-how'. Anderson then made a parallel distinction between declarative and procedural knowledge, but the latter lacked the notion that knowing how to do things necessarily had a theoretical base as is required in the sort of knowledge in professional education especially and that we call functioning knowledge.

On threshold concepts

Davies, P. and Mangan, J. (2007) Threshold concepts and the integration of understanding in economics, *Studies in Higher Education* 32,4: 711–26.

Meyer, J.H.F. and Land, R. (2003) Threshold concepts and troublesome knowledge (1): Linkages to ways of thinking and practising within the disciplines. http://www.utwente.nl/so/vop/nieuwsbrief_17/land_paper.pdf (accessed 2 February 2011).

Meyer, J.H.F. and Land, R. (2006) *Overcoming Barriers to Student Understanding.* London: Routledge.

Meyer and Land (2003) explain threshold concepts and their application in various areas, notably science, and their book (2006) focuses on blocks and problems some students have in various content areas, and what teachers might do to overcome these problems. Davies and Mangan apply the concept of threshold concepts to their area of economics and how they might be used to improve teaching.

On the SOLO taxonomy

Hattie, J. and Purdie, N. (1998) The SOLO model: addressing fundamental measurement issues.

Boulton-Lewis, G.M. (1998) Applying the SOLO taxonomy to learning in higher education,

These are Chapters 7 and 9 respectively in Dart, B. and Boulton-Lewis, G. (eds) (1998) *Teaching and Learning in Higher Education.* Camberwell, Victoria: Australian Council for Educational Research.

Hattie is concerned with the specific use of SOLO in testing and educational measurement whereas Boulton-Lewis is more general, showing how SOLO may be used from thinking generally about what we want students to be able to do, to the assessment of learning outcomes.

Atherton. J. (2010) Learning and Teaching: SOLO Taxonomy. http://www.learningandteaching.info/learning/solo.htm (accessed 2 February 2011). This URL has been up for some time but James Atherton has revised it and has hyperlinks to some interesting discussion on threshold concepts and troublesome knowledge and some good references.

As SOLO might apply to children's ethics and to zoology, from the University of Queensland's TEDI: http://www.tedi.uq.edu.au/downloads/Biggs_Solo.pdf (accessed 2 February 2011).

A paper by Hargreaves and Grenfell on SOLO and 'The use of assessment strategies to develop critical thinking skills in science': http://www.unisa.edu.au/evaluations/Full-papers/HargreavesFull.doc (accessed 2 February 2011).

And Google 'SOLO taxonomy' but be selective as there is a lot there.

6

Constructively aligned teaching and assessment

Constructive alignment arose out of an experiment with portfolio assessment. Students were asked to place items in a portfolio as evidence that their professional decision making had been improved by the theory they had been taught in class. The students couldn't be 'taught' the evidence, they had to reflect on their experience and provide it themselves. The teaching method followed from a series of negotiations as to how that evidence might best be obtained, the assessment was on the basis of the quality of the evidence provided. The course was a success, results provoking a rethink of the design of teaching. It seemed that two principles were involved: a *constructivist* theory of learning, and *alignment* between the intended learning outcomes of the course, the teaching/learning activities and the assessment tasks. Enter constructive alignment.

How did constructive alignment come about?

Constructive alignment came about as a result of an experiment with portfolio assessment in a bachelor of education programme. The course, entitled *The Nature of Teaching and Learning*, was a senior-level course in educational psychology for in-service teachers. Initially, the course followed the usual model: topics from the psychology of learning and development that were considered relevant to the improved practice of teaching were taught. The students were assessed in terms of how well the theory, and the relevance of the topics to education, were understood and explained in written assignments.

Then, following a visit to Canada by the teacher of that course, the penny dropped. Writing about the application of psychology to education was not – or should not have been – what the course was about. The course was intended for in-service teachers to improve their own teaching in the classroom, whereas the assessment had nothing to do with their experience or their workplace. The assessment provided no evidence on the question of whether the course was indeed improving the professional competence of those taking it. What caused the penny to drop and events that happened thereafter are contained in Box 6.1.

Box 6.1 How constructive alignment came into being

In 1994, one of the authors, John, returned to the University of Hong Kong from study leave in Canada, very impressed with the use of assessment portfolios in Canadian elementary schools. He was to resume teaching an evening course in a part-time BEd programme, which was about how knowledge of psychology might improve teaching. In preparing for the course next time round, it struck him that portfolio assessment was worth trying. As the students were teachers during the day, they had plenty of opportunities to see how their knowledge of psychology might be influencing their teaching decisions, which after all was what the course was intended to do. Right, so the students would be assessed on how they could demonstrate that psychology had been influencing their teaching and they were to compile a portfolio of examples of this. When John told the students that this is how they would be assessed, they reacted negatively:

> How am I supposed to do it well when I'm not sure exactly what the professor wants to see in it? . . . though he did say that we can put what means much to us in the portfolio, yet how can I be sure that he agrees with me?

John suggested item types for their portfolios and after a trial run, they got the idea. When they finally submitted their portfolios, John was stunned. They were rich and exciting, the class achieved more A and B grades than ever before, the student feedback was the best he'd ever received. Here is an excerpt from one diary:

> All [the teacher] said was 'show me the evidence of your learning that has taken place' and we have to ponder, reflect and project the theories we have learnt into our own teaching . . . If it had only been an exam or an essay, we would have probably just repeated his ideas to him and continued to teach the same way as we always do!

John didn't know it at the time, but he'd just implemented an example of outcomes-based teaching and learning.

Only he'd called it 'constructive alignment'.

Source: Biggs (1996b)

John thought that the experiment with portfolio assessment had worked so well for two reasons. The first was that the knowledge *about* psychology did not draw from the students' experience, while the knowledge that was to drive their teaching led to action by the students that was very much within their experience. That gap, between a static body of declarative knowledge and personal action, had to be bridged. On one side of the gap was what Leinhardt et al. (1995) called 'university' knowledge, and on the other side was 'professional' knowledge. University knowledge is abstract declarative knowledge, and what the student has to do here is to label, differentiate, elaborate and justify. On the other hand, 'professional' knowledge is functioning knowledge, which requires the practising professional to execute, apply and prioritize (Leinhardt et al. 1995). Bridging that gap has traditionally been left to the student to do, 'out there', after graduation. That job should be done before graduation, and this is what the portfolio helped students to do. The portfolio experiment and Leinhardt's analysis were fifteen years ago. Nowadays, as we shall be seeing, that contrast is not nearly as striking as it was then, as graduate outcomes address the sorts of things that professionals need to know, an issue we shall be dealing with in the next chapter.

The second, not unrelated, reason why the portfolio scheme had worked so well was because of alignment between theory and practice that was so lacking in Leinhardt's analysis of university teaching and professional requirements. In the portfolio, the learning activities indicated in the intended outcomes were mirrored both in the teaching/learning activities the students undertook, and in the assessment tasks, so that the learning activities the students engaged were those that directly addressed what it was they were supposed to be learning.

What is constructive alignment?

The portfolio experiment was generalized to a design for teaching that was called 'constructive alignment' (CA). 'Constructive' comes from the constructivist theory that learners use their own activity to construct their knowledge as interpreted through their own existing schemata. 'Alignment' is a principle in curriculum theory that assessment tasks should be aligned to what it is intended to be learned, as in criterion-referenced assessment. Constructive alignment extends in a practical way Shuell's statement that 'what the student does is actually more important in determining what is learned than what the teacher does' (1986: 429). The intended outcomes specify the *activity* that students should engage if they are to achieve the intended outcome as well as the content the activity refers to. The teacher's tasks are to set up a learning environment that encourages the student to perform those learning activities, and to assess student performances against the intended learning outcomes.

Focusing on what and how students are to learn, rather than on what topics the teacher is to teach, requires that an intended learning outcome, or ILO, specifies not only *what* is to be learned, the topic, but *how* it is to be learned and to what standard. The outcome statement thus specifies a verb that informs students how they are expected to change as a result of learning that topic, for example 'reflect on X', or 'apply theory to Y'. That verb, or verbs, should then be addressed in the teaching/learning activities (TLAs), and in the assessment task (AT).

In constructive alignment, the intended learning outcomes are written to include an activity, not just a topic: for example, to *explain* a particular concept. That activity, *explain*, is then specified in the teaching context so that it is activated in order to achieve the outcome. Likewise, that activity, *explain*, is specified in the assessment task, to ascertain if the outcome has been achieved and how well. The target verb *explain* is represented in the teaching/learning context and in the assessment. Likewise in driving instruction, the intention is that the learner learns how to drive a car. The teaching focuses on the learning activity itself: driving a car, not giving lectures on car driving, while the assessment focuses on how well the car is driven. The alignment is achieved by ensuring that the intended verb in the outcome statement is present in the teaching/learning activity and in the assessment task.

The idea of aligning assessment tasks with what it is intended that students should learn is old – it is criterion-referenced assessment, which is how anyone outside an educational institution assesses what has been learned when teaching anyone else anything. A mother assesses how well her child can tie a shoe, not on how well her child performs compared to the kid next door. Yet, as we see in Chapter 10, educational institutions generally became enamoured of norm-referenced assessment, which tells us who learns better than who. That is an important function when selecting from many people for few positions, such as making an appointment to a job from a large field of applicants, or awarding a limited number of university places or scholarships. However, when the aim of teaching is that students learn specified content to acceptable standards, aligning the assessment of learning to what is to be learned is not only logical, it is more effective in getting students to learn. Cohen (1987), after a comprehensive review, was so impressed that he called alignment between the assessment and the intended learning outcome the 'magic bullet' in increasing student performance.

That is all very well for a skill like car driving, you might say, where the learner's activities are explicit, but how can that apply to something that is conceptually of a high level and abstract like learning a theory? The example of *The Nature of Teaching and Learning* course (see Box 6.1, p. 96) illustrates that it can.

The theory in any subject is not only meant to be 'understood', whatever that all-purpose word might specifically mean, but, as was argued in the previous chapter, it is intended to change the way students see the world and thence to change their behaviour towards it. This is obviously the case in professional courses, as we have seen, but virtually all sound learning, whether in medical education or in subjects like pure physics, gives the student a different view of the world, together with the power to change some aspects of it, such as being able to solve novel or unseen problems. That view, and instances of the empowerment that learning gives the student, should guide the design of the intended learning outcomes for a course or programme.

All good teachers have some implicit idea of how they want their students to change as a result of their teaching so that they can work towards achieving that change when teaching. Constructively aligned teaching systematizes what good teachers have always done: they state upfront what they intend those outcomes to be in the courses they teach – always allowing that other, unintended but desirable, outcomes will emerge that they may not have anticipated. As explained later, we use outcomes statements and open-ended assessment tasks that allow for unintended but desirable outcomes. Unlike some outcomes-based education, such as competency-based, constructively aligned teaching is not closed loop, focusing only on what is predetermined.

Another difference between constructive alignment and other outcomes-based approaches is that in constructive alignment, the connections between ILOs, TLAs and assessment tasks ATs are aligned intrinsically, a 'through train' if you like, on the basis of the learning activities expressed in the outcomes statements. In other outcomes-based models, alignment exists through criterion-referencing the assessment tasks to the ILOs, but not additionally between the ILOs and the TLAs.

Constructively aligned teaching is likely to be more effective than unaligned because there is maximum consistency throughout the system. Like all traditional teaching, the curriculum lists the content topics that are judged desirable for students to learn, but then those topics are translated into outcome statements and the teaching/learning activities steer the students' learning towards those intended outcomes, with the assessments tasks and their rubrics acting as signposts along the way. All components in the system address the same agenda and support each other. As Hattie (2009b: 6) says: 'Thus, any course needs to be designed so that the learning activities and assessment tasks are aligned with the learning outcomes that are intended in the course. This means that the system is consistent.'

The students are 'entrapped' in this web of consistency, optimizing the likelihood that they will engage the appropriate learning activities, helping the Roberts learn *more like* the Susans but leaving them free to construct their knowledge their way. We emphasize the 'more like' because Susan has a richer knowledge base that enables her to create more elaborate constructions than Robert is likely to, but at least Robert can engage in more appropriate learning activities than he would otherwise have done.

Where assessment is not aligned to the intended or other desired outcomes, or where the teaching methods do not directly encourage the appropriate learning activities, students can easily 'escape' by engaging in inappropriate learning activities, which become a surface approach to learning, as exemplified by Ramsden's psychology student (see pp. 24–5).

Cowan (2004) has a related idea to alignment that he says goes 'beyond alignment to integration'. He uses the idea of 'sound standard' assessment which in effect integrates the criteria of assessment and the intended learning outcomes. The teacher clearly outlines what criteria make a piece of work higher or lower than a sound standard for a pass. The student and other students assess a piece of work becoming very clear as to what constitutes various grades of pass. Wherever possible, teacher-designed TLAs are replaced with student learning activities based on various kinds of reflection.

A critic of the first edition of this book described constructive alignment as 'spoon feeding'. On the contrary, spoon feeding, like the other Level 1 metaphors with their curious affinity to metabolic processes – 'regurgitating', 'chewing it over', 'stuffing them with facts', 'ramming down their throats', 'getting your teeth into' – puts a hold on the student's cognitive processes. Spoon feeding does the work for the students, so that they have little left to do but obediently swallow. Constructive alignment, by way of contrast, makes the students themselves do the real work, the teacher simply acts as 'broker' between the student and a learning environment that supports the appropriate learning activities.

It is also important to remember that while the term 'intended' learning outcomes is used, the teaching and assessment should always allow for desirable but unintended outcomes, as these will inevitably occur when students have freedom to construct their own knowledge. The assessment tasks should be open enough to allow for that: an issue we address in Chapters 10 and 12.

Design of constructively aligned teaching and assessment

Let us now unpack the prototypical example of constructive alignment in the course *The Nature of Teaching and Learning*. There are four stages in the design:

1 describe the *intended learning outcome* in the form of a verb (learning activity), its object (the content) and specify the context and a standard the students are to attain;
2 create a learning environment using *teaching/learning activities* that address that verb and therefore are likely to bring about the intended outcome;
3 use *assessment tasks* that also contain that verb, thus enabling you to judge with the help of rubrics if and how well students' performances meet the criteria;
4 transform these judgements into standard grading criteria.

Intended learning outcomes (ILOs)

The ILOs are statements, written from the students' perspective, indicating the level of understanding and performance they are expected to achieve as a result of engaging in the teaching and learning experience. The ILOs for *The Nature of Teaching and Learning* course, with the learning activities or verbs italicized, follow:

1 *explain* why a particular course topic is important to teaching;
2 *apply* a course topic to your own teaching;
3 *reflect* on your teaching in terms of a working theory you have gained from the course;
4 *evaluate* a situation that has gone wrong and *apply* a solution.

Each of these verbs addresses 'understanding' at some level: which is why using 'understand' as the verb for your ILOs won't work, because it does not give any indication of the level of understanding required. In the following chapter we shall elaborate on this important question of the level of the outcomes by presenting taxonomies of verbs that are classified in terms of their cognitive level. For the moment, let us stay with explain, apply, reflect and evaluate.

Note that the first ILO, 'explain', refers to declarative knowledge whereas all the rest, 'apply', 'reflect' and 'evaluate and apply', refer to functioning knowledge. In addressing the second ILO, 'apply', the students may choose the same topic as in (1), say expectancy-value theory, but in (1) they explain it verbally while in (2) they are required to apply to their own teaching. 'Reflect' in the third ILO is at a higher cognitive level, requiring students to apply that framework they have constructed from the course to their own teaching as reflective practice. The fourth ILO, 'evaluate and apply', requires the students to spot a problem, evaluate it, then suggest how it might be rectified in light of material taught in the course: this too is at a high cognitive level. The last is an example of the 'reflect–plan–apply–evaluate' sequence of action research. The next question is how students were helped to engage these verbs.

Teaching/learning activities (TLAs)

The verbs the students needed to enact are italicized in our list of ILOs. The TLAs were obtained through negotiation with the students when they saw that the teacher lecturing to them wasn't going to help them achieve the outcomes of the course. The following dialogue, condensed from several sessions, illustrates how this happened (S are students, T is teacher):

S How do we show we can reflect?
T Keep a reflective diary or journal.
S What do we put in it?
T What you think are critical incidents in your teaching, anything that might indicate how your teaching has been improved, such as samples of conversations with your students, lesson plans, samples of student work.
S That's too vague. We need help to decide what to put in.

T Talk it over with your colleagues. A learning partnership's a good idea. Choose a friend, maybe two, and get their phone number, sit next to them in class. Talk it over together. You can help each other. You can see me in a group if you are in real difficulty.

S Wouldn't it be better if we had discussion groups of students teaching the same subjects as we do? Then we can share experiences on similar problems.

T Certainly. I've already booked the room next door. You can meet there.

S But we'll need direct teaching on some things. Won't you lecture us?

T Yes, but only to clarify issues that you raise. There's a topic for each session and I'll give you pre-reading rather than lecture on it. We can clarify each topic in the lecture, as necessary.

And so on.

In short, instead of the teacher doing the work for the students, the students were helped to do what *they* needed to do in order to meet the intended learning outcomes of the course. TLAs included independent learning with the pre-reading with self-addressed questions ('What was the most important idea in today's session?'), and small group learning and collaborative learning with learning partners, a reflective diary, and most important, as all were practising teachers, their workplace, so that all the learning activities mentioned in the ILOs were embedded in the TLAs in one way or another. Box 6.2 summarizes the alignment between ILOs and the TLAs.

Box 6.2 Intended learning outcomes (ILOs) for *The Nature of Teaching and Learning* and aligned teaching/learning activities (TLAs)

1 *Explain* why a particular course topic is important to teaching.
  TLAs: plenary sessions with pre-readings and notes used for learning information, clarification and elaboration. Discussion on application to teaching with partners and in small groups.
2 *Apply* a course topic to your own teaching.
  TLAs: independent problem solving in workplace, recorded in reflective diary.
3 *Reflect* on your teaching in terms of a working theory you have gained from the course.
  TLAs: keep reflective diary on critical incidents; discuss with group/ learning partner.
4 *Evaluate* a situation that has gone wrong and *apply* a solution.
  TLAs: use workplace resources, group/learning partner comparing perspectives on evaluating and applying.

Assessment tasks (ATs)

The assessment portfolio comprised items selected by the students that they thought addressed each ILO. The students were to decide on the evidence for their achievement of the ILOs in the form of items for their portfolio and to explain why they thought the portfolio as a whole met the ILOs. Specifically, the requirements were:

1 four pieces of evidence selected by the student, which they thought addressed most of the ILOs;
2 a reflective journal, including answers to the self-addressed questions for each plenary session;
3 a justification for selecting each portfolio item and the overall case they were supposed to make as a learning package, showing how each ILO had been addressed one way or another. This provided further evidence of students' reflective awareness of their learning.

A list of suggested item types was provided, but original items were encouraged.

Box 6.3 shows the alignment between the ILOs and the items in the portfolio.

Box 6.3 ILOs for *The Nature of Teaching and Learning* **and aligned assessment tasks (ATs)**

1 *Explain* why a particular course topic is important to teaching.
   AT: Set yourself a 2000-word essay on one of two nominated topics.
2 *Apply* a course topic to your own teaching.
   AT: Written report explaining relevant diary entries concerning the application, problems encountered, student reactions.
3 *Reflect* on your teaching in terms of a working theory you have gained from the course.
   AT: Present selected parts of diary with comments: explain how your portfolio items meet ILOs and self-evaluate.
4 *Evaluate* a situation that has gone wrong and *apply* a solution.
   AT: Write a case study of a critical incident in your own teaching and how you dealt with it.

One student referred to the assessment portfolio as 'a learning tool'. In fact, it was difficult to separate what was a TLA and what an AT, as is the case in an aligned system. For example, students learned how to reflect by using the journal, which was used later as evidence of reflection; the self-addressed questions (such as 'What was the most important idea?') are both learning activities that can also provide evidence for the quality of learning.

Grading

The final step is to obtain a final grade for the student from the evidence presented in the portfolio as to how well the ILOs have been achieved. There are normally two aspects to grading: assessing the student's outputs against the stated criteria and combining results from several ATs to form a final grade. This can be done quantitatively, as is usually the case, or qualitatively: these issues and the pros and cons are discussed in Chapter 10.

In the case of *The Nature of Teaching and Learning*, a qualitative approach was taken as being the most suitable for the task and the context. Each letter grade represents a qualitatively different level of thinking, as follows:

A Able to reflect, self-evaluate realistically, able to formulate and apply theory to problematic classroom situations, clear mastery of course contents.

B Can apply theory to practice, a holistic understanding of course and components, barely failed **A**.

C Can explain the more important theories, can describe other topics acceptably, barely failed **B**.

D Can only explain some theories, barely failed **C**.

F Less than **D**, plagiarism.

The grading was simple, involving no quantitative 'marking' or averaging to calculate a final grade. The portfolio items were assessed as to whether they provided 'evidence' for A qualities, B qualities and so on. If the evidence collectively did not reveal realistic self-evaluation, for example, but did show an ability to form a working theory and apply it to classroom situations, then here was a clear B.

Constructive alignment: an overview

This chapter describes how constructive alignment came about and how the course in which it was first used illustrates the important steps in implementing constructive alignment. We generalize by reference to Figure 6.1, which can be used as a general framework for teaching. Although constructive alignment arose in a professional programme, it can be implemented in virtually any course at any level of university teaching.

The intended learning outcomes are central to the whole system. Get them right and the decisions as to how they are to be taught and how they may be assessed follow. We express the ILOs in terms of what constructive activities are most likely to achieve them. Activities are *verbs*, so, practically speaking, we specify the verbs we want students to enact in the context of the content discipline being taught.

Turn back to Figure 1.1 (p. 6). We see that Susan tended spontaneously to use high level outcome verbs such as theorize, reflect, generate, apply, whereas Robert used lower level outcome verbs such as recognize, memorize,

Figure 6.1 Aligning intended learning outcomes, teaching and assessment tasks

describe. Their level of engagement is expressed in the cognitive level of the verbs used: reflection is high level, memorizing low level. Note that these verbs are examples only. Precisely what is meant by 'level', and how to determine it, is a key issue addressed in Chapter 7.

Those verbs take objects, the content topic taught. We explicitly reject the one-dimensional notion of 'covering' the topics in the curriculum. Rather we need to specify the *levels* of understanding or of performance (see Chapter 5).

Once we have sorted out the ILOs, we design TLAs that are likely to encourage students to engage the verbs that are made explicit in the ILOs. By so doing, we optimize the chances that the intended outcomes will be achieved. Next, we select assessment tasks that will tell us whether and how well each student can meet the criteria expressed in the ILOs. Again, this is done by embedding the verbs in the ILOs in the assessment tasks. ILOs, teaching and assessment are now aligned, using the verbs in the ILOs as markers for alignment.

Finally, a grading scheme needs to be constructed according to how well the ILOs have been met. A grade of A denotes a quality of learning that is the best we can reasonably expect for the course. Obviously, that level will become increasingly higher from first year to more senior years. In the final year, one would expect the sorts of verbs that are in the top box of Figure 5.1 (p. 91, 'generalize', 'reflect') to define an A. B is highly satisfactory, but lacks the flair that distinguishes A. C is quite satisfactory, while D denotes what is minimally acceptable; anything less is fail (F). What that range will be for any particular course and year level is a matter of judgement by the teacher or programme committee. The criteria, or rubrics, defining the final grades will need to be much more specific than this and will need to be developed for each course. The important thing is that the categories are defined by a particular *quality* of learning and understanding, not by the accumulation of marks or percentages.

Grading on the *quality* of learning is not new. It has been used to define levels of honours and postgraduate dissertations for years. The level of honours as it has typically been used captures the idea that a student with first class honours *thinks differently* from a student with an upper second. This difference is not captured by saying that a first has to obtain more marks than an upper second. We have more to say on this in Chapter 10.

To sum up, in a constructively aligned system of teaching, the teacher's task is to see that the appropriate learning activities, conveniently expressed as verbs, are:

1 nominated in the intended learning outcome statements;
2 embedded in the chosen teaching/learning activities so that performing them brings the student closer to achieving the ILOs;
3 embedded in the assessment tasks enabling judgements as to how well a given student's level of performance meets the ILOs.

Because the TLAs and the ATs now access the same verbs as are in the ILOs, the chances are increased that most students will engage with the appropriate verbs. This is by definition a deep approach. Had Ramsden's psychology teacher (see pp. 24–5) included in the ILOs such verbs as 'theorize', 'generalize' or 'explain the contribution of particular founders of modern psychology', an assessment task that required only paraphrasing 'a bit of factual information for two pages of writing' would immediately be seen to be inadequate.

Constructive alignment is common sense. Mothers, like driving instructors, use it all the time. What is the intended outcome? That the child can tie her shoes. What is the TLA? Tying her shoes. What is the assessment? How well she ties her shoes. Why is most university teaching not so aligned? There are several reasons:

1 Traditional practices of teaching and assessment ignore alignment. A common method of determining students' grades depends on how students compare with each other (norm-referenced), rather than on

whether an individual's learning meets the intended outcomes (criterion-referenced). In the former case, there is no *inherent* relation between what is taught and what is tested. The aim is to distribute or spread students' performances so that we clearly separate the good students from the less good, not to see how well individuals have learned what they were supposed to have learned.

2 'If it ain't broke, don't fix it.' Some teachers believe there's nothing wrong with current practice. As we saw in Chapter 1, however, there are problems of teaching that are arising in the rapidly changing university scene. In any case, a situation doesn't have to be 'broke' before we try to make it work better. The difference between reflective and unreflective teachers is that the former teachers believe they can always teach better than they are doing at present. Indeed, a major feature of award-winning university teachers was that they were continually seeking feedback from students on ways in which they could improve their teaching (Dunkin and Precians 1992).

3 Resource limitations appear to dictate large classes with mass lecturing and multiple-choice testing. These make alignment more difficult, certainly, but not impossible. However, policies that require teachers to use norm referencing by grading on the curve do make alignment impossible. If constructive alignment is to be implemented such policies and practices need be changed, as we discuss in Chapter 13.

4 These issues of alignment may not have occurred to teachers.

5 Other teachers might like to use the principle but they don't know how to.

These points are addressed throughout this book. We shall see how the principle of alignment can be applied to the design of most courses. Finally, in Chapter 13, we look at the evidence for the effectiveness of constructive alignment.

Now try Task 6.1 to see how aligned your teaching and assessment are to the intended learning outcomes of a course you are currently teaching.

Task 6.1 Constructive alignment in your current teaching and assessment

Take a course that you are teaching.

A What are three of the things that you expect your students to be able to do at the end of the course?

1 _____

2 _____

3 _____

B   How do you *teach* your students to do these things?

For 1 _____

For 2 _____

For 3 _____

C   How do you *assess* your students on doing these three things?

For 1 _____

For 2 _____

For 3 _____

Your reflection:

What do you think of the alignment between A, B and C above?

_____

_____

Summary and conclusions

How did constructive alignment come about?

Constructive alignment was born in a psychology course for teachers. Teachers learn psychology so that they may teach better, but the evidence that they do as a result of learning psychology is not specifically collected. In this class, the student teachers were asked to provide such evidence from their own teaching and place it in a portfolio. The class's response resulted in their engaging in learning activities that could help them meet this new assessment task, which became their curriculum. They focused their learning on obtaining evidence that psychology was helping them to teach more effectively. Enter constructive alignment.

What is constructive alignment?

Constructive alignment is based on the twin principles of constructivism in learning, and alignment both of teaching and of assessment tasks to the intended learning outcomes. The intended outcomes specify the *activity* that students should engage in if they are to achieve the intended outcome, the teacher's tasks then being to set up a learning environment that encourages the student to perform those learning activities, and to assess the students' performances against those intended learning outcomes. Focusing on what and how students are to learn, rather than on what topics the teacher is to teach, requires that an intended learning outcome, or ILO, specifies not only *what* is to be learned, the topic, but *how* it is to be learned and to what standard. The outcome statement thus specifies a verb that informs students how they are expected to change as a result of learning that topic, for example 'reflect on X', or 'apply theory to Y'. That verb, or verbs, should then be addressed in the teaching/learning activities (TLAs), and in the assessment task (AT).

Design of constructively aligned teaching and assessment

Constructive alignment requires the design of: the *intended learning outcomes* using a verb indicating a standard of performance, and the content to be learned; the *teaching/learning activities* that address that verb; *assessment tasks* that also contain that verb with rubrics that enable one to judge how well the standard of the students' performances to meet the criteria. Each of these stages is illustrated from the original course on teaching psychology, and how they were aligned to the ILOs.

Constructive alignment: an overview

In a constructively aligned system, all components – intended learning outcomes, teaching/learning activities, assessment tasks and their grading – support each other, so the learner is enveloped within a supportive learning system. In Part 2 of this book we turn to the details of designing such a system, and in Part 3 we look at its implementation.

Further reading

Biggs, J.B. (1996b) Enhancing teaching through constructive alignment, *Higher Education*, 32, 1: 1–18.

Tyler, R.W. (1949) *Basic Principles of Curriculum and Instruction*. Chicago: University of Chicago Press.

Biggs's paper outlines in detail the original course that gave rise to constructive alignment. At the time, he did not know that Ralph Tyler had said something rather similar over 50 years ago:

1 What educational purposes should the school seek to attain?
2 How can learning experiences be selected which are likely to be useful in attaining these objectives?
3 How can learning experiences be organized for effective instruction?
4 How can the effectiveness of learning experiences be evaluated?

Tyler's book was widely prescribed in US teachers' colleges and worldwide; it went to 36 editions, while Tyler himself was educational guru to Presidents Truman, Eisenhower and Johnson. But essentially nothing changed. The problem was that educators generally at that time were obsessed with norm-referencing and there was no way they were going to give that up, so that on the issue of aligning assessment to effective learning, Tyler received respectful lip service only. His book is under one hundred pages in length and is well worth a read, for old time's sake.

Film

Teaching Teaching & Understanding Understanding, an award-winning film available on DVD from the University of Aarhus, Denmark, written and directed by Claus Brabrand. In less than 20 minutes, Claus takes the viewer through the basics of constructive alignment with Doina and Rune, Danish versions of Susan and Robert. Available from Aarhus University Press (www.unipress.dk) in English, French, Spanish, Italian, Portuguese, German and Danish.

Websites

The Engineering Subject Centre, Higher Education Academy, UK. http://www.engsc.ac.uk/er/theory/constructive_alignment.asp (accessed 2 February 2011).

An excellent overview of constructive alignment, with links to related topics such as 'Assessment', 'Approaches to learning', etc.

If you want more, Google 'constructive alignment' and browse – but be selective as there is a lot there.

Part 2

Designing constructively aligned
outcomes-based teaching and learning

7

Designing intended learning outcomes

Intended learning outcomes (ILOs) apply at the *institutional* level as graduate attributes, or as we prefer, graduate outcomes, and at the *programme* and *course* levels.* Graduate outcomes provide useful guidelines for designing programme outcomes, which are in turn addressed by the outcomes of specific courses. Most of this chapter is taken up with the design and writing of course ILOs, as they are central to the design of teaching and assessment. It is necessary to stipulate the kind of knowledge to be learned, declarative or functioning, and to use a verb and a context that indicate clearly the level at which it is to be learned and how the performance is to be displayed for assessment.

Intended learning outcomes at different levels

As we saw in the previous chapter, an ILO is a statement describing what and how a student is expected to learn after exposure to teaching. Such an outcome statement can be made at three levels:

- the *institutional* level, as a statement of what the graduates of the university are supposed to be able to do;
- the degree *programme* level, as a statement of what graduates from particular degree programmes should be able to do;
- the *course* level, as a statement of what students should be able to do at the completion of a given course.

Let us now look at each in turn.

---

* We use 'programme' to refer to the whole degree pattern. Some universities refer to this as a 'course', as in a course of study. We use 'course' to refer to the units of study making up a programme, whereas others refer to this as a 'unit', 'module' or 'subject'.

Graduate outcomes

It has long been believed that university study has an effect on the way graduates think and act, over and above the knowledge and skills that have been learned in the official curriculum of the degree programme. For example, graduates are thought to feel a need to seek and evaluate evidence before coming to a conclusion, not to accept 'spin' as readily as nongraduates, to question the status quo, to show intellectual curiosity about the physical or social world. Public opinion used to expect certain moral behaviour from graduates, as in such statements as: 'He ought to have known better with his education!' The public service, too, used to recruit graduates, without stipulating any particular area of study, on the grounds that they would be employing a certain sort of person, a person who thinks like a graduate. This view reminds us of a famous saying by Albert Einstein: 'Education is what remains after one has forgotten what one has learned in school.'

In somewhat similar vein, the Higher Education Council (HEC) of Australia defined the attributes a graduate should possess as: 'The skills, personal attributes and values which should be acquired by all graduates regardless of their discipline or field of study. In other words, generic skills should represent the central achievements of higher education as a process' (HEC 1992: 20).

The Dearing Report (1997) was more specific in referring to qualities that responsible citizens in a global society should have, such as 'critical thinking', 'ethical practice', 'creativity', 'independent problem solving', 'professional skills', 'communications skills', 'teamwork', 'lifelong learning' and the like. But what are these qualities really and, more to the point, how are they supposed to be acquired and manifested in such varied fields as accountancy, veterinary science or social work? Or are they simple generic abilities that apply across the board to any subject?

And here lies the problem. We are clearly dealing with more specific residues than what is left after you've forgotten everything you were ever taught. There are several different conceptions of graduate outcomes, which makes it difficult for universities to agree on an institution-wide policy in fostering them (Barrie 2004). Barrie, after a phenomenographic analysis of teachers' conceptions of graduate outcomes, arrived at a hierarchy of conceptions. The lowest sees graduate outcomes as *generic* foundation skills that are unrelated to any particular discipline area, such as numeracy and communication skills that can be taught in standalone courses. At the other extreme are attributes as abilities that are deeply *embedded* in particular disciplines: for example, problem-solving strategies that involve thinking like a physicist won't be of much help in solving problems of medical diagnosis. Teachers who hold the view that graduate outcomes are embedded in their discipline are not going to be very concerned about fostering a generic problem-solving ability. Their concern is to make sure that their students are required to show evidence of the appropriate problem-solving strategies in their academic performances, especially in the higher years. Otherwise, they do not see developing generic graduate outcomes as their responsibility.

How we teach these graduate outcomes thus depends on whether we see them as generic or embedded. Some graduate outcomes can reasonably be seen as generic and standalone, such as literacy skills, generic problem-solving strategies and critical-thinking skills, can work across different content areas and may be taught as standalone subjects (Hattie 2009a, 2009b). It is therefore helpful to provide some generic courses in study skills and metacognitive study strategies (pp. 175–77) as enabling outcomes, but not as substitutes for teaching problem solving or creativity in embedded contexts. Such enabling outcomes are lower order, instrumental in helping students achieve higher order outcomes. For instance, generic metacognitive problem-solving strategies could be seen as an enabling outcome for lifelong learning. However, like many such generic outcomes they should also be addressed in the context of a subject or topic. In fact, extended abstract outcomes such as 'far transfer' from one domain to another, should be in the intended learning outcomes of many higher level courses.

A rather ruthless approach to the assessment of graduate outcomes is given by Yuen-Heung et al. (2005) in a US university. These graduate outcomes, or 'university learning goals' as they were called, are not an atypical list: 'leadership', 'independent lifelong learning', 'values-based decision making', 'develop service potential', 'critical thinking' 'logical reasoning', 'written communication' and 'oral communication'. Students are rated by teachers on goals and each goal's sub-goals. Independent lifelong learning has 14 sub-goals, critical thinking 13, and so on, making 74 goals and sub-goals in all. Students not meeting a satisfactory level on any goal or sub-goal are 'lifted' until they do. One must be forgiven for thinking that the time and effort going into this might be better spent in teaching those goals in context.

Embedded outcomes, such as creativity and lifelong learning, on the other hand, require significant substantive knowledge in a given area, and so should be built into the intended learning outcomes of particular programmes and courses, which is an issue we address in detail in later chapters.

Schwartz (2010) takes a holistic view of graduate outcomes, seeing them as going beyond professionally related skills to comprise 'wisdom', which may be acquired at university through the Confucian ideas of reflection, having a suitable role model and relevant personal experience, not by anything gained from a single course. He recommends a final year capstone course called 'Practical Wisdom' to help students reflect on the getting of wisdom. Knight (2006), likewise, says that graduate outcomes such as reasoning, creativity, ethical practice, teamwork and collaboration and so on are complex 'achievements' or 'wicked competencies' that develop rather than are taught. They have no single cause, are slow growing, and need a complex environment, an *ethos* – a particular climate, a sequence of role models – in which to develop. They are unlikely to be achieved if they are only addressed in one or a few courses. Their assessment cannot be measured with what Knight calls 'high-stakes' assessment instruments of high reliability, such as tests. Self- and peer-assessment, and particularly portfolios, in which students make claims that they themselves try to substantiate are more suitable. In this view, graduate outcomes need continually looking to, such that they are fostered in teaching over a range of subjects and interactions with students.

Most universities want both kinds of graduate outcomes to be addressed, as do quality assurance agencies, not to mention employers who want to be assured that graduates have achieved the claimed graduate outcomes. One problem is that if outcomes such as creativity or critical thinking are embedded in general teaching and not taught in generic foundation courses, they are less visible, whereas graduate outcomes in standalone courses (e.g. Critical Thinking 101) can be seen to have been addressed and assessed, so the quality assurance committee is duly impressed at the next institutional audit or process review. The fact that the critical thinking may not necessarily apply in depth to the content area in which the graduate has studied, but only to across-the-board exercises addressed in the standalone class, may easily be overlooked.

How do we resolve these contradictory positions and derive an internally consistent policy for any given institution? This will be a matter of policy, that will differ from university to university according to their mix of attributes and their policies on addressing them. At this stage we would distinguish three levels of addressing graduate outcomes:

1 The institutional climate itself has a formative effect on some graduate outcomes. Ethical behaviour, lifelong learning, creativity and so on are more likely to thrive in a Theory Y institutional climate that itself values such outcomes in the very real sense that it enacts them in its own policies and procedures.
2 Graduate outcomes built into degree programme outcomes, which are addressed as appropriate in constituent courses. An example of this approach in a first year management course is given by Green et al. (2006).
3 Standalone generic courses for enabling outcomes such as study skills, language and communication, numeracy and IT skills. Such skills are often part of higher order graduate outcomes such as lifelong learning, which comprises several generic skills such as surfing the net selectively, and communication and numeracy skills. Such courses may be particularly useful for students with special needs.

Intended learning outcomes at the programme level

In translating graduate outcomes to programme outcomes, two aspects need to be reconciled: mapping the graduate outcomes onto the programme, and designing the programme ILOs from the aims of the particular degree programme itself. Any degree programme is established in order to achieve a definite aim, which will be served by the course ILOs – and many academics will see these programme specific ILOs as more important than ILOs generated to serve graduate outcomes. These contrasting needs can be met by embedding the graduate outcomes in the content and teaching of the programme.

Let us start with the aims of the programme itself: what is it meant to achieve, and what is its focus and its context? For example, take a bachelor of business management, BBM (accountancy) programme. The focus, let us say, is on accounting and the programme graduates are to serve the professional, commercial and industrial sector. This aim is served if graduates can achieve the following outcomes:

1 explain the conceptual and contextual framework and practical skills of the accounting profession;
2 analyse this framework of accounting and apply the practical skills to manage real-life accounting situations, and solve problems in accountancy;
3 communicate effectively as a professional with clients and colleagues in real-life accounting situations;
4 operate effectively and ethically as a team member in real-life accounting situations.

These programme ILOs are in effect the reasons for establishing the programme. We see most of the outcomes are about functioning knowledge, except the first. There would usually be only a few programme ILOs; rarely would they exceed, say, six. A common problem at this level is to force an *a priori* template on programme ILOs, such that outcomes must address knowledge, skill, values and social concerns (e.g. Ewell 1984). It is fair enough to see that graduate outcomes address such concerns, but to insist they be applied willy-nilly to all programme outcomes is to invite confusion and bottleneck. This problem gets worse at course level and so we return to it below.

Having derived these programme-specific ILOs, the next question is how to reconcile these with general graduate outcomes. A simple solution is to see that programme committees and course teachers check that where *possible and appropriate* the intended learning outcomes address the listed graduate outcomes, but grounded in the content and context of the degree programme. Thus degrees in education, social work, fine arts, computing science or business and management would address different mixes of graduate outcomes. The 'creativity' outcome, say, is then confined to the particular areas the student has studied – with hopefully some overflow to a way of thinking, but no promises. Thus, all degree programmes would address 'creativity' in some way or another. The graduate outcomes are used only to jog the memory when writing ILOs and deriving the criteria for assessing assessment tasks. Hardliners on accountability may not consider this rigorous enough, but it makes most educational sense.

One problem with being too rigorous about applying graduate outcomes is that, particularly in the social/value domain, they have varying degrees of relevance to different programmes. Empathy, say, is highly appropriate in a social work degree, rather less so in, say, computer programming. A social worker lacking empathy clearly should not be awarded a degree in social work, but one would be inviting big trouble withholding a degree from a computer scientist on the basis of lack of empathy. To insist that inappropriate or irrelevant graduate outcomes are forced into all programmes irrespective of suitability is to invite resistance and cynicism from students.

Reconciling specific programme ILOs with the requirements of the university's graduate outcomes policy is a question specific to each institution and there are various ways of handling it (Bath et al. 2004; Sumsion and Goodfellow 2004). The College of Business in one Hong Kong university developed an intermediate set of outcome statements at the College level that were stringently mapped with the university's graduate outcomes and that were then used to guide the development of individual degree programme ILOs. The intermediate College set of graduate outcomes made the mapping process to programme and then to course ILOs that much easier.

However, it is the course ILOs to which teaching and assessment are aligned.

Intended learning outcomes at the course level

In the first edition of this book, we used the term 'curriculum objectives' or just 'objectives' for the intended outcomes of a course. We now think the term 'intended learning outcome' (ILO) is better because it emphasizes more than does 'objective' that we are referring to what the student has to learn rather than what the teacher has to teach. 'Intended learning outcome' clarifies what the student should be able to perform after teaching that couldn't be performed previously – and there may well be outcomes that are a positive outcome of teaching that weren't intended. The term 'objective' was intended to have the latter, student-centred, meaning but ILO makes it absolutely clear that the outcomes are from the student's perspective. The term 'objective' also may recall in older readers the problems associated with 'behavioural objectives'.

'The student will understand expectancy-value theory' might be a teaching objective, but it is not an ILO. Likewise the following example, taken from the objectives for an occupational therapy course: 'At the end of this course, students will be able to understand the concept of muscle tone and its relation to functional activity.' What does it mean 'to understand the concept of muscle tone'? What learning activities are involved? What level of understanding are the students to achieve?

With an ILO we need to make a statement about what students' learning would look like after they have learned expectancy-value theory to the acceptable standard. Defining that standard of the outcome of learning is important. Verbs like 'understand', 'comprehend', 'be aware of' are unhelpful in ILOs because they do not convey the *level* of performance we require if the ILO is to be met. Even the quite common 'demonstrate an understanding of' leave important questions unanswered: what does the student have to do to demonstrate 'an' understanding? What level of under-standing does the teacher have in mind – simple acquaintance? Able to point to an instance of? Apply in a real-life situation? One of the key criteria of a good ILO is that the student, when seeing a written ILO, would know what to do and how well to do it in order to meet the ILO. Box 7.1 presents the conventional objectives of a course in engineering, then the same course expressed in ILOs.

Box 7.1 From objectives to intended learning outcomes in an engineering course

Objectives (old)

1 To provide an understanding of the kinematics and kinetics of machines and the fundamental concepts of stress and strain analysis.

2 To develop an analytical under-standing of the kinematics and kinetics and elastic behaviours of machine elements under loading.

ILOs (new)

1 To *describe* the basic principles of kinematics and kinetics of machines and the fundamental concepts of stress and strain analysis.

2 Using given principles, to *solve* a mechanical problem that involves loading and motion.

3 To *select* relevant principles to obtain the solutions for mechan-ical problems.

4 To *present* analyses and results of experiments in a proper format of a written report such that a tech-nically qualified person can follow and obtain similar findings.

Source: Patrick Wong and Lawrence Li, Department of Manufacturing Engineering and Engineering Management, City University of Hong Kong

---

The main reasons for teaching a course – as with the reasons for developing a programme – usually amount to no more than five or six. Each ILO might be regarded as addressing one of these reasons. A set of five or six well-designed course ILOs communicates an integrated and holistic overview of the course. The more ILOs there are, not only will it be more likely to fragment the holistic view of what the course is basically about, it would also become more difficult to align teaching/learning activities and assessment tasks to each. Trying to impose a knowledge + skill + value + attitude template, with all their sub-domains, is even more inappropriate at the course level as we saw it is at the programme level. We have come across institutions requiring all outcomes to be balanced in terms of the three domains addressed in Bloom's taxonomy of educational objectives: the cognitive domain (Bloom 1956), the affective domain (Krathwohl et al. 1973), and the psychomotor domain (unfinished by Bloom but see Simpson 1972). However, the affective domain and/or the psychomotor domain may not be applicable to all courses, and to include them unnecessarily increases the number of outcomes and their TLAs and ATs – when they are irrelevant to the course! At the programme and graduate outcome levels, however, all three domains may be relevant at some stage or another, and it is useful to have Bloom to remind us to think about this possibility, but they certainly should not be prescribed in fixed proportions at either programme or course level. The proportion of different kinds of outcome domain should not be ordained before designing ILOs but left to the programme and course committees to decide their relevance.

Another problem we have come across is that teachers start with the topics to be taught and then they try to write outcomes for those topics. In delivering a course, there might be say ten topics to be taught, but in writing several outcomes for each topic, a massive set of 30 or more outcomes would be created, which is unmanageable; you can't align teaching/learning activities and assessment tasks to 30 outcomes! There might well be ten topics in the curriculum for a course, but ILOs can be designed that group topics so that more than one topic can be addressed by one ILO. You therefore start with the aims of the course in relation to the programme as a whole, then list the important topics that are to be addressed – usually, these will include the threshold concept(s) and core concepts. The important thing is to decide what students are to *do* with these topic concepts. Some may need only declarative treatment, such as 'explain', while others are to be treated as functioning knowledge, such as 'apply'. The ILOs are then written, no more than five or six, that deal appropriately with the chosen topics.

With these caveats, we turn to writing course ILOs.

Designing and writing course ILOs

In designing outcomes, there are several points to consider.

Decide what kind of knowledge is to be involved

Is the ILO in question about declarative knowledge: knowing about phenomena, theories, disciplines, specific topics? Or is it about functioning knowledge: requiring the student to exercise active control over problems and decisions in the appropriate content domains? The ILO should be clear as to what kind of knowledge you want and why.

Declarative knowledge in a professional education programme may be taught for various reasons:

- As general 'cultural' content, as in the liberal arts notion of an educated person; e.g. a business management student must take an arts subject for 'broadening'. There is no functioning knowledge involved here.
- As content specifically related to the profession: e.g. the history of western architecture in an architecture degree. This is important background for architects to have, but again there may be little direct bearing on functioning knowledge.
- As content that does bear on functioning knowledge, but is not a key priority. In this case, students might be taught the basic outlines and where to go for more details as and when the need arises.
- As content that definitely bears on everyday decision making. The ILO should be written specifically for underwriting the functioning knowledge concerned. In fact, as we discuss in the next chapter, the declarative knowledge may well be subsumed under the functioning knowledge ILO.

All these different purposes for teaching a topic or course require careful thought as to the balance between coverage and depth. The curriculum is not a plateau of topics, all 'covered' to the same extent, but a series of hills and valleys. In an international phone call, which is expensive and usually made for a specific purpose, you don't just chat about the weather. We need similarly to prioritize our classroom communications by deciding the depth, or level of understanding required, for each topic, as discussed later.

Select the topics to teach

Selecting the actual topics to teach is obviously a matter of specific content expertise and judgement. You, as the content expert, are best able to decide on this, but when doing so note the tension between coverage and depth of understanding.

There is almost always strong pressure to include more and more content, particularly when teachers share the teaching of a course and in professional faculties where outside bodies validate courses. All concerned see their own special topic or interest as the most important. Over-teaching is the inevitable result. But, to quote Gardner again:

> The greatest enemy of understanding is coverage – I can't repeat that often enough. If you're determined to cover a lot of things, you are guaranteeing that most kids will not understand, because they haven't had time enough to go into things in depth, to figure out what the requisite understanding is, and be able to perform that understanding in different situations.
>
> (Gardner 1993: 24)

If we conceive the curriculum as a rectangle, the area (breadth × depth) remains constant. Take your pick. Breadth: wide coverage and surface learning giving disjointed multistructural outcomes. Depth: fewer topics and deep learning giving relational and extended abstract outcomes. Do you want a curriculum 'a mile wide and half an inch deep', as US educators described the school mathematics curriculum following the abysmal performance of US senior high school students in the Third International Mathematics and Science Study (quoted in Stedman 1997)? Or do you want your students to *really* understand in the sense that they are able to effectively use what you have taught them?

Actually, the area of the curriculum needn't be entirely constant. Good teaching increases the area, maintaining depth. But there are limits, and there is little doubt that most courses in all universities contain more content than students can handle at little more than the level of acquaintance – which, it is to be hoped, is not an intended outcome. However, when modes of assessment go no deeper than acquaintance, as is likely with multiple-choice tests, the problem remains invisible.

Level of understanding intended

Is the ILO for an introductory or an advanced course? Brabrand and Dahl (2009) used SOLO to demonstrate that in undergraduate science courses in two Danish universities the level of outcomes expected increased from first to final year, but there were large differences between disciplines. In first year, an extended abstract or theoretical level of understanding of a topic may be too high for even an A grade. The answer also varies according to why students are enrolled in a common first-year subject. Anatomy 101, for example, might contain students enrolled in first-year medicine and students enrolled in a diploma in occupational therapy. The required levels of under-standing in the ILOs may need to be different for each group.

Next, it is necessary to ask why you are teaching this particular topic:

- to delineate boundaries, giving students a broad picture of what's 'there';
- to inform on a current state of play, to bring students up to date on the state of the topic or discipline;
- to stockpile knowledge, of no perceived use for the present, but likely to be needed later; or
- to inform decisions that need making in the near future, as in problem-based learning?

Each of these purposes implies a different level and kind of understanding; each can be nominated by identifying the appropriate outcome action verbs.

One way of addressing the importance of a topic is to spend more or less time on it. A better way is that important topics should be *understood at a higher level* than less important topics. An important topic might be understood so that students can use it or solve problems with it; a less important topic, just that it is recognized. We can signal importance by choosing a verb at the appropriate level of understanding for each topic.

The verb in the ILO has two main functions: it says what the student is to be able to do with the topic and at what level. In Figure 5.1, depicting SOLO, you will recall that there were some typical verbs for each SOLO level. Table 7.1 gives several more.

This gives us a wide range of levels that can be adapted to the levels appropriate to particular courses, from first to senior years. Particular content areas and topics would have their own specific verbs as well, which you would need to specify to suit your own course. Some verbs could be either extended abstract or relational, depending on, for example, the degree of originality or the context in which the verb was deployed: 'solve a problem', for example. And whether 'paraphrase' is relational or multistructural depends on how the student goes about paraphrasing: replacing with like-meaning phrases or rethinking the meaning of the whole text and rewriting it. Writing ILOs is one thing, but when it comes to assessing them it needs to be done in a context so that these ambiguous verbs can be pinned down: to 'show your working', as maths teachers are wont to say.

For another set of verbs, based on Bloom's revised taxonomy (Anderson and Krathwohl 2001), see Table 7.2.

The original Bloom taxonomy was not based on research on student learning itself, as is SOLO, but on the judgements of educational administrators, neither is it hierarchical, as is SOLO. Anderson and Krathwohl's revision is an improvement, but even then under 'understanding' you can find 'identify', 'discuss' and 'explain', which represent three different SOLO levels. This is exactly why 'understand' and 'comprehend' are not helpful terms to use in writing ILOs. However, the Bloom taxonomy is a useful adjunct for suggesting a wider list of verbs, especially for a range of learning activities.

Table 7.1 Some verbs for ILOs from the SOLO taxonomy

Unistructural	Memorize, identify, recognize, count, define, draw, find, label, match, name, quote, recall, recite, order, tell, write, imitate
Multistructural	Classify, describe, list, report, discuss, illustrate, select, narrate, compute, sequence, outline, separate
Relational	Apply, integrate, analyse, explain, predict, conclude, summarize (précis), review, argue, transfer, make a plan, characterize, compare, contrast, differentiate, organize, debate, make a case, construct, review and rewrite, examine, translate, paraphrase, solve a problem
Extended abstract	Theorize, hypothesize, generalize, reflect, generate, create, compose, invent, originate, prove from first principles, make an original case, solve from first principles

Table 7.2 Some more ILO verbs from Bloom's revised taxonomy

Remembering	Define, describe, draw, find, identify, label, list, match, name, quote, recall, recite, tell, write
Understanding	Classify, compare, conclude, demonstrate, discuss, exemplify, explain, identify, illustrate, interpret, paraphrase, predict, report
Applying	Apply, change, choose, compute, dramatize, implement, interview, prepare, produce, role play, select, show, transfer, use
Analysing	Analyse, characterize, classify, compare, contrast, debate, deconstruct, deduce, differentiate, discriminate, distinguish, examine, organize, outline, relate, research, separate, structure
Evaluating	Appraise, argue, assess, choose, conclude, critique, decide, evaluate, judge, justify, monitor, predict, prioritize, prove, rank, rate, select
Creating	Compose, construct, create, design, develop, generate, hypothesize, invent, make, perform, plan, produce

Source: Anderson and Krathwohl (2001)

Table 7.3 Some typical declarative and functioning knowledge verbs by SOLO level

	Declarative knowledge	*Functioning knowledge*
Unistructural	Memorize, identify, recite	Count, match, order
Multistructural	Describe, classify	Compute, illustrate
Relational	Compare and contrast, explain, argue, analyse	Apply, construct, translate, solve near problem, predict within same domain
Extended Abstract	Theorize, hypothesize, generalize	Reflect and improve, invent, create, solve unseen problems, extrapolate to unknown domains

Table 7.3 lists typical verbs at different SOLO levels illustrating each of declarative and functioning knowledge.

Writing the course ILOs

We are now in a position to start writing course ILOs. These need to be stated in such a way that they stipulate:

- the *verb* at the appropriate *level* of understanding or of performance intended;
- the topic *content* the verb is meant to address, the object of the verb in other words;
- the *context* of the content discipline in which the verb is to be deployed.

The ILOs for the course *The Nature of Teaching and Learning* illustrate these points:

1 *Explain* why a particular course topic is important to teaching.
2 *Apply* a course topic to your own teaching.
3 *Reflect* on your teaching in terms of a working theory you have gained from the course.
4 *Evaluate* a situation that has gone wrong and *apply* a solution.

The first refers to declarative knowledge: the students have to reach a level of understanding that requires them to *explain* something, not just describe or list it: the latter only display multistructural levels of understanding, but explaining requires students to be able to relate the topic to the context of teaching and is at a relational level of understanding. The second is a functioning knowledge example also at the relational level as it requires a level of understanding that enables the student to apply the topic to teaching.

The other two are also about functioning knowledge and should be at the relational to extended abstract level of understanding, depending on the originality of the student's response. The content in (3) is the student's own working theory and the context the student's own teaching, and in (4), the content is the theory used in evaluating and the context the problematic situation in teaching.

As a note on the number of ILOs per course, we stated earlier that there should be no more five or six ILOs for any course, even though there may be up to ten topics that need addressing. The answer is to write *integrating* ILOs that address several topics, or, as in ILOs (1) and (2) above, the ILO allows the student to select just one topic for demonstrating ability to achieve the ILO. Another thing to watch out for are redundant ILOs, such as 'Describe and explain . . .'. 'Describe' is redundant because if the student can explain the topic, he or she can certainly describe it.

The other matter one should keep in mind at this stage is that desirable but *unintended* outcomes, or outcomes unforeseen by the teacher, may emerge. This is the nature of extended abstract responses by the student, and they will be accounted for in the normal assessment, but others may simply be things that the student sees as important and relevant learning. This matter becomes a practical issue during assessment, and we address it in Chapter 10.

You should now be in a position to design and write your own ILOs for a course you are teaching (Task 7.1).

Task 7.1 Writing course ILOs

Take a course that you are teaching. Consider the course aim and write the course ILOs by identifying:

a the kind of knowledge to be learned (declarative or functioning).
b the content or topic to be learned.
c the level of understanding or performance to be achieved.
d any particular context in which the outcome verb is to be enacted.

The following grid may be a useful framework to help you think.

Kind of knowledge *Declar/function*	*Level of* *understanding* *(outcome verb)*	*Content topic*	*Context*

Now go across the rows and write out the course ILOs by stating the intended level of understanding or performance (outcome verb), topic and the context in which the verb is to be enacted. There is no need to include the kind of knowledge in the ILO as that is defined by the verb(s) you use.

To recap an example of a course ILO from our course *The Nature of Teaching and Learning*:

Students should be able to:
Reflect (*level of understanding and performance*) on your teaching (*context*) in terms of a working theory you have gained from the course (*content*).

Now write your course ILOs.

Students should be able to:

ILO1: _____

ILO2: _____

ILO3: _____

ILO4: _____

ILO5:_____

ILO6:_____

Review the ILOs to see whether:

a the kind of knowledge, content and level of understanding or performance are relevant to achieve the course aim.
b they cover all the main reasons for teaching the course.
c they are clearly written, especially in identifying the level of understanding or performance to be achieved by the students, and the context (if appropriate).
d the number is manageable for designing aligned teaching/learning activities and assessment tasks.

How does this new set of course ILOs compare to your existing course 'objectives'? Does the existing set need to be rewritten?

Aligning ILOs at three levels: curriculum mapping

Now that we have written the course ILOs, we have the task of checking to see that the three levels of intended outcomes, graduate, programme and course, are aligned. We can achieve this by curriculum mapping (Huet et al. 2009), which is a systematic means of ensuring alignment between programme ILOs and graduate outcomes, and course ILOs and programme ILOs.

Graduate outcomes and programme ILOs

Table 7.4 shows a simply way of checking the alignment between graduate outcomes and programme ILOs.

The table is a device to ensure that the match between programme ILOs and graduate outcomes has at least been considered. Programme ILOs should not be forced to match graduate outcomes that don't belong in the programme. Because of the different natures of different disciplines or professions, different programmes may have different emphases in addressing the graduate outcomes. It is not necessary that every programme should address all graduate outcomes to the same extent because some may not be relevant to the programme. Programme ILOs are simply the reasons that the programme is being taught, which is a matter of professional and academic judgment. However, university policy will prevail on this.

Task 7.2 parallels Table 7.4: it asks you to align programme ILOs with the graduate outcomes of your university, if it has any. If the programme ILOs haven't yet been articulated, discuss them with the programme coordinator and derive a set, then match them with the graduate outcomes. This should give you a clearer idea of how graduate outcomes can suitably be addressed in your teaching. How does your attempt gel with your university's policy on this?

Gelade and Fursenko (2007) also describe a tool for systematically mapping courses and programmes for graduate outcomes.

Table 7.4 An example of aligning programme ILOs with graduate outcomes

Graduate outcomes	Programme ILO
Competent in professional practice	Analyse and apply principles to real-life accounting situations
Communicate effectively	Communicate as a professional with clients and colleagues in real-life accounting situations
Teamwork	Operate effectively and ethically as a team member in real-life accounting situations
Ethical professional	As above

Task 7.2 Aligning programme ILOs with graduate outcomes

1 Take a programme in which you are teaching and *either* list the programme ILOs if they are already articulated *or*, if they are not, sit down with the programme coordinator or programme committee chairperson and first write the aims of the programme and a list of programme ILOs that meet those aims.

2 What are the graduate outcomes of your university? List them in the left-hand column in the grid below.

3 In the right-hand column list the programme ILOs that would address the graduate outcomes.

Are all graduate outcomes addressed somewhere? Which are not? Does it matter?'

Graduate outcomes	Programme ILO
1	
2	
etc.	

Programme ILOs and course ILOs

The next level of alignment is between the programme and the course ILOs. As each programme is served by its constituent courses, it is important that, when aligning course ILOs to the programme ILOs, the course ILOs in total address all aspects of the programme ILOs. Often a programme ILO will be addressed by several courses, from different and increasingly more complex angles. You may attempt this in Task 7.3.

Task 7.3 Aligning course ILOs with programme ILOs

For individual teachers

1 List the programme ILOs of the programme.

2 List the course ILOs of the courses that you are teaching in a given programme.

3 Consider what programme ILO(s) each of the course ILOs addresses in the following table.

Programme ILOs	Course 1 ILOs	Course 2 ILOs	Course 3 ILOs
1			
2			
3			
4			

Do your course ILOs address all the programme ILOs?

For the programme coordinator

After all the courses of the programme have been considered, the programme coordinator needs to consider the following:

1 Are all the programme ILOs being addressed by all the courses as a whole?

2 Is the alignment between the programme ILOs and the course ILOs balanced? In other words, are any of the programme ILOs being overemphasized or vice versa?

3 Are there any gaps in the programme ILOs that are not being addressed?

The great advantage of this level of alignment is that it guards against complaints:

- from students that through sloppy programme design the same issue is addressed at the same level in different courses;
- from employers or professional bodies that some important issues aren't addressed at all by any course.

Course ILOs, teaching/learning activities and assessment tasks

The final alignments are between the course ILOs and (a) the teaching/learning activities (TLAs); and (b) the assessment tasks (ATs). These are the critically important tasks for the design of a constructively aligned curriculum. They are dealt with in the rest of Part 2.

Summary and conclusions

Intended learning outcomes at different levels

Intended learning outcomes exist at three levels: as graduate outcomes, as programme outcomes and as course outcomes. Graduate outcomes are conceived mainly in two ways: as generic skills or abilities that are to be displayed in all circumstances or as attributes embedded in the content area of a discipline. Reconciling these interpretations and dealing with them in an accountable way is a complex issue. Programme ILOs need to address the graduate outcomes in an accountable way and to reconcile this with the reasons that the degree is being offered in a substantive sense. They are expressed as the central outcomes intended for the programme and that are to be met by the particular courses in a balanced way. Course ILOs determine the teaching and assessment that takes place in the classroom and consequently need to be designed and written with a view to the kind of knowledge, the content and the level of understanding intended.

Designing and writing course ILOs

Before designing particular ILOs it is necessary to:

1 decide what kind of knowledge is to be involved;
2 select the topics to teach, but beware: 'The greatest enemy of understanding is coverage';
3 decide the purpose for teaching the topic, and hence the level of understanding or performance desirable for students to achieve. We need to prioritize, by requiring that important topics are understood at a higher level than less important topics.

Prioritizing ILOs is done in terms of the verbs related to each level of understanding: important topics are assigned a higher level of understanding than less important ones. The SOLO taxonomy is useful for providing a 'staircase of verbs' that can be used selectively to define the ranges of understanding needed. Using verbs to structure the ILOs emphasizes that learning and understanding come from student activity and they are used to align ILOs, teaching/learning activities and assessment tasks.

Aligning ILOs at three levels

Once ILOs have been finalized, they need aligning: programme ILOs with graduate outcomes, course ILOs with programme ILOs, and teaching/learning activities and assessment tasks with course ILOs. These last alignments with course ILOs are dealt with in following chapters.

Further reading

Toohey, S. (2002) *Designing Courses for Universities.* Buckingham: Open University Press.

Toohey focuses more on programme (which she calls 'course') design than on course ('unit') design, which usefully complements the present chapter, whereas we concentrate more here on writing ILOs for courses.

Graduate outcomes

Higher Education Research and Development, 23, 3: August 2004. This whole issue is devoted to graduate outcomes, or, as they were then called, graduate attributes.

The Graduate Attributes Project, Institute for Teaching and Learning, University of Sydney: http://www.nettl.usyd.edu.au/GraduateAttributes/ (accessed 2 February 2011), and how each faculty has developed its own statement of graduate attributes based on the university's framework: http://www.nettl.usyd.edu.au/GraduateAttributes/interpretations.cfm (accessed 2 February 2011).

How the Faculty of Commerce and Economics contextualizes the UNSW graduate attributes: http://wwwdocs.fce.unsw.edu.au/fce/EDU/part3.pdf (accessed 2 February 2011).

Writing programme ILOs

http://www.tuning.unideusto.org/tuningeu/index.php?option=com_frontpage&Itemid=1
http://www.altc.edu.au/standards/FAQs (accessed 2 February 2011).

The Tuning Project addresses generic and subject competences that European degree programmes are meant to address. The Australian Learning and Teaching

Council aims to define minimum or threshold learning outcomes that would make Australian degree programmes internationally comparable, and will be overseen by the Tertiary Education Quality and Standards Agency (TEQSA) from 2011.

Writing course ILOs

The following guides to writing ILOs elaborate the above:

Higher Education Academy: http://www.heacademy.ac.uk/ (accessed 2 February 2011).

Oxford Brookes University: http://www.brookes.ac.uk/services/ocsd/2_learntch/ writing_learning_outcomes.html (accessed 2 February 2011).

University of Glasgow: http://www.gla.ac.uk/services/senateoffice/qae/progdesign approval/progdesign/ilosguidelines/ (accessed 2 February 2011).

One great thing about the HE Academy is that it has subject centres (see top of its home page) where information about writing ILOs, teaching in various contexts (group, large class, and so on) and assessment and grading are presented as appropriate for a large number of subject areas. Throughout Part 2 of this book, readers are advised to go there for more about applications in their own content area.

8

Teaching/learning activities for declarative intended learning outcomes

We discuss aligning teaching/learning activities (TLAs) to ILOs relating to declarative knowledge in this chapter, and to ILOs relating to functioning knowledge in the following one. Teaching declarative knowledge by lecture, followed by tutorial, has become so established that 'lecturing' has become the generic term for university teaching, to be carried out in 'lecture theatres', particularly for dealing with large classes. We suggest that the term 'lecture' describes a situation, not a teaching/learning activity, and that within the situation of the large class there are far more effective ways of achieving course ILOs than talking at students. In this chapter, we show how interactive teaching, which is a highly effective mode of teaching, can be used in even large classes. We also deal with interactive learning, and teacher questioning, in smaller classes.

What teachers do, what students do, with declarative knowledge

Let us say teaching takes place in a typical lecture situation, where the intended outcome contains that very common declarative verb 'explain'. What are teacher and student most likely to be doing (see Table 8.1)?

The teacher talks to the usual structure of the lecture: introduces the topic, explains, elaborates, takes questions and winds up. The students are engaged in receiving the content, listening, taking notes, perhaps asking a question – but they are probably not engaged in 'explaining', although this is what the students are intended to be able to do. Here, the teacher is doing all the explaining. The students are usually only required to explain the theory or topic in question when it comes to exam time – but by then it's too late. The students haven't been given systematic opportunities to learn how to explain but they are assessed on their ability to explain. There's a distinct lack of alignment between the ILO and the students' learning-related activities.

Table 8.1 What teachers and students do in a lecture leading to an ILO containing 'explain'

Teacher activity	Student activity
Introduce	Listen
Explain	Take notes
Elaborate	Understand (but correctly? deeply enough?)
Show some PPT slides	Watch, note points
Questions on slides	Write answers to questions
Wind up	Possibly ask a question

What does it mean to 'explain', as opposed to, say, 'describe'? In order to 'explain' something, the student must be able to tell how the components of the topic/theory are related to each other. To 'describe', on the other hand, requires only that the components of the topic be outlined, not necessarily how they interconnect. The first is a relational level of understanding, the second multistructural. In the typical lecture situation, the teacher's task is therefore to present both the information itself and how it is structured; the student's is to receive the information and to make the logical interconnections that structure the information. In our example, neither teacher nor Robert monitors that double task. Susan would structure her understanding enough for her to be able to explain the topic but only because that's what she usually does by reflectively explaining to herself while reviewing and revising. Susan's learning-related activities are aligned to the ILO, if only by default, whereas Robert's are not. In constructively aligned teaching, the teacher might use teaching/learning activities such as peer teaching or buzz groups within the class to ensure that everyone does some explaining; the TLAs are then aligned to the ILO containing that verb 'explain'.

We should now consider teaching/learning activities that relate to constructing a base of declarative knowledge.

Constructing a declarative knowledge base

Building a well-structured knowledge base involves what Ausubel (1968) calls 'reception learning', that is, the reception of declarative knowledge and structuring it meaningfully. As we have seen in the 'explain' example, lecturing by the teacher leaves that structuring activity up to the student – Susan does it well, Robert usually does it poorly if at all. It is important to use TLAs that help all students, particularly the Roberts.

Teaching/learning activities for reception learning can be managed by the teacher, by groups of students or by the individual student:

- *teacher managed with little student participation*: lecturing, tutorials;
- *teacher managed with some student participation*: setting assigned readings or textbooks, laboratories, concept mapping, minute papers, teaching study skills in context (these are explained below);
- *teacher managed with active student participation*: peer teaching, peer-assisted study sessions (PASS), interactive work in class, bulletin boards, various group work;
- *student managed*: collaborative learning groups, chat rooms;
- *individually managed*: reading, searching the web, soliciting advice, listening to a lecture, and strategic management of these activities using metacognitive and study skills.

Many of the teacher managed activities are not teaching/learning *activities* so much as teaching/learning *situations*, in which the appropriate student learning-related activities may or may not occur. The situation – be it lecture, tutorial, laboratory or excursion – simply defines the broad parameters within which learning takes place. Specific learning activities targeting the ILO need to be deployed within the situation. It would be a poor physiotherapist who told a patient with a problematic knee joint: 'Go to the gym and do some work with weights.' The proper response would be to find out what the problem was: that, say, one of the muscles supporting the kneecap was weak so the kneecap 'wandered'. Working the whole of the knee in the gym would exacerbate the problem because the other muscles would do the work for the weak one, thus worsening the imbalance. The weak muscle needs to be singled out and exercised.

Just so, hitting all the ILOs with one method, lecturing, is likely to call out the learning activity of memorizing to do the work meant for genuine understanding – especially is this so if the assessment is by examination. In short, the learning activity most appropriate to each ILO needs to be singled out and 'exercised'. Dumping the student in a teaching/learning situation with non-aligned student learning activities will in many cases result in over-exercising inappropriate learning 'muscles'.

Let us illustrate with that very common situation, the large class lecture followed by a tutorial, as a means of constructing a base of well-structured declarative knowledge.

Teaching to declarative intended learning outcomes

The lecture

A lecture is where the subject matter expert tells the students about the major topics that make up the discipline or professional area, and what the latest thinking is on a topic or discipline. The flow of information is one way, the students' contributions usually being limited to questions and requests for clarification. Elaborating the material, removing misconceptions, applying to specific examples, comparing different interpretations, are left to the complement of the lecture, the tutorial. This seems like a good combination for effective reception learning: the lecture is like the Tasmanian tiger making the kill, the tutorial like the Tasmanian devil doing the mopping up. The simile is even more apt: the tiger is already extinct, and the devil is heading that way.

Probably because it conveniently accommodates large fluctuations in student numbers, the lecture has become the method for all seasons. It is assumed that if you know your subject, and do not have any speech defects, you can deliver a passable lecture. But take the case of Dr Fox, who did a circuit of several US university medical faculties. He was hugely successful; the student ratings were highly positive and he was praised as an inspirational teacher in total command of his subject matter. It turns out that Dr Fox was a professional actor, whose only knowledge of the field was supplied by a *Reader's Digest* article (Ware and Williams 1975). Dr Fox's escapade has been used to support several conflicting positions:

- Good teaching isn't a matter of how much you know but of how well you put it across. (Wrong on both counts. 'Putting it across' is not what good teaching is.)
- It just goes to show how unreliable student ratings are: they only want to be entertained. (It doesn't show this: these students were rating a one-off presentation, not a complete semester of teaching.)
- Lecturers should be trained in thespian skills or at least in public speaking, as in Box 8.3 (pp. 153–4). (Helpful, no doubt, but could the majority of academics, however well trained, perform centre stage, day after day, inspiring students every time?)
- We should subcontract large class lecturing to professional actors. (Why not, if an academic writes the script?)
- Lectures may motivate and inspire students – if they have the appropriate thespian skills. (Partly correct.)
- There must be better ways of teaching large classes than lecturing. (Correct.)

Years ago Donald Bligh (1972) reviewed nearly 100 studies comparing lecturing with other methods, mostly group discussions or reading. He found the following:

1 Lectures are relatively effective for *presenting information*, but unsupervised reading is more effective. Accessing information using search engines is now much easier still.
2 Lectures are quite ineffective for stimulating *higher order thinking*.
3 Lectures cannot be relied on to inspire or to change students' attitudes favourably, although many lecturers believe their own lectures do.
4 Students like *really good* lectures; otherwise they prefer well-conducted group work.

Psychological constraints on learning

Why are lectures so ineffective? Here are some pointers from the nature of human learning:

1 Sustained and unchanging low level activity lowers concentration. Sitting listening to a lecture is such an activity yet it requires concentrated effort to follow lecture content.
2 The attention of students is typically maintained for about 10 to 15 minutes, after which learning drops off rapidly (see Figure 8.1).
3 A short rest, or a change in activity, every 15 minutes or so restores performance almost to the original level (see Figure 8.1).
4 A period of consolidation after prolonged learning greatly enhances retention. Getting students to review at the end of the lecture what has been learned leads to much better and lasting retention than simply finishing and dismissing the students (see Figure 8.2).

Figure 8.1 Effect of rest or change of activity on learning

Source: Bligh (1972)

Figure 8.2 Effect of consolidation at end of lecture on retention

Source: Bligh (1972)

The time periods in Figure 8.1 depend on the students, the skill of the lecturer, the pace of the lecture, the difficulty of the material, the use of educational technology involving a change of activity, the time of day and so on. But the basic point remains: do not talk for longer than 15 or 20 minutes without a pause unless you are *certain* you still have their attention. When you pause, get the students to change their activity.

The effect of consolidation in Figure 8.2 may be achieved by asking students to *actively review* what they had just learned. That does not mean that you tell them what you've just told them, as in the conventional summary: that's you being active. The students are the ones who should do the reviewing: get them to tell you or a neighbour their take on what you have just told them. The problem is that both teacher and students see the lecture as a matter of teacher performance, not of learner performance. It is a perception that has to be reversed. Today, there's a further argument against the lecture: students are so mixed and selective, and so media wise, they far prefer to obtain information at their own pace from the web, rather than at the pace dictated by someone talking at them (Laurillard 2002).

Given all this, how can we justify relying so heavily on the lecture? Can the lecture do *anything* that books and the web cannot? It can.

Many university teachers, through their research and scholarship, have developed a perspective on their field of expertise that is not to be found in textbooks. Through publication lag, textbooks are easily two or more years out of date while active researchers are not. In any event, textbooks do not usually have an 'angle', a perspective, but are typically a multistructural list of things that every first-year student might ever need to know. Who better to provide a critical perspective on that bland smorgasbord of knowledge than the teacher at the cutting edge of the topic and in person? The best defence of the lecture, particularly in senior undergraduate years, thus lies not in doing what other media do as well – and usually better – but in exposing students to the most recent developments in the field, and to the ongoing workings of a scholarly mind.

The teacher should be an agent for transforming knowledge, helping students to interpret and to construct their own knowledge, not a passive substation that relays preformed messages to them. Unfortunately, as noted in Chapter 1, the credit transfer system in universities may well result in courses being designed to be equivalent to courses taught in other universities, a consequence that would severely discourage cutting-edge teaching of the kind we are talking about here. The pressure is to teach in style and content that is compatible with what is being taught in other universities, not to build on locally concentrated excellence.

And where does this discussion leave lecturers who *aren't* frontline researchers? Looking for alternatives to just lecturing, we hope. Heaven forbid that teachers have reached the demeaning point where all that remains for them to do is to tell students about content that they can read more effectively for themselves.

Since practicalities dictate that large numbers of students will be scheduled to meet one teacher in a big room, it is better to see this as a *plenary session* in which – and out of which – excellent learning can take place, using teaching/learning activities that directly address the intended learning outcomes.

So how can we transform the lecture theatre into a learning theatre?

Making the lecture theatre a learning theatre

The teaching of Eric Mazur

Eric Mazur (1998) asked himself that last question. He was lecturing in physics at Harvard and regularly received good student evaluations. Then he read an article saying that when physics students were lectured to, they relied on memory not on understanding. Not in my class they don't, Eric thought, and tested them on basic principles. The result told him that they were, indeed, relying on memory.

He decided to stop lecturing, forcing the students to rely not on memory but on understanding. He set readings that had to be read before the class. He also gave the students two or three simple questions to be answered by email the night before the class: no answers, no admission to class. His email also said: 'Please tell us what you found difficult and confusing. If you found nothing difficult or confusing, please tell us what you found most interesting.' Thus he discovered what might need clarifying in class. He emailed replies to each student, with an appropriate comment from a database of generic comments.

In class the next day, the students were presented every 10 minutes with a multiple-choice question based on the readings. Each student seat in the theatre had a personal digital assistant (PDA) so that students could record their response to each question; responses were automatically tallied for the whole class and projected on a screen. Other questions addressed a 'trick' physical phenomenon, for example: 'A flat plate of cast-iron, two feet square and one inch thick, has a large circular hole, diameter four inches, drilled in the center. The plate is then heated. Does the hole in the center (a) increase in diameter, (b) decrease, or (c) remain the same, as the plate expands with heating?' While all the relevant physical principles were known by this stage, a wide diversity of opinion as to the outcome of the heating occurred. The students were asked to find someone nearby who voted differently and then to convince their neighbour that their own response was the correct one. After discussion, another vote was taken and this time there was usually much more consensus, in the direction of the correct answer. Mazur reports that the learning was powerful and the students enjoyed it. He was consistently voted best teacher of the year.

Two features of Mazur's approach stand out: feedback and good alignment requiring student activity relevant to the course ILOs. He wanted high level understanding, he gave the students teaching/learning activities that required them to think about novel problems and apply the knowledge they had gained from reading – not from listening to his lectures – and each student received feedback individually from himself and from other students.

Course preparation assignments

David Yamane (2006), like Mazur, was also bothered by the inefficiencies of lecturing. He was bothered by the fact the material could be read before class more efficiently than listening to it in class. The problem was that students didn't read when they were told to. His subject was sociology. He posted 'course preparation assignments' (CPAs) on the course web page to be completed before each class, the time in class being spent in discussions on the assignment in groups of about four. The CPA required students to read and think about a chapter in the course textbook and to produce a written response to a question or problem based on the reading. The CPAs had the following general structure:

1 an introductory statement
2 an objective (ILO) for the assignment
3 the background information for the topic
4 the written assignment.

The first 10 minutes of class were spent in small groups, where individual members pooled their assignments and synthesized one for the group, which was then presented to the whole class. Yamane acted as coordinator and produced a large diagram on the whiteboard that drew together all the points raised and led to a conclusion about the problem. This product was frequently used as the starting point for the next CPA.

This is an example, like the concept map, where what is usually an assessment task – the assignment – becomes the teaching/learning activity. However, instead of assessing the assignment, Yamane looks at each one to check that it has been carried out honestly. If it has, he awards a pass and, if not, the student has to repeat it (all repeats pass in his experience).

This technique worked well within classes of 30 to 80, but Yamane does not recommend it in classes larger than this. He compared the CPA method with a lecture course, taught by himself and using the same material, on students' responses to a questionnaire on their level of thinking and their sense of responsibility and involvement and found strong evidence for the effectiveness of the CPA approach.

Box 8.1 gives an example of an adaptation of CPA by Catherine Chiu in her teaching of sociology at City University of Hong Kong.

How the large class lecture can become interactive

Mazur's, Yamane's and Chiu's teaching are examples of getting students relevantly active with teaching/learning activities that facilitate the intended

---

Box 8.1 Course preparation assignments in the teaching of sociology

Introduction to sociology

Course preparation assignment for Week 5

Lecture two: Culture

Read Macionis, Chapter 2, and familiarize yourself with these key concepts:

a Culture, symbols, language, values, beliefs, norms, mores, folkways, cultural integration
b Cultural changes, cultural lag
c Cultural diversity, subculture, counterculture
d Ethnocentrism, cultural relativism

Assignment 1

1 Objective (ILO): To define the key values of Hong Kong culture.
2 Background: On pp. 43–44, you read that Robin Williams identifies two key values of US culture.
3 Assignment: Identify at least five key values of Hong Kong.

Assignment 2

1 Objective (ILO): To apply two theoretical approaches to explain why certain key values exist in Hong Kong.
2 Background: On pp. 54–56, Macionis presents analysis of culture using two perspectives – structural-functional and social-conflict.
3 Assignment: Pick two of the key values of Hong Kong you have identified and explain why they exist in Hong Kong from the structural-functional point of view. Then do the same by using the social-conflict approach.

Source: Catherine Chiu, City University of Hong Kong

---

outcomes. Such teaching, along with formative feedback, has the largest effect on student learning (Hattie 2009a). We now look at a range of TLAs that are suitable in large class teaching for constructing a declarative knowledge base in different content areas.

Concept maps

Concept maps were originally designed both to present a structure and to find out how students see the structure (Novak 1979). They can be used by teachers for both teaching and assessment purposes and by students for organizing their ideas, for example for reviewing the semester's work, for planning and writing essays or for clarifying difficult passages. They are useful for ILOs that require students to see the whole, to perceive relationships, to integrate and to organize. Concept maps can be demonstrated and used by students inside or outside the classroom.

In creating concept maps, students singly or in groups are presented with a core concept or principle. Either they themselves generate sub-concepts that relate to it, or the sub-concepts are supplied. The students then arrange the sub-concepts, either drawing them or arranging cards on which they have been written, in a way that makes best sense to them. The distance between sub-concepts reflects their perceived degree of interrelation. Lines are then drawn linking sub- and central concepts, with a brief explanation of what the link or relationship is.

Creating concept maps is a learning experience for the students, helping them to explicitly structure their thinking and, at the same time, the resulting maps give an indication of how the student sees the way in which individual concepts relate to each other. They can therefore also be used for assessment purposes (pp. 243–4). As concept maps present an overall picture, a holistic representation of a complex conceptual structure, they are best evaluated by judging the complexity of the arrangement and the correctness of the interrelations, rather than by analytic 'marking' (see Chapter 10). They can be used as feedback, to see how teaching might be adjusted, as part of the final assessments of student learning or for students in their own studying.

Santhanam et al. (1998) found that first-year science and agricultural students saw the value of using concept maps but not their relevance. They thought that memorization was the best approach to study in first year and so did not use concept mapping in their own studying; a depressing finding, suggesting that the students had obtained the wrong cues from the way they had been taught and assessed (see also Ramsden et al. 1986).

Learning partners

A great help for both students and teacher, especially in large classes, is to require students to form a partnership with another student or a small group of students. Partnerships are not a TLA as such, but they provide a convenient context for a range of TLAs and for general mutual support. Students need someone to talk to: to share concerns, to seek clarification over assignment requirements, to check their own insecure interpretations of procedure or of content (Saberton 1985).

Partners could be matched by the teacher, perhaps on the basis of the way students complement each other (high performing/at risk, international/ local, mature age/straight from school, those with access to desirable resources/those with little access). Alternatively, students could each choose their own partners, which has some advantages but particularly with the presence of international students, there are excellent reasons for ethnically mixed partnerships. Partners then agree to sit next to each other in class and to consult out of class, exchanging telephone numbers, email, etc. They can also collaborate on suitable assessment tasks. Partnerships that do not work because of personal chemistry should be reformed. Some students may prefer to remain loners and that should be respected: it is their loss, which in time they may come to realize.

Learning partners permanently sitting next to each other makes life much easier for the teacher when implementing the kinds of note swapping, activities and discussions such as active review mentioned earlier. The teacher's out-of-class time in dealing with queries is actually rather more than halved, because the chances are that one partner can put the other partner straight without consulting the teacher.

Minute paper

The minute paper (Angelo and Cross 1993) is a technique whereby students write brief answers to such questions as:

At the start of the lecture: What do I most want to find out in this class?
Towards the end: What is the main point I learned today?
Also at the end: What was the main point left unanswered in today's session?

Allow a couple of minutes for students to swap and read what their neighbour said. The students' responses may be handed in, with names, and each can be read in a few seconds. The answers can be used as formative feedback both for them and for you – and as an attendance check. The cumulative record gives a very good, and quick, indication of the development of students' thinking through the course.

These ultra-short essays at the beginning of the class forces students, as did Mazur, to actually *do* the pre-reading and to reflect on it. The second question can tell you something about their learning and your teaching: if some quite minor aside by you is seen as 'the main point', either you or they have a problem. In either case, it will need to be addressed in the next class. The third question ('What was the main point . . .') also provides a good starting point and review for the next class. Students are provided with feedback on how their thinking is in line with other students' thinking and with your own. You can no doubt think of other questions that would better suit your intended outcomes. Some may find it more convenient for students to use PDAs to record and transmit their minute papers.

Note taking

Note taking is widely misused when students take notes for the purpose of obtaining a record of what the teacher says. Students, especially the Roberts, have a twofold problem: of following what they are hearing and of writing notes for later reference. They can't do both simultaneously so they alternate between listening and writing. But while they are writing the gist down, the lecturer is sentences ahead. Their notes are therefore a random sample of a fraction of what the teacher was saying. And with only a fraction of the trees, they have to reconstruct the whole wood. Difficult. If note taking is primarily intended as a record for later revision, it is both inefficient and wasteful. Why not just hand out readings?

Note taking may, however, be a useful TLA, for example for immediate review and reflection. If students are to take notes, comprehension time should be separated from recording time, and students should be allowed a time slot to check their notes. Students can swap notes with their neighbour, discuss differences and rewrite their own notes. They can thus review the main ideas about what has been said and elaborate their own understanding to their neighbour and reflect on their neighbour's interpretation if it is different from their own.

Note taking should be used as a teaching/learning activity, in other words, not as a horribly inefficient recording device. The sorts of notes students might best take depend on the content area, the use to which they are to be put and any ILOs they are to serve. For these reasons, the skills and purposes of note taking, as with other study skills, are usefully incorporated into the teaching of particular content (Chalmers and Fuller 1996): we discuss this further later (p. 176).

Think-aloud modelling

When presenting new tasks or problems, it can be very helpful for the teacher to think out loud while handling it, so that the students are clearer about what they are supposed to be doing. The teacher is doing the self-analysis and reflection publicly, letting the students know how an expert does it, so that eventually they do it their way themselves. Many teachers think aloud for their students automatically, but many others do not. Modelling is handy whenever you get the inevitable: 'But what are we supposed to do?' But then, for it to be an active TLA, they must then be required to do it, not just watch a demonstration.

A computer and imager enables you to face and interact with the class while thinking out loud, showing your notes and revisions and mistakes. For example, you could show how you write an article at the various stages of planning, composing and revising, to demonstrate the various techniques that academic writers use. Students are brought face to face with processes and possibilities that they themselves would not think of and, if the class is not too large, the students can call out contributions to the ongoing composing or problem-solving process. In large classes, you could nominate a particular row or rows of students to call out their suggestions.

Work-along exercises

Olivia Leung, of the Department of Accountancy at City University of Hong Kong, links student activity to her lecturing by devising work-along exercises that accompany her discussion of each topic. These exercises help students follow the lecture closely and actively visualize the application of concepts. Box 8.2 shows some examples of work-along exercises used in an accounting class of over 200 students.

Box 8.2 Some examples of work-along exercises for a class in accounting of over 200 students

Review question: Debit and credit effects on assets and liabilities

What accounts below are decreased by debits?

- Inventory
- Accounts payable
- Dividends
- Cash
- Notes payable
- Accounts receivable

Answer: _____

Why? _____

Review question: Adjusting entry supplies

The trial balance shows supplies of $2000 and supplies expense of $0. If $750 of supplies are on hand at the end of the period, what is the adjusting entry?

Account	Debit	Credit
	$1250	
		$1250

The balance in supplies after adjustment is $750, the amount remaining unused. The amount used is transferred to expense.

Review question: Closing entries

Which of the following accounts will have a zero balance after the closing process?

- Unearned revenue
- Advertising supplies
- Prepaid insurance
- Rent expense
- Income summary

Answer: _____
are temporary accounts. All temporary accounts are closed and thus have a zero balance after the closing process.

Source: Olivia Leung of City University of Hong Kong

Changing activities

As for other large class activities, remember that concentration flags after 15 minutes or so, particularly if the ongoing activity is straight listening. You might set a timer to ring every 15 minutes; when it rings, stop talking and change the activity or consolidate (Gibbs et al. 1992). Here are some suggestions for student activities:

- Students reflect on what they think they have just learned, then in pairs tell each other what they saw as the most important point in the preceding 15 minutes of lecturing. Here's a TLA that gets *them* to 'explain'.
- Each student writes down a question or a comment sparked by the previous 15 minutes for their neighbour to respond to. They can hand in their question/comments sheet at the end of the session; it will also be useful feedback to you – and an attendance check.
- You pose questions for them to answer, either individually or discuss with a neighbour.
- You set a problem based on the content discussed for them to work on, either individually or in discussion with a neighbour.
- Towards the end of the lecture, allow five minutes for each student to tell their neighbour or learning partner (see pp. 142–3) what they think was the thrust of the session. This achieves the consolidation by active review and also gives them a different perspective to think about, other than their own interpretation of your perspective. Further, they are giving and receiving feedback, and enacting that ubiquitous ILO 'explain'.

Linking diagrams and key points can be achieved by handouts using PowerPoint software, three or so slides per page, with space beside each where the students can write their notes and comments. This gives students accurate basic notes and diagrams, but requires them to actively search for the main idea, and put it in their own words with an example or two.

The various techniques just mentioned meet many of the objections raised about the lecture yet they can take place in the lecture situation and focus on what the *students* are doing, rather than on what the teacher is doing. Students are not confronted with loads of information at too great a rate for many of them to handle, but are required to work with that information, to elaborate, correct and consolidate it.

Peer teaching

What do you perceive when you enter the door of a large crowded lecture theatre: 400 students sitting there waiting to be taught by you or 400 teaching assistants waiting to be brought in on the action? Peer teaching is a very powerful ally when you have large classes to teach. There may be no single best method of teaching, 'but the second best is students teaching other students' (McKeachie et al. 1986: 63).

Both tutor and tutee benefit academically under peer teaching, the tutor more than the tutee, while the tutor is also likely to have increased social skills and attitudes to study and self (Goodlad and Hirst 1990; Topping 1996). The reasons for these benefits are clear:

- The content to be taught has to be viewed from the perspective of someone whose conceptions of the topic to be taught are different from and almost certainly less well developed than one's own. Changing one's perspective is enriching.
- The teacher reflects on how the students learned the topic, which means that peers, being closer to that process and more aware of the traps and difficulties than the expert, can teach more empathically.
- The teacher 'owns' the material, publicly taking responsibility for its validity. There is heavy loss of face if they get it wrong – so they are more careful about getting it right.

Two New Zealand tertiary institutions give course credit for peer tutoring, the practical work being carried out tutoring secondary school students (Jones et al. 1994). No, not education students, destined for a teaching career, but law, science, and business students. The assumption is simply that teaching the subject deepens students' understanding of it. Compared to teacher-led groups, student-led groups range wider in their discussion and produce more complex outcomes (McKeachie et al. 1986; Tang 1998). In cross-year tutoring, the tutor is in a higher year than the tutee. Both tutors and tutees like the process, and the achievement of the tutees is little different from conventionally taught (Topping 1996): a positive and cost-effective finding, when you think about it.

In developing academic mentoring and peer-tutoring programmes, Brown et al. (2008) suggest that we need to identify the specific outcomes intended for the mentoring programme, understand the context within which the programme is embedded, decide on the mentoring model to be used, whether it is a one-on-one or small group peer-tutoring, and clearly define the roles of the participants. Support to prepare students as peer tutors is necessary to enable them to acquire the desired benefit from participating in the peer-tutoring scheme (Nestel and Kidd 2005). In participating in a peer-tutoring scheme, both the tutors and tutees benefit in improved understanding and performance in the subject area involved, improved confidence and study skills, as well as ongoing friendships (Beasley 1997). Beasley also reports improved course grades and positive evaluations of both tutors and tutees.

For peer tutors to benefit through peer tutoring to enhance their self-monitoring of comprehension, integration of new and prior knowledge, and elaboration and construction of knowledge, support and training need to be provided so that they adopt a *reflective knowledge-building* mode through explaining and questioning rather than simply *knowledge-telling* focusing more on delivering knowledge than on developing it (Rosecoe and Chi 2007).

The peer assistance supplementary scheme or peer-assisted study sessions (PASS in either case) is a common scheme for cross-year tutoring, designed to alleviate the problem of large first-year classes. The tutors are second-year or third-year students who passed the first-year subject exceptionally well and are judged to have the appropriate personal qualities for tutoring. They are trained to 'model, advise and facilitate' rather than to address the curriculum directly and are either paid or given course credit. Data involving 295 courses in the USA show improved achievement and higher re-enrolment and graduation rates (National Center for Supplemental Instruction 1994). Outcomes in the UK are likewise encouraging (Topping 1996).

At the University of Queensland, in samples comprising thousands of students, regular attendees of PASS averaged a whole grade higher than students who did not attend, while of the students gaining high distinctions, 85% attended PASS, 14% did not (Chalmers and Kelly 1997). PASS employs two tutors or student leaders per group of 25 first years and they are paid also to attend at least one lecture that the tutees receive (Watson 1996, 1997; Chalmers and Kelly 1997). Leaders receive one full day of training and ongoing weekly meetings with the staff coordinator. Leaders are required to keep a reflective diary, with which they provide feedback to the departmental staff coordinator. This ongoing information was found to be far more useful to lecturers in meeting problems than end-of-semester course evaluations. Attendance from the first-year classes is voluntary, ranging from 20% of the class to over 80%. The agenda is up to the students, but it frequently involves a review of what has gone on in class that week. No new material is presented.

Following are some of the benefits that students see (Chalmers and Kelly 1997):

- a friendly environment in which they can comfortably ask 'the dumbest questions';
- weekly study that keeps them up to date;
- insight into the range of material other students are covering and the difficulties they have;
- a mentor who can give information and who has inside knowledge of how they coped;
- international students particularly like the opportunity to discuss without staff present.

PASS is considered particularly useful in:

- large classes, particularly when unsupported by other group work;
- subjects with a high technical content;
- classes with a failure rate of more than 10%;
- classes with high international student enrolments;
- a service role as a core subject for a number of degree courses.

To sum up, then, that lecture theatre can indeed become a learning theatre if two major principles are adopted:

1 keep the students active with relevant teaching/learning activities;
2 supply them regularly with feedback from yourself, from other students, and from reflective self-assessment.

Where does this leave the tutorial?

Active learning of this kind meets many if not all of the outcomes the tutorial is intended to achieve – elaboration and clarification of what the students had understood from the preceding lecture. And given that 'tutorials' of 30 and 40 students, as sometimes occurs, can't possibly do what they are supposed to do, and that tutors are frequently the least experienced staff members, one begins to question why we should have tutorials at all. Essentially, the tutorial is a relic of an older academic ecosystem, when the Susans outnumbered the Roberts.

If we replace the lecture with more flexible teaching/learning activities involving interactive learning, as suggested earlier, the conventional tutorial, like the poor Tasmanian devil, may follow the Tasmanian tiger into extinction unless its function and its structure are rethought. In the School of Experimental Psychology at the University of Sussex, for example, tutorials are mainly student-led tutorials. Students give a brief 15-minute presentation that has been assessed by the teacher beforehand; each tutorial has assigned questions for discussion and each student must put to the group at least one point in the lectures they didn't understand. Beyond that, the students run the main proceedings themselves, except that the teacher turns up for the last 10 minutes, which has a good effect on morale and allows unresolved issues to be put to the teacher (Dienes 1997).

Interactivity in smaller classes

In classes under 30, sometimes the formal lecture becomes the formal lecture with a looser, more conversational script. Some inspirational lecturers like students to interrupt with comments or ask unplanned questions. They can think up answers on their feet: the lightning riposte, *that's* the stuff of good teaching! Maybe, but the attention in this case is on the teacher, not on what the students are supposed to be doing. The students may just become the means for showing how brilliant the teacher is.

Good interactive teaching nevertheless requires on-the-spot improvisation in response to events as they occur. Questions and comments from students can be the basis for rethinking and reconstructing new and exciting ideas, if the ball is picked up and taken in an appropriate direction. Papers have originated that way. The experience gives the phrase 'the social construction of knowledge' real meaning.

Dealing with questions from students

In more intimate surroundings than the large lecture theatre, questioning by students presents a different challenge. Dealing effectively with questions requires a knowledge of topic structure that is sufficiently rich and flexible that you can recognize the students' perspective of it and their access to it. It's a matter not only of having expert knowledge of your subject – that goes without saying – but also of understanding where they are coming from in asking it in the way they did, and how the understanding they displayed in asking the question can be orchestrated in harmony with your own expert knowledge. Student questions may well open the gateway for you to start negotiating their way to understanding threshold concepts (pp. 83–4).

Questions put to students

Convergent questions

Convergent questions are asked with a correct answer in mind and students are steered towards that answer. Such questions are not necessarily low level. Socratic questioning is a case in point. The teacher goes round the class asking questions that lead subtly to the answer the teacher requires. This is the social construction of knowledge, where all contribute and agree on the structure as it emerges.

Divergent questions

Divergent questions, unlike convergent questions, are open-ended. They are useful for probing student experiences and using such experiences for constructing fresh ideas and interpretations, for incorporating them as examples of the case in point and for student reflection. In professional programmes, where the students have hands-on experience, there is a wealth of functioning knowledge to be tapped, to be located in a conceptual structure and generalized. Divergent questions can also lead to aimless rambling and that needs controlling. Good questioning skills are required.

High- or low-level questions

High-level questions probe the high-level verbs: theorizing, reflecting, hypothesizing; low-level questions enact the low-level verbs: recalling factual answers. High-level questions need *wait time*. High-level thinking takes more time than low-level thinking. Whether out of fear of silence, impatience or bad judgement, the fact is that in most classrooms nowhere near enough wait time is allowed. When allowed unlimited time to answer, tertiary students averaged nine seconds to answer a convergent question, over 30 seconds to answer a divergent question (Ellsworth et al. 1991). The longer students took, the better the quality of the response. If you might feel embarrassed by 30 seconds of silence, work out ways of not being embarrassed.

The fact that high-level responding needs time is a major advantage of the asynchronous use of educational technology, that is, when students respond to online questions and issues in their own time (see Chapter 4).

Now for a reflective task about who is doing what in your classes (Task 8.1). How would you redesign your next large class 'lecture' (Task 8.2)?

Task 8.1 What happened in your large class session?

Reflect on a session you gave to a large class in the last semester. What are the learning outcomes that you intended the students to achieve in the session?

_____

_____

_____

_____

Write down what activities occurred during that session and who was (were) engaged in those activities ('the doers')?

Activities	*The 'doers'*			
	Teacher	*Students as a class*	*Students as peers*	*Students individually*

Now compare the activities and who the 'doers' of those activities are, with the intended outcomes of the session. Who was (were) doing the activities that led to achieving the intended outcomes?

Your reflection:

_____

_____

Task 8.2 Redesigning your next large class session

Take your next large class session, in which you would normally regale your students with a long and carefully prepared lecture. Now have a go at restructuring the session. Assume the time for the session is one hour. If more than this, make allowance in your plan.

First write down the intended learning outcomes that you would like the students to achieve in the session:

_____

_____

_____

_____

Write down the activities and the 'doers' of those activities.

1 At the beginning of the session

Activities	The 'doers'			
	Teacher	Students as a class	Students as peers	Students individually

2 During the main part of the session

Activities	The 'doers'			
	Teacher	Students as a class	Students as peers	Students individually

3 Before the end of the session

Activities	The 'doers'			
	Teacher	Students as a class	Students as peers	Students individually

What changes have you made for this session compared to the 'lecture' that you did for Task 8.1? Why would you make those changes?

Your reflection:

_____

_____

Managing large class teaching

Large classes require effective and quite specific management skills. It is quite shameful that the least experienced and junior staff members are often allocated to the largest classes to spare the more experienced teachers from this unpopular teaching situation.

Large classes need *meticulous preparation*. The larger the class, the slower things get done. A spur-of-the-moment change of direction, perhaps in response to a student question, highly desirable and manageable with a group of 30, becomes perilous with 300. Most teachers find large class teaching a 'performance', with the increased likelihood of stage fright (see Box 8.3).

Box 8.3 Dons struggle with stage fright

It happens to the best of them. As lecture time approaches, on come the cold sweats and the nerves as confidence departs.

An underperforming student, scared of being found out? No. An experienced lecturer, who has been in the limelight for years, with stage fright? Yes.

One who knows plenty about it – and who wants to know more – is University of Canberra marketing communication lecturer Amanda Burrell.

Ms Burrell has a degree in creative arts (acting) from the University of Wollongong and was a professional performer for a decade before turning to lecturing about 10 years ago.

Returning to the lectern this year for the first time in 15 months after having a baby, Ms Burrell found herself in dread of fronting a class. . . . A straw poll of colleagues revealed that many felt the same way. 'People told me stories about losing confidence, how they lost their voice in a presentation, how they fainted or got so muddled they couldn't read their notes,' Ms Burrell said. 'I thought: "There's something worth looking at here".'

Ms Burrell believes stage fright among lecturers is a widespread but little talked about problem. She has set herself the task, as a research project, to find out how many suffer and how they cope. She even rigged up a colleague with a heart-rate monitor to check stress levels. The woman, whose resting heart rate was 80 beats per minute, was described by a third-party observer to be 'as cool as a cucumber' during a presentation. But her heart rate had peaked at 175 bpm.

Ms Burrell said she wanted universities to include public speaking as part of their training for new lecturers. Ms Burrell has plans to visit acting schools. 'I'd like to see how the training of professional actors can inform our practice,' she said.

Source: Brendan O'Keefe, *The Australian Higher Education,*
19 April 2006

As few teachers have any training in public speaking, providing such training would no doubt be helpful. However, even with training, the majority of academics would be pushed to be able to perform centre stage, day after day, inspiring students every time: even Dr Fox (p. 136) would have trouble doing that.

This slow-heaving hulk needs to be carefully directed otherwise it will crush your plans. Establish your procedural rules at the outset: signals for silence, procedures for questioning (how are you going to deal with the forest of hands or with the clown who always asks questions to class groans?), signals for starting and stopping, if you are going to use buzz groups who is to discuss with whom, who is to be spokesperson on report back, and how to bring them back to order when it's time. Establish these rules in the first session.

The size and buzz of a large class require a smooth start:

- Don't just sail straight in. Signal that class has started and wait for quiet. Try playing music while students enter, then when you are ready to start, stop the music. It creates a nice air of expectancy.
- Start with a proper introduction: 'Following from last week when we . . . What we are going to do today.' Why lecture when the topic is in the textbook? Because you are going to do something the textbook can't? What is that? Tell them. Then they'll know what they should be getting from this particular lecture (Gibbs et al. 1984).
- If lecture you must, preview with a slide giving the subheadings of the lecture, and some explanation of the sequences of subheadings, or a diagram if that is appropriate.

Following are a few points to watch while talking to a large class:

- Eye contact students while talking; no head buried in notes.
- Ensure clarity: project the voice, check it can be heard at the back. Cordless radio mikes are best.
- Focus on the 'U' rather than the 'T'. Susan and her friends tend to sit along the front row and up the middle (the T), Robert and his friends at the back and down the sides (the U). Focus on grabbing Robert and you will automatically include Susan.
- Handouts should be distributed on entry or exit. If possible, organize the schedule at least a week ahead so that the end of the previous session can be used for handouts for the next. Distributing handouts during class is messy and time wasting.

- Consider putting any lectures on your institution's e-platform and then ask yourself this question: why give that lecture at all if they all have access to it anyway? Can't you use that time more effectively than merely repeating what they can read at their own pace? Yes, you can: we've just been through that. But if the material is essential for the next plenary session with the students, make sure you have some exercises or other way of ensuring that they will read the material purposefully.

Questions may easily provide a break that many students perceive as chat-to-neighbour time while the nerd has a heart-to-heart with the teacher. To prevent this, the whole class must be included and involved. This means *distancing* yourself, not doing the personable thing and leaning towards the questioner. Move back so that the questioner is part of the class, repeat the question so that it becomes a whole class question. In a very large class, it may be better to ask students to write down their questions and pass them up to the front, rather than shouting them at you. You could take them on the spot or answer them in the introduction to the next session. In *very* large classes – what have we come to? – you might use the large meeting technique, with microphone stands in the aisles.

Most students dislike the *impersonality* of large class teaching: it's a short step from there to a cold Theory X climate. To warm things up a bit, try the following (Davis 1993):

- Stand in front of the lectern, not behind it. Walk about, up and down the aisles if feasible. Get students to leave a few rows empty, so you can move along them. Convey accessibility, not distance, but stand still when delivering important points.
- Do not in your friendly wandering be seduced by a *sotto voce* question. Make it a question coming from the whole class (see earlier).
- At the beginning of the class get neighbouring students to introduce themselves to each other. These may or may not lead to formal learning partnerships, as described above.
- Get students to complete a short biographical questionnaire, giving names, reasons for taking the course, hobbies, etc. You can then refer to students by name occasionally, selecting examples to illustrate points to match their interests. They'll feel good about that, although not everyone may get a mention.
- Arrive early, and/or leave late, to talk with students. Make your hours of availability in your office known and keep those times sacred. Some teachers may be comfortable with inviting groups of students, in circulation to cover everyone, to coffee.
- Where tutors assess assignments and not you, make sure you read a sample and discuss points in class. Let them know you are not delegating entirely.
- Use humour and topical references but take care where there are large numbers of international students. They are likely to be confused by topical references, colloquialisms and culturally specific jokes.

Eric Mazur, he who decided lectures were a waste of time (pp. 139–40), kept the photographs of the 160 students in his physics class in his address file. When they emailed in their answers to his questions on reading, the tasks were such that errors fell into few categories, so that there were essentially only five generic emails to be sent, to groups of 30 or so students. By clicking on the student's address, up would come their face reminding him who he was talking to. He then tuned the opening and the close to the individual: 'Hi there Jenny. You slipped up a bit here, after last week's great effort. Here seems to be the problem . . . (then he pasted the appropriate generic email). Let me know if it's not clear now. Best.'

Large class teaching is difficult, but it doesn't have to follow the pattern of the standard lecture. If you are not convinced already, read *Twenty Terrible Reasons for Lecturing* (Gibbs 1981). Certainly, large class sizes provide no reason to abandon the principle of alignment, either in designing teaching/ learning activities to suit your intended learning outcomes or, as we shall see in Chapter 11, in selecting the assessment tasks needed.

Before leaving this chapter, you can now try to design TLAs for some of your course ILOs relating to declarative knowledge. Task 8.3 gives a framework that would help you.

Task 8.3 Teaching/learning activities for declarative ILOs

Select two of your course ILOs relating to declarative knowledge. Design TLAs that would facilitate achievement of these ILOs.

Course ILO1: _____

Course ILO2: _____

Number of students in the course: _____

Course ILO	Teaching situation	Teaching activities (what the teacher does)	Learning activities (what the students do)

Now double-check if the student learning activities are aligned to the verbs nominated in the respective course ILOs. What is your observation?

_____

_____

> Compared with the teaching situations that you have been using so far for the same course ILOs:
>
> **a** What changes have you made?
> **b** What do you expect to achieve through these changes?

Summary and conclusions

What teachers do, what students do, with declarative knowledge

The term 'lecture' is teacher centred: it says what teachers do. The important thing is what students are doing while the teacher is lecturing. Even in a simple ILO involving the verb 'explain', students are unlikely to be doing any explaining themselves in the typical lecture situation. This needs turning around, so that the ILO prescribes what *students* should be doing in a teaching/learning situation if they are to build a solid, well-structured knowledge base that is prerequisite to achieving ILOs, especially higher order ILOs.

Teaching to declarative intended learning outcomes

Lecturing is logistically convenient, in that it enables teachers to handle large numbers of students simultaneously. However, its only educational advantage over other teaching situations is that when given by an active researcher, it exposes students to a scholar's ongoing thinking. Otherwise the learning that takes place in lecturing is demonstrably worse than in other teaching situations. Interactive teaching provides a more articulated focus on ILOs and the TLAs that foster them.

Making the lecture theatre a learning theatre

Interactive teaching and learning can be brought to the large class quite readily. The most prolific resource in large classes is the students themselves. Using them appropriately engages verbs that address a range of ILOs that teacher-directed TLAs can only address with difficulty or not at all. Creating semi-permanent learning partnerships can make life easier for both you and the students, providing a continually accessible resource for discussing, reciprocal questioning and mutual support in an otherwise anonymous environment. In resource starved times, it is amazing that peer teaching in its various forms, including the use of paid students as in PASS, is not used more widely. In smaller classes, interactivity between teacher and students is more personal and requires, in particular, effective questioning skills. When large class teaching becomes more interactive, it is effectively doing what the tutorial was supposed to do, which then raises the question of whether tutorial-type sessions should be restructured or be dropped altogether.

Managing large class teaching

Large classes raise management problems of their own. A plenary session demands management strategies quite different from those appropriate to small classes. It is important to work out in advance such things as how to commence the session, effective strategies of talking and questioning during the session, ensuring that students know what to do and who is to report back after student–student interaction sessions. A management issue of a different kind is overcoming the anonymity and alienation that many students feel and dislike in large classes.

Further reading

On lecturing in large classes

Bligh, D.A. (1972) *What's the Use of Lectures?* Harmondsworth: Penguin.
Elton, L. and Cryer, P. (1992) *Teaching Large Classes.* Sheffield: University of Sheffield Teaching Development Unit.
Gibbs, G. and Jenkins, A. (eds) (1992) *Teaching Large Classes in Higher Education.* London: Kogan Page.
O'Neill, M. (Project Director) *Teaching in Large Classes.* A very comprehensive CD-ROM, produced at the University of Western Australia, showing examples of expert teachers in action at all stages of teaching, from getting prepared for lecture to closing elegantly. Interviews with novice teachers, expert teachers and students are presented at each teaching stage.
Teaching and Educational Development Institute, University of Queensland, Project on Teaching Large Classes: http://www.tedi.uq.edu.au/largeclasses/

There is a wealth of material on the problem of large class teaching. Bligh is interesting background reading on why lectures don't do what is generally expected of them. The other references suggest how more fruitful use might be made of that plenary session, misguidedly called the 'lecture'.

On interactive teaching

Chalmers, D. and Fuller, R. (1996) *Teaching for Learning at University.* London: Kogan Page.
Race, P. and Brown, S. (1993) *500 Tips for Tutors.* London: Kogan Page.

been trained to do it: the professional does what she does because she has thought about it and has made an informed decision to do it this way and not that way.

There are thus two broad tasks in educating students for such professional decision making. The first task is to build up the appropriate declarative knowledge base, and the second is to put that to work. These tasks may be done in the traditional fill-up-the-tanks model: declarative knowledge is built up first, the application of that knowledge follows. Another model is just-in-time learning: the student's declarative knowledge base is built up as need arises. This is the case in problem-based learning (PBL), where professional knowledge is rooted in practice from the outset. PBL is used in many professional programmes and we deal with it in a later section. Just-in-time learning is now conceived more broadly in connection with lifelong learning in the workplace, with particular reference to the role of information technology (Brandenburg and Ellinger 2003).

Unfortunately, many ILOs in professional education are addressed with TLAs more suitable for declarative knowledge. For example, in dealing with an ILO containing the verb 'apply', teachers may only *talk about* applying the knowledge instead of getting the students to *do* the applying (see Table 9.1).

After first addressing the ILOs that establish the relevant declarative knowledge, let us say that the teacher, when addressing the ILO 'apply', discusses what is meant by 'application' in the context in question and models an example or gives a demonstration. Here, the students are doing what they do when taught declaratively: they listen and take notes. They are not doing any applying themselves and, as always, it is more important that the students' activities are aligned to the ILO in question than the teacher's. The students may be required to 'apply' in the final examination but by then, as we saw with 'explain' in the last chapter, they were not explicitly given that

Table 9.1 What teachers and students do in a lecture addressing an ILO containing 'apply'

Teacher activity	Student activity
Introduce	Listen
Explain	Listen, take notes
Elaborate	Understand (but correctly? deeply enough?)
Discuss application in area	Listen, take notes
Give examples of application	Listen, take notes
Show some PPT slides	Watch, note points
Questions on slides	Write answers to the questions
Wind up	Possibly ask a question

opportunity before they were assessed. In our consulting work, we have come across teachers who are quite convinced that they are dealing with 'application' as mentioned in the ILO – but *they* are dealing with it, not the students. It's that mindset, once again, that sees teaching being about what teachers do, not about what learners do.

In later sections of this chapter, we suggest teaching/learning activities that are more clearly aligned to ILOs for functioning knowledge. Table 9.2 suggests some of the teaching/learning situations where each is likely to be developed.

We see that the teaching/learning situations are now highly diverse, some located in the classroom, but others are best located in the workplace or its substitute, the placement or practicum, while others again can be at home, in front of the computer or virtually anywhere. Certainly we can move out of those large lecture theatres. We can gather with our students in more personably arranged rooms, sprawl under the trees in companionable groups, log into chat rooms in the comfort of our homes and, perhaps most important, let our students report back to us about their learning in the world of work.

The task is to develop TLAs within these teaching/learning situations to suit the ILOs, which now are quite specific to the particular professional programme concerned. We can only discuss general principles with a few particular examples here. In designing TLAs it helps to consider them as the assessment tasks as well – then you have excellent alignment. For example, say the ILO requires the application of a concept to a real-life case, the teaching/learning activity is simply applying that concept to a case study and the most appropriate assessment task is how well that concept is applied to the case study.

Let us say we are teaching a course in client relationships in a bachelor programme of social work and the ILO is to establish rapport with a client.

Table 9.2 Some areas for developing functioning knowledge with sample ILOs and the teaching/learning situations where they may be located

Graduate outcomes	Sample course ILOs	Teaching/learning situations
Professional competence	Apply, solve problems	Laboratory, workplace, placement
Creativity	Design, invent	Workplace, home, studio
Communication	Explain, write	Everywhere
Teamwork	Cooperate, lead	Workplace, classroom, computer simulations
Lifelong learning	Reflect, develop	Everywhere
Ethical sense	Explain codes of practice	Classroom
	Behave ethically	Workplace, placement

We could give a lecture explaining what rapport is and then give the students a written test on what they think good rapport is. This is poor alignment: the students learn *about* rapport, not necessarily how to *create* rapport, which is one intended outcome of the course. No, let us give the lecture by all means – but call it an explanation of the need for rapport or a briefing – but the most appropriate learning will take place when the students are themselves required to create rapport with a client and the assessment is how well they do that. Here you have perfect alignment throughout: the intended outcome becomes the activity of teaching and of learning, the TLA, and it is also the assessment task. A different assessment task might address an ILO about their ability to explain why rapport is essential.

Let us now take a few ILOs for functioning knowledge, starting with 'apply'.

Teaching/learning activities for 'apply'

'Apply' is one of the most common verbs, but it is too wide ranging on its own and is focused down to apply *something* to *something* or to *someone*. We offer a range of teaching/learning situations where application is involved, some of which will better suit a particular context than others.

Case-based learning

Case-based learning (CBL) of one kind or another has been around for some time in law and business schools. CBL is concerned with bridging the gap between theory and practice, between declarative and functioning knowledge, and accordingly can apply to most professional education. Cases need to be relevant in that they address the ILOs in a sufficiently complex way, realistic by including everyday 'noise' as well as the essentials of the case, engaged by appropriate TLAs, and sufficiently challenging to allow students to hypothesize and to reflect on their management of the case (McCabe et al. 2009). There are several variants, a common one having two stages: (i) presenting cases that have already been carried out and (ii) requiring students to carry out their own cases.

Documents presenting the case to students may be in the form of narratives, outlining a real-life situation or an event – the court proceedings, the person or business with a problem – and through teacher–student, and student–student interactive discussion, draw out what happened, who the participants were and their differing perspectives of the issues. Many ILOs could be addressed: application, the role of theory in the decision making involved in the case, the role of teamwork and collaboration, critical thinking, creativity. Box 9.1 presents a case in environmental education.

Box 9.1 A case in environmental education

The ILOs addressed in this case study are:

1 *Apply* relevant ecological principles to conservation and exploitation of natural resources to *solve real-life problems* and *explain* the rationale for doing so.
2 *Critically evaluate* the merits, limitations and future trends and *apply* techniques in environmental conservation and resources management.

Mr Wong and his family are indigenous villagers in Yuen Long. Mr Wong owns three hectares of land and five hectares of fishponds inherited from his ancestors. With assistance of his two sons, Mr Wong manages to produce vegetables and freshwater fish for sale at the local markets. To keep up with production, he, like many farmers and fishermen in the New Territories, has been applying fertilizers and pesticides to the field, and trying to stock as many fish as possible in his ponds. However, in recent years, he sees his harvest decline gradually. One day, he woke up to discover that a great quantity of his fish were floating belly up. He could not believe his eyes!

What is going wrong? What can he do? How can he be assured that he is doing the right thing?

Provide reasons to support your answers.

Source: Dr Paul Shin, Department of Biology and Chemistry,
City University of Hong Kong

Case-based learning can be used to illustrated particular issues or, as in problem-based learning (see later), it can be used throughout a course to address the whole syllabus, the cases being carefully selected so that the content areas that are to be addressed are represented and sequenced in the logic of the build-up of knowledge.

Case-based learning may however lead to excessive workloads for both teacher and student (McNaught et al. 2007; McCabe et al. 2009). McNaught et al. found that in the first run of a service science course in first-year physics students achieved higher level learning outcomes than previously, but in the course evaluation the students complained of too heavy a workload, which was also reflected in a significant increase in surface approach scores in the Study Process Questionnaire. This problem was taken into account in subsequent runs of the course.

Group work

Case-based learning makes a great deal of use of group work, so here is a good place to discuss various kinds of group. Most TLAs for functioning knowledge make use of student–student interaction, both in the form of role play or of a variety of kinds of group work, which require students to apply their knowledge and to address functioning knowledge in general learning.

Although the essence of group work is student–student interaction, the initiating, orchestrating and managing of many kinds of group need to be performed by teachers. Student–student learning interactions in small groups are effective in producing the following outcomes (Collier 1983; Johnson and Johnson 1990; Topping 1996):

- *Elaboration of known content.* Students hear of different interpretations, things they themselves hadn't thought of. This facilitates:
- *Deriving standards for judging better and worse interpretations.*
- *Reflective awareness of how one arrives at a given position.* How did he arrive at that conclusion? How did she? How did I get to mine? Which is better?
- *Applying theory to practice.*

The reflective aspects are sharpened because students readily identify with each other's learning in a way they do not do with top-down teacher-directed learning (Abercrombie 1969). Abercrombie herself used this style of group work with medical students in applied areas such as interpreting X-rays, as described below.

In all group work, the students must have sufficient background to contribute, either from reading enough to have an informed discussion or where the topic relates directly to personal experience. Above all, the group leader needs to be able to create the right sort of atmosphere so that students can discuss uninhibitedly. Some teachers find it hard not to correct a student, not to be seen as the expert or to arbitrate in disputes between students. But to become the expert arbitrator kills the point of the exercise, as students then tend to sit back and wait to be told what to think.

As to the optimal size of a group, there is no set answer as it depends on the nature of the group task and the group dynamics. The principle is that each member should feel responsibility and commitment. The larger the group, the more likely 'social loafing' will take place, one member leaving it to the others to do the work. Interestingly, this is a western phenomenon – in ethnic Chinese groups, members work harder in larger groups (Gabrenya et al. 1985). If the architecture permits, students can be allocated to groups of 10 or so in the same room, but it can be awkward where lecture rooms are tiered, with fixed seats – outside under the trees is preferable, weather permitting. When the groups have reached their conclusions, one person speaks to the plenary session on their behalf, making sure that spokesperson is nominated in advance. When reporting back, individuals then need not feel shy about saying something others might criticize: it comes from the group.

In forming groups, Yamane (2006) strongly recommends assigning students to groups randomly. He found groups formed by friends or voluntary membership are much more likely to gossip or otherwise discuss off-task. Random assignment 'solved the problem', as he puts it.

Buzz groups

Students are given a question, problem or issue to discuss in the course of a class or asked to apply theory to analyse and solve a case study. The success of free ranging discussion depends on the size of the group and making absolutely sure the students are clear about what they have to do. Brainstorming groups have a topic and no rules, except to say whatever comes to mind. Brainstorming can be used wherever the verbs 'generate', 'hypothesize', 'speculate' and the like are being addressed.

Jigsaw groups

Here the groups are allocated sub-tasks and the plenary is to put the finished sub-tasks back together to solve the main task. This is a good way of getting a complex task handled where every person has had some active input into the solution. The downside is that each group only gets to see the working of their own sub-task, and may miss the whole. Again, assessment is the answer: the assessment task must address the whole. Each student could be asked to write a reflective report on the task and their role in it. Concept maps are also useful here, as they are what the whole complex is about, not just the sub-concept.

Learning cells

Learning cells are dyads formed not so much for mutual support, as are learning partners, but for working jointly on a problem or skill. The justification is simply that students work better when working in pairs (McKeachie et al. 1986). This is particularly useful in laboratory situations, learning at the computer terminal or question–answer on set tasks.

Problem-solving groups

Abercrombie (1969) worked with medical students in problem-solving groups. Her groups consisted of 10 or so students, and the task was diagnosis, mostly using X-ray films as content (about what the X-ray may be of and what it might mean). The principle is applicable to any situation where students are learning to make judgements, and where there is likely to be a strong difference of opinion. Students have to construct a hypothesis where the data are insufficient to reach an unambiguous conclusion. Different individuals typically seize on different aspects of the data or use the same data to draw different conclusions, so that astonished students find themselves at loggerheads with others equally convinced of the correctness of their own interpretations. The shock of that discovery can be powerful, forcing students to examine closely the basis of what theories they used and how they arrived at their own conclusions. Students taught in this way made better diagnoses, based more firmly on evidence, and they were less dogmatic, being more open to consider alternative possibilities (see also Abercrombie 1980). In addition to increased professional competence, Abercrombie found motivational and social outcomes that are also professionally relevant, such as increased self-concept, communication skills and self-knowledge.

Syndicate groups

These are formed out of a class of 30 or so into four to eight students each (Collier 1983). Each group has an assigned task, which could be part of a larger project, a problem or a case study. The heart of the technique is the intensive debate that is meant to go on in the syndicates. The assignments are designed to draw on selected sources as well as on students' first-hand experiences, so that everyone has something to say. The syndicates then report back to plenary sessions led by the teacher to help formulate and to consolidate the conceptual structures that have emerged from each group. Collier reports that student motivation is high, and that higher level skills are enhanced, as long as they are addressed in assessment.

Many of the common group structures discussed earlier can be replicated online. Some groups work better online, some worse. For example, going from student to student, seeking the opinion of each on the discussion topic, works much better asynchronously online than synchronously, either online or face to face. In the asynchronous use, students are not under pressure to say something – anything – when it is their turn, but rather they can take their time to think out their view first and then post it on the bulletin board after due reflection. Buzz groups, on the other hand, work better face to face, where oral spontaneity is an important feature (Maier and Warren 2000). Syndicates also work well online, which can work synchronously at first, then subgroups may confer and then report back, which can be synchronously for some phases and asynchronously for others.

Reciprocal questioning

Students are trained to ask generic questions of each other, following the teaching of a piece of content (King 1990). Generic questions get to the point of the content; in SOLO terms they are relational. For example:

- what is the main idea here?
- how would you compare this with . . .?
- but how is that different from . . .?
- now give me a different example.
- how does this affect . . .?

King compared answers to these kinds of question presented in the reciprocal teaching situation to answers to the same questions presented in open-ended discussion that took the same time. While the latter were often longer, they were almost all low level. On critical thinking and high-level elaboration, the reciprocal questioning groups were far superior. These findings emphasize that when getting students to interact in order to reach specific outcomes, make sure there is a clear and high-level agenda for them to address.

Spontaneous collaboration

Some student groups are unofficial, formed spontaneously to focus on coping with specific tasks, such as set assignments (Tang 1996, 1998). Tang studied spontaneous collaborative learning among physiotherapy students, who, after the announcement of an assignment, formed their own groups, deciding who would check out what set of references, what ideas might be included and so on. The collaborative effort extends variously through the planning phase of the assignment or project, but the final detailed plan and write-up is conducted individually. Over 80% of Tang's students collaborated to some extent and those who did showed greater structural complexity (higher SOLO levels) in their assignments. Such a high proportion of spontaneous collaboration may not occur with western students, but Goodnow (1991) reports that Australian students at Macquarie University formed syndicates, mainly for the purpose of exchanging wisdom on examination questions. An interesting question is how far teachers might encourage, or have any interaction with, these spontaneously formed groups (Tang 1993).

Facebook, MSN and Twitter are used by students mainly for non-academic purposes, but many students use them for spontaneous collaboration over set work such as assignments.

Workplace TLAs

Workplace learning, variously known as 'placement', 'attachment', 'practicum', 'clinical' or 'internship' according to discipline, is an integral component, even the apex of, professional education.

Depending on the nature of individual professions, each professional education programme has its own specific ILOs. However, the major ILOs of workplace learning which would likely be applicable to many professional programmes are for the students to be able to:

1 *integrate* knowledge and skills learned in university to real-life professional settings;
2 *apply* theories and skills to practice in all aspects of professional practice;
3 *work collaboratively* with all parties in multidisciplinary workplace settings;
4 *practise* with professional attitudes and social and ethical responsibilities in their respective professions.

Workplace learning is an active learning experience focusing on student participation in situated work activities (Billet 2004). It provides a teaching/learning situation where students learn through active participation (usually under supervision) in various aspects of professional practice situated in the real-life professional context. It could be a hospital clinical placement of internship in medical and healthcare programmes, field placement in social work, industrial attachment in business and engineering or law firm placement for law students. This teaching/learning situation is most suited to facilitate the functioning ILO of applying theories and concepts to perform professional practice such as making clinical decisions and diagnosis, planning and implementing treatment or intervention programmes, conducting industrial projects, producing a stage play and making a legal case, etc.

To enable students to achieve these outcomes, teaching/learning activities that are aligned to the ILOs must be designed. In most workplace learning situations, these activities include the following.

Teaching activities, conducted by placement educators:

1 plan and coordinate the logistics of the placement;
2 design appropriate learning activities;
3 select cases or projects;
4 provide appropriate level of guidance and scaffolding to learning;
5 provide feedback to learning;
6 assess the learning outcomes.

Learning activities, conducted by the students either in groups or individually:

1 assess or interview a patient or client to collect relevant data;
2 analyse the data to identify a situational problem or issue;
3 formulate solution to the problem through application of theory to the problem or situation in hand;
4 implement actions to effect the solution;
5 evaluate effectiveness of intervention or project;
6 implement improvement or changes based on evaluation;
7 collaborate with other team members either intra- or inter-disciplinarily;
8 reflect on own performance to identify areas for improvement.

It is important to ensure the alignment between these student learning activities and the ILOs for that particular workplace learning situation. Walsh argues that: 'constructive alignment could help to identify the similarities between the learning experience in the institution, which is highly structured, and the learning experience in the workplace, in which the student needs a clear indication of learning expectations and the way to achieve these' (Walsh 2007: 82).

Workplace learning involves experiences in the workplace that can lead to positive learning outcomes – and higher starting pay (Blair and Millea 2004). However, workplace experience can be stressful. It needs to be closely integrated with classroom learning, with ILOs that are clearly defined and understood by all parties concerned (Hu et al. 2009). In particular, the need for students to integrate and apply theory to practice should be explicitly emphasized to help them understand the link between classroom and workplace learning. It is important that students should see the common ILOs in both workplace and classroom and how they are interrelated and mutually supportive to provide a holistic professional learning experience. Because of the gap between formal learning in the classroom and relatively unstructured learning in the workplace, the student is required to be reflective and to learn from experience or as Gray (2001: 316) puts it, 'the acquisition of meta-competence – learning to learn'.

The success or otherwise of work placement is very dependent on the supervisor, who may hold quite different views on what is important and what is to be learned from those held by the university teaching staff. What the latter may define as ILOs may not be what the workplace actually requires. All this points to close cooperation between institution and workplace, and that the latter will provide the learning opportunities required to meet the ILOs, and that the supervisor uses appropriate rubrics for assessing student performance.

A learning contract, a negotiated agreement between the student and the placement educator regarding the particular learning experience, may well form part of the placement. In such contracts, students are actively involved in designing their learning experience, in identifying their learning needs, their ways of fulfilling those needs and how they will be assessed. A learning contract provides an authentic and contextualized learning experience that students will encounter in a real-life situation.

Teaching/learning activities for creativity

Creativity is not only an intended learning outcome in the fine or performing arts, as the graduate outcomes of most universities stipulate. So what is meant by creativity in higher education? Cropley and Cropley (2009) see creativity as about generating and evaluating new ideas, and innovation as implementing those ideas to produce *effective novelty*. Likewise, Cowdroy and De Graaff (2005) from an architectural background see creativity as 'inspired design' that takes a design further than has previously been reached. Seen thus, creativity is essential in all professions.

We have already used the terms 'convergent' and 'divergent' in connection with student questioning. They were originally coined by Guilford (1967) to describe two different forms of ability:

- *convergent* ability, as in solving problems that have a particular, unique answer, as in most intelligence and ability test items. Convergent thinking is 'closed'. A common perception is that convergent thinking is what academic ability is about: knowing a lot and getting it right, but that should be only part of the academic story.
- *divergent* ability, as in generating alternatives, where the notion of being correct gives way to other assessments of value, such as aesthetic appeal, originality, usefulness, self-expression, creativity and so on.

We prefer to see the terms 'convergent' and 'divergent' as describing *processes*, ways of going about thinking, that are involved in most high-level thinking and in professional work, rather than as simple abilities. However, it is difficult to 'generate', 'hypothesize', 'theorize' or 'reflect' without prior content mastery. You have to know what you are to hypothesize about or to reflect on. But, by the same token, having a solid knowledge base is no guarantee that one will be creative in using it. Many, perhaps most, academics focus on establishing that knowledge base, but neglect the next step of making it function creatively.

Creativity also requires, or at least is accompanied by, intense interest and involvement in a specific area, the end result of which is a product, a 'creative work', as Elton (2005) puts it, comprising something new, a synthesis that didn't exist quite like that before. The job of teachers is thus not to help students 'be' creative, but to help them create works, products, outputs, that are founded in the discipline or area and that add to it in an original and innovative way. The essence of creativity is to concentrate on process, and produce outcomes that are unexpected and often unintended (Jackson 2005).

A common perception is that outcomes-based teaching and learning is antithetical to creativity on the ground that the outcomes are predetermined, specified in advance and so form a 'closed loop'. This is true when the intended outcomes are low level, such as competencies, or are convergent, working towards the one correct answer. However, when the outcomes are high level, at the extended abstract end, they contain verbs such as 'design', 'invent' or the verb 'create' itself. Here the outcome is itself an open-ended process, the product not being predetermined at all.

Addressing open-ended verbs like these with an appropriate teaching/ learning activity is igniting a creative process with an unspecified outcome. A common TLA for the ILOs just examined is brainstorming in groups, after which students can individually work on their ideas and possibly regather to provide mutual feedback. There are many ways of triggering the creative verb, as appropriate for each discipline or area: an engineering TLA for 'design' will obviously be very different from a TLA for a creative writing course for 'create a character . . .'. 'The Imaginative Curriculum' is a large-scale project designed to help teachers, whatever their teaching area, to foster students' creativity through specific examples of teaching practice (Jackson et al. 2006).

Some areas, such as dramatic art, require situations in which TLAs are reflective and improvised. Box 9.2 provides an example.

Box 9.2 An example of teaching/learning activities in acting skills

TLAs in drama involve private rehearsal and reflection and public interaction with the teacher in workshop, skills classes and before-the-camera situations. Both student and teacher are looking for organic application and generation. The quality of reflection, whether intuited or consciously thought through, can be measured by repeating the exercise; and by making sure that the doing of the exercise is connected/ aligned to the thinking of the reflection. Self-control, which includes extensive private preparation, is paramount.

ILO: *Create a character and establish credible relationships.*

TLA: *Character object exercise.* The student seeks the core of the character by being in a character-familiar space (e.g. bedroom), using meaningful objects and carrying out physical activities, e.g. getting dressed.

ILO: *Achieve an organic perception of action and of the sequence 'reaction–action–variation'.*

TLA: *Playing the action:* Generating interaction through trying to make another *character* do something, as opposed to simply saying the lines and 'indicating' (not effecting an activation). When an action is played, the actor induces curiosity and, most significantly, becomes a storyteller, i.e. what will happen next? The TLA ought to be self-controlled or the student will lack ownership/authenticity. An element of peer control can be a great support. If the partner is activated, the student will at least receive a good energy-inviting reaction, which also amounts to interaction (the result of action playing). Proaction and reaction are the two halves of activation (or action playing). In dramatic terms, action playing, with its character-informed variations, naturally represents alignment.

A good piece of material can be found in Act I, scene vii of *Macbeth*. Lady Macbeth tries to make Macbeth kill the king. That is her action. To get what she wants, she must be proactive. She will have to use more than one approach or variation (otherwise, the scene would be resolved after only a line or two) and that is obtained by drawing on a range of so-called psychological activities (transitive verbs). These must generate tempo rhythms that can organically affect and potentially change a partner. High-level verbs must be sought, e.g. flatter, rebuke, encourage, humiliate. 'Beg' is self-indulgent, 'persuade' or 'question' are generalizations, 'shout' is intransitive. Applying these verbs and then reflecting on the exercise with a view to progressing should be givens. But sometimes the student may only pay lip service to the verbs; or struggle with reflection.

Source: Alan Dunnett, Drama Centre, Central Saint Martins, University of the Arts, London

Powerful TLAs for creativity can be constructed using educational technology. In her discussion of e-learning, Laurillard (2002) outlines *adaptive* media that change their state in response to users' actions, thus giving intrinsic feedback, internal to the action, as opposed to a commentary which is external. Simulations allow students to change parameters and see what happens, which encourage the 'what would happen if?' enquiry. *Productive* media allow students to construct micro-worlds, where they may build their own systems.

Unfortunately, it is much easier to stifle creativity than to encourage it. Whatever the TLAs relevant to a creative ILO, the right climate for encouraging creativity is one where the students can feel they can take risks and can feel free to ask 'what would happen if?' without being ridiculed either by the teacher or by other students for making a 'silly' response (Box 9.3).

Box 9.3 How not to encourage creativity

Teacher: And now, who can tell me what infinity means? (*Silence*). What is infinity?

Billy: Uh, I think it's like a box of Creamed Wheat.

Teacher: Billy, you're being silly.

Source: Jones (1968: 72)

Billy is, of course, quite right, infinity *is* like a box of Creamed Wheat breakfast cereal, on which there is a picture of a man holding a box of Creamed Wheat who is holding a box of Creamed Wheat . . . *ad infinitum*. It is likely, however, that Billy will in future keep his insights to himself, at least in that teacher's class. This homely example illustrates some further points that also apply to tertiary teaching. Snap value judgements by teachers are not a good idea. The teacher in the box might better have picked this up with (laughs): 'Good, but can anyone explain what Billy might mean?' and an enlightening discussion could ensue. We can too easily dismiss an insight that at first glance seems irrelevant.

A Theory X climate of criticism, mistrust and high anxiety is death to creative responses from most people. An example of this, familiar to all academics, is the difference in adventurousness, originality and freshness between a term assignment and the answer to a question on the same topic held under invigilated examination conditions: we return to this later when discussing the assessment of creativity.

Teaching/learning activities for lifelong learning

Lifelong learning, the ultimate aim of university teaching, has the generic and the embedded meanings of many other graduate attributes (pp. 114–15). The generic meaning – that graduates can learn to handle whatever life throws at them – is vacuous, empty rhetoric. The embedded meaning, however, that students can learn to handle unseen problems in their chosen field of study, is significant and attainable. One somewhat blinkered interpretation is that lifelong learning is 'a political response to a need to upskill the working population in order to obtain a competitive advantage in the economy' (Burns and Chisholm 2003: 179).

Burns and Chisholm relate lifelong learning to work-based learning in the context of engineering. They propose an ongoing interface between educational institutions and engineering firms, but they claim their models of work-based learning can be applied to any professional area. The general principle is just-in-time learning where, as in PBL but now in the workplace proper, people seek to learn what they have to know when need arises, most frequently now with the aid of e-technology (Brandenburg and Ellinger 2003).

A somewhat related but more flexible idea is the *emergent* curriculum (Jackson et al. 2006). The 'curriculum' here comprises problems that emerge in real life and that cannot be predicted and that usually require ongoing 'conversations' to invent, create and implement new enterprises that work in a business sense. As Jackson (private communication) elaborates:

> No-one knows where we are heading until an idea or a perception of needs begins to crystallise. We are trying to establish the conditions and resources for co-operative just-in-time learning and then respond to what emerges. We have students on year long placements scattered all over the world experiencing a multitude of cultures and problem working situations. The emergent curriculum is driven by a highly contextualised situation and need and the way it is met is not through text-book knowledge but by creating conditions, relationships and networks for purposeful and sympathetic conversation informed by experiences of dealing with similar situations or operating from principle-based positions.

These views of work-based and just-in-time learning can apply to pre-university, undergraduate, postgraduate and continuing professional development in the workforce. A related idea is life-wide learning; which is, as it were, the horizontal axis of lifelong learning: that while students are learning within, and in formal situations without, the classroom, they are simultaneously experiencing a huge range of important learning activities that impinge upon their lives (Jackson and Law 2010). Important though such learning is, however, we must limit ourselves here to our focus: what can be achieved within the general run of institutional undergraduate programmes.

The role of the institution in this context is twofold: what it can achieve externally by locating aligned teaching/learning activities and assessments in work-based placements wherever feasible; and what it can achieve internally on campus in providing students with the skills needed for independent lifelong and just-in-time learning. The latter addresses both second-tier attributes of 'information literacy' and 'personal and intellectual autonomy' that Barrie (2004) suggests comprise 'lifelong learning'. Students need to learn how to seek new information, how to utilize it and evaluate its importance and how to solve novel, non-textbook, professional problems. They will need high-level reflective skills and an abstract body of theory on which to deploy them, so that they can judge how successfully they are coping with novel problems, and how they may do better. Action learning for life, if you like.

As for Barrie's 'personal and intellectual autonomy', we are dealing with three levels of self-directed learning:

1   generic study skills;
2   study skills that relate to learning particular content;
3   reflective learning.

Generic study skills

Study skills are ways of managing time and space. For example:

- keeping notes and references neatly and systematically so that they can be found when needed;
- apportioning time and keeping track of deadlines, so that all topics and subjects are given adequate time, and in proportion to their importance;
- seeking new information without being overwhelmed, using search engines strategically and relevantly, prioritizing searches.

Adults are very much better at such organizing and planning than are students straight from school, while women are generally better than men (Trueman and Hartley 1996). Teaching generic study skills, particularly long-term planning, has positive effects on performance (Hattie et al. 1996).

Study skills that relate to learning particular content

These skills include:

- underlining/highlighting the key words in a passage;
- reading for main ideas, not details, as in SQ4R (Thomas and Robinson 1982);
- taking notes properly, by capturing the main idea of several sentences in own words, rather than copying every second or third sentence;
- using concept maps to derive a major structure;
- composing essays according to a pre-planned structure, reviewing and revising, not submitting the first draft.

But consider this experiment. Ramsden et al. (1986) taught study skills to first-year undergraduates from a variety of faculties, focusing on reading and note taking, examination preparation and writing skills. The effects were the opposite of what was intended: in comparison to a control group, the students increased their use of *surface* approaches. Subsequent interviews with the students revealed that they believed that to be successful in first year you needed to retain facts accurately, so they selected from the study skills course just those strategies they believed would help them memorize better. You will recall first-year students rejected concept maps for the same reason (p. 142). Students get these ideas from the way they have been taught and assessed and from the general culture of the class. No doubt the teachers did not at all intend that the students would interpret their first-year experience in this way, but they did.

This misalignment, between what the teachers intended and what the students perceived, can be overcome if teachers embed useful study skills in their teaching so they are not only teaching *what* they want their students to learn, but *how* to learn it. Chalmers and Fuller (1996) suggest teachers teach strategies for *acquiring* information (note making, memorizing, skim reading), strategies for *working with* information (explaining ideas, organizing ideas, writing summaries), strategies for *confirming* learning (handling assessment tasks) and so on. These are adapted to suit the particular unit or course content.

If study skills are supported by the context in which they will be used, it becomes clear why those strategies are useful. Building knowledge is so much more effective when the tools needed for building are used on the spot, thoughtfully.

Reflective learning

Lifelong learning and just-in-time learning require *informed self-direction*. That is, students need to operate from a sound knowledge base and use reflective or metacognitive skills to work strategically towards solving novel problems, to self-monitor their emerging solutions. It will be recalled that such learning is among the most effective (see Table 4.1, p. 59). The outcomes are not spelled out, they are emergent: one doesn't know what the intended outcome is to be until it emerges from a fuzzy problem situation. The teaching/learning activities are entirely self-managed or negotiated with others in the field and the ongoing formative feedback has also to be entirely self-managed. The judgement has to be made that *this* is the best solution in these complex circumstances.

When faced with such a novel situation, the learner might consider the following questions:

- This is a 'fuzzy' problem; how can I reformulate it in a way that relates to first principles leading to good solutions?
- What do I know that might be relevant? What problems like this have I met before? What did I do then?
- How can I find out further information? From where? How do I test it?
- I'll try this solution; does it work? How could I improve it?

These constitute a different order of question, using reflective skills in order to organize and conceptualize what is known prior to *re*-conceptualizing it.

The verbs involved are open ended and extended abstract: planning, theorizing, hypothesizing, generating.

Alongside these divergent processes, it is also necessary to monitor what is going on, to test ongoing outcomes for adequacy, to see that learning is on track. Evaluating one's own work, of prime importance in everyday professional life, is one skill that graduates feel their university education least prepared them to do (Boud 1986). Self-evaluation or self-monitoring skills therefore need to be addressed. Accordingly, self- and peer-assessment are as much teaching/learning activities as assessment tasks. Other relevant TLAs are reflective diary, selecting critical incidents and suggesting how to deal with them.

If dealing with emergent problems is what graduates are supposed to be able to do, undergraduate teaching should foster self-managed learning and assessment. The generic and content-specific study skills mentioned earlier only challenge students to apply, generalize and refine their understanding of what is given. Reflective learning skills and strategies require students to go further: to manage problems and questions that they have *not* previously addressed. This is also the aim of problem-based learning.

E-portfolios may be used to structure students' reflections on their learning at both undergraduate and graduate levels. The aim is to help students align their own learning outside as well as inside the classroom to their career goals (Cheung et al. 2009).

Now try Task 9.1 to see how well your students are prepared for lifelong learning.

Task 9.1 Teaching/learning activities to prepare students for lifelong learning

In the context of your own institution, identify:

A The elements deemed to be relevant to lifelong learning.
   1 _____
   2 _____
   3 _____
   4 _____

B The intended learning outcomes that students need to address the above elements and to develop lifelong learning.
   1 _____
   2 _____
   3 _____
   4 _____

C Reflect on the current teaching and learning activities within either your course or your programme and identify those that would facilitate students achieving those intended learning outcomes.

ILOs for lifelong learning	Course/ programme	Teaching/learning activities	
		Teaching activities	Learning activities

Your reflection:

Are your students adequately prepared for lifelong learning in your course/programme? If not, what changes would you make?

_____

_____

Problem-based learning

Problem-based learning (PBL) reflects the way people learn in real life; they simply get on with solving the problems life puts before them with whatever resources are to hand. In real life we do not stop to wonder at the 'relevance' of what we are doing, or at our 'motivation' for doing it: it is the traditional model of education that gives birth to these questions.

Education for the professions for years followed the fill-up-the-tanks model of knowledge acquisition and much of it still does. The disciplines are taught first, independently of one another, and, armed with all that declarative knowledge and with some professionally relevant but atheoretically taught skills, the student is accredited as ready to practise as a professional. Professional practice, however, requires functioning knowledge that can be put to work on the spot. Traditionally taught graduates manage to do that with varying degrees of success and, with experience in the real world, become increasingly better at it. However, if students graduate with that functioning knowledge already to hand, their induction into real-life professional practice is that much quicker. The problem in the traditional model is that the graduate and programme outcomes nominate professional competence on graduation but high levels of declarative knowledge are the main output: intended learning outcomes, teaching and assessment are not aligned.

PBL is alignment itself. If the aim is to become a doctor – PBL originated in a school of medicine – then the best way of becoming one is being one, under appropriate guidance and safeguards. If the ILO is to make clinical diagnoses then making clinical diagnoses is the obvious teaching/learning activity and how well they are made is the obvious assessment task. And so it goes for any professional problem.

Although PBL is used most commonly in education for the professions, it can also be used in the teaching of basic disciplines (see 'Further reading' at end of this chapter, where a couple of websites on PBL for teaching physics and biology are provided).

Goals of PBL

There are several modifications and versions of what is called 'PBL', but all should address the four goals distinguished by Barrows (1986):

1 *Structuring knowledge for use in working contexts*: professional education is concerned with functioning knowledge. PBL is concerned with constructing knowledge that is to be put to work.
2 *Developing effective reasoning processes*: such processes refer to the cognitive activities required in the professional area concerned and include: problem solving, decision making, hypothesizing, etc. Each professional area has its own specific processes to be developed as relevant problems are solved.
3 *Developing self-directed learning skills*: included here are the three levels of skill mentioned earlier (pp. 175–8): generic study skills, content-specific study skills and especially the reflective or self-management skills for life-long learning that are specifically addressed in PBL, where they are learned in context, as they should be.
4 *Increased motivation for learning*: students are placed in a context that requires their immediate and committed involvement. Thus, in terms of motivational theory (see Chapter 3), the value is high, the expectation of success is high, as problems and cases are selected in which students are likely to be successful, and so motivation is high.

To these four may be added a fifth:

5 *Developing group skills, working with colleagues*: many professions require teamwork, so this becomes a goal in many PBL programmes. It might be noted that such teamwork takes place in a workplace-like context, unlike much group project work.

PBL varies according to two major variables (Barrows 1986):

1 *The degree to which the problem is structured*: some problems are tightly struc-tured, with all the information needed to solve them. Others have some

facts provided, the student having to find the rest. Open or 'ill-defined' problems present no data, it being entirely up to the student to research the case and decide what needs to be found out and what to do to handle it.

2   *The extent of teacher direction:* the most conservative case, arguably not PBL, is where the teacher controls the amount and flow of information. In the case of 'ill-defined' problems, teacher direction is minimal, the students going off on their own to solve the problem. Variations in between depend on how much the teacher provides clues and support for handling information.

Savin-Baden (2000) argues that problem-based learning is commonly confused with problem-solving learning. The latter simply means setting problems for students to solve after they have been taught conventionally and then discussing them later. In PBL, on the other hand, 'the starting point for learning should be a problem, query or a puzzle that the learner wishes to solve' (Boud 1985: 13). The problem, or a series of problems, is where learning starts and, in going about solving those problems, the learner seeks the knowledge of disciplines, facts and procedures that are needed to solve the problems. The traditional disciplines do not define what is to be learned, the problems do. However, the aim is not only to solve those partic-ular problems, but in the course of doing so, the learner acquires knowledge, content-related skills, self-management skills, attitudes, know-how: in a word, professional wisdom. This means the problems have to be carefully selected.

Nature and construction of the problems

A good problem has the following characteristics (Johnston 2002):

1   It calls on different disciplines and integrates them in solving the problem.
2   It raises options that promote discussion.
3   It activates and incorporates previous knowledge.
4   It requires new knowledge the students don't yet have.
5   It stimulates participants to elaborate.
6   It requires self-directed learning.
7   And, of course, it meets the course ILOs.

Such problems are open ended and 'ill structured', that is, they do not present the students with enough information.

Here's a problem for you: 'You plan to use PBL in teaching your course for the first time. What are you going to do?' Ill structured, definitely. You may see straight away that you don't have enough information, and that seeking a solution involves higher order thinking, such as hypothesizing, evaluation, reflection. It also involves divergent thinking, as there is likely to be more than one way of reaching a solution. A sensible first step, then, might be to read the rest of this chapter, then some of the readings. Are there any colleagues in your institution using PBL? If so, talk to them.

Steps in designing a good problem are given in Box 9.4.

Box 9.4 Designing a problem

1 Map all the *concepts* likely to be involved from different disciplines, including the *knowledge* and *skills* required to solve the situation. Maybe a knowledge tree would help.

2 Write the *ILOs*. What do you expect the students to do with the new knowledge and skills?

3 Identify a *real problem* from a real-life situation that is important to students, such as one they are likely to meet in their future employment. Authenticity is highly motivating.

4 Repeat (3) until all your ILOs are addressed.

5 When *writing* problems make sure to:

- Use the present tense. Otherwise problems look like another textbook exercise.
- Provide a context and specific role of practitioner: what, when, where.
- Provide specific rather than vague data.
- Require the students to deliver something: a decision or report.

6 Many situations or problems *evolve over time*. It might be appropriate to provide an extended problem (called the 'roll-out' problem or case). Such a problem is in parts, covering a sequence of events or the problem is addressed in stages as more data become available and may last over more than one semester.

7 Write a *facilitator guide* for others involved in the PBL, including:

- the problem
- the ILOs
- the learning issues, including all the new knowledge you expect participants to learn and discuss
- content background information for the facilitators
- suggested resources for students.

Source: David Johnston, former Director, Hong Kong Centre for PBL, with permission

---

A typical PBL sequence goes like this:

- The *context* is pressing. In a typical medical programme, students in their first week of their first year are faced with the responsibility for a real patient with, say, a broken leg. The felt need to learn is strong.
- Learners become *active* very quickly. They are assigned to small problem-solving groups and begin *interacting* with teachers, peers and clients (who present the problem).

- Learners start from what they already know and *build a knowledge base* on that. They learn where to go to check what they know and to seek out more. They are variously guided towards resource materials, including films, videos, the library and lecture room. Knowledge is *elaborated and consolidated.* Students meet with a tutor and discuss the case in relation to the knowledge they have obtained.
- The knowledge is functioning: it is *applied* to the problem in hand. *Feedback* is ongoing.
- The problem is reviewed and learners develop *self-management* and *self-monitoring skills*, which they review throughout the programme.

The italicized words may remind you of some of the more important characteristics of a rich learning context described in Chapter 4.

The optimal amount of structure of the problem, and of teacher direction, depends at least initially on the educational philosophy of the teachers and tutors participating, and what freedom the students can initially handle (Ryan 1997). In a study at the Polytechnic University of Hong Kong, modifications were introduced to fit the aims of six departments and the different expectations of full- and part-time students (Tang et al. 1997). The full-time students found most difficulty with assessment, not surprisingly given their exam-dominated school background. As one student put it, 'It is difficult to guess what is the marking scheme of the lecturer' (Tang et al. 1997: 586). Part-time students, by way of contrast, took to PBL straight away because it mimicked the workplace: 'When I encounter a problem, I will have a solution, like that in my workplace' (Tang et al. 1997; Tiwari et al. 1999).

For those interested in trying PBL, you can now handle Task 9.2.

Task 9.2 Getting going with PBL

Take a topic you are teaching and turn it into PBL. Be guided by Box 9.4.

We deal with assessment issues in PBL in Chapter 12.

Does PBL work?

Albanese and Mitchell (1993) conducted a major meta-analysis of all studies published between 1972 and 1992 and reached the following conclusions:

1 Both staff and students rate PBL higher in their evaluations and enjoy PBL more than traditional teaching.

2 PBL graduates perform as well and sometimes better on clinical performance. More PBL (medical) graduates go into family practice.
3 PBL students use higher level strategies for understanding and for self-
directed study.
4 PBL students do worse in examinations of basic science declarative
knowledge.
5 PBL students when compared to traditionally taught students become
progressively deeper in their approaches to learning (Newble and Clarke
1986; McKay and Kember 1997).

PBL requires a *different way* of using knowledge to solve problems. Hmelo
et al. (1997) distinguish two strategies in clinical decision making:

- *Data driven*: 'This patient has elevated blood sugar, therefore he has diabetes.'
- *Hypothesis driven*: 'This patient has diabetes, therefore blood sugar should
be up, and rapid respiration, "fruity" breath odour . . .'

Experienced and expert doctors use the data-driven strategy, except for
unfamiliar or complex problems. Novice doctors, such as students in training,
lack that experience and should therefore work top-down from first principles, with longer reasoning chains: 'If this, then because of that, it would
follow that we should find symptoms X, Y and Z . . .' The traditionally taught
students tried to follow the experts – but couldn't because they didn't have
the background. PBL taught students increasingly used hypothesis-driven
reasoning, with longer and clearer reasoning chains. PBL students also used
a wider variety of knowledge resources, whereas traditionally taught students
stuck with the textbook.

An important aspect of evaluating PBL is its implementation, particularly
cost benefits. The economies of large lectures are offset by the economies of
self-directed learning and on the size and number of tutorial groups comple-
menting the lectures. Albanese and Mitchell (1993) estimate that for fewer
than 40, and up to around 100 students, PBL once set up can be equivalent
in cost to traditional teaching. Savin-Baden (2000) is more optimistic still,
saying that because of the move to mass education, fee-paying students from
diverse backgrounds are more likely to be attracted to interesting ways of
learning, like PBL, than to mass lectures.

Let's hope so.

Problem-based problems

PBL is particularly sensitive to context and climate. Remember the
disastrous effect a know-it-all tutor had on the questioning strategy needed
for the problem-solving process ('That's for me to know and for you to find
out') (p. 65). An equally devastating effect was achieved in another case
when the course coordinator decided to retain the traditional final-year
examination, leaving the students unsure whether their conclusions drawn

from solving the problem would be relevant to the final exam. They weren't. Not surprisingly, performance was low and the course evaluation of PBL was unfavourable (Lai and Tang 1999).

Both cases are examples of poor alignment. The tutor was creating affective misalignment in that the climate created was incompatible with the spirit of PBL, while the coordinator was creating curricular misalignment in that the assessment matched neither the ILOs nor the TLAs used.

In PBL, students cover only 80% of the traditional syllabus and do not perform as well in standard examinations (Albanese and Mitchell 1993). That worries traditional critics more than PBL teachers because when PBL graduates know their declarative knowledge is insufficient, they have the self-directed skills to know just in time where to go and how to acquire what knowledge they will require when attending to a particular case – which is an essential part of lifelong learning.

PBL is undoubtedly an effective approach to teaching. It exemplifies a high degree of alignment. To practise as a particular professional requires solving problems that belong to that profession. Thus, professional knowledge and skill are the intended learning outcomes, professional practice comprises the teaching/learning activities, professional knowledge and skill are what are assessed (among other things). PBL is distinguished from apprenticeship in that it is theory based; it is not just a matter of performing the skills in an uninformed manner.

There are two major reasons why PBL is not used more widely. First, PBL requires teachers to adopt a different philosophy of professional education: that education is something more than the acquisition of separate bodies of knowledge, in one of which the teacher is professed expert. The teacher has to be prepared to drop the role of expert. Many find this hard to do: their very career path is expedited by demonstrating their specific expertise. It is much easier for experts to give lectures on their speciality, leaving integration and application as the students' problem to solve. Most students probably will, but years down the track.

Second, PBL requires considerable institutional flexibility. Most universities are organized into departments with specific content foci. PBL is multidisciplinary as usually the problems presented require knowledge from several areas: it therefore challenges the traditional model of university organization.

So where do you place the horse – before or after the cart?

Now design TLAs to help your students put knowledge to work (Task 9.3).

Task 9.3 ILOs and TLAs to put knowledge to work

Take one of your course ILOs relating to functioning knowledge, where students are expected to put knowledge to work in practical contexts. Identify what teaching/learning situations you use and identify the teacher and student activities. Are the student activities aligned to the ILO? Would those TLAs really help the students achieve that ILO?

ILO relating to functioning knowledge in my course:

_____

Teaching/learning situation	TLAs	
	Teacher activities	Student activities

Who is performing the ILO verb(s)? _____

Do I need to change the TLAs? _____

What changes would I make? _____

_____

_____

Before we leave the teaching/learning activities, let us revisit Task 5.3 (p. 92) as Task 9.4.

Task 9.4 *Threshold* and *core concepts* revisited

In Task 5.3, we asked you to identify a *threshold concept* and its related *core concepts* of a subject that you teach and explain what level of understanding or performance you intend your students to achieve and how they have been taught. Now that we have looked at TLAs for both declarative and functioning intended learning outcomes, what TLAs would you use to teach these concepts?

Intended level of understanding/performance in relation to:

Threshold concept: _____

_____

Core concepts: _____

_____

Threshold/core concept	Teaching/learning situation	TLAs	
		Teacher activities	Student activities

Your reflection:

What changes have you made?

_____

_____

Why have you made those changes?

_____

_____

Summary and conclusions

Functioning knowledge and professional education

Professional education is chiefly concerned with putting knowledge to work as functioning knowledge. The usual means of doing this is to build the declarative knowledge base first, as we saw in the last chapter, but in problem-based learning, that knowledge base is built in the process of its being applied. 'Apply' is the most typical verb in functioning knowledge. It is important to see that the TLAs used ensure that the students themselves do the applying and not just watch someone else doing it or telling them about it. Functioning knowledge may be used in teacher-managed, student-managed or self-managed situations.

Teaching/learning activities for 'apply'

Case-based learning has had a long history in applying theory to practice. A common teaching/learning situation for 'apply', depending on applying what to what, is groupwork. We looked at different types of group: brainstorming, buzz groups, jigsaw, learning cells, reciprocal questioning, syndicate to name a few. Some students may on their own initiative set up their own spontaneous learning groups. The suitability of which type of group will, of course, depend on the ILO in question. Workplace learning is used precisely because it is concerned with application and also in service of lifelong learning.

Teaching/learning activities for creativity

Almost all graduate attributes mention 'creativity' in some form or another, but most university teaching emphasises convergent rather than divergent thinking. Both ways of thinking are important in all high-level functioning. Creativity is characterized by open-ended thinking based on a sound knowledge base, resulting in products with some degree of originality. Such creative work can be positively encouraged in a number of ways. Unfortunately, it is all too easily discouraged by insisting on a regimen of correct answers rather than experimenting with ideas, and by creating a Theory X type of climate in which students are fearful of taking risks and exploring different possibilities.

Teaching/learning activities for lifelong learning

Lifelong learning opens a range of learning: just-in-time learning, work-based learning, continuing professional education and related, life-wide learning, all of which go well beyond undergraduate education. Undergraduate courses can, however, prepare students for later just-in-time and work-based learning – as indeed PBL has already been doing for many years. TLAs for ILOs preparatory for lifelong learning need to emphasize learner information literacy and reflective self-direction. The latter may be achieved by teaching students both generic and content-specific study skills and by reflective practice. Students need to be able to manage their space and time effectively, to be able to seek new information, especially by using search engines strategically and to carry out effectively those strategies that are specific to their content area. Additionally, they need to be able to reflect on past practice, with the intention of improving what they have done and of solving new problems they haven't met before.

Problem-based learning (PBL)

PBL is an example of a total approach to the main aims of lifelong learning. Students learn the skills for seeking out the required knowledge as the occasion demands. The problems are selected so that by the end of the programme, the learner is ready to move directly into the workforce. Less content may be covered than in a traditional programme, but the knowledge the students do have is acquired in a working context, is put back to use in that context and where the students have insufficient knowledge they have the metacognitive skills to know what they don't know and where to go to get it and how then to use it. Students taught by PBL reason more effectively, they have greater self-awareness and self-direction, and they enjoy learning more, as indeed do their teachers. However, PBL is sensitive to insensitive teaching. An institutional problem is that the infrastructure for PBL is not discipline based, whereas most universities are organized on disciplinary lines. Teachers tend to identify themselves as scholars in their home discipline and PBL might seem to threaten their academic identity.

Further reading

On case-based learning

Colbert, J., Trumble, K. and Desberg, P. (eds) (1996) *The Case for Education: Contemporary Approaches for Using Case Methods.* Boston: Allyn and Bacon.
Lynn, L.E. (1996) *What is the Case Method? A Guide and Casebook.* Tokyo: The Foundation for Advanced Studies on International Development.
www.queensu.ca/ctl/goodpractice/case/resources.html (accessed 2 February 2011).

These two books and the website discuss various theoretical and practical issues in using case-based learning. On the effectiveness of case-based learning: http://www.cuhk.edu.hk/sci/case-learning/doc/reflections.pdf (accessed 2 February 2011).

On group work

Abercrombie, M.L.J. (1980) *Aims and Techniques of Group Teaching.* London: Society for Research into Higher Education.
Collier, K.G. (1983) *The Management of Peer-Group Learning: Syndicate Methods in Higher Education.* Guildford: Society for Research into Higher Education.
Johnson, D.W. and Johnson, R.T. (1990) *Learning Together and Alone: Cooperation, Competition and Individualization.* Englewood Cliffs, NJ: Prentice-Hall.

The first two are very practical accounts of using groups effectively. Johnson and Johnson is the classic on setting up cooperative learning groups.

Working in Groups – A Note to Faculty and Quick Guide for Students. Derek Bok Centre for Teaching and Learning, Harvard University.

On workplace learning

The Journal of Workplace Learning: http://www.emeraldinsight.com/info/journals/jwl/jwl.jsp (accessed 2 February 2011).

On creativity

Cropley, A. and Cropley, D. (2009) *Fostering Creativity: A Diagnostic Approach for Higher Education and Organizations.* Cresskill, NJ: Hampton Press.

Jackson, N. (2010) Developing creativity through life-wide education. http:// imaginativecurriculumnetwork.pbworks.com/f/Developing+creativity+through +life-wide+education+version+5++15+06.pdf (accessed 2 February 2011).

Jackson, N., Oliver, M., Shaw, M. and Wisdom, J. (eds) (2006) *Developing Creativity in Higher Education: The Imaginative Curriculum.* London: Routledge.

Cropley and Cropley start with the assumption that creativity is essential in innovations in all professional areas – their main concern is with engineering – and that higher education can enhance students' creativity and their awareness of their creative potential. Jackson et al. are concerned that current quality assurance, peer review, pressures on research output and so on discourage innovation and creativity, and in this book academics teaching across all disciplines show how creativity can be integrated into normal university teaching. The chapters by Jackson and Sinclair on a pedagogy for creativity and Baillie on art, science and engineering are noteworthy for deriving TLAs. Jackson's 2010 paper discusses the development of creativity in 'life-wide' contexts, using events that happen to one contemporaneously with formal education.

Mycoted, on teaching for creativity: 'The A to Z of creativity techniques'. http://www. mycoted.com/creativity/techniques/ (accessed 2 February 2011).

The link to creativity on the Higher Education Academy website: http://www. heacademy.ac.uk/creativity.htm (accessed 2 February 2011).

Mycoted has an extensive range of 'creativity techniques' that will provide a source of ideas; the Higher Education Academic website has many useful links.

On lifelong and life-wide learning

Jackson, N. and Law, R. (eds) (2010) Enabling a More Complete Education: Encouraging, Recognising and Valuing Life-Wide Learning in Higher Education. Conference held 13–14 April, University of Surrey. http://life-widelearningconference.pbworks.com/ (accessed 2 February 2011).

Knapper, C. and Cropley, A. (2000) *Lifelong Learning in Higher Education.* London: Kogan Page.

http://www.lifelonglearning.co.uk/ (accessed 2 February 2011).

Knapper and Cropley's book is one of the classics in this area. The two home pages are of lifelong learning sites, one in the UK, the other in Australia, with plenty of links. The Jackson and Law URL takes you to a collection of papers and discussions at a conference by eminent academics addressing issues related to learning 'life-wide'.

On reflective learning

A Roadmap to University Success. https://eportal.cityu.edu.hk/bbcswebdav/orgs/ L_EPORTFOLIO_WORKSHOP/Generic-Structure/general_qualifications.html (accessed 2 February 2011).

On problem-based learning

Boud, D. and Feletti, G. (eds) (1997) *The Challenge of Problem-based Learning.* London: Kogan Page.

Savin-Baden, M. (2000) *Problem-based Learning in Higher Education: Untold Stories.* Buckingham: The Society for Research into Higher Education/Open University Press.

Research and Development in Problem Based Learning. The Australian Problem-Based Learning Network c/o PROBLARC, CALT, The University of Newcastle, NSW 2308.

Boud and Feletti contains contributions by users in many different areas. Savin-Baden introduces a little-discussed aspect: what happens *inside* when teachers and students experience PBL. Both books are important for anyone seriously interested in PBL. The last is a serial publication of the Australian Problem-Based Learning Network, which holds biennial conferences, of which these volumes are the proceedings.

Waters, L. and Johnston, C. (2004) Web-delivered, problem-based learning in organisation behaviour: a new form of CAOS, *Higher Education Research and Development,* 23, 4: 413–31.

An e-version of PBL in teaching organizational behaviour is based on *Case Analysis of Organisational Situations.*

PBL in biology (20 case examples): www.saltspring.com/capewest/pbl.htm

PBL in physics, chemistry, biology and criminal justice: www.udel.edu/pbl/problems (accessed 2 February 2011).

10

Aligning assessment tasks with intended learning outcomes: principles

What and how students learn depends to a major extent on how they think they will be assessed. Assessment practices must send the right signals to students about what they should be learning and how they should be learning it. Current practice, however, is distorted because two quite different models of summative assessment have, for historical reasons, been confused and the wrong signals to students are often sent. In this chapter, these issues are clarified. We examine the purposes of assessment, the relation between assessment and the assumed nature of what is being assessed, assessing for desirable but unintended or unexpected learning outcomes, and who might usefully be involved in the assessing process. The underlying principle is that the assessment tasks should comprise an authentic representation of the course intended learning outcomes.

Some case studies

Let us do some cased-based assessment. Task 10.1 presents six assessment dilemmas. These are the sorts of issues that teachers are likely to face and that they will need to resolve, one way or another. We need a theory of assessment if we are to resolve such issues satisfactorily and this is what this chapter is meant to provide. Go through these cases and write your responses down. When you have completed this chapter you might like to revisit what you wrote to see if your thoughts have changed.

Task 10.1 Some cats to place among your collegial pigeons: Six assessment dilemmas for you to consider

Case 1. Misunderstanding the question

You are assessing assignments and find that one student has clearly misunderstood the question, the only one to have done so. It is now past the due date for handing in. If you assess it as it is, she will fail. What do you do?

a Fail her.
b Hand it back, explain that she has misunderstood and give her an extension.
c As in (b), but assess it pass/fail only or deduct a grade.
d Set her another assignment, to be assessed later. Meantime record 'result withheld'.
e Other. What?

What is your decision and what are the reasons for it? _____

_____

_____

_____

Would you have decided differently if she would otherwise graduate with distinction?

_____

_____

Case 2. Grading on the curve

The guidelines for awarding a grade of A are outlined in a programme document:

> *Outstanding.* Demonstrates thorough understanding and interpretation of topics and underlying theories being discussed, and shows a high level of critical thinking and synthesis. Presents an original and thorough discussion. Well organized and structured, fluently written and correctly documented. Substantial coverage of the literature.

You use these guidelines in grading the assessment tasks of your class of 100 students and find to your delight that 35 (35%) meet these criteria, so you award A to all of them. Your departmental head, however, is unhappy about this because you are 'not showing enough discrimination between students and we don't want this department to get a reputation for easy marking'. The results have not been announced yet, so he suggests that you regrade so that only 15% of your students are given an A. What do you do? Why?

a You agree you must have been too lenient, so you do as he says, giving A to the first 15 only, the remaining of the original As being given B.
b You compromise, splitting the difference: you give As to 25 students.

c You say something like: 'Sorry, but the guidelines are clear. I must in all conscience stick with the original. The conclusion to be drawn is that this was an exceptionally good group of students and that they were taught well.'

d 'I must stick with the guidelines. However, I am prepared to entertain a second opinion from a colleague whose judgement you trust. If I can be persuaded that I have been too lenient, I will change my grades.'

e Other.

What is your decision and what are the reasons for it? _____

_____

_____

_____

Case 3. A matter of length

It is policy that the maximum word length of assignments is 1000 per credit point. You are teaching a 2-credit point module. One of your better students has handed in an assignment of 2800 words. What do you do and why?

a Count up to 2000 words, draw a line and mark or assess up to that point only.

b Hand it back to the student with the instructions to rewrite, within the limit, with no penalty.

c As for (b) but with a penalty. (What would you suggest?)

d Hand it back unassessed.

e Assess or mark it but deduct a grade or part-grade, or marks, according to the excess.

f Other.

What is your decision and what are the reasons for it? _____

_____

_____

Would your decision have been any different if it were a poor student?

_____

_____

Case 4. Exam strategy

You are discussing the forthcoming final exam with your first-year class. You explain that, as usual, there will be five sections in the paper, each section covering an aspect of the course, and there are two questions per section. They are to choose one of the two, making a total of five questions, to be completed in three hours. You alone will be doing the assessing. A student asks: 'If I think I will run out of time, is it better to answer four questions as best as I can, or to attempt all five, knowing I won't finish most questions?'

What do you say in reply and why? _____

_____

_____

_____

Case 5. Interfering with internal affairs?

You are the head of a department that has decided to use PBL in the senior level subjects. In PBL, the emphasis is on students applying knowledge to problems, rather than carrying out detailed analyses of the research literature, as has been the tradition in the past. Faculty regulations require you to set a final examination for the major assessment of the course, despite your own judgement and that of your staff that this format is unsuitable for PBL. It is therefore decided that the final exam will contain questions that address application to problem solving rather than questions that require students to demonstrate their familiarity with the literature.

On seeing the paper, however, the external examiner insists that the questions be reworded to address the research literature. You argue, but he insists that 'academic standards' must be upheld. If they are not reworded, you know that he will submit an adverse report to the academic board, where there are vocal critics of your foray into PBL.

What do you do and why? _____

_____

_____

_____

Case 6. What is the true estimate of student learning?

A department is trying to arrive at a policy on the proportion of final examination to coursework assignments. In discussing the issue, the head collates data over the past few years and it becomes very clear that coursework assessments are consistently higher than examination results. In discussing this phenomenon, the following opinions are voiced.

a Such results show that coursework assessments may be too lenient and because the conditions under which they are undertaken are

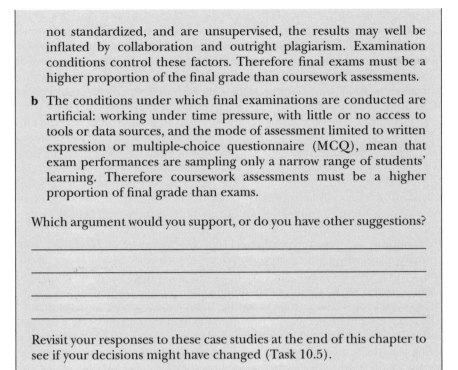

not standardized, and are unsupervised, the results may well be inflated by collaboration and outright plagiarism. Examination conditions control these factors. Therefore final exams must be a higher proportion of the final grade than coursework assessments.

b The conditions under which final examinations are conducted are artificial: working under time pressure, with little or no access to tools or data sources, and the mode of assessment limited to written expression or multiple-choice questionnaire (MCQ), mean that exam performances are sampling only a narrow range of students' learning. Therefore coursework assessments must be a higher proportion of final grade than exams.

Which argument would you support, or do you have other suggestions?

_____

_____

_____

_____

Revisit your responses to these case studies at the end of this chapter to see if your decisions might have changed (Task 10.5).

Formative and summative assessment

There are many reasons for assessing students: selecting students, controlling or motivating students (the existence of assessment keeps class attendance high and set references read), satisfying public expectations as to standards and accountability, but the two most outstanding reasons are for *formative feedback* and for *summative grading*. Usually – and perhaps unfortunately – both are referred to as types of 'assessment'. Both are based on seeing how well students are doing or have recently done, which is what assessment is, but the purposes of the two forms of assessment are completely different.

In formative assessment, the results are used for *feedback* during learning. Students and teachers both need to know how learning is proceeding. Formative feedback may operate both to improve the learning of individual students and to improve the teaching itself. Formative feedback is inseparable from teaching: as we have already noted (pp. 64–6), the effectiveness of different teaching methods is directly related to their ability to provide formative feedback. The lecture itself provides little. The improvements to the lecture mentioned in Chapter 8 were almost all formative in function: they got the students learning actively and feedback was provided on their activity, either from teacher or from peers. Formative feedback is a powerful teaching/learning activity that uses error detection as the basis for error correction: if error is to be corrected, it must first be detected. Thus, students must feel absolutely free to admit error and seek to have it corrected. Students also need to learn to take over the formative role for themselves, just as writers need to spot error and correct it when editing a text by reflecting critically on their own writing. Self- and peer-assessment are particularly helpful TLAs for training students to reflect on the quality of their own work.

In summative assessment, the results are used to grade students at the end of a course or to accredit at the end of a programme. Summative assessment is carried out after the teaching/learning episode has concluded. Its purpose is to see how well students have learned what they were supposed to have learned. That result, the grade, is final. Students fear this outcome; futures hinge on it. They will be singularly unwilling to admit their mistakes. Error no longer is there to instruct, as in formative assessment; error now signals punishment. This difference between formative and summative reminds us that continuous assessment (see later) is problematic when it is used for both formative and summative purposes. What then do students do about admitting error? Do they reveal their uncertainties so that they may be addressed and corrected, or do they conceal them so they don't lose marks?

Nevertheless, there is one similarity between formative and summative assessment: in both we match performance as it is, with performance as it should be. When the student is aware of the immediate purpose to which it is being put, the same task can act as a TLA, in the formative sense, and as the assessment task when it is time to do the summative assessment: 'When the chef tastes the sauce it is formative assessment; when the customer tastes, it is summative' (anon.). Figure 10.1 places tasting the sauce in a classroom context.

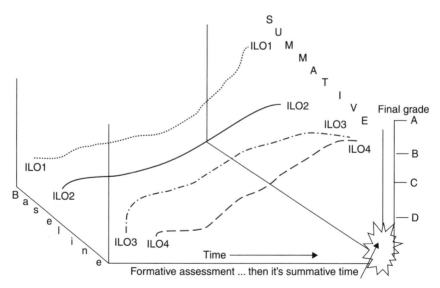

Figure 10.1 Learning in four topics and their formative and summative assessment

Say four topics are to be learned in a semester. The intended learning outcomes of each are symbolized as ILO1, ILO2, ILO3 and ILO4. At the start of the semester (labelled 'baseline') students enter with little or some knowledge, which the TLAs nurture until the end of the semester. Formative assessment checks that growth and sees that it is on track. Then it is time to see where each student now stands with respect to each of the four ILOs; this is the task of summative assessment. Finally, there is the administrative matter of converting those four positions into a grade, taken here as A, B, C and D.

A caution in interpreting Figure 10.1. While the same assessment task may be used formatively throughout the course and summatively at the end, it must be clear to the students when it is being used for what purpose. To use it for *both* formative and summative purposes, as may happen in continuous assessment, creates a conflicting situation for the students: they are being asked to display and to hide error simultaneously. When assessment is continuously carried out throughout a course, and it is intended to use some of the results summatively, the students must be told *which* assessment events are formative and which summative. They can then decide how they will handle the task to best advantage.

Effects of assessment on learning: backwash

We teachers might see the intended learning outcomes as the central pillar in an aligned teaching system, but our students see otherwise: 'From our students' point of view, assessment always defines the actual curriculum' (Ramsden 1992: 187). Students learn what they think they will be tested on. This is *backwash*, a term coined by Lewis Elton (1987: 92), to refer to the effects assessment has on student learning. Assessment determines what and how students learn more than the curriculum does.

Backwash is usually seen negatively, as in 'teaching to the test' (Crooks 1988; Frederiksen and Collins 1989). Recall the 'forms of understanding' that Entwistle and Entwistle's (1997) students constructed to meet presumed assessment requirements (see p. 85). Negative backwash always occurs in an exam-dominated system. Strategy becomes more important than substance. Some teachers deliberately teach exam-taking strategies, such as telling students to attempt all questions even if they don't finish any because they gain more marks than they would by thinking deeply over a question and providing a well-argued answer. Students go through previous papers, best-guessing what questions they will encounter and then rote learning answers to them. This sort of backwash leads inevitably to surface learning. Yet it is inevitable that students learn for the sort of assessments they expect; students would be foolish if they didn't. So, what do we do about it?

Backwash can work positively by encouraging appropriate learning when the assessment is aligned to what students should be learning (Figure 10.2).

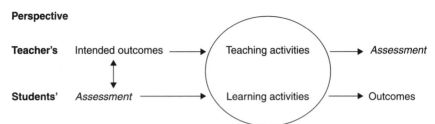

Figure 10.2 Teacher's and student's perspectives on assessment

From the teacher's perspective, summative assessment is at the end of the teaching–learning sequence of events, but from the student's perspective the assessment is at the beginning. However, if the intended outcomes are embedded in the assessment, as indicated by the downward arrow, the teaching activities of the teacher and the learning activities of the student are both aligned towards achieving the same goal. In preparing for the assessments, students will be learning the intended outcomes.

It sounds easy, but there is a long tradition of thinking about assessment, and some time-honoured assessment practices, that complicate matters. In this chapter, we clarify some of the conceptual issues involved; in the next, we deal with designing and grading assessment tasks for declarative knowledge and, in the chapter after that, designing and grading assessment tasks for functioning knowledge.

Measurement model of assessment

Two quite different models of assessment underlie current thinking and practice: the *measurement* model and the *standards* model (Taylor 1994). Understanding the difference between the two models is basic to effective assessment.

In the Chinese Han Dynasty, established in 206 BC, the purpose of education was selective. Students were required to master a huge classical curriculum, in order to put into effect Confucius's belief that 'those who excel in their study should become officials' (quoted in Zeng 1999: 21). The winners, however lowly their background, were motivated by a rich prize: a lifetime of wealth and prestige. The idea was to select the best individuals in terms of stable characteristics: 'not only intelligence, but also character, determination, and the will to succeed' (Zeng 1999: iv).

Twenty-three centuries later, psychologists in the nineteenth century also became interested in sorting people out on certain stable characteristics. Sir Francis Galton found that physical and mental differences such as height, weight and performance on various mental tests, which he called 'traits', were distributed in 'an unsuspected and most beautiful form of regularity' (Galton 1889: 66). He was of course referring to the normal curve, a distribution that occurs inter alia as a result of the extent of the polygenetic inheritance of such traits. Galton's assumptions, not only about statistical techniques, but also about the inheritance of ability and of educability, were built into the burgeoning industry of mental testing in the early part of the twentieth century.

Educability was assumed to be about how bright people were, and, back to the Han Dynasty, education was seen as a device for sorting people out, usually the brightest, but sometimes to sort out those who weren't educable in normal schools. It was in fact for this last reason that one hundred years ago Alfred Binet designed one of the first intelligence tests. But Galton's influence is even today far-reaching. So-called 'parametric' statistical procedures, such as correlation and factor analysis, which are used for constructing educational tests and establishing their reliability and validity, are based on Galton's work on individual differences and the normal curve. Taylor (1994) refers to this individual differences model as 'the measurement model' of educational assessment.

The measurement model was originally adapted by psychologists to measure stable traits and abilities along a graduated scale, so that individuals could be compared, either against each other or against population norms. This is fine for research, or for diagnosis when dealing with individuals – for example to say how atypical a person is on reading ability – but the model was hijacked and applied to assessing *educational* outcomes in the form of norm-referenced assessment (NRA).

In NRA, results of assessment are reported in terms of comparisons between students. The rank order is the simplest example, which tells who performs better than who, but there are sophisticated versions of NRA, such as grading on the curve, which we discuss later.

For now, let us examine some of the assumptions on which the measurement model is based when it is applied to assessing classroom learning.

Some assumptions of the measurement model

(*Note*: Beware the following subheadings. All are either wrong or misleading.)

Knowledge can be quantified

Measurement requires that the learning outcomes of individual students are quantified as scores along a single dimension or continuum so that individuals may be compared with each other. In practice, this means that learning is evaluated according to *how much* material has been learned correctly. Good learners know more than poor learners. The Level 1 view of teaching makes essentially quantitative assumptions, as we noted in Chapter 2: teaching involves transmitting the main points, assessment involves marking students on their ability to report them back accurately. The uni- and multi-structural levels of the SOLO taxonomy are quantitative, where learning is a matter of finding out more and more about a topic. But if you assess using only quantitative techniques, what happens to the higher levels of the SOLO taxonomy, to those of our ILOs that address critical analysis or hypothesizing?

Percentages are a universal currency

One of the commonest forms of quantification is the percentage, derived either as the ratio of number correct to maximum possible multiplied by 100, or as sets of ratings the maxima of which total 100. When this transformation is carried out, it is assumed that percentages are a universal currency, equivalent across subject areas and across students, so that different students' performances in different subjects can be summed, averaged and directly compared. This is completely unsustainable, yet that doesn't stop university senates having long and earnest debates about one faculty using 75% as the cut-off for an A grade and another using 70% as the cut-off: 'We must level the playing field across faculties! It's not fair if it's easier to get an A in arts than it is in science!' Such debates are silly: they assume that you can extract certainty from the unknowable. There is simply no way of knowing if 75% in physics is the 'same standard' as 75% in history; or even if a student's result of 75% in Psychology 201 this year represents an improvement over 70% the same student obtained in Psychology 101 the previous year.

Educational tests should be designed to clearly separate the high and low scorers

Measurement experts used to maintain that a good attainment test yields 'a good spread', following the bell curve (back to Galton). However, grades follow the bell curve only if two conditions apply: that ability is normally distributed, and that ability is the sole determinant of academic attainment. But the ability of our students is not likely to be normally distributed because university students are not randomly selected – not quite yet, anyway. And neither is ability the sole determinant of students' learning outcomes. Other factors are called 'teaching' and 'learning'. As argued in Chapter 1, good teaching narrows the initial gap between Robert and Susan therefore producing a *smaller* spread of final grades than that predicted by the initial spread of ability. The distribution of results after good teaching should not be bell shaped but skewed, with high scores more frequent than low scores. At university level there is therefore every reason *not* to expect a bell curve distribution of assessment results in our classes. Forcing assessment results to follow the curve actually prevents us from seeing how students are really performing.

Quantitative approaches to assessment are scientific, precise and objective

Numbers mislead. The measurement model yields an extended continuous scale that invites us to make minute distinctions between students, but we have to be careful. The error of measurement in our usual class sizes is bound to be rather more than one percentage point. Worse, the way we use the scales prevents them from being equal interval scales, that is, where the difference between any two adjacent numbers is the same as that of any other two. This is an *essential* property if we are to average and accumulate marks. The difference between 73 and 74, say, must be the same as the difference between 79 and 80, if marks are to be added or averaged. But the difference between 79 and 80 often becomes zero if first class honours is awarded to a dissertation of 79 marks when the cut-off is 80 (see Box 10.3, pp. 211–12). When teachers and boards of examiners are faced with the borderline case, it is commonly argued that as the scale is not accurate to one mark, 'we'll give the student the benefit of the doubt.' This, however, makes our scale elastic, distinctly more rubbery at some points along the scale than at others.

Do such decisions show how human we are or how sloppy? We are both and neither. We are being wonderfully inappropriate, like cooking dinner in the chemistry lab. The precision of the parametric measurement model is just as out of place in the classroom as is weighing sugar in milligrams. It is worse, actually, because the procedure of quantifying qualitative data, such as shifts in students' understandings, requires arbitrary judgements as to what is a 'unit', what is 'worth' one mark, what is worth five or however many marks. These judgements are not only subjective; they often do not even have an explicit and examinable rationale, beyond a vague norm referencing: 'I am marking out of ten; this is the best so it should get ten but I'll give it nine because no answer can be perfect. This answer is average so that makes it five marks.' What the *criteria* are that allow the judgement that this answer is 'best' and that one is 'average' may not be examined.

What happens, then, is that a series of independent minor subjective judgements – a mark for this, a mark for that – accumulate. The big decision – pass or fail?, first class or upper second? – is made on the aggregate of numbers, which includes the aggregate of error in all those minor judgements. That big decision should be made, not on the accumulation of unknowably flawed minor judgements, but on a reasoned and publicly sustainable judgement about the performance itself. This requires a holistic judgement made on publicly stated criteria.

The application of a precise, scientific model, derived from the psychology of individual differences, to an area where it does not apply cannot be scientific.

University education is selective

Comparing students with each other assumes that universities are a selective device to find the intellectuals in the population, as in Han Dynasty China, or that the purpose of the undergraduate years is to weed out the 'pass' level students from the potential postgraduate research students.

The only place for assessing students selectively in the university context is for entry to university or to graduate school. At entry, a convenient estimate of scholastic ability is obtained by summing a student's best three, or best five, HSC or A level subjects, with or without adjustments for second attempt.

What you get is a measure of scholastic ability, which is robust enough to allow direct comparisons between students in different subject areas. It is rough, but it works over large numbers. Once students have been selected, however, the aim of undergraduate teaching is to get students to learn what is in the curriculum, an enterprise in which the measurement model has no place.

But, you may well ask, shouldn't the entry into university, and especially into graduate school, be based on whether the students are able to meet the criteria or standards necessary for doing graduate work? Indeed so; and you don't answer that question by comparing students with one another. Comparing students only arises if there are more applicants than places but you don't have to norm-reference the whole procedure to solve that problem.

The above assumptions, derived from the measurement model, give rise to some common practices.

Grading on the curve

After ranking, a common form of norm-referenced assessment is 'grading on the curve'. The top 10% of the class, say, are awarded 'high distinction', the next 15% 'distinction', the next 25% 'credit' and 45% 'pass'. The results will appear to be stable from year to year and from department to department. If there is a query from the odd student about the grade awarded, it is easy to point to an unarguable figure: all objective, very precise. 'You didn't earn enough marks to beat the others. They were too good for you. Sorry.'

The very term 'high distinction' is itself comparative, applicable only to that blessed few who are highly distinguished. This puts a semantic brake on the number of HDs awarded. Even if one-third of the class met the criteria set for obtaining a high distinction, it would be seen by colleagues on the board of examiners, with the bell curve tolling in their heads, as a contemptible fall in standards, not, as it should be, a cause for congratulation. Rather than calling the highest grade a 'high distinction', the neutral term 'A' makes it easier to accept that a high proportion of students could reach that high standard.

Many people, teachers, administrators, and even students, feel it 'fitting' that a few should do extremely well, most should do middling well and a few do poorly, some failing. This feeling comes straight from the assumptions that ability is the only factor that determines learning outcomes and that ability is normally distributed. Both assumptions are untenable, as we have seen.

Unfortunately, grading on the curve is so easy. All you need is a test that will rank order the students – a quick and dirty multiple-choice question-naire will do – and then you simply award an A to the first 10%, B to the next 25%, or whatever has been decided, and so on. The actual quality of the students' performance is irrelevant.

Grading on the curve also appeals to administrators, because it conveys the impression that standards over all departments are 'right', not too slack, not too stringent, so that a few do really well, most middling and a few poorly: we have got it *right*, year after year. But that result is an artefact: the distribution has been defined that way, whatever the actual standards reached in any given year or department.

Grading on the curve precludes aligned teaching and criterion-referenced assessment. It is a procedure that cannot be justified on educational grounds.

Marking

Marking is an assessment procedure that comes directly from quantitative assumptions and is so widespread as to be universal. It is, however, a procedure that needs to be examined closely. By 'marking' we mean quantifying learning performances, either by transforming them into units (a word, an idea, a point), or by allocating ratings or 'marks' on a subjective (if not arbitrary) basis. For marking to be acceptable, we have seen that one mark must be 'worth' the same as any other, so that they can be added and averaged and a grade is awarded on the number of marks accumulated. Two most peculiar phenomena are associated with marking:

1 It does not matter *what* items are correct, as long as there are enough of them.
2 Half the total number of marks available is almost universally accepted as the pass mark.

Multiple-choice tests enact these assumptions exactly. Learning is represented as the total of all items correct. Students quickly see that the score is the important thing, not how it is comprised, and that the ideas contained in any one item are of the same value as in any other item. The strategy is to focus on the easy or trivial items; and of the alternatives you don't know, tick the ones that seem vaguely familiar. You'll almost certainly get more than half correct – and by defintion you'll pass.

The essay format, technically open ended, does not preclude quantitative means of assessment. When multiple markers use marking schemes, they give a mark or two as each 'correct' or 'acceptable' point is made, possibly with bonus points for argument or style. This too sends misleading messages to students about the structure of knowledge and how to exploit its assessment. A good example is the strategy in timed examinations of attempting all questions and finishing none. The reasoning is that the law of diminishing returns applies: the time spent on the first half of an essay nets more marks than the same time spent on the second half. The more facts the more marks, never mind the structure they make. But students don't learn 'marks', they learn such things as structures, concepts, theories, narratives, skills, performances of understanding. These are what should be assessed, not arbitrary quantifications of them. It is like examining architects on the number of bricks their designs use, never mind the structure, the function or the aesthetic appeal of the building itself.

Assessment separated from teaching

In the measurement model, assessment is a standalone activity, unrelated to teaching as such. Accordingly, it attracts its own context and culture. One such feature is the need for standardized conditions including the same assessment tasks for all, a necessary condition when students are to be compared with each other. Guaranteeing standardized procedures leads to a Theory X, bureaucratic assessment climate, which, as we shall see, in turn prescribes decontextualized assessment tasks, which most frequently address only the lower order ILOs.

In universities that work in this way, teaching occupies the greater part of the academic year, assessment a frantic couple of weeks at the end. Both the present writers can recall, now with shame, not even thinking about the final examination until the papers were due to be sent to the central examinations section. You teach as it comes, you set an examination when you are asked to, the examination centre invigilates it for you, you allocate the marks.

Alignment doesn't come into it.

Backwash from the measurement model

Measurement model procedures send unfortunate messages to students:

- *The trees are more important than the wood.* Maximizing marks is the important thing, not seeing the overall structure of what is being learned. Put another way, the measurement model encourages multistructural, not relational or extended abstract thinking.
- *Verbatim responses will gain marks.* Although a verbatim replay of a unit in the text or in the lecture may not be very noble, it has to be given some credit when using a multistructural marking scheme, given that cheating has been ruled out. This happens even when the teacher has warned the class that verbatim responses will be penalized (Biggs 1973, regrettably).
- *Success or failure is due to factors that are beyond the student's control.* An individual's result under norm-referenced assessment depends on the competition, who is more able than who. Thus, in the event of a poor result, the student can either blame bad luck or, more damagingly, come to the conclusion that he or she is simply not as able as the other students. Students can't do anything about luck or ability, so why bother?

The case against the measurement model is pretty convincing, so why do its procedures remain? Box 10.1 suggests some answers.

Box 10.1 Why measurement model procedures remain

1 *Tradition, habit:* why question what has worked well in the past, especially when administrative structures and procedures make change difficult?

2 *Bureaucratic convenience*

- Dealing with numbers gives the illusion of precision. Any appeal or disagreement is over trivial issues. Let the numbers make the big decisions.
- Grading on the curve gives the illusion of consistent standards, no egregious departments or results.
- The language of percentages is generally understood (another illusion).
- Given the tight security of exams, avoidance of plagiarism can be assured.
- Combining results from different departments needs a common framework: the percentage and normalized scores (both illusions).

3 *Teaching convenience*

- You teach, the exam questions can be left until well into the semester, exams section will see to the details. It is flexible on coverage, what questions you set.
- You can easily average and combine marks across tasks and across courses.
- You can use marks for disciplinary purposes (deduct for late submission).
- It's easy to argue with students on the basis of numbers in case of dispute.

4 *Genuine belief in the measurement model:* my job *is* to sort the sheep from the goats.

Let us now turn to the alternative, the standards model.

Standards model of assessment

The standards model of assessment is designed to assess changes in performance as a result of learning, for the purpose of seeing what, and how well, something has been learned. Such assessment is criterion-referenced (CRA), that is, the results of assessment are reported in terms of how well an individual meets the criteria of learning that have been set. This model is the relevant one for assessment at university (Taylor 1994). The point is not to identify *students* in terms of some characteristic, but to identify *performances* that tell us what has been learned, and how well. Unlike in norm-referenced assessment, one student's result is quite independent of any other student's.

In 1918, the educational psychologist R.L. Thorndike made it very clear that criterion-referenced assessment was most appropriate for educational purposes, and predicted that CRA would displace NRA from public schooling (Airasian and Madaus 1972). Thorndike was right about the first point, but, unfortunately, his prediction was wrong. The idea still lurks that education *is* a selective exercise, and that norm-referenced assessment is the way to go. But even where this idea is not explicit, the procedures of constructing and administering tests, establishing reliability and validity and interpreting and reporting test scores are based on parametric statistics. The biological assumptions of polygenetic inheritance, which produce the normal curve, are assumed to be appropriate for educational assessment. They are not. As already argued, for purposes of classroom assessment such statistics as the correlation and the usual tests of reliability and validity, which assume that test scores are normally distributed, are entirely inappropriate. Reliability and validity of assessments are important, but they have entirely different meanings in the standards model, as we explain below.

Outside educational institutions, the standards model is assumed whenever anyone teaches anyone else anything at all. The teacher has a standard, an intended outcome of their teaching, which the learner is to learn satisfactorily. Parents intend their children to learn to dress themselves to a given standard of acceptability, swimming instructors have standards they want their learners to achieve. Parents don't lecture a toddler on shoe tying, and give a multiple-choice test at the end to see if their child ties her shoes better than the kid next door. The parent's intended learning outcome, the teaching/learning activity and the assessment are all the same: it is tying a shoe. In the case of driving instruction it is driving a car. The alignment is perfect. Constructively aligned teaching and learning places this approach back into the institution.

The logic is stunningly obvious: say what you want students to be able to do, teach them to do it and then see if they can, in fact, do it. There is a corollary: if they cannot do it, try again until they can. This principle is used in 'mastery learning' (Bloom et al. 1971) and the Keller Plan, a mastery model for universities (Keller 1968). Students are allowed as many tries at the assessment as they need – within reason – in order to pass the preset standard. Some students pass in short order, others take longer. The main objections to mastery-learning models were not to the principle, but to the fact that the preset criteria were defined quantitatively, mainly because quantitative criteria are easy to define. In one study with high school biology students, the Roberts who focused on memorizing detail performed well in such a mastery-learning approach, but not the Susans who were bored stiff (Lai and Biggs 1994).

Such objections do not apply when the standards are defined *qualitatively*. Qualitative assessment does not directly address the question of *how much* the student knows, but *how well*. This requires an explicit classification of learning quality that needs to be derived for each topic or skill taught. The SOLO taxonomy is a general model of learning quality that can be adapted to suit particular content (see Chapter 5).

Let us now look at the assumptions needed to make the standards model of assessment work.

Some assumptions of the standards model

We can set standards (criteria) as intended learning outcomes of our teaching

Yes we can, as outlined in Chapter 7. If the intended learning outcomes are written appropriately, the job of the assessment is to enable us to state how well they have been met, the 'how well' being expressed not in 'marks' but in a hierarchy of levels, such as letter grades from 'A' to 'D', or as high distinction through credit to conditional pass, or whatever system of grading is used. Deciding at the level of a particular student performance is greatly facilitated by using explicit criteria or rubrics (examples on p. 240 – Table 11.1, p. 242 – Table 11.3, p. 264 – Table 12.2). These rubrics may address the task, or the intended learning outcome.

Different performances can reflect the same standards

While standardized conditions are required when individuals are to be compared to each other, when we are seeking to find the optimum performance of individuals, the more standardized the conditions the less valid the test is likely to be for any given individual. Individuals learn and perform optimally in different conditions and with different formats of assessment. Some work better under pressure, others need more time. As in professional work itself, there are often many ways of achieving a satisfactory outcome. Individual students demonstrate their best work in different ways; assessment tasks such as portfolios allow for that.

Teachers can judge performances against the criteria

This is critical when using the standards model but it is skirted when using the measurement model. In the latter, teachers need to answer the following question: 'How many marks do I give this section?' and in the former: 'How well does this performance as a whole meet the criteria for awarding an A (or whatever)?' In order to make these holistic judgements teachers need to know what is poor quality performance, what is good quality, and why.

Constructive alignment operates on these same assumptions and addresses how they may work in practice.

Backwash from the standards model

The backwash from the standards model is quite different from that of the measurement model.

- *The wood is more important than the trees.* The students have to focus on learning and performing the whole task, not pieces of it, and they are assessed on their understanding the whole.
- *Students will readily see the relevance of the assessment tasks because they authentically represent what they are intended to learn.*
- *Students should be quite clear about what they are expected to be able to do and about the grading criteria for different levels of performance.* This knowledge provides a signpost, encouraging students to reflect on the learning progress and to be metacognitive about improving their performance.
- *Success or failure is due to factors that are relatively controllable by students, rather than on luck or the ability of others.* 'Here is what I am supposed to have achieved, I didn't achieve it, so what went wrong?' The answer to that could be: 'I didn't put in enough effort', or 'I didn't know how to do it.' Both attributions can lead to self-management. 'I am dumb' becomes the attribution of last resort.

Norm- and criterion-referenced assessment: let's get it straight

Differences between NRA and CRA

Because many NRA practices in assessing students are so common, despite the educational logic of CRA, we should be quite clear about the differences between NRA and CRA. To recap briefly:

1 In NRA, the results are expressed in terms of comparisons between students after teaching is over. CRA results are expressed in terms of how well a given student's performance matches criteria that have been set in advance.
2 NRA makes judgements about *people*, CRA makes judgements about *performance*.

Task 10.2 presents a criterion-referenced test to sort the sheep from the goats (joke).

Task 10.2 NRA or CRA?

A teacher assesses two students in a CRA system and notes that Robert has been awarded a B and Susan an A. On a recheck of the papers, the teacher notes with a shock that Robert's paper *is* as good as Susan's! He is reassessed and given an A too.

Is this reassessment of Robert NRA (comparing students) or CRA (judging on standards)? Why?

_____

_____

_____

The answer is at the end of this chapter.

A summary of the differences between CRA and NRA is captured in Table 10.1, which lists a lexicon of NRA and CRA terms. And the only term common to both is: summative assessment.

Nevertheless, it is easy to blur the two models. Task 10.3 represents a valiant attempt by an arts faculty at one university to move towards the standards model. Previously, a marks system was used to define 'A+', 'A' and 'A–' and so on, and the attempt was made at faculty board to devise a scheme that defined the grading categories, avoiding marks. The resulting scheme was issued to all teachers in the faculty.

Table 10.1 Two lexicons

Norm-referenced assessment

Mark, percentage, decile, rank order, decontextualized assessment, standardization, 'fairness', quantitative, average, grade-point average, normal/bell curve, normal distribution, grading on the curve, a good spread of scores, parametric statistics, test–retest reliability, internal consistency, discrimination, selection, competition, high flier, ability, summative assessment.*

Criterion-referenced assessment

Assess, authentic/performance assessment, contextualized, standards, formative, assessment criteria, individualization, optimal performance, student-centred, qualitative, grading categories, ILOs, alignment, judgement, distribution-free, non-parametric statistics, effort, skill, learning, competence, expertise, mastery, summative assessment.*

* The one word in common!

Task 10.3 Faculty Office suggests how final grades should be determined

The following guidelines were issued to all staff in the faculty. They were to use these in arriving at their final grade distributions:

A (A+, A, A−)	Excellence, up to 10% of students. The student must show evidence of original thought as well as having a secure grasp of the topic from background reading and analysis.
B (B+, B, B−)	Good to very good result, achieved by next 30% of students who are critical and analytical but not necessarily original in their thinking and who have a secure grasp of the topic from background reading and analysis. Occasionally, a student who shows originality but is less secure might achieve this result.
C (C+, C, C−)	Satisfactory to reasonably good result. The students have shown a reasonably secure grasp of the subject but probably most of their information is derivative with rather little evidence of critical thinking. Most students will fall into this category.
D	Minimally acceptable. The students have put in effort but work is marred by some misunderstandings, but not so serious that the student should fail. Students falling into this category, and outright failures, would not normally comprise more than about 10%.

Source: Faculty of Arts Handbook, the University of . . .

What is the problem here? _____

_____

_____

_____

You work out what the problem is. Then turn to Box 10.2 (but no peeking!) (p. 211).

A double problem

Despite the prevailing norm-referenced cast of mind at undergraduate level, the logic of criterion-referenced assessment is generally seen in assessing theses and dissertations. We expect a dissertation to display certain characteristics: coverage of the literature, definition of a clear and original research question, mastery of research methods, and so on. The categories of honours (first class, upper second, lower second) originally suggested qualities that students' work should manifest: a first was qualitatively *different* from an upper second, it was not simply that the first got more sums right. Today, this

---

Box 10.2 The problem in Task 10.3

The intention is to assess according to quality, but the thinking is still measurement model. Where there is a conflict, it seems that the NRA guidelines would be expected to prevail. For instance, if 30% of students 'showed evidence of original thought as well as having a secure grasp, etc.' that would be seen in this scheme to be anomalous, but as teachers we should be happy if this is what we found. Likewise, we should be disappointed, if not ashamed, that most students displayed 'derivative information' (C): it looks like they hadn't been taught properly, but here we are told that that is what we should expect. What is wrong here is that the definitions of learning outcome appear to be based on expected distributions of ability. Major departures from that distribution suggest either that there is something wrong with our teaching or that we are too soft in assessing.

---

approach might be in jeopardy, as these categories seem increasingly to be defined in terms of ranges of marks, which is unfortunate. In Box 10.3 we see a doubly unfortunate instance: defining the level of honours in terms of marks, and allowing non-academic factors to influence the judgement of academic quality.

Box 10.3 How not to 'mark' a dissertation

A student's postgraduate thesis, carried out at an Australian university, was submitted late, and given a mark of 76. However, during an oral examination, in which the student left the room in tears, one examiner persuaded the other two examiners that because of 'supervisory difficulties', the thesis be upgraded to 79, which meant a classification of second class honours for the degree. The student then raised other issues, including sexual harassment and claimed her thesis was worthy of first class honours. An internal enquiry suggested that 79 be converted to 80, so the dissertation was now awarded first class honours. But the case was then referred to the State Deputy Ombudsman, who advised that the 'real' mark should have been 73, when readjusted for lateness and the bonuses for stress.

A 'real' mark is surely that which reflects the genuine worth of the work done, but here we have a thesis variously marked at 73, 76, 79 and 80,

---

ranging from second to first class honours. The variation is due not so much to differences in staff opinion on the intrinsic academic worth of the thesis, as to differences in opinion on non-academic matters – lateness, stress, supervisory difficulties and sexual harassment – which were factored in arbitrarily and after the event. The public, employers, other universities – not to mention the poor student – would simply have no idea whether the thesis demonstrated those qualities of flair and originality that are associated with first class honours or of the less dazzling but high competence that is associated with good second class honours. It is ironic that a lay person, the deputy ombudsman, seems to have been the one who was least swayed by non-academic issues.

Source: 'From a flood of tears to scandal', *The Australian*, 26 January 2001, p. 4

Had the standards model of assessment been used, this double problem could not have occurred. The ILOs would refer to academic qualities only, not sexual harassment, lateness or anything else, and the assessment would be aligned to those ILOs. There are other and more appropriate ways of dealing with the non-academic issues than by adjusting final grades.

Some important concepts in assessment

Authentic and performance assessment

In assessing functioning knowledge in particular, the assessment tasks need to represent the knowledge to be learned in a way that is authentic to real life. Verbal retelling is not often authentic; for example, we do not teach psychology or any other subject just so that students can tell us in their own words what we have told them. We need some sort of 'performance of understanding' (see pp. 84–6) that reflects the kind of understanding that requires an *active demonstration* of the knowledge in question, as opposed to talking or writing about it. This is referred to as 'authentic assessment' (Wiggins 1989; Torrance 1994). The term 'authentic' assessment may imply that all other forms of assessment are inauthentic, so many prefer the term 'performance assessment' (Moss 1992). It reminds us of what we already know in aligned teaching, that the assessment task should require students to do more than just tell us what they know – unless, of course, declarative knowledge is all that we require in this instance.

When aligning the assessment tasks to different ILOs, particularly those addressing functioning knowledge, a variety of assessment tasks will be used. Hernandez (2007) taught a class for writing in Spanish as a second language and used a range of aligned tasks, which included individual group and paired writing tasks, a learning journal, a portfolio and an exam (but only because he had to). Students reported that these tasks not only resulted in increased writing competence but also self-efficacy, self-regulation and lifelong learning skills. This is an excellent example of the backwash from the assessment tasks when the latter are also learning activities.

Decontextualized assessment

Authentic or performance assessment raises the issue of contextualized as opposed to decontextualized assessment tasks.

1 Performance assessments include the practicum and case-based and work-based assessment, which are suitable for assessing functioning knowledge in its appropriate context.
2 Decontextualized assessments include written exams and term papers, which are suitable for assessing declarative knowledge, and do not necessarily have a direct connection to a real-life context.

While both contextualized and decontextualized learning and assessment each have their place, in practice decontextualized assessment has been overemphasized compared to the place declarative knowledge has in the curriculum. We need to assess both, as appropriate. A common mistake is to assess only the lead-in declarative knowledge, not the functioning knowledge that emerges from it.

Holistic and analytic assessment

Analytic marking of essays or assignments is a common practice. The essay is reduced to independent components, such as content, style, referencing, argument, originality, format, and so on, each of which is rated on a separate scale. The final performance is then assessed as the sum of the separate ratings. This is very helpful as *formative* assessment (Lejk and Wyvill 2001a); it gives students feedback on how well they are doing on each important aspect of the essay, but the *value* of the essay is how well it makes the case or addresses the question as a whole. The same applies to any task: the final performance, such as treating a patient or making a legal case, makes sense only when seen as a whole.

A valid or authentic assessment must be of the total performance, not just aspects of it. Consider this example from surgery. You want to be sure that the student can carry out a particular operation with high and reliable competence. An analytic assessment would test and mark knowledge of anatomy, anaesthesia, asepsis and the performance skills needed for making clean incisions and then add the marks to see if they reach the requisite 50% (or in this case perhaps 80%). Say a student accrues more than the number of marks needed to pass but removes the wrong part. On the analytic model a pass it must be.

Absurd though this example may seem to be, in an analytic marking scheme some aspects of knowledge are inevitably traded off against others. The solution is not to blur the issue by spreading marks around to fill in the cracks, but to require different levels of understanding or performance, according to the importance of the sub-topic. In this example, the student's knowledge of anatomy was insufficient to allow the correct performance, hence the proper judgement is 'fail'. Assessment of components certainly should be undertaken as formative assessment but, at the end of the road, assessment should address the whole.

In making holistic assessments, the details are not ignored. The question is whether, like the bricks of a building or the characters in a novel, the specifics are tuned to create an overall structure or impact. This requires a *hermeneutic* judgement; that is, understanding the whole in light of the parts. For example, an essay requiring reasoned argument involves making a case, just as a barrister has to make a case that stands or falls on its inherent plausibility. The judge does not judge the barrister's case analytically: uses legal terms correctly (+10 marks), makes eye contacts with jury members (+5 marks), eye contacts jury for too long (−3 marks) and then aggregates, the counsel with most marks winning the suit. The argument, as a whole, has to be judged. It is the whole dissertation that passes, the complete argument that persuades, the comprehensive but concise proposal that gets funded, the applicant's case that wins promotion. That is what holistic assessment is about.

Critics argue that holistic assessment involves a 'subjective' judgement. But as we have seen, awarding marks is a matter of judgement too, a series of mini-judgements, each one small enough to be handled without qualm. The numbers make the big decisions: if they add up to 50 or more, then it is a pass. At no point does one have to consider what is the *nature* of a passing grade as opposed to a fail or of a distinction level of performance as opposed to a credit. One of the major dangers of quantitative assessment schemes is that teachers can shelter under them and avoid the responsibility of making the judgements that really matter: What is a good assessment task? Why is this a good performance? (Moss 1992).

The strategy of reducing a complex issue to isolated segments, rating each independently, and then aggregating to get a final score in order to make decisions, seems peculiar to schools and universities. It is not the way things work in real life. Moss (1994) gives the example of a journal editor judging whether to accept or reject a manuscript on the basis of informed advice from referees. The referees don't give marks, but argue on the intrinsic merits of the paper as a whole and the editor has to incorporate their advice, resolve conflicting advice and make a judgement about what to do with the whole paper: reject it, accept it or send it back for revision. Moss reports that one of her own papers, which argued for a hermeneutic approach to educational assessment, was rejected by the editor of an educational journal on the grounds that a hermeneutic approach was not the model of assessment accepted in the educational fraternity. Moss gleefully pointed out that the editor had just used a hermeneutic approach to arrive at that conclusion. Her paper was accepted.

In order to assess learning outcomes holistically, it is necessary to have a conceptual framework that enables us to see the relationship between the parts and the whole. Teachers, like journal editors, need to develop their own framework, a process in which the SOLO taxonomy can be useful (see pp. 122–4 above; Boulton-Lewis 1998; Hattie and Purdie 1998; Lake 1999).

Convergent and divergent assessment: unintended outcomes

We used the terms 'convergent' and 'divergent' in Chapter 9 in connection with teaching for creativity. A Level 1 view of teaching sees all assessment as convergent: get right what I have just taught you. When essays are marked with a checklist, marks are awarded only for matching the prescribed points, none for other points that might be just as good or better. This is not what assessment should be about. Virtually all university-level subjects require at least some divergent assessment. Setting only closed questions is like trying to shoot fish in murky water. We need to use open-ended assessment tasks that allow for *unintended outcomes*, that follow from such verbs in the ILOs as 'hypothesize', 'create', 'design', 'reflect' and the like.

A student teacher provided the following metaphor for assessment:

> When I stand in front of a class, I don't see stupid or unteachable learners, but boxes of treasures waiting for us to open.
> (an inservice teacher education student, University of Hong Kong)

What 'treasures' students find in their educational experience is something that can surprise, delight and, of course, disappoint too. When we assess using closed questions something like this occurs:

Teacher How many diamonds have you got?
Student I don't have any diamonds.
Teacher Then you fail!
Student But you didn't ask me about my jade.

Students' treasures need not be just in diamonds. If you only ask a limited range of questions, then you may well miss the jade: the treasure that you didn't know existed because you didn't ask. Of course, if the ILOs are expressed only in diamonds that is one thing, but frequently they are not, or ought not to be if they are.

Any rich teaching context is likely to produce learning that is productive and relevant, but unanticipated. The value of many formal activities lies precisely in the surprises they generate, such as field trips, practica or lab sessions, while informal activities bring about unanticipated learning in infinite ways. The student talks to someone, reads a book not on the reading list, watches a television programme, browses the net, does a host of things that sparks a train of thought, a new construction. Such life-wide learning probably will not fit the questions being asked in the exam, but these learnings could be highly relevant to the course ILOs. Most important discoveries came about as a result of paying attention to unintended outcomes. Howard Florey was creative enough to see that the mould that had attacked his samples was not the problem but the solution; it was called penicillin. Here was an unintended but highly desirable outcome.

Assessment practices should allow for such rich learning experiences, but rarely do. The psychology professor of one of the authors included the following in the final exam paper: 'Based on the first-year syllabus, set and answer your own question on a topic not addressed in this paper.' Another was: 'Psychology. Discuss.' You had to answer these questions extremely well. He also used the instruction: 'Answer *about* five questions.' The conservative or insecure students answered exactly five. The more daring answered three, even two. They were, of course, the deep learners. Other ways of assessing unintended outcomes are reflective journals, critical incidents and the portfolio. We look at these in due course.

Some may see a problem of 'fairness' here. Shouldn't all students be assessed on their performance in the same task? This complaint has weight only in a norm-referenced context, when you are comparing students with each other. Then, yes, you have to standardize so that all have a fair crack at however many As or HDs have been allocated. In portfolio assessment, however, the complaint of unfairness is irrelevant. If one student can meet the ILOs by submitting task X, while another student meets the same ILOs with task Y, where is the problem?

> To treat everyone the same when people are so obviously different from each other is the very opposite of fairness.
>
> (Elton 2005, on assessing student learning)

If the ILOs specify creativity and originality and the assessment does not allow for them, now that *is* unfair.

Who takes part in assessing?

Three stages are involved in assessing students' performances:

1 *setting the criteria* for assessing the work;
2 *selecting the evidence* that would be relevant to submit to judgement against those criteria;
3 *making a judgement* about the extent to which these criteria have been met.

Traditionally, the teacher is the agent in all three assessment processes. The teacher decides in advance that the evidence for learning comprises correct answers to a set of questions that again in the teacher's opinion addresses and represents the essential core content of the course and the teacher makes the final judgements on meeting the criteria.

Students can and often should be involved in all three stages (Harris and Bell 1986; Boud 1995). Students can be involved in discussing with the teacher what the criteria might be, which need not be the same for all students, as happens in a learning contract system (p. 170). Students can also be involved in (2), that is, as the ones responsible for selecting the evidence to be put up against the criteria, as happens with assessment by portfolio. Finally, students can be involved in making the summative judgement (3). This can be as self-assessment (SA) or as peer-assessment (PA), and either or both can be used as a teaching/learning activity and as an assessment task. Their judgements may also be included in the final grade. All these possibilities are discussed in due course.

Self- and peer-assessment also provide TLAs that engage crucial and otherwise neglected aspects of student learning:

1 First-hand knowledge of the criteria for good learning: students should be quite clear about what the criteria for good learning are, but when the teacher sets the criteria, selects the evidence and makes the judgement of the student's performance against the criteria, the students may have little idea as to what they should have been doing and where they went wrong. It is too easy for the students just to accept the teacher's judgement and not reflect on their own performance. They should be more actively involved in knowing what the criteria really mean. They should learn how to apply the criteria, to themselves and to others.

2 What is good evidence for meeting the criteria and what is not? Telling students may not engage them. They need to learn what is good evidence by being actively involved in selecting it.

3 Making judgements about whether a performance or product meets the given criteria is vital for effective professional action in any field. Professionals need to make these judgements about their own performance (SA) and that of others (PA). It is the learning experience professionals say is most lacking in their undergraduate education (Boud 1986). Brew (1999) argues that students need to distinguish good from poor information now they are faced with an incredible overload of information from the net: an essential skill in lifelong learning (pp. 176–7). A more general argument along these lines is that conventional assessment disempowers learners, whereas education is about empowering learners and assessment can be made to play an empowering role (Leach et al. 2001).

Reliability and validity

A frequent criticism of qualitative assessment is that it is 'subjective' and 'unreliable'. This is the measurement model talking. Let us rephrase so that the concepts of reliability and validity can be applied to both models of assessment. The questions are:

1 Can we rely on the assessment results – are they reliable?
2 Are they assessing what they should be assessing – are they valid?

Can we rely on the assessment results?

In the measurement model, reliability means:

- *Stability*: a test needs to come up with the same result on different occasions, independently of who was giving and marking it. Thus the procedure of test–retest reliability: give the same test to the same group again and see if you get the same result.
- *Dimensionality*: the test items need to measure the same characteristic, hence the usual measures of reliability: split-half, internal consistency (Cronbach α).
- *Conditions of testing*: each testing occasion needs to be conducted under standardized conditions.

Here reliability is seen as a property of the test. Such tests are conceived, constructed and used within a sophisticated framework of parametric statistics, which requires that certain assumptions be met, for example that the score distributions need to be normal or bell shaped.

However these concepts do not apply to the standards model. Being able to rely on the assessment results in this case involves:

- *Intra-judge reliability:* does the same person make the same judgement about the same performance on two different occasions?
- *Inter-judge reliability:* do different judges make the same judgement about the same performance on the same occasion?

Here reliability is not a property of the test, but of the ability of teachers/judges to make consistent judgements. This requires that they know what their framework of judgement is and how to use it: the criteria need spelling out in what are now known as grading criteria or *rubrics*, which are simply clear criteria of grading standards. We deal with these in Chapters 11 and 12.

Reliability here is not a matter of statistical operations, but of being very clear about what we are doing, what learning outcomes we want, what is to be the evidence for those outcomes and why. In other words, reliable assessments are part and parcel of good teaching.

Do the assessment results assess what they should be assessing?

In the measurement model, the test needs to be validated against some external criterion to show that the trait being measured behaves as it should if it were being measured accurately. Thus, the scores could be correlated with another benchmark test or used as a variable in an experimental intervention, or in predicting an independent outcome.

In the case of the standards model, by way of contrast, validity resides in the *interpretations and uses* to which test scores are put (Messick 1989), that is, in the test's alignment with the total teaching context. For example, if sitting an exam results in students rote-learning model answers, then that is a consequence that invalidates the test. An aligned, or properly criterion-referenced assessment task is valid, a non-aligned one is invalid. The glue that holds the ILOs, the teaching/learning environment, and the assessment tasks and their interpretation together is *judgement*. There is now quite a good deal of agreement about reliability and validity in qualitative assessment (Frederiksen and Collins 1989; Moss 1992, 1994; Shepard 1993; Taylor 1994).

Table 10.2 draws all these points together, contrasting the measurement and standard models.

Task 10.4 is a reflective exercise to help you see where you stand in your thinking about your assessment practice.

Table 10.2 Comparing the measurement and standards models

	Measurement model	*Standards model*
Theory	Quantitative. Classic test theory, assuming scores follow the normal curve	Qualitative. A theory of learning enabling consistent judgements. No assumptions about distributions
Stability	Scores remain stable over testing occasions	Scores after teaching should be higher than before teaching
Dimensionality	The test is unidimensional. All items measure the same construct	Test is multidimensional (unless there is only one ILO). The items address all the course ILOs
Testing conditions	Conditions need to be standard for all learners	Conditions need to be optimal for individual learners
Validity	External: how well the test correlates with outside performances	Internal: how well scores relate to the ILOs and to the target performance domain
Use	Selecting students. Comparing individuals, population norms. Individual diagnosis	Assessing the effectiveness of learning, during and after teaching and learning

Task 10.4 Where does your assessment stand?

Reflect on your assessment practice so far, put a cross on the continuum at a point that best represents what you currently do in assessing your students:

Formative	_____	Summative
Involving your students	_____	All teacher controlled
Using open-ended assessment tasks	_____	Using closed-ended assessment tasks
Authentic tasks	_____	Decontextualized tasks
Criterion-referenced	_____	Norm-referenced
Using grading criteria	_____	Using model answers
Awarding grades for quality	_____	Awarding marks for quantity
Assessing the task as a whole	_____	Assessing individual components of the task

If you were to adopt constructively aligned assessment, what changes would you need to make in your assessment practice?

Task 10.5 Follow-up to Task 10.1

Now take a second look at Task 10.1 (pp. 191–5). Would you make different decisions now?

Answers to Task 10.2 The NRA/CRA problem

CRA. Despite the fact that Susan's and Robert's performances were compared, the purpose of comparing was not to award the grades but to check the consistency of making the judgement. What happened here was that the initial judgement of Robert's performance was inaccurate, very possibly because of a halo effect: 'Ah, here's Robert's little effort. That won't be an A!' It took a direct comparison with Susan's effort to see the mistake. The standards themselves were unaltered.

Summary and conclusions

Formative and summative assessment

The first thing to get right is the reason for assessing. There are two paramount reasons for assessing students: formative, to provide feedback during learning; and summative, to provide an index of how successfully the student has learned when teaching has been completed. Formative assessment is basic to good teaching, and has been addressed in earlier chapters. Our main concern in this chapter is with summative.

Effects of assessment on learning: backwash

The effects of assessment on learning are usually deleterious. This is largely because assessment is treated as a necessary evil, the bad news of teaching and learning, to be conducted at the end of all the good stuff. Students second-guess the assessment and make that their curriculum, and will underestimate requirements if the assessments tasks let them, so they get by with low-level, surface learning strategies. In aligned teaching, to the contrary, the assessment reinforces learning. Assessment is the senior partner in learning and teaching. Get it wrong and the rest collapses. This and following chapters aim to help us get it right.

Measurement model of assessment

The measurement model of educational assessment was hijacked from individual differences psychology, which is concerned with measuring stable characteristics of individuals so that they can be compared with each other or with population norms. However, when this model is applied to assessing educational outcomes, numerous problems arise. Unfortunately, many procedures deriving from the measurement model remain in current practice: grading on the curve so that students have to compete for the higher grades; marking, despite its universality, has implications for the nature of knowledge that are unacceptable; separating assessment from teaching, which ignores alignment and imposes a separate culture of assessment as apart from the culture of teaching and learning. The backwash from the measurement model sends unfortunate messages to students about the nature of knowledge and about what assessment preparation strategies to use and that lead to surface learning.

Standards model of assessment

The standards model of educational assessment defines forms of knowledge to be reached at the end of teaching, expressed as various levels of acceptability in the ILOs and grading system. This framework requires higher levels of judgement on the part of the teacher as to how well the students' performances match the ILOs than does quantitative assessment. The assessment tasks need to be 'authentic' to the ILOs, stipulating a quality of performance that the assessment tasks demand. The backwash from the standards model is summed as assessment for learning, as much as assessment of learning. Having a clear target and the knowledge of the standards expected for different grades encourages students to be more reflective about their learning.

Norm- and criterion-referenced assessment: let's get it straight

Although norm- and criterion-referenced assessment are logically different, there is still room for confusion. The key distinction is whether the criteria or standards for awarding summative grades exist prior to the assessment, or grades are awarded not on the basis of pre-existing standards but on how students compare to each other.

Some important concepts in assessment

Several concepts are important in thinking about and implementing constructive alignment. Authentic assessment directly engages the student with functioning knowledge in its context, decontextualized assessment is more suitable for declarative knowledge. While formative feedback often should be analytic by informing students how well they are managing different aspects of the task, the summative judgement should be of the whole, not the sum of its parts. Open-ended assessment tasks allow for unintended, desirable and divergent outcomes, and students themselves need to be involved in the various stages of assessment, in both peer- and self-assessment.

Reliability and validity

Measurement modelists accuse qualitative assessment methods of being 'subjective' and 'unreliable'. What they fail to recognize is that the concepts of reliability and validity are not the exclusive domains of number crunchers. As the quantitative scaffolding is dismantled, we find that notions as to reliability and validity depend more and more on the teacher's basic professional responsibility, which is to make judgements about the quality of learning.

Further reading

Many of the concepts underlying a theory of assessment are dealt with in the following two chapters, and a general reading list is provided at the end of Chapter 12. Below are some readings that are specific to this chapter:

Dart, B. and Boulton-Lewis, G. (eds) (1998) *Teaching and Learning in Higher Education.* Camberwell: Australian Council for Educational Research.

Moss, P.A. (1994) Can there be validity without reliability?, *Educational Researcher*, 23, 2: 5–12.

Taylor, C. (1994) Assessment for measurement or standards: the peril and promise of large scale assessment reform, *American Educational Research Journal*, 31: 231–62.

Torrance, H. (ed) (1994) *Evaluating Authentic Assessment: Problems and Possibilities in New Approaches to Assessment.* Buckingham: Open University Press.

The Taylor and Moss articles are seminal, outlining the principles of the rethink on assessment, where the criteria that are qualitatively defined are included. Taylor traces the historical and conceptual roots of NRA and CRA, clearly outlining where the confusions in current practice have crept in, while Moss goes into the conceptual issues in terms of assessment theory. Torrance's book contains some commentaries on qualitative assessment. Dart and Boulton-Lewis contains chapters by Boulton-Lewis, Dart, and Hattie and Purdie, which specifically deal with SOLO as a conceptual structure for holistic assessment.

11

Assessing and grading for declarative intended learning outcomes

In this chapter, we discuss some general practical points about designing assessment tasks and grading students' performance, and then we focus on intended learning outcomes relating to declarative knowledge. Assessing declarative knowledge is overwhelmingly by the written essay, under either invigilated or open conditions, and by multiple-choice testing. An important problem in grading the written essay format is its unreliability. We discuss eliminating halo effects and other sources of unreliability and suggest the use of assessment criteria, or rubrics, to use in both the analytic and the holistic assessment of extended prose. The multiple-choice questionnaire (MCQ) has its uses but typically it addresses only low-level outcomes. We look at the ordered-outcome item, which is an objective format that aims to assess high level ILOs. Assessment in large classes raises some challenges but there are better ways of assessing than cramming large numbers of students into examination halls and relying heavily on MCQs.

Designing assessment tasks

We now turn to designing assessment tasks that are to be aligned to the learning outcomes we intend to address. An appropriate assessment task (AT) should tell us how well a given student has achieved the ILO(s) it is meant to address and/or how well the task itself has been performed. Assessment tasks should not sidetrack students into adopting low-level strategies such as memorizing, question spotting and other dodges. The backwash must, in other words, be positive, not negative. It will be positive if alignment is achieved because then, as we saw in the previous chapter, the assessment tasks require students to perform what the ILOs specify as intended for them to learn.

In designing appropriate assessment, the following need to be taken into account:

1 The criteria for the different grades, assigned to describe how well the assessment tasks have been performed, should be clearly outlined as rubrics that the students fully understand. These rubrics act as signposts to students for preparing for assessment (Norton 2004): for examples of rubrics, see Tables 11.1 (p. 240) and 11.3 (p. 242). After assessment, students can compare their actual grade with the criteria for higher grades and thus reflect on why their actual grade may not be as high as they would have liked. They wouldn't have the faintest idea of what was good or what was poor about their performance if they received a grade such as 'You were in the 60–70% range.'

2 One assessment task may address several ILOs. One AT per ILO can easily lead to an overload of assessment for the student. *Synoptic* assessment is where a large task addresses several ILOs and may even be used to assess ILOs in different courses, as in a research project or a capstone project. We deal with these modes of assessment in the next chapter. A final exam is traditionally used synoptically, but this is likely to be effective only when the ILOs are all declarative and all the students are Susans.

3 By the same token, one ILO may be addressed by more than one assessment task. For example, an assignment and a reflective diary may each have something to say about an ILO 'reflect and improve'. It helps to see each AT as a *source of evidence* of a student's achievement of any ILO. An ILO can be addressed by one source of evidence or several, just as one assessment task may provide evidence relating to more than one ILO.

4 In selecting assessment tasks, the time spent by students performing them and by staff assessing students' performances, should reflect the relative importance of the ILOs. This is frequently breached when there are compulsory final examinations ('70% of the final grade must be by final examination'). In this case, most of the assessment is likely to be focusing on ILOs addressing only declarative knowledge ('describe', 'explain', 'argue'). Other and possibly more important ILOs, which can't be easily assessed in the exam situation ('apply', 'design', for example), are assessed by tasks worth only 30% of the final grade.

5 An important practical point is that the assessment tasks have to be *manageable*, both by students in terms of both time and resources in performing them and by staff in assessing students' performances. For example, a portfolio would be impracticable in a large class.

Now for a major question: are we assessing and grading the *task* or the *intended learning outcomes*? In outcomes-based teaching and learning we should be assessing the ILOs, but the near universal practice is that we assess the task: the exam paper, the assignment, the lab report. Students for their part want to know how well they did in the exam, in their assignment, in their lab report.

In this chapter, then, we deal with assessing and grading the task, with our main focus on declarative knowledge, and return later to the question of assessing the ILO.

Assessing and grading using extended prose

How important is the format of the assessment task?

Typical declarative ILOs would include: identify, describe, list, explain, argue, compare and contrast. In these, the student is required orally or in writing to say something *about* a topic or body of knowledge, not necessarily to *do* anything with that topic. There are two main formats of assessment addressing these ILOs: questions that probe the student's knowledge base, to which students write extended prose in answer; and objective format, usually in the form of the MCQ.

How important is the format of assessment? In a word: very. Different formats produce typical forms of backwash. In preparing for exams, students use memorization-related activities and for assignments, application-related activities (Tang 1991). Tang found that an assignment required deep learning from the students with respect to one topic; the exam required acquaintance with a range of topics, which allowed a high degree of surface learning. The teachers concerned realized the assignment better addressed their ILOs, but only with respect to one topic. They accordingly adopted a policy to use both: short answer exams to ensure coverage, the assignment to ensure depth.

As for MCQs, students see them as requiring low cognitive level processes and so they avoid a deep approach when studying for them, while they see essays as requiring higher level processes and so use them (Scouller 1996, 1998). Some students were actually angry at being assessed by MCQs, feeling they did not do justice to their learning (see Box 11.1).

Box 11.1 Two examples of students' views on multiple-choice tests

I preferred MCQ . . . It was just a matter of learning facts . . . and no real analysis or critique was required, which I find tedious if I am not wrapped in the topic. I also dislike structuring and writing and would prefer to have the answer to a question there in front of me somewhere.

A multiple choice exam tends to examine too briefly a topic or provide overly complex situations which leave a student confused and faced with 'eenie, meenie, minie, mo' situation. It is cheap and, in my opinion, ineffectual in assessing a student's academic abilities in the related subject area.

Source: Scouller (1997)

So, format is important. In some areas such as in the mathematics and the sciences carefully designed MCQ items can assess high level problem solving ILOs, but with that proviso, MCQ items are best avoided. Too readily they address lower order ILOs, calling in verbs such as 'memorize', 'recognize', 'identify', 'match'. Essays have a better potential for assessing higher level understandings of declarative knowledge such as 'explain', 'argue', 'analyse' and 'compare and contrast'.

Let us deal first with what is the most common format for assessing declarative knowledge, essay-type answers to specific questions, first in invigilated situations – the typical exam – and then in open situations, such as the assignment.

Assessment under timed invigilation: the exam

The major reasons for the ubiquity of the standard examination have less to do with assessment theory and more to do with management issues. Because the situation of invigilating students in a timed context effectively minimizes plagiarism, many universities require a percentage at least of the summative assessment leading to a student's final grade to be assessed in this situation (we deal with the question of plagiarism later; pp. 270–3).

Assessment in this context is quite extraordinary when you think about it. It is about the only situation, outside TV quiz shows, when somebody is asked to answer questions to which the person who asked the questions already knows the answers! Nobody is telling anything new to anybody. This is not what good communication is about, which implies that new information is conveyed. Such assessment is hardly in keeping with a graduate outcome requiring communication skills.

However, there is a place for such convergent assessment in order to check the breadth and accuracy of students' knowledge. We can't ask all the questions that would tap the sum total of a student's knowledge, but we can sample areas of it. It is a little like shooting those fish in murky water and concluding that the number of fish you hit is an indication of how many fish are there. That metaphor reminds us that we should also be thinking of complementary formats of assessment that are open to considering evidence that we ourselves had not thought of. For example, portfolio assessment allows students to tell us what they consider to be evidence for their learning in relation to the ILOs and that they would like us to consider.

But apart from the problem of those missed fish, it is very *convenient* to have a time and a place nominated for the final assessment. Teachers, students and administration can work around that: everyone knows where they stand. Further, nobody has an 'unfair advantage': all is standardized (but do you then allow question choice in a formal examination?).

It is sometimes claimed that the time constraint reflects 'the need in life to work swiftly, under pressure and well' (Brown and Knight 1994: 69). However, in real-life situations where functioning knowledge is time stressed – the operating theatre, the bar (in law courts, that is), or the classroom – this point is better accommodated by performance assessment, rather than by pressurizing the assessment of declarative knowledge in the exam room.

Alignment suggests that time constraints be applied only when the target performance is itself time constrained.

Time constraint creates its own backwash. Positively, it creates a target for students to work towards. They are forced to review what they have learned throughout the course, and possibly for the first time see it as a whole: a tendency greatly enhanced if they think the exam will require them to demonstrate how holistic their view of the course is and not just a series of easy-to-predict questions about particular topics. The format can be open ended, so theoretically students can express their own constructions and views, supporting them with evidence and original arguments. The reality, however, is often different.

The more likely backwash of timed exams is negative, with students memorizing specific points to be recalled at speed (Tang 1991). Even so, there are different ways of memorizing: Susan creates a structure first, possibly involving 'knowledge objects' (p. 24), then she memorizes the key access words ('deep memorizing'), while Robert simply memorizes unconnected facts (Tang 1991). So while timed exams encourage memorizing, this is not necessarily *rote* memorizing or surface learning. Whether it is or not depends on the students' typical approaches to learning and on what they expect the exam questions to require.

Open-book examinations remove the premium on memorization of detail, but retain the time constraint. Theoretically, students should be able to think about higher level things than getting the facts down. Baillie and Toohey (1997) moved from a traditional examination in a materials science course to a 'power test' – an open-book exam, with opportunities for collegial interaction – with positive results on students' approaches to learning. Students need, however, to be very well organized and selective about what they bring in, otherwise they waste time tracking down too many sources.

Does the time constraint impede divergent responses? Originality is a temperamental horse, unlikely to gallop under the stopwatch or to flourish in the climate of a stern regimented silence. One needs only to compare the quality of a term assignment with that of an exam response on the same topic to see that difference. In our experience, Susans excepted, exam texts are dull, crabbed and cloned; most students focus on the same content to memorize and use the same examples as given in class or in the text. And isn't it so boring for us to be told over and over what we know already? The assignments of the same students, contrariwise, are often fresh, frequently telling us something we didn't know before, and sometimes even appear to have been written with pleasure.

It is possible for students to display originality in examinations – especially if they can prepare their original answers at leisure. But then they need to know the questions, at least in general outline. You can encourage this high-level off-track preparation by making it known you intend asking open questions ('What is the most important topic you studied in the course this semester? Why?') or by telling the students at the beginning of the semester what the exam questions will be – but then, of course, they have to be complex questions, open to different interpretations and this strategy is open to the criticism that it could encourage plagiarism and memorization of the plagiarized source. Assessing divergent responses cannot be achieved by using a model-answer checklist, because it does not allow for the well-argued surprise.

In short, while the exam can elicit high-level responding from Susan, Robert underperforms in the timed, invigilated setting, especially when he knows that he can get by with memorization. As we shall see in the section on assessing in large classes (pp. 243–9), there are better ways of using that invigilated space than asking for written answers to closed questions. When universities require a proportion of invigilated assessment in the final grade, it is all the more important that alternatives to the closed-answer format are used.

Exams are almost always teacher assessed, but need not be. The questions can be set in consultation with students, while the assessing and awarding of grades can be done by the students themselves and/or their peers. Boud (1986) describes a conventional mid-session examination, where students in an electrical engineering course were, after the examination, provided with a paper of an unnamed fellow student and a detailed model answer and asked to mark it. They then did the same to their own paper, without knowing what marks someone else might have given it. If the self- and peer-assessed marks were within 10%, the self-mark was given. If the discrepancy was greater than 10%, the lecturer remarked the script. Spot checking was needed to discourage collusion ('Let's all agree to mark high!'). Student learning was greatly enhanced, as the students had access to the ideal answer, to their own match to that and also the perspective of someone else on the question – and teacher marking time was slashed by nearly a third.

Assessing and grading extended prose under open conditions

The essay assignment is one of the most common forms of assessment. It enables students to construct their response to a question or issue and to display originality and their ability to make a case or argument. But there are traps for the unwary teacher (Box 11.2).

Box 11.2 A warning from an ancient history essay

Question: In what ways were the reigns of Tutenkhmen and Akhnaton alike and in what ways were they different?

   The student who obtained the highest marks in the class listed the life histories of both pharoahs and was commended by the teacher for her effort and depth of research. But her lists didn't answer the question, which required a compare-and-contrast structure.

Source: Biggs (1987b)

The student who gained top marks hadn't addressed the question. Her teacher had failed to distinguish between 'knowledge telling' and 'reflective writing' (Bereiter and Scardamalia 1987). Knowledge telling is a multistructural strategy that can all too easily mislead those assessing the essay. Students tell all they know about the topic content by listing in a point-by-point form. When marking bottom-up, as is so often done by tutors using a common template for a marking scheme, it is very hard not to award high marks for knowledge telling when in fact the student hasn't properly addressed the question.

Reflective writing, on the other hand, transforms the writer's thinking. The novelist E.M. Forster put it thus: 'How can I know what I think until I see what I say?' The act of writing externalizes thought, making it possible to unleash a learning process. By reflecting on what is written, it can be revised in so many ways, creating something quite new, even to the writer. That is what the best academic writing does.

Reflective writing, not knowledge telling, is what the essay should be about. Tynjala (1998) suggests that writing tasks should require students to transform their knowledge actively, not simply to repeat it. The writing should require students to undertake open-ended activities that make use of existing knowledge and beliefs, that lead them to question and reflect on that knowledge and to theorize about their experiences and to apply theory to practical situations, and/or to solve practical problems or problems of understanding. Tynjala gave students such writing tasks, which they discussed in groups. When compared with students who did not do these tasks, the reflective writers had the same level of knowledge as the other students but were far better than the latter in the *use* to which they could put their thinking.

Assessing the discourse structure of the essay requires a framework within which that structure can be judged. SOLO helps in making that judgement. Listing, describing and narrating are multistructural structures; arguing a case, compare and contrast, causal explanation and interpretation are relational. Inventive students create their own structures, which when they work can make original contributions: these are extended abstract. The facts and details play their role in these structures in like manner to the characters in a play. And the play's the thing. You do not ignore details, but ask of them:

- Do they make a coherent structure (not necessarily the one you had in mind)? If yes, the essay is at least relational.
- Is the structure the writer uses appropriate or not? If yes, then the question has been properly addressed (relational). If no, you will have to decide how far short of satisfactory it is.
- Does the writer's structure open out new ways of looking at the issue? If yes, the essay is extended abstract.

If the answer is consistently 'no' to all of these questions, the essay is multistructural or less and should not be rated highly, no matter how numerous the details. If you want students to 'identify' or 'list', the short answer and

MCQ are more appropriate formats, as they are easier for the student to complete and for the teacher to assess. It may be appropriate to award the grades on this basis: D (bare multistructural), C– to C+ (increasingly better multistructural, hints of relational), B– to B+ (relational), A– to A+ (extended abstract). Each grade is qualitatively different from the next, but within each grade, one can use the '+' and '–' modifiers for a bare C or an excellent C. Table 11.2 (p. 241) can be used to convert the letter grade to a number for collating purposes and for calculating the grade-point average (GPA).

The essay assignment can be a powerful tool for learning as well as an assessment task. If it is not used for the purpose of reflective writing, thus addressing ILOs with higher relational and extended abstract verbs, it is simpler to use a listing format.

Now let us look at the downside of the essay. Many years ago, Starch and Elliott (1912; Starch 1913a, 1913b) originated a devastating series of investigations into the reliability of assessing essays. Marks for the same essay ranged from bare pass to nearly full marks. Sixty years later, Diederich (1974) found things just as bad. Out of the 300 papers he received in one project, 101 received every grade from 1 to 9 on his nine-point marking scale.

The problem was that the judges were not using the same criteria. Diederich isolated four families of criteria:

- *ideas*: originality, relevance, logic;
- *skills*: the mechanics of writing, spelling, punctuation, grammar;
- *organization*: format, presentation, literature review;
- *personal style*: flair.

The judges had disagreed about their relative importance, some applying all the criteria, others applying one or few.

Maximizing stable essay assessment and grading

The horrendous results reported by Starch and Elliott and by Diederich occurred because the criteria were unclear, unrecognized or not agreed on. There should have been some kind of moderation procedure, where teachers need collectively to clarify what they really are looking for when assessing different tasks and use an agreed set of criteria or rubrics. The reliability of their interpretations of the criteria by each may be tested by assessing a sample of the same scripts and repeating this procedure until they reach a high degree of consensus, say of the order of 90% within a range, say, of ± 1 grade. The criteria not only need to be used, the levels of acceptability (A to F) in meeting the criteria need to be defined. In Diederich's criteria, 'ideas', for example, has three subscales: originality, relevance and logic. How do you define an 'A' level of originality, or a 'B' level? Table 11.1 (p. 240) gives an example of a set of rubrics for assessing an assignment on arguing a case.

Halo effects are a common source of unreliability. Regrettable it may be, but we tend to judge the performance of students we like more favourably than those we don't like. Halo effects also occur in the order in which essays are assessed. The first half-dozen scripts tend to set the standard for the next half-dozen, which in turn reset the standard for the next. A moderately good essay following a run of poor ones tends to be assessed higher than it deserves, but if this same essay follows a run of very good ones, it is assessed at a lower level than it deserves (Hales and Tokar 1975).

Halo and other distortions can be greatly minimized by discussion. There is some really strange thinking on this. A common belief is that it is more 'objective' if judges rate students' work without discussing it. In one fine arts department, a panel of teachers independently awarded grades without discussion, the student's final grade being the undiscussed average. The rationale for this bizarre procedure was the postmodern argument that the works of an artist cannot be judged against outside standards. Where this leaves the assessment process itself is a thought to ponder.

Disagreement between external examiners for research dissertations is best resolved by discussion before the higher degrees committee adjudicates, but this is comparatively rare in our experience. Such disagreements are more commonly resolved quantitatively: by counting heads or by hauling in additional examiners until the required majority is obtained. In one university, such conflicts were until recently resolved by a vote in senate. The fact that the great majority of senate members hadn't even seen the thesis aided their detachment, their objectivity unclouded by mere knowledge.

Once the criteria or rubrics for assessment have been decided (see Table 11.1, p. 240, for an argue-a-case assignment), the moderation procedures just mentioned should be implemented, whereby all assessors agree on the interpretation and application of the rubrics.

Sophisticated computer assessment can augment if not entirely replace assessment by humans. Shermis and Burstein (2003) report that newer automated essay scoring programmes scored content and understanding far more successfully than humans, while the quality of the feedback from the essays was much superior. Hattie (2009b) asked teachers and a computer program to score student essays and found the computer scoring to be faster, more detailed, and more reliable and valid.

To sum up, the following precautions in any summative criterion-referenced assessment procedure suggest themselves:

- Before the assessment itself, the wording of the questions should be checked for ambiguity and clarity by a colleague.
- Criteria or rubrics for grading should be clearly established and understood by all parties concerned.
- All assessment should be 'blind', the identity of the student concealed.
- All rechecking should likewise be blind, the original assessment concealed.
- Each question should be assessed *across* students, so that a standard for each question is set. A common practice is to assess all the questions the same student has written in the exam book, then move on to the next

student's book. However, assessing student by student allows more room for halo effects than assessing answer by answer.

- Between questions, the papers should be shuffled to prevent systematic order effects.
- Grade into the full letter grades, A, B, C, and D first, then discriminate more finely into A+, A, A– etc.
- Recheck borderline cases.
- Check out the possibilities of computer scoring.

Objective formats of assessment

The objective test is a closed or convergent format requiring one correct answer. It is said, misleadingly, to relieve the marker of 'subjectivity' in judgement. But 'judgement' won't go away. In objective tests, judgement is shifted from scoring items to choosing items and to designating which alternatives are correct. Objective testing is not more 'scientific' nor is it less prone to error. The potential for error is pushed to the front end, in producing items that can address higher order ILOs, which is difficult and time consuming to do properly – and doing it properly includes pilot testing items. The advantage is that the cost benefits rapidly increase the more students are tested at a time. With machine scoring, it is as easy to test 1020 students as it is to test 20: a seductive option.

There are many forms of the objective test: true–false, MCQ, matching items from two lists and ordered outcome. We consider the MCQ, and its lookalike, but very different, ordered-outcome format.

Multiple-choice questions

The MCQ is widely used. Theoretically, it can assess high-level verbs, but practically it rarely does. As we saw, some students look back in anger at the MCQ for not doing so (see Box 11.1, p. 226).

MCQs usually assess declarative knowledge, often in terms of the least demanding cognitive process, recognition. But probably their worst feature is that MCQs encourage the use of game-playing strategies, by both student and teacher:

Student strategies
1 In a four-alternative MC format, never choose the facetious or obviously jargon-ridden alternatives.
2 By elimination, you can usually reduce to a binary choice, which gives the pig ignorant a 50% chance of being correct.
3 Does one alternative stimulate a faint glow of recognition in an otherwise unrelieved darkness? Go for it.
4 Longer alternatives are often a better bet than the shorter ones.

Teacher strategies

1 Student strategies are discouraged by a guessing penalty: that is, deducting wrong responses from the total score. (Question: Why should this be counterproductive?)
2 The use of facetious alternatives is patronizing if not offensive (I-can-play-games-with-you-but-you-can't-with-me). Not nice.
3 You can reword existing items when you run out of ideas: it also increases reliability (if you want that sort of reliability, see p. 218).

MCQs allow enormous coverage – that 'enemy of understanding', as Gardner (1993) put it. One hundred items can cover a huge range of topics. Exclusive use of the MCQ greatly misleads as to the nature of knowledge, because the method of scoring makes the idea contained in any one item the same value as that in any other item (see Box 11.3). Knowledge itself is nuanced, but MCQs are not.

Box 11.3 What do you remember of Thomas Jefferson?

An MCQ was given to fifth-grade children on the 200th anniversary of the signing of the US Constitution. The only item on the test referring to Thomas Jefferson was: 'Who was the signer of the Constitution who had six children?' A year later, Lohman asked a child in this class what she remembered of Thomas Jefferson. She remembered that he was the one with six children, nothing of his role in the Constitution.

What else did this girl learn? She learned that:

There is no need to separate main ideas from details; all are worth one point. And there is no need to assemble these ideas into a coherent summary or to integrate them with anything else because that is not required.

Source: Lohman (1993: 19)

The message is clear. Get a nodding acquaintance with as many details as you can, but do not be so foolish as to waste your time by attempting to learn anything in depth.

MCQs can be useful as a minor supplement to other forms of assessment and for quick quizzes. Eric Mazur used them as a TLA, publicly displaying the range of responses and getting their students to discuss them (p. 139). Their potential for wide coverage means items can address anything dealt with in class: they are therefore useful in encouraging class attendance.

When used exclusively, however, they send all the wrong signals.

Ordered-outcome items

An ordered-outcome item looks like an item from an MCQ, but instead of opting for the one correct alternative out of the four or so provided, the student is required to attempt all sub-items (Masters 1987). The sub-items are ordered into a hierarchy of complexity that reflects successive stages of learning that concept or skill. The students ascend the sequence as far as they can, thus indicating their level of competence in that topic.

The stem provides sufficient information for a range of questions of increasing complexity to be asked. In the given example (Box 11.4), devised by one of the authors (CT), the SOLO taxonomy was used as a guide to the levels of complexity: (a) is declarative unistructural, (b) and (c) are increasingly complex declarative relational and (d) addresses functioning knowledge at a relational level. The levels do not need to correspond to each SOLO level or to SOLO levels at all; here, SOLO is simply a way of helping structure increasingly high level responses that *make sense* in the particular context.

Box 11.4 An ordered-outcome item for physiotherapy students

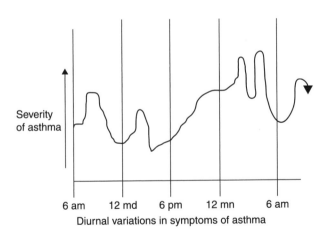

Diurnal variations in symptoms of asthma

a When is the asthma attack most severe during the day?
b Is a patient with asthma physically fitter at 1 pm or 8 pm?
c Do you expect a patient with asthma to sleep well at night? Give your reasons.
d Advise a patient with asthma how to cope with diurnal variation in symptoms.

A guide to constructing ordered-outcomes items, using a SOLO sequence, follows:

a   *Unistructural:* use one obvious piece of information coming directly from the stem. Verbs: 'identify', 'recognize'.
b   *Multistructural:* use two or more discrete and separate pieces of information contained in the stem. Verbs: 'list' and, in this example, 'compare', which is nearer relational.
c   *Relational:* use two or more pieces of information each directly related to an integrated understanding of the information in the stem. Verbs: 'interpret', 'apply'.
d   *Extended abstract:* use an abstract general principle or hypothesis that can be derived from, or suggested by, the information in the stem. It is sometimes possible to use a one-correct-answer format ('Formulate the general case of which the preceding (relational) item is an instance') or to use a divergent short-answer sub-item ('Give an example where (c) – the preceding item – does *not* occur. Why doesn't it?'). Verbs: 'hypothesize', 'design', 'create' (not in the Box 11.4 example).

An example from chemistry is given in Box 11.5.

Box 11.5 An ordered-outcome item for chemistry students

In a space shuttle, the exhaled air from an astronaut is circulated through lithium hydroxide filters to remove carbon dioxide according to the following equation:

$$2LiOH(s) + CO_2(g) \rightarrow Li_2CO_3(s) + H_2O(l)$$

(Relative atomic masses: H = 1.0, Li = 6.9, C = 12.0, O = 16.0, K = 39.0; molar volume of a gas at the temperature and pressure of the space shuttle = 24 dm^3).

a   State whether the lithium hydroxide in the filters is in the form of a solid, liquid or gas.
b   How much greater is the relative molecular mass of carbon dioxide compared to that of lithium hydroxide?
c   Calculate the volume of carbon dioxide that could be absorbed by 1gm of lithium hydroxide.
d   Suggest how the spent lithium hydroxide in the filters can be conveniently regenerated after use.

[Solubility data: LiOH (slightly soluble), NaOH (soluble), Li$_2$CO$_3$ (insoluble)]

Source: Holbrook (1996)

In the ordered-outcome item, we are seeing what ILOs a student can meet that apply to a single situation. The ordered-outcome format sends a strong message to students that higher is better: recognition and simple algorithms won't do. Using this format with mathematics items, Wong (1994) found students operated from theory rather than applying algorithms, while Lake (1999) found an ordered-outcome format in biological sciences led students from the basic skills of data retrieval to the advanced skills of critical analysis.

In constructing ordered-outcome items so that we can achieve one final score at the end, the items need to form a staircase: unistructural items must be easier than multi-; multi- easier than relational; relational easier than extended abstract. This can be tested with trial runs, preferably using the Guttman (1941) scalogram model, or software is available (Masters 1988). Hattie and Purdie (1998) discuss a range of measurement issues involved in the construction and interpretation of ordered-outcome SOLO items.

In scoring ordered-outcome items as a normal test, it is tempting to say (a) gets 1 mark if passed, (b) 2 marks, (c) 3 marks and (d) (let's emphasize extended abstract) 5 marks. We then throw the marks into the pot with all the other test results. While this is convenient, it misleads as to a student's level of understanding. If the score is less than perfect, a nominal understanding of one level could be averaged with a high understanding of another, yielding 'moderate' understanding across all levels, which was not the case at all.

Alternatively, we could say that as the items are for all practical purposes perfectly ordered, the final score is the highest level addressed, as all the preceding levels may be presumed to have been passed.

For those who are interested to try out some ordered-outcome items, you can complete Task 11.1.

Task 11.1 Writing ordered-outcome items

Try the following steps to write some ordered-outcome items for your course.

1 Identify the content area and the ILOs that you expect your students to achieve with that content area.

Content area: _____

ILOs: _____

_____

_____

_____

2 Design the stem to provide adequate information for the students to answer the range of questions. The stem could be in the form of written information, a diagram, a chart or any other form of presentation.

---

3 Now design four or five questions that the students need to answer based on the information given in the stem. These questions should be of increasing complexity of the ILOs. Double-check if the answers to the questions do reflect the successive stages of learning of the concept or skill as indicated in the ILOs.

---

4 Now decide how you are going to score the items.

This discussion of ordered-outcome items has raised two major issues:

1 Do we assess how well each ILO has been addressed or how well the task has been performed?
2 Do we assess quantitatively or qualitatively?

Let us turn to these two questions.

Assessing and grading the task

At the beginning of this chapter we raised the question of whether we should be assessing and grading the ILO or the task. When each ILO is assessed by only one assessment task, there is no problem: the assessment of the task becomes the grade. When there are several tasks that might address one ILO or when one task addresses several ILOs that the question arises of how we arrive at a final grade for the task.

Several positions may be taken:

1 The task is aligned to the ILOs and is assessed quantitatively, or 'marked', in the traditional way; that is, ratings or percentages are given in the way they always have been. Some teachers feel that this is already adequate for their particular subjects and will continue to assess this way, Chapter 10 notwithstanding. This is a minimally acceptable position, as at least alignment is present.
2 The task is assessed and graded qualitatively but analytically by using rubrics (see Table 11.1), and converted to percentage points for obtaining the final grade for a task or for a course.
3 The task is assessed holistically and graded directly.

Point 1 is standard practice, and nothing further need be said about that. We do, however, need to say more about points 2 and 3.

Assessing and grading qualitatively, but reporting quantitatively

Table 11.1 gives an example of point 2, assessing and grading qualitatively using rubrics, and then converting to a quantitative scale, for an assignment in which a case is argued, evidence for and against is marshalled, a conclusion is reached and a letter grade from F to A is to be given.

You may notice that the general structure from D to A is in terms of SOLO as applied to the four components of introduction, argument, conclusions and references. Each component is assigned a range of points, weighted so that the argument, the most important component, is allocated most points. Note that the gap between grades is greater than the gap between levels within grades, to emphasize that achieving a grade is more important than achieving a fine grade within grades. Thus, a grade is first awarded according to the rubrics, after which the conversion to a number is made. The task, in other words, is graded qualitatively, it is not 'marked'. The conversion to points is only for administrative purposes. (And notice: we used the term 'points', not 'marks'.)

For example, let us say the introduction in one case describes the topic, refers to past work with some passing evaluation of it but then goes on to state the present case, with no logical progression to the topic. This meets the C criteria generally, hinting at a B–, so let us say C+, or seven points. Each component is then assessed in this way and totalled. Table 11.2 gives a range of percentage points for a letter grade.

Say a student scored 67 for this assessment task. This is closest to a B (Table 11.2), so B it is. The second row in Table 11.2 is for arriving at the final grade point average (GPA) for a student for the year. The mean percentage points over all courses is calculated and converted to a typical GPA-type scale. All this is fairly arbitrary, but then using numbers to quantify qualitative data always is. Numbers just happen to be very convenient for determining final results over a number of tasks or a number of courses.

The third position, where the task is assessed holistically and graded directly, has already been illustrated in Chapter 6, in the original constructively aligned course, where the portfolio items were searched for evidence of the ILOs (p. 104). We return to this in portfolio assessment (pp. 256–60).

Assessing and grading the intended learning outcome

We now turn to the issue of assessing and grading the ILO as opposed to assessing and grading the task. Sometimes the task itself is so important that

Table 11.1 Grading criteria (rubrics) for an argue-a-case assignment

	Percentage points	D 1–3	C– C C+ 5–7	B– B B+ 9–11	A– A A+ 13–15
Introduction	15	Gives enough to tell what the topic is but little prioritizing	Describes topic, refers to past work, what is proposed to do here	As in C, but shows what past work has done/not done; logical progression to topic	Interesting and complex account of why this topic, what questions need to be addressed, foretaste of original contribution
Argument	50	Some relevant points in descriptive lists, mainly either pro or con 5–20	More relevant points drawn from literature, lists both pros and cons, but has difficulty in making a convincing case 24–28	Most/all relevant points from mainstream literature; uses appropriate structure to resolve issues in convincing argument 32–38	As in B, but makes an original case in own voice, well supported by resources/references going well beyond the mainstream literature 42–50
Summary and conclusions	20	Summary is a list of either pros or cons leading to a lopsided conclusion 2–4	Summary recognizes differences but unable to resolve them, weak conclusion or jumps to conclusion 7–10	Summary is balanced leading to well-reasoned conclusion 13–17	Summary leads to a surprise or original conclusion generating new issues 18–20
References	15	Sparse; little evidence of library skills Incorrect formatting	Evidence of some search skills Standard references in mostly correct formatting	Comprehensive, showing care in researching the issue, format correct and clear 9–11	As in B, but uses unusual references to bolster an original argument Formatting as in B
		1–3	5–7		13–15

Table 11.2 Conversions between percentage points, letter grades and GPA

Fail	D	C–	C	C+	B–	B	B+	A–	A	A+
> 45	46–50	52	55	60	65	68	70	75	80	80+
For GPA	1.0	1.7	2.0	2.3	2.7	3.0	3.3	3.7	4.0	4.3

it is an ILO. 'Write a laboratory report' is an example: keeping proper records of laboratory procedures is an intended outcome in itself. Usually, however, assessment tasks are a means, not an end: 'pass the examination' is not an intended learning outcome in itself but a means by which we can assess whether particular learnings have occurred or not.

It could be argued that since the assessment tasks have been aligned to one or more ILOs, that is good enough: alignment is present and so we assess the task, as we have always done. However, where there is more than one task relevant to any given ILO, we would not then know what contribution each task made to that ILO; and where one task addresses several ILOs, assessing the task doesn't give much idea of how well a student has met any particular ILO.

The alternative to assessing and grading the task is to use the evidence supplied by the assessment tasks to assess and grade each student's performance with respect to each ILO. The argument here is that since the ILOs are statements of what the student is intended to learn, it makes most sense to report the results of the assessments in terms of the ILOs for each course rather than for the assessment tasks themselves. Again, if there is only one AT per ILO, there is no issue, but where there are several the question becomes: 'What does the available evidence say about this student's performance on the ILO in question?'

Having said that, it is not, of course, a good idea to multiply assessment tasks – we need to watch both our workload and the students' – but an AT that is set primarily to address a particular ILO often has something to say about a student's performance on another ILO. For example, a common verb like 'explain' a particular concept or 'be able to communicate' may be evidenced in an examination and again in an assignment. Do we ignore the evidence from a secondary AT or do we incorporate it in our assessment of how well the student has met the ILO?

Assessing by ILO cannot meaningfully be performed quantitatively, that is by 'marking' the ILO. It is a question of what the evidence from the assessment tasks says about how well the ILO has been achieved by a given student, which has to be a matter of *judgement*. In order to keep our own judgements stable, and in order to obtain maximum reliability between teachers making these judgements, rubrics need to be spelled out clearly. Table 11.3 gives a sample set of rubrics for the verb 'explain' although, of course, these will need to be adjusted according to what is being explained and in what context.

Here, we moved straight from whatever evidence is available to making a graded judgement of how well the student addresses the ILO itself. This

Table 11.3 Example of criteria (rubrics) for grading a declarative ILO

	Marginal	Adequate			Good			Excellent		
	D	C−	C	C+	B−	B	B+	A−	A	A+
Scale score	1.0	1.7	2.0	2.3	2.7	3.0	3.3	3.7	4.0	4.3
ILO Explain	Able to identify and briefly write about limited points. Very little evidence of using these points to provide reasoning to why they are interrelated	Able to identify a number of relevant points with some details. Use these points to provide a fair reasoning or causality. No evidence of a comprehensive overview of reasoning or causality			Able to identify a full range of relevant points with details. Supported by relevant literature. Points are organized to provide a comprehensive and cohesive reasoning or causality			As in 'good' but provides views on possible alternative causes and/or results depending on changes of conditions. Able to link current reasoning to situations in real-life professional contexts		

could be used as formative feedback to the student or summatively. If the latter, as this is only one ILO out of five or so for a given course, we will need to state a final grade for that course and to calculate a student's overall grade for the ILO. The 'scale score' is actually taken from one university's conversion from grade to GPA-type scale: notice that again as in Table 11.1 (p. 240), the gap between grades is greater than the gap within grades in terms of scale score. When the final result has been calculated, we can convert to GPA score using Table 11.2 (p. 241), as before. It would in fact be most meaningful if on the student's transcript all the assessments of all the course ILOs were retained rather than overall GPA. This would give a potential employer, or the dean of graduate school, for instance, a detailed account of the student's strengths and weaknesses.

In practice, students at present want to know 'How did I do on that midterm assignment?' rather than 'How did I do on the "explain" ILO?' To some extent, then, it will be necessary to assess both the task itself to give student feedback, as well as the ILOs it may address. In time, however, when students and the public generally become used to outcomes-based teaching and learning it may well be that a profile of grades on the ILOs will become perfectly meaningful to all.

Assessing in large classes

Many teachers see no alternative to the final exam and the MCQ when assessing large classes. Using varied assessment tasks for higher level ILOs, especially those addressing functioning knowledge, is seen by many teachers as impractical in large classes.

However, it need not be thus. Of course, assessing the projects, assignments and portfolios of 400 students between the end of semester and submission of grades to the faculty board of examiners may be logistically and humanly impossible. But there are alternatives.

Cloze tests

These were originally designed to assess reading comprehension. Every seventh (or so) word in a passage is deleted and the student has to fill in the space with the correct word or a synonym. A text is chosen that can only be understood if the topic under discussion is understood, rather like the gobbet (p. 244). The omitted words are essential for making sense of the passage.

Concept maps

We have seen concept maps as a teaching/learning activity (pp. 141–2). They can also be used for assessment. They are particularly useful for giving an overview of the course. They need not take a long time to prepare and the teacher can tell at a glance if a student has an impoverished knowledge structure relating to the topic or a rich one.

Gobbets

Gobbets are significant chunks of content with which the student should be familiar and to which the student has to respond (Brown and Knight 1994). They could be a paragraph from a novel or of a standard text, a brief passage of music, a Venn diagram, an archeological artefact, a photograph (a building, an engine part) and so on. The student's task is to identify the gobbet, explain its context, say why it is important, what it reminds them of or whatever else you would like them to comment on.

Gobbets should access a bigger picture, unlike short answers that are sufficient unto themselves. That big picture is the target, not the gobbet itself. Brown and Knight point out that three gobbets can be completed in the time it takes one essay exam question, so that to an extent you can assess both coverage and depth. They could assess either declarative or functioning knowledge. Box 11.6 gives two examples of gobbets for assessing ILOs for declarative knowledge.

Box 11.6 Two examples of gobbets

For assessing the ILOs 'identify' and 'explain' in Law

A piece of legislation is provided. Students are asked to identify the context of the legislation, explain its importance, and its possible impact on a current legal crisis.

For assessing the ILOs 'analyse' and 'recommend' in Occupational Health and Safety

Students are given a photograph of a section of a construction site in function.

Students are asked to analyse the situation, identify any potential health and safety hazards and recommend measures to improve the situation.

Group assessment

Group assessment is appealing in large classes. With four students per assessment task, you get to assess almost a quarter the number you would otherwise. But there are problems, particularly of plagiarism and its equivalent, freeloading. It is necessary to be very careful about who does what in the project, which is where peer-assessment helps, and that each student obtains an overview of the whole task, not just of their particular contribution, for example by writing a reflective report on how well each thinks they have achieved the ILOs (pp. 254–5).

Letter-to-a-friend

This is written by the student to a friend, imaginary or real, who is supposedly thinking of enrolling in the course in the following year (Trigwell and Prosser 1990). These letters are about a page in length and are written and assessed in a few minutes. The student should reflect on the course and report on it as it affects them. Letters tend to be either multistructural or relational, occasionally extended abstract. Multistructural letters are simply lists of course content, a rehash of the course outline. Good responses provide integrated accounts of how the topics fit together and form a useful whole (relational), while the best describe a change in personal perspective as a result of studying the course (extended abstract). Letter-to-a-friend also provides a useful source of feedback to the teacher on aspects of the course. Like the concept map, letters supplement more fine-grained tasks with an overview of the course.

Minute paper

The minute paper appeared as a TLA for large class teaching and as a learning activity and as feedback for the teacher (p. 143). It can just as easily be used summatively for grading purposes, but if so, the students should be told first as their strategies will be different. An obvious advantage is that the three-minute essay can be answered and assessed in, er, three minutes.

Peer- and self-assessment

Peer- and self-assessment can slash the teacher's assessment load quite drastically, even when conventional assessments such as exam or assignment are used (p. 229). An additional benefit is that self- and peer-assessment are particularly well suited for assessing functioning knowledge and values ILOs such as teamwork and cooperation, because such assessments are what are required in real life.

Let us recap the advantages:

1 Self- and peer-assessment give the students first-hand, active involvement with the criteria for good learning.
2 Students learn how to select good evidence.
3 Judging whether a performance or product meets given criteria is vital for effective professional action.

It is important that these educational justifications are made clear to the students, not only because the rationale for all teaching and assessing decisions should be transparent, but because it is necessary to get the students on side. A common belief is that assessment is the *teacher's* responsibility and some students resent being required to do the teacher's dirty work (Brew 1999). Peer-assessment can also be stressful to some students (Pope 2001). It should be noted too that good students under-assess themselves, compared to how their peers would rate them, while poor students over-assess themselves (Lejk and Wyvill 2001b).

How well do self- and peer-assessments agree with teacher assessments? Falchikov and Boud (1989), reviewing 57 studies, found that agreement was greatest with advanced students, least in introductory courses; and in convergent content subjects, such as science, medicine and engineering, rather than in arts and social science. Good agreement requires explicit criteria of assessment and discussion and training in using them (Fox 1989).

As an operational rule of thumb, Boud (1986) suggests that if self- and/or peer-assessments agree within a specified range, whether expressed as a qualitative grade or as a number of marks, the higher grade is best awarded (collusion can be mitigated by spot checking). He estimates this procedure can cut the teacher's load by at least one-third. Gibbs (1999) cut marking time for the teacher by 18 hours a week by using peer-assessment, while summative marks increased by 20% simply because peer-assessment is itself a powerful TLA.

Random assessment

One way of ensuring that students are motivated to put effort into a series of ATs is to use random assessment. In Gibbs (1999), 25 reports through the year were required, but as each was worth only a trivial 1%, the quality was poor. When the requirements were changed, so that students still submitted 25 reports as a condition for sitting the final exam, but only four reports selected at random were marked, two benefits resulted. The students worked consistently throughout the term and submitted 25 good reports, and the teacher's marking load was one-sixth of what it had previously been.

Short-answer examinations

These are answered in note form. This format is useful for getting at factual material, such as interpreting diagrams, charts and tables, but is limited in addressing main ideas and themes. The examiner is usually after something quite specific, and in practice operates more like the objective format than the essay (Biggs 1973; Scouller 1996). However, it has advantages over the standard MCQ in that it is less susceptible to test-taking strategies: the answer can't be worked out by elimination, it requires active recall rather than just recognition and it is easier to construct but not as easy to score.

Venn diagrams

A simple form of concept map, where the boundary of a concept is expressed in a circle or ellipse, and interrelations between concepts expressed by the intersection or overlap of the circles (see Box 11.7). Venn diagrams, like concept maps, are very economical ways of expressing relationships. They can be used for teaching purposes, in conveying relationships to students, and for assessment purposes, so that students may convey their ways of seeing relationships between concepts. Getting students to draw and briefly explain their own Venns, or to interpret those presented, can be done quickly, where the target of understanding is relationships between ideas.

Box 11.7 represents an item for an educational psychologist course ILO relating to professional interaction. There are three domains: psychologist, student and school, with each of which the psychologist has to interact at various times. For the student to be able to explain examples of the inter-actions (1) through (3) would indicate a high level of understanding of the

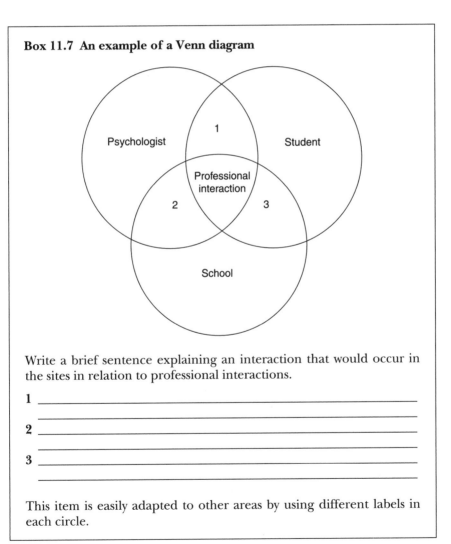

Box 11.7 An example of a Venn diagram

Write a brief sentence explaining an interaction that would occur in the sites in relation to professional interactions.

1 _____
   _____
2 _____
   _____
3 _____
   _____

This item is easily adapted to other areas by using different labels in each circle.

psychologist's role. This item could be adapted to virtually any situation: just label the circles differently. Task 11.2 asks you to think about precisely that.

For those who need to assess declarative ILOs for a large class, Task 11.2 asks you to design a gobbet, a concept map or a Venn diagram as an assessment task.

Task 11.2 Design a gobbet, concept map or Venn diagram for assessing declarative ILOs for large classes

Consider some the ILOs for declarative knowledge in your course, design a gobbet, a concept map or a Venn diagram as an assessment task.

For the gobbet

ILOs to be assessed:

_____

_____

1 The content information you are going to give to your students.

_____

_____

_____

2 Questions or tasks your students need to answer or complete in relation to the content information.

_____

_____

_____

For the concept map or Venn diagram

ILOs to be assessed:

_____

_____

1 The concepts or information to be given to the students (if appropriate).

_____

_____

_____

2 Questions or tasks your students need to answer or complete in relation to the concept map or Venn diagram.
3 Presentation of the concept map or Venn diagram.

Educational technology (ET) can help in rapid assessment, as well as in assessment generally (see Chapter 12).

Before we end this chapter, Task 11.3 is an exercise on designing assessment tasks for declarative knowledge of your course.

Task 11.3 Design an assessment task or tasks for one of your course declarative ILOs

Select one ILO relating to declarative knowledge of your course and design assessment task(s) that will appropriately assess this ILO. To help you check the alignment between the task(s) and the ILO, identify what the students are required to do in order to complete the assessment task(s). The task requirements should be aligned to the ILO.

Course ILO: _____

Number of students in the course: _____

Assessment task	Student activities to complete the task
1	
2	

Now double-check whether the student activities are aligned to the verb(s) nominated in the respective course ILO.

After designing the task(s), you will need to write the grading criteria for either the ILO or for each of the tasks.

Summary and conclusions

Designing assessment tasks

In designing assessment tasks (ATs) there are several things to bear in mind. Clear assessment criteria or rubrics need to be established for each task, or for the ILO(s) each AT is meant to address. It is useful to think of ATs as a *source of evidence* of a student's achievement of any ILO. You can have one source of evidence or several, just as one task may provide evidence on more than one ILO. However, the ATs have to be *manageable*, both by students in terms of both time and resources in performing them and by staff in assessing students' performances.

Assessing and grading using extended prose

Declarative knowledge is typically assessed by writing answers to set questions or in essay-type or objective formats. The format chosen matters because it can affect the way students react to the task. Writing is either in the timed and invigilated 'exam' or unrestricted, as in the typical essay assignment. The stress typically felt in the 'exam' situation produces its own distortion in the quality of work done, especially by the Roberts of this world. A particular problem with assessing extended writing is the lack of reliability between assessors. Several suggestions are made to improve this.

Objective formats of assessment

The lack of reliability of assessing essays, plus the time they take to assess, has led many teachers to use objective formats, particularly the MCQ. The major problem with the MCQ, however, is that it is not at all suited to addressing high-level outcomes and that it is prone to encouraging strategic rather than knowledge-driven responding. An exception is the ordered-outcome format, which encourages students to target higher rather than lower level items.

Assessing and grading the task

Once the AT is aligned to the ILO(s) it is meant to address, the question becomes how, operationally, is the student's performance assessed? Is it assessed against the task or against the ILO(s) the task is meant to address? Teachers and students are used to task assessment and that is what many teachers will continue to do. There are three ways of task assessment: quantitatively, as has been the case traditionally; by assessing and grading the task analytically, addressing the task components using rubrics for each component; or by assessing the task as a whole and grading qualitatively.

Assessing and grading the ILO

The most logical, and operationally the simplest, way of assessing is by using the evidence gained from the various tasks directly to assess the ILO itself, by using rubrics designed for each ILO. The main objection to this method is simply that teachers and students are not yet used to it.

Assessing in large classes

Assessing large classes need not mean exams and MCQs. Cloze tests, concept maps, gobbets, group assessment, letter-to-a-friend, minute paper, peer- and self-assessment, random assessment, and Venn diagrams and are all ways in which rapid assessments of higher order ILOs, involving little time in either sitting or assessing, can be made.

Further reading

Computer scoring of essays

Rudner, L. and Gagne, P. (2001) An overview of three approaches to scoring written essays by computer, *Practical Assessment, Research and Evaluation,* 7: 26. http://pareonline.net/getvn.asp?v=7&n=26 (accessed 2 February 2011).

Shermis, M. and Burstein, J. (eds) (2003) *Automated Essay scoring: A Cross-disciplinary Perspective.* Hillsdale, NJ: Erlbaum.

Much of the background and enrichment material for this chapter is the same as for the next. Please refer to the Further Reading section in Chapter 12.

12

Assessing and grading for functioning intended learning outcomes

In this chapter we discuss assessment tasks that address ILOs for functioning knowledge, and how they may be graded. Functioning knowledge has particular relevance to professionally related programmes. We look first at a range of assessment formats, including individual and group projects, presentations, case studies, portfolios and capstone projects. We then discuss the assessment of some common graduate outcomes: creativity, lifelong learning and problem solving. E-assessment is useful for both declarative and functioning knowledge but especially for the latter as some very complex and lifelike simulations can be created. Finally we take a look at the general problem of plagiarism, which is the major reason for invigilating students during assessment. Plagiarism is of increasing concern in today's universities for a variety of reasons. We look at some of the issues here and how plagiarism may be minimized.

Formats for assessing functioning knowledge

Assessing functioning knowledge is in principle much easier than assessing declarative knowledge. Just look at these verbs: 'apply', 'design', 'create', 'solve unseen problem', 'perform a case study', 'reflect and improve' and many others that put knowledge to work. These verbs work as performances of understanding in a context, and in professional faculties, that context is about dealing with real-life professional problems. The assessment in these cases is much more direct than when assessing decontextualized declarative knowledge. How well do the students carry out a case study? Get them to carry out a case study and see how well they do it. How well do the students design a piece of systems software? Get them to design a piece of software and see how well they do it.

Such tasks are, as in real life, often divergent, ill formed or 'fuzzy', in the sense that there are no single correct answers. For example, there are many acceptable ways a software program could be written for use in a real estate office. 'Real life' imposes limitations relating to budget, the costs of a range of materials, time and space and so on, that allow different alternatives. Assessment involves how well the design or creation works within those limitations. What is important is that the student shows a 'real-life' understanding of the situation: how the problem may reasonably be approached, how resources and data are used, how previously taught material is used, how effectively the solution meets likely contingencies and so on. Clearly, this needs open-ended assessment, where students are free to structure their performances as they best see fit.

Various formats may be used for assessing and grading of functioning knowledge in terms either of the ILOs addressed or the task itself. As in the case of declarative knowledge, it is a matter of whether the rubrics apply to the task, to the ILO, or to both.

Capstone or final-year projects

Capstone projects are versions of final-year projects with the specific intention of addressing programme ILOs that may not have been assessed in individual courses. It is, in fact, a flaw in much programme design that programme ILOs are often seen in practice if not in intention as no more than the sum of individual course ILOs. However, many programme ILOs, 'to make informed professional decisions' for example, may not be addressed by any particular course ILO, but by a combination of several ILOs. Many important outcomes – most graduate outcomes for example – are not easily teachable in a single semester, but emerge over the years more as a result of 'immersion' than of direct teaching (Knight and Yorke 2004). For this reason, Knight and Yorke recommend that students keep long-term portfolios of their work in which this development may be tracked.

Addressing these broad ILOs, or combinations of ILOs, requires *synoptic* assessment, that is, an assessment that straddles several course ILOs. This is what the capstone project attempts to do. Synoptic assessments enable students to integrate their experiences, providing them with important opportunities to demonstrate their creativity (Jackson 2003). If students' creativity is inhibited by having to address course-specific ILOs throughout their undergraduate courses – or if they *feel* it has been inhibited – then they can really let fly in their final-year or capstone projects.

The capstone project is thus designed to span several final-year courses or possibly courses over all years, so that students have a chance to show that they can put it all together and use it or, more generally still, to show how they have developed in line with the institution's graduate outcomes and of the programme ILOs, which otherwise may never be satisfactorily and holistically assessed. It is particularly well suited to assess those evolving, 'fuzzy' ILOs that are not readily amenable to direct teaching such as lifelong learning and creativity.

Case study

In some disciplines, a case study is an ideal way of seeing how students can apply their knowledge and professional skills. It could be written up as a project or as an item for a portfolio. Case studies might need to be highly formal and carried out under supervision or be carried out independently by the student. Possibilities are endless.

Assessing the case study is essentially holistic, but aspects can be used both for formative feedback and for summative assessment. For example, there are essential skills in some cases that must be got right, otherwise the patient dies, the bridge collapses or other mayhem ensues. The component skills here could be pass–fail; fail one, fail the lot (with latitude according to the skill and case study in question). Having passed the components, however, the student then has to handle the case itself appropriately and that should be assessed holistically.

McNaught et al. (2007) systematically built in assessment tasks throughout the case study experience in a case-based science course, most of which were formative but some being summative. While these tasks improved the quality of performance, the students complained of excessive workload, which underlines the need for care in designing these sorts of assessment. A similar caution is necessary in the case of portfolios, see below.

Critical incidents

Asking students to keep records of critical incidents in their workplace experience and later to discuss their significance can be very powerful evidence of how well their knowledge is functioning. They might explain why these incidents are critical, how they arose and what might be done about it. This gives rich information about how students (a) have interpreted what they have been taught and (b) can make use of the information in the workplace.

Such incidents might be the focus of an assessment interview, of a reflective journal or be used as portfolio items (see later).

Individual and group projects

Whereas an assignment usually focuses on declarative knowledge, the project focuses on functioning knowledge applied to a hands-on piece of research. Projects can vary from simple to sophisticated or carried out individually or by a group of students.

Group projects are becoming increasingly common for two major reasons: they aim to teach students cooperative skills, in line with ILOs or graduate outcomes relating to teamwork; and the teacher's assessment load is markedly decreased. They are not, however, always popular with students: they often find it difficult to coordinate times; the assessment may not take into account individual contributions, on the one hand, or group processes, on the other; workplace cooperation involves individuals with distinct roles and they may not be assessed individually on their contribution (Morris 2001). The common practice of simply awarding an overall grade for the outcome, which each student receives, fails on all counts.

Group projects need to be used carefully. Peer evaluation of contribution is certainly one way to make them more acceptable, but giving that 'a miserly 5% towards the final grade' is not enough to overcome the problem, as one student, quoted in Morris (2001), put it. Lejk and Wyvill (2001a, 2001b) have carried out a series of studies on assessing group projects, this question of assessing contribution of members being one aspect. They found that self-assessment was not very effective and suggest that the fairest way is to use peer-assessment following an open discussion between students about relative contributions – but the peer-assessment should be conducted in secret, not openly.

Most attempts to assess relative contribution use quantification. A simple version might be to award a global 60%, say, to a particular project. If there are four participants, this means that 240 marks need to be allocated. You may make this allocation, on the basis of interviews with the students, or get them to do it. One problem is that they may decide to divide them equally – some hating themselves as they do so, knowing they are selling themselves short. Lejk and Wyvill use an elaborate matrix where students rate each other on aspects of the task and derive an index for each student, which is used to weight the calculation of the grade of each. The reliability of peer-assessment in assessing group projects is an interesting and neglected issue that is handled by Magin (2001).

A problem with collaborative projects is that individual students too easily focus only on their own specific task, not really understanding the other components or how they contribute to the project as a whole. The idea of a group project is that a complex and worthwhile task can be made manageable, each student taking a section they can handle. However, the tasks should not be divided according to what students are already good at: Mario has read widely, so let him prepare the literature review, Sheila is good at stats so let her do the analysis of results. The problem with this is that little *learning* may take place. We want students to learn things other than what they already know, so a better allocation is that Sheila does the literature review and Mario the stats. This is likely to end up with both helping one another and then everyone learns with some peer teaching thrown in to boot.

Most important, we want the students to know what the whole project is about and how each contribution fits in. To ensure this, an additional holistic assessment is necessary. Students might be required individually to submit a reflective report, explaining where and how their contribution fits into the project as a whole and explaining how they think they have achieved the ILOs through their participation in the project.

Learning contracts

Contracts replicate a common everyday situation. A learning contract would take into account where an individual is at the beginning of the course, what relevant attainments are possessed already, what work or other experience and then, within the context of the course ILOs, he or she is to produce a needs analysis from which a contract is negotiated: what is to be done and how it is proposed to be done and how it is to be assessed. Individuals, or homogeneous groups of students, would have a tutor to consult throughout and with whom they would have to agree that the contract is met in due course. The assessment problem hasn't gone away, but the advantage is that the assessments are tied down very firmly from the start and the students know where they stand (Stephenson and Laycock 1993). Learning contracts help students to commit to progress and to develop ownership over their learning, through planning, negotiating, implementing and reflecting (Brewer et al. 2007).

A more conventional and less complicated learning contract is little different from clear criterion referencing: 'This is what an A requires. If you can prove to me that you can demonstrate those qualities in your learning, then an A is what you will get.' This is basically what is involved in portfolio assessment (see later).

See Further Reading at end of chapter for examples of learning contracts.

Portfolio assessment

Portfolios have long been used in the art world and in job applications: individuals place their best work in a portfolio for judgement. They also need to be wisely selective: dumping in items that do not address the job specifications and qualifications will not impress. Just so, students need to be wisely selective in placing in their portfolios what they think best addresses the ILOs and to explain why. Portfolios allow the student to present and explain his or her best 'learning treasures' and are therefore ideal for assessing unintended outcomes (pp. 215–16). When students give their creativity free rein, portfolios are full of complex and divergent surprises, aligned to the course or programme ILOs in ways that are simply not anticipated by the teacher.

In their explanations for their selection of items, students explain how the evidence they have in their portfolios addresses the course ILOs or indeed their own personal intended aims and outcomes of learning. One danger with portfolios, as with case studies, is that students may go overboard, creating excessive workload both for themselves and for the teacher. Limits must be set (see later).

Assessing portfolio items can be deeply interesting. It may be time consuming, but that depends on the nature and number of items. Many items, such as concept maps, can be assessed in a minute or so. In any event, a whole day spent assessing portfolios is existentially preferable to an hour of assessing lookalike exam papers.

Following are some suggestions for implementing portfolio assessment:

1 *Make it quite clear in the ILOs what the evidence for good learning may be.* The ILOs to be addressed should be available to the students at the beginning of the semester and discussed with them.
2 *State the requirements for the portfolio:*

- *Number of items:* this depends on the scope of the portfolio, whether it is for assessing one course or several, and the size of the items. Four items is about the limit in a semester-long course, but that is flexible.
- *Approximate size of each item:* some items, such as a reflective essay, may reach 2000 words or more, while other items, such as concept maps or other diagrams, require less than a page. A rule of thumb: the total portfolio should not be much longer than a normal project or assignment.
- *A list of sample items* is most helpful when the students are new to portfolios (see Box 12.1) but they should be discouraged from using that list only. Students should show some creativity by going outside the list.
- *Any compulsory items?* This depends on the nature of the course. In most professional courses, a reflective journal is probably a good basis even if only extracts are submitted in the end.
- *Source of items:* items may be specific to a course or drawn from other courses in the case of assessing programme ILOs. In some problem-based courses, students will be continually providing inputs, often on a pass–fail basis, over a year, or two years. The final evaluation could then comprise – *in toto* or in part – samples of the best work students think they have done to date.
- *Grading the portfolio:* portfolios are best assessed as a whole (the 'package'), not by marking individual items.

Box 12.1 Sample items that went into an assessment portfolio in a course for teachers

- Critical incidents from a reflective diary
- Lesson plans, constructed on principles dealt with in class
- Teaching checklists on how teachers may (unconsciously) encourage surface approaches in students as rated by a colleague
- A videotaped peer discussion on teaching with each participant writing up his/her perspective
- Accounts of exemplary teaching/learning experiences and the lessons to be drawn
- Concept maps of the course
- Letter-to-a-friend about the course
- Reviews of articles, self-set essays, to address the declarative ILOs
- A questionnaire on motivation and self-concept.

Source: Biggs (1996b)

On the last point, if items are graded separately and averaged, the main value of the portfolio is lost: the situation is the same as combining different assessments in the usual way to arrive at a final grade (see p. 239). While each item might address one or more different ILOs, the whole addresses the thrust of the course. The student's selection of items is in effect saying: '*This* is what I got out of your class. I have learned these things, and as a result my thinking has changed in the following ways.' If their package can show that, they have learned well indeed.

Box 12.2 gives a concrete example from a course for educational psychologists at a Hong Kong university; Table 12.1 gives general guidelines for grading a portfolio.

Box 12.2 An example of assessing and grading a portfolio holistically

Curriculum and instruction: a subject in a course for educational psychologists

Grading will be based on your attaining the following ILOs:

1 Apply the principles of good teaching and assessment to chosen contexts.
2 Relate selected aspects of curriculum design and management to the educational system in Hong Kong.
3 Apply the content and experiences in this subject to enhance your effectiveness as an educational psychologist.
4 Show examples of your reflective decision making as an educational psychologist.

Final grades will depend on how well you can demonstrate that you have met all the ILOs (only grades A, B, C and F were awarded):

A Awarded if you have clearly met all the ILOs, provide evidence of original and creative thinking, perhaps going beyond established practice.
B Awarded when all ILOs have been met very well and effectively.
C Awarded when the ILOs have been addressed satisfactorily or where the evidence is strong in some ILOs, weaker but acceptable in others.
F Less than C, work plagiarized, not submitted.

Assessment guidelines

Show evidence that you have learned according to the criteria in the ILOs. Keep a *reflective journal* to record useful insights as you progress through the course. Use as a database. The evidence will be presented in the following forms:

- A *paper*, drawing on principles of curriculum and good teaching, explaining how you would like to see the Hong Kong educational system implement any major educational reforms. You should have ILO (2) in mind.
- A *report* specifically addressing ILOs (3) and (4), a review of those aspects of the course that you think will probably enhance your work as an EP. This can refer both to your way of thinking about your role, as much as to actual skills. Your reflective journal will be an important source for this.
- Your *own rationale* of your group presentation, taking into account the evaluation made at the time of presentation. You should have ILO (1) in mind.
- A *self-evaluation* showing how you have addressed each of the ILOs.

Place these in a portfolio, which will be graded as above. Take 5000 words as a guideline for the complete portfolio.

Handout for students in a masters course for educational psychologists

Table 12.1 Holistic grading of a portfolio of items

Marginal	*Adequate*	*Good*	*Excellent*
D	*C– C C+*	*B– B B+*	*A– A A+*
1.0	*1.7 2.0 2.3*	*2.7 3.0 3.3*	*3.7 4.0 4.3*
The pieces of evidence are relevant and accurate, but are isolated, addressing one aspect of the course. Demonstration of understanding in a minimally acceptable way. Poor coverage, no originality, weak justification of portfolio items.	The evidence is relevant, accurate and covers several aspects of the course. Little evidence of an overall view of the course. Demonstrates declarative understanding of a reasonable amount of content. Able to discuss content meaningfully. Good coverage but little application or integration. Fair justification of items.	The evidence presents a good appreciation of the general thrust of the course. Good coverage with relevant and accurate support. A clear view of how various aspects of the course integrate to form a thrust or purpose. Good evidence of application of course content to practice. Portfolio items well justified.	As in 'good' but with higher degree of originality and evidence of internalization into personalized model of practice. Good evidence of reflection on own performance based on theory. Generalizes course content to new and unfamiliar real-life contexts.

Notice that the final grade is awarded on the basis of the student's profile on all the ILOs: there is no need for counting and averaging, which greatly simplifies the usual procedure. Because of these points, portfolios are very appropriate for capstone projects (p. 253).

Educational technology has enabled the development of e-portfolios with items involving multimedia presentations.

If you are interested in implementing portfolio assessment, try completing Task 12.1.

Task 12.1 Design portfolio assessment for functioning ILOs

Have a go at designing portfolio assessment for functioning ILOs for your course by following the steps below:

1 Identify the ILOs relating to functioning knowledge that are to be assessed.
2 Indicate the number of items to be included in the portfolio and the size of each item.
3 Give a list of sample items for students' consideration. However, students should be encouraged to include items outside the list and ones that they think will best evidence their achievement of the course ILOs.
4 Write the grading criteria of the portfolio.

Before you implement the portfolio assessment, discuss with your students so that they clearly understand the rationale, procedural details of the assessment and the grading criteria. It would be helpful if students have access to some samples of portfolios produced by previous students. You should allow them a trial item on which you provide formative feedback and a provisional summative grade. If they are happy with that result they can include it in the final summative assessment. If they are not happy, they can have another try.

Presentations

Student presentations

As opposed to the traditional seminar, student presentations are best for functioning rather than declarative knowledge. Peer input can be highly appropriate in this case. In one fine arts department, students present a portfolio of their best work to an examining panel that comprises teachers, a prominent local artist and a student (rotating), who view all the student productions. The works are discussed and a final, public, examiners' report is submitted. This is not only a very close approximation to real life in the gallery world, but actively involves staff and students in a way that is rich with learning opportunities.

Poster presentations

Poster presentations also follow a real-life scenario: the conference format. A student, or group of students, displays their work, according to an arranged format, in a departmental or faculty poster session. This provides excellent opportunities for peer-assessment and for fast feedback of results. Poster assessment was introduced as an additional element of the assessment of final-year project in an optometry programme to facilitate and assess reflection and creativity (Cho 2007). Apart from teacher assessing the posters, self- and peer-assessment were also used. To motivate students to do well in the poster assessment, opportunity was given to present the students' posters at a regional conference and a cash reward was awarded to the best poster. Student feedback shows that designing the posters was fun and helped them to be more creative and reflective of what they were doing in the project. The experience of self- and peer-assessment also helped them learn from an assessor's perspective. However, posters 'must be meticulously prepared' (Brown and Knight 1994: 78). The specifications need to be very clear, down to the size of the display and how to use back-up materials: diagrams, flow-charts, photographs. Text needs to be clear and highly condensed. Assessment criteria can be placed on an assessment sheet, which all students receive to rate all other posters. Criteria would include substance, originality, impact and so on.

Reflective journal

In professional programmes in particular, it is useful if students keep a reflective journal, in which they record any incidents or thoughts that help them reflect on the content of the course or programme. Such reflection is basic to proper professional functioning. The reflective journal is especially useful for assessing ILOs relating to the application of content knowledge, professional judgement and reflection on past decisions and problem solving with a view to improving them. One teacher told us she had tried journals but found them useless, because the students wrote what was in effect a diary of routine events – which is *not* what a reflective journal should contain. One needs to be very clear about what course or programme ILOs the journals are meant to be addressing. In a course of contact lens clinic in one of the universities in Hong Kong, reflective writing was used as one of the components of assessment to encourage and assess students' reflection during their clinical placement (Cho and Tang 2007). Students were asked to keep reflective diaries on their learning experience from clinical cases, interaction with and feedback from supervisors and peers and application of theory to practice. Students were briefed on this new form of assessment and were also involved in giving suggestions on the design and assessment weighting of reflective diaries. Quantitative and qualitative feedback from students indicated that students found that they learned more because of the reflective component of the assessment, their learning experience was sharpened through the reflective writing. They were motivated to communicate more frequently with their supervisors and peers to critique their own practice and also the application of theory to practice.

Assessing journals can be delicate, as they often contain personal content. For assessment purposes it is a good idea to ask students to submit selections, possibly focusing on critical incidents and on entries that relate to particular ILOs, the students explaining why they think that they do. Journals should not be 'marked' as a task, but taken as sources of evidence for the ILOs in question, especially useful for the verb 'reflect' to see if the students are able realistically to evaluate their own learning and thinking in terms of course content.

One of the authors used reflective diaries to assess transformative reflection applied to teaching in an inservice master of education course for tertiary teachers (Tang 2000). As one of the learning activities, students were asked to keep a reflective diary of their learning for every session of the course. They were required to select and include two such diaries as part of their assessment portfolio. Feedback from the students showed that the diaries were a useful tool for transformative reflection, providing them with opportunities to search for and express their learning in a personal way and to relate and apply their learning to their own teaching.

Venn diagrams

In the previous chapter we saw how Venn diagrams could be used for assessing declarative ILOs. In Task 12.2 you are asked to design a Venn diagram for an ILO in functioning knowledge and align TLAs and ATs accordingly.

Task 12.2 Venn diagram of TLAs and ATs for functioning knowledge

Functioning ILOs to be addressed by this Venn diagram:

_____

_____

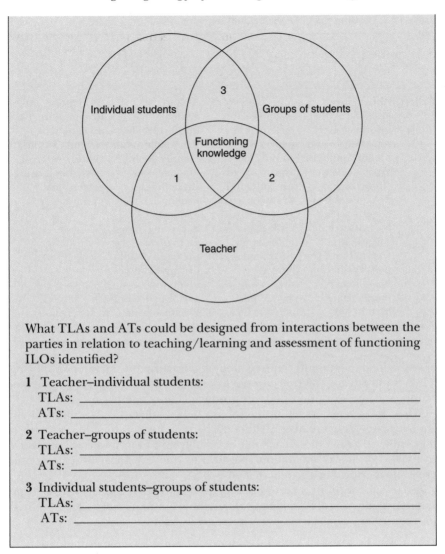

What TLAs and ATs could be designed from interactions between the parties in relation to teaching/learning and assessment of functioning ILOs identified?

1 Teacher–individual students:
   TLAs: _____
   ATs: _____

2 Teacher–groups of students:
   TLAs: _____
   ATs: _____

3 Individual students–groups of students:
   TLAs: _____
   ATs: _____

Assessing 'reflect and improve'

As an example of using rubrics to assess functioning ILOs, Table 12.2 presents possible rubrics for the ILO 'reflect and improve'.

Assessing creativity

A deep-seated ambiguity about the nature of creativity and its assessment exists: whether creativity is conceived as generic, applying across contexts, or

Table 12.2 Grading the ILO 'reflect and improve'

	Marginal *D* *1.0*	*Adequate* *C– C C+* *1.7 2.0 2.3*	*Good* *B– B B+* *2.7 3.0 3.3*	*Excellent* *A– A A+* *3.7 4.0 4.3*
Reflect	Able to use available information to self-evaluate and identify limited aspects of own strengths and weaknesses in a general sense. No evidence of suggestions of ways to improve performance. No evidence of theory being used in self-evaluation.	Able to use available information to self-evaluate and identify more aspects of own strengths and weaknesses in a general sense. Little application of theory in self-evaluation and limited suggestions of ways to improve performance.	Able to use available information to self-evaluate and identify the full range of own strengths and weaknesses. Self-evaluation is improving, based on theory. Increasingly able to suggest ways to improve performance in a specific real-life context.	As in 'good'. Able to generalize self-evaluation to beyond existing context. Suggest ways of improving professional performance.

as embedded in students' chosen area of specialization. As when discussing TLAs for creativity, then, we are not assessing here how creative people are, but the creative work that students produce (Elton 2005).

While most teachers in all disciplines believe that it is possible to help students use their creative abilities to better effect, rather fewer think it is possible to assess these capabilities reliably and even fewer are prepared to try and do it. Yet evaluation is critical to the very idea of creativity and creativity is critical in all areas of study.

Let us start with an area where creativity is expected: University College London Slade School BA in Fine Art, Student Handbook 2003/2004 (quoted in Elton 2005). The assessment criteria are as follows:

> You will be assessed on the evidence of ambition, experimentation, innovation and understanding of the subject and its contexts, as developed in the work. Your progress in and development of the following will be taken into account:
>
> • critical awareness
> • relevant use of processes and materials
> • the depth and scope of investigation
> • the ability to realise ideas
> • contribution to and participation in the course

'Experimentation and innovation' and 'the ability to realise ideas' imply what creativity psychologists like Guilford (1967) and Hudson (1966) refer to as divergent thinking or originality: the ability to create something different on a foundation of the known. This can take the form of recombining known elements in a new way or seeing connections between ideas that others have missed. 'Critical awareness' is similar to transformative reflection (p. 45): it looks at what is known with a view to seeing what it might become.

These criteria suggest a sequence, starting with a foundation of solid knowledge, prising it open and generating new possibilities, in a SOLO-type progression from relational to extended abstract. Extended abstract verbs are open ended, such as hypothesize, generate, design, reflect and improve: all are built on prior sound knowledge and they require an object and a context relating to that knowledge. Assessing creativity in this way applies to all disciplines, from accounting to zoology and, accordingly, can be built into course or programme ILOs as appropriate. In higher years, such open-ended assessment should be appropriate whatever the area of study.

Two major conditions apply to assessing creativity:

1 The assessment tasks have to be open ended. Invigilated examinations are not good formats for displaying creativity, but portfolios, web pages (an e-version of portfolios), blogs, solving 'far' or 'fuzzy' problems, designs, projects, case studies, posters, narratives, reflective journals offer excellent opportunities for students to display their creativity in thinking about and applying their learning.

2 The climate must be such that students are encouraged to take risks, to dare to depart from the established way of doing things. A Theory X climate, with an insistence on students being *right*, discourages creativity.

Assessments in some areas must insist that students do things the established way: surgery, laboratory practice, for example. But when the ILOs address creativity, the assessment tasks must be open ended.

But to continue with our strategy of assessment, what about the rubrics for assessing such outcomes? Isn't asking creative work to be assessed against set criteria something of an oxymoron? Not really, but as Elton (2005) says, the criteria have to be interpreted 'in light of the work'. One aspect of this, he says, is connoisseurship, the ability of experts to assess work in their own field of expertise, the willingness to employ judgement. Balchin (2006) adds to the reliability of judgement by using consensual assessment by several judges.

An important ingredient of creativity is the *originality* of the product and we can estimate that: is it totally surprising and unexpected, is it original-ish but rather ho-hum or is it somewhere in between? Another key attribute of genuine creativity is *appropriateness*. Creative work falls within a context. A design that doesn't work, be it ever so 'imaginative', should not receive an A; a hypothesis that is off the wall as far as the research literature is concerned is not likely to be much of a contribution to knowledge. The rubrics will need to address the constraints that have to be met but be open enough to allow students to display their originality. What other specific aspects of a creative work may need to be taken into account in assessment will depend to a large extent on the discipline area.

John Cowan (2006) suggests a rather more radical model for assessing creativity, based on students' self-assessment according to their own conceptions of what creativity means. The assessment by the teachers is not of the student's creativity on the basis of the creative works the student produces, but to 'decide if they are sufficiently persuaded by the learner's making of their judgement to endorse the learner's self-assessment of their own creative processes, thinking and outcomes, made against the learner's chosen and stated criteria, and following the method of judging which the learner has outlined' (Cowan 2006: 161). To achieve this requires workshopping with students to help them formulate their ideas of creativity and what constitutes the kind of creative works they might produce and how to self-assess it.

Assessing lifelong learning

Lifelong learning is also one of the graduate outcomes that can only really be assessed in its embedded form. The summative assessment of lifelong learning generically will by definition occur rather late in the day for the learner. However, the embedded components of lifelong learning, such as the ability to work independently, to source information selectively, to monitor the quality of one's learning, to reflect transformatively and improve decision making, to use sensible strategies for tackling unseen problems, are assessable in well-designed capstone or independent research projects.

A particular aspect of lifelong learning is workplace learning, of which the practicum is a foretaste. The practicum, if properly designed, should call out all the important verbs needed to demonstrate competence in a real-life situation. Examples include practice teaching, interviewing a patient or client in any clinical session, handling an experiment in the laboratory, producing an artistic product. It should be quite clear that the student has to perform certain behaviours to a specified standard. Videotaping students at work is useful, as then students can rate their own performance against the criteria before discussing the supervisor's rating.

The closer the practicum is to the real situation, the greater its validity. The one feature that distorts reality is that it is, after all, an assessment situation and some students are likely to behave differently from the way they would if they were not being assessed. This may be minimized by making observation of performance a continuing fact of life. With plenty of formative feedback before the final summative assessment, the student might nominate when he or she is 'ready' for the final, summative, assessment. This might seem labour intensive, but recording devices can stand in for *in vivo* observation, as can other students.

In fact, this is a situation ideal for peer-assessment. Students will become accustomed to being observed by one another when they give and receive peer feedback. Whether student evaluations are then used, in whole or in part, in the summative assessment is a separate question but one worth considering.

In Chapter 9, we discussed some teaching/learning activities for facilitating functioning knowledge in workplace learning focusing on ILOs such as:

1 *integrate* knowledge and skills learned in university to real-life professional settings;
2 *apply* theories and skills to practice in all aspects of professional practice;
3 *work collaboratively* with all parties in multidisciplinary workplace settings;
4 *practise* with professional attitudes and social responsibilities in their respective professions.

Because of the multifaceted nature of the different workplace learning situations, there can be no one fixed format of assessment. Assessment tasks and formats must be designed or selected to appropriately address the ILOs. Some common assessment tasks in workplace learning may include:

- observation of students' workplace performance
- placement case reports
- placement case/seminar presentations
- performance records
- reports from other staff in the placement centre
- feedback and evidence from others' relevant sources
- e-portfolio.

The ILOs, and the criteria or rubrics by which they are assessed, should be clearly defined and understood by all parties concerned before the commencement of the workplace learning placement. In most cases, assessment is conducted either by the workplace educators or as a combined effort of the institute academics and the workplace educators. These assessments are teacher-centred. However, we should consider the possibility and feasibility of involving the students in assessing their own performance through peer- and/or self-assessment. These student-centred assessments enable students to have a clearer understanding of the ILOs, have a shared control of their learning and also better equip them for lifelong learning.

Assessing problem solving

Assessing problem solving can vary considerably. Standard problems usually call out a relational response, using conventional and correct paradigms. But even in these problem types, an 'elegant' (extended abstract) solution that is original and concise obviously should be given greater credit: this is creative work even if the format is conventional.

'Fuzzy' problems are those to which there is no definitive correct solution, only better or worse ones. Deciding whether a solution is 'better' or 'worse' depends on the context. All sorts of criteria could come into play: degree of originality, 'elegance', loose strings left hanging, cost etc. Each teacher will have to decide each case on its merits. In this open and complex area, as in the case of creativity, we return to the notion of connoisseurship: the expert should be able to recognize excellence in their field of expertise.

One area where assessing problem solving has well-established practices is problem-based learning itself. The essential feature of a teaching system designed to emulate professional practice is that the crucial assessments should be performance based, holistic, allowing plenty of scope for students to input their own decisions and solutions (Kingsland 1995). Some version of the portfolio, as open ended, may be useful in many programmes, but essentially the assessment has to be suitable for the profession concerned.

Medical PBL developed the 'triple jump' (Feletti 1997), but the structure applies to professional education generally:

1 *dealing with the initial problem or case*: diagnosing, hypothesizing, checking with the clinical database, making use of information, reformulating;
2 *review of independent study*: knowledge gained, level of understanding, evaluating information gained;
3 *final problem formulation*: synthesis of key concepts, application to patient's problem, self-monitoring, response to feedback.

While these steps emulate real life, Feletti asks:

- Do all steps have to be passed or can you average?
- Is there an underlying 'problem-solving ability'?
- Should performance at the various steps correlate together or not?

Possibly sounding like the previous UK prime minister Margaret Thatcher, we would answer 'no', 'no' and 'no':

- 'No', you cannot average because that may mask a crucial weakness.
- 'No', we are not interested in underlying problem-solving abilities, we are interested in whether the student can solve the problems in question.
- 'No', the steps or rather outcomes may well correlate but as teachers that is not our business. We are interested in the answers to each outcome step independently of any other.

All of which goes to show just what a grip measurement model thinking has had on our thinking: even on best practice PBL practitioners.

E-assessment

E-assessment has much potential in assessing both declarative and functioning knowledge. Computer-assisted assessment (CAA) is directed towards declarative knowledge, using the power of the computer to assess conventionally but more efficiently in objective format. There are commercial MCQ banks, or the teacher can design and use them through WebCT or Blackboard.

CAA has several advantages over the usual pencil-and-paper format (Maier et al. 1998) because it:

- allows more than one attempt;
- can supply hints;
- provides immediate feedback;
- can guide reading as a result of the test;
- may be either formative or summative;
- can present questions in random or standard order.

There can be a databank of several questions on a topic and, when a student logs on, a different sample of questions can be presented each time and the difficulty level each student is getting correct can be recorded, diagnoses made and suggestions provided as to how learning may be improved.

A concern with using CAA summatively is that, in time, students can rote learn the correct responses, bypassing the mental process required to work out the correct response. This can be mitigated by randomizing the alternatives at each presentation. When used on a pass–fail basis, 'pass' requiring 90% correct responding, CAA is identical with mastery learning. And that is the problem: it is too easy to equate good learning with 'knowing more', if that is all CAA is used for.

E-assessment's most exciting use is in assessing functioning knowledge. Complex real-life situations can be given in multimedia presentations and students asked to respond. A video clip, with multiple-choice alternatives, could show a professional scenario, say a psychologist interviewing a client, and the student is required to choose from the alternatives what type of situation is represented (Maier and Warren 2000); or in an open-ended version, asking the student to comment on what is going on, a critical analysis of the exchange, what steps the psychologist might take next and so on. Essay assessment can be facilitated by the teacher inserting comments from a bank of comments in appropriate parts of the essay.

Students may be required to set up their own web pages and post their learnings as they would in a learning portfolio and in portfolio assessment. The advantage here is that all the other students in the course can access it and post their own evaluative comments, thus providing formative feedback and self- and peer-assessment much more readily than when assessments are made in hard copy. The UK Open University uses a student-created website in place of a traditional exam; details and discussion of the issues involved such as plagiarism, are provided in Weller (2002). In one university, each student has their own PDA that they use in a wide variety of ways throughout the course. They are able to take photographs and videos and post them on the net, communicate with their teacher and with one another, thus potentially turning every relevant experience into a learning event, a TLA, that can also be used as an assessment task.

Educational technology can be very sophisticated, as in *productive media*, using microworlds where the student builds his or her own system (Laurillard 2002): here TLA and assessment are intertwined as in real-life learning. In fact, the uses of ET in assessment are limitless, mimicking as it can much authentic assessment and by virtue of its interactivity allowing creativity of a high order.

As far as large class e-assessment is concerned, however, one must sound a caution. At first blush it sounds like the answer to assessment of high-order ILOs of functioning knowledge in large classes because the students can work away in their own time, but someone has to visit the websites and make the assessments. Certainly a large part of this burden can be solved by self- and peer-assessment and no doubt too programs like Scardamalia and Bereiter's (1999) Knowledge Forum can help to organize the mass of responses and evaluate the contribution individual students make to the forum.

ET may handle both quantitative and qualitative modes of assessment, with considerable logistical and managerial advantages. The potential of ET in assessment is most valuable in open-ended responding, in rich and contextualized situations, particularly with the advent of software like Knowledge Forum, which facilitates both formative and summative assessment at either individual or group level.

A problem with using ET for summative assessment is that one needs to be sure that the person at the keyboard is the student who should be there. However, the problem of plagiarism exists in both conventional and ET modes.

Let us now consider that problem.

Plagiarism

Many students do not see plagiarism as a moral issue or that it undermines assessment (Ashworth et al. 1997). In some universities, up to 90% of all students plagiarize their work (Walker 1998). In 2002, the Australian Vice-Chancellors Committee commissioned a survey that found that 14% of students are plagiarists, but the figure is probably much higher because much goes unreported.

Susskind (2006) in a summary of various reports on plagiarism suggests that plagiarism in university essays is so rife that bringing back compulsory exams may be the only way to stop it: 'Plagiarism has knocked the stuffing out of the essay assignment,' Melbourne University's Simon Marginson is quoted as saying. 'It has contaminated the essay badly, making it a waste of time as an educational project. Things have moved beyond the current regimes of assessment. The system has broken down.'

Susskind summarizes the driving forces behind current plagiarism levels:

- The first is the Internet, with 8 to 10 billion pages of information freely available.
- Since universities have gone corporate, passing students affects funding, so that teachers are not encouraged to report plagiarism, because of the fear of scandal and loss of funds from failed students. In one Australian university, the senior administration dismissed the claims made by an external examiner that several students had plagiarized their work as

motivated by 'spite', although that examiner had actually supplied the web addresses from which the students had downloaded their papers. This particular case ended in an independent enquiry that took the administration severely to task, resulting in much clearer definitions of plagiarism and tougher procedures, but the fact that this case even occurred is evidence of the extent to which some institutions not only may tolerate but even condone plagiarism.

- Globalization in Australia has brought an influx of about 560,000 foreign university students, or 25% of the student body, many of whom struggle with English. Many feel it preferable to copy from sources rather than trust their own writing skills.
- Generation Y's tendency to question the value and legitimacy of copyright and intellectual property is another factor. Brimble and Stevenson-Clark (reported in Lane 2006) found that 40% of students from four Queensland universities thought that faking the results of research was just 'minor cheating', while 11% did not even regard it as cheating. Students were also very tolerant of copying another student's assignment or downloading from the web.

The true occurrence of plagiarism is hard to estimate: we have estimates here ranging from 14% to 90%. Probably both figures, and all in between, are true in different universities. Plagiarism among international students presents a different problem, due to uncertainty about writing skill. In some cultures, students are taught that it is disrespectful to alter the words of an expert (Ballard and Clanchy 1997).

The remedy is not necessarily to go back to compulsory examinations as such – the educational cost of that in terms of sound assessment would be huge – but to use the invigilated situation more effectively. For example, videos can easily be played in the invigilated situation, either publicly or using controlled individual PDAs with earphones. The student watches the video and is to apply a theory to interpret what is going on. This is a version of the gobbet with a more applied intent. The scenario could be of a social worker interacting with a client, a teacher in a classroom during a critical incident, a scene from a play, a historical re-enactment . . . the possibilities are endless.

Oral assessments are used most commonly in the examination of dissertations and theses but they can be used in undergraduate assessments. The interview is not used in undergraduate assessment as widely as it might be. A properly constructed interview schedule could see a fruitful interview through in 20 minutes or so, while carefully run group interviews could deal with four or five students at a time. Interviews are not necessarily as time consuming as they appear to be and they are even more plagiarism proof than an invigilated exam. Unstructured interviews can be unreliable, but a major advantage of interviewing, that it is interactive, is lost if the interview is too tightly structured. Teachers are able to follow up and probe, while students are able to display their jade, pearls and opals – their unanticipated but valuable learning treasures. Oral assessments should be tape recorded so that the assessment itself may be made under less pressure, and the original assessment can be checked in case of dispute when student and an adjudicator can hear the replay.

A longer-term remedy for plagiarism is to change the culture of the institution. Students are much readier to cheat if they perceive the staff to be setting 'make-work' assignments or if they know that their assignments will be marked by tutors and part-timers whose heart isn't in it: surface approaches on one side breed surface approaches on the other. Setting worthwhile assessment tasks that draw meaningfully on the experience of the students, such as reflective journals, is much more likely to be treated respectfully.

Smythe (2006) describes a way of successfully reducing plagiarism by requiring students to choose a research topic and a proposal, which is submitted early in the semester. Students are thus forced to think about the assignment from the start and to work on it until about the middle of the semester, when they hand in a first draft. This is not graded but comments and guidelines suggested, which are then built into the final version that is graded. Smythe's technique is labour intensive – 'only manageable in classes of under 100' – but the advantages are that students feel a personal commitment and they have to follow the guidelines provided.

Smythe's technique contributes to addressing the fundamental problem. Teachers need to convey a culture of scholarship and what research means. Brimble and Stevenson-Clark's finding that students condone cheating in research simply shows that they don't understand the nature of research or scholarship in general. It doesn't mean producing the results that the corporations who finance the research want to see. It means following the rules of empirical evidence gathering and of their replicability, of logical argument and of recognizing the work of other scholars and building on that in a transparent way: making clear what are the source data, what is the researcher's contribution and its originality. The conventions of citation always make it clear what is previous work and what is the researcher's.

What applies to scholars at the forefront of knowledge applies to undergraduate students when they submit their work. They need to be taught – and to see by example – what the nature of scholarship is and how, therefore, we need to be careful in citing others' work to make clear what is and is not the work of others. Many students plagiarize out of ignorance. They really don't understand the nature of the game.

The game, however, isn't always clear even to academics. Wilson (1997) points out that plagiarism proceeds in stages (that interestingly follow the SOLO levels):

- *Repetition*: simple copying from an unacknowledged source. Unistructural and unacceptable.
- *Patching*: copying, with joining phrases, from several sources. Some general, non-specific, acknowledgement. Weak multistructural and still unacceptable, but harder to spot.

- *Plagiphrasing*: paraphrasing several sources and joining them together. All sources may be in the reference list, but the source pages are unspecified. Still multistructural and still unacceptable, technically, but a plagiarism programme would not detect it because no single sentence or paragraph can be traced, yet the ideas are all second-hand. This shifts almost imperceptibly to the next stage.
- *Conventional academic writing*: ideas taken from multiple sources and repackaged to make a more or less original and relational type of synthesis. Quotes properly referenced, general sources acknowledged; the package may be new but are the *ideas* new? Unoriginal academic writing is plagiphrasing that is properly referenced.
- The extended abstract level would involve a 'far' transformation from the sources – genuine originality – which conventional academic writing should, but does not necessarily, incorporate.

Repetition and patching are clearly unacceptable, but students with poor writing skills of whatever cultural background find it hazardous to attempt to 'put it in your own words' when they are not confident in their use of the language. Lack of confidence in writing skill, especially in second-language international students who may have a good *content* understanding, can easily lead to 'innocent' patching. Such cases need augmented modes of assessment, such as a brief interview, or a less verbal medium such as a concept map.

Plagiphrasing should be unacceptable, but as it is not verbatim it is difficult to detect with software. However, the shift from plagiphrasing to conventional academic writing (presumably acceptable) is not always clear. While it may be sometimes difficult to decide what constitutes genuine and culpable plagiarism, repetition and patching are definite no-nos.

Teachers, on both local and international fronts, need therefore to be extremely clear about these levels of plagiarism and what the rules of referencing and of citation are. And, of course, what the penalties are. The culture of going soft on suspected plagiarism cannot be tolerated as it is antischolarship. In the corporatized world, a firm known for its cheating or false labelling in the end loses its market.

In summary, plagiarism can be minimized by the following means:

1 creating a culture that emphasizes scholarly values;
2 alerting students to the rules and the penalties for infringing them;
3 using assessment tasks that use reflective diaries and other tasks based on personal experiences;
4 using oral assessment and peer- and group assessment;
5 checking assignments using software. *Turnitin*, licensed to 29 Australian universities, can detect plagiarism from web-based sources;
6 increased invigilation as a last resort, but widening the range of assessment tasks within that context from the conventional written examination.

To wind up this chapter on assessing and grading functioning knowledge, you might care to tackle Task 12.3.

Task 12.3 Design an assessment task or tasks for one of your course functioning ILOs

Select one ILO relating to functioning knowledge of your course and design assessment task(s) that will appropriately assess this ILO. To help you check the alignment between the task(s) and the ILO, identify what the students are required to do in order to complete the assessment task(s). The task requirements should be aligned to the ILO.

Course ILO: _____

Number of students in the course: _____

Assessment task	Student activities to complete the task (individually)	Student activities to complete the task (in group)
1		
2		

Now double-check whether the student activities are aligned to the verbs nominated in the respective course ILO.

After designing the task(s), you will need to write the grading criteria for either the ILO or for each of the tasks.

Summary and conclusions

Formats for assessing functioning knowledge

Functioning knowledge is readily assessable because it is deployed most often in the student's real-life experience. Assessment tasks include critical incidents, projects and reflective journals; case studies mirror professional life, while the formats of assessment such as the portfolio and contract are used in real-life assessment situations. Often, high-level functioning knowledge is not addressed by one course ILO but by several, or by the whole programme, so assessment needs to be synoptic, addressing several ILOs. The portfolio and the capstone project are such assessment tasks.

Assessing creativity

Creativity is not something ineffable and unassessable: it is involved in all subject areas, especially in higher years, and needs to be assessed. Creative thinking requires a sound knowledge base, but beyond that requires critical awareness or reflection and the ability to generate original ideas or products that address critical reflection on what is the case. Assessment needs therefore to be open ended, allowing students to spring their surprises on us, but they also need to be surprises that are assessed within parameters that each situation would define as relevant. One suggestion for assessing creativity without any external 'impositions' of what creativity might be is to monitor students' self-assessments of their own creativity using their own standards of what creativity implies.

Assessing lifelong learning

One highly defined area of lifelong learning is assessment of work-based learning, starting with the practicum, which is a representation of professional experience. Lifelong learning can also be assessed through its components: ability to work independently, to source information selectively, to monitor the quality of one's learning, to reflect transformatively to improve decision making, to use sensible strategies for tackling unseen problems and the like, all of which are variously assessable in open-ended formats.

Assessing problem solving

Assessing students' ability to solve 'far' or 'fuzzy' problems is similar to assessing the components of lifelong learning. A detailed technology of assessment has developed in problem-based learning itself.

E-assessment

E-assessment has two main roles. Computer-assisted assessment makes the most out of the standard situation of asking standard convergent questions and providing feedback. Beyond that, interactive e-assessment allows students to give free rein to their creativity by constructing models, using web pages, blogs and chats. Moreover, these formats can use self- and peer-assessment readily.

Plagiarism

Plagiarism is an ancient problem but it seems to be becoming easier and more rife with the use of the Internet, with pressures on universities not to fail students and with cultural changes among Gen Yers and some international students in views of what constitutes intellectual property. The best answer to this is to institute a culture of scholarship in which the way of doing research, of submitting assignments and of setting assessment tasks as authentic and personally relevant, becomes the accepted norm. There are better ways of minimizing – but admittedly not eliminating – plagiarism than by increased invigilation.

Further reading

General assessment tasks

Brown, S. and Glasner, A. (eds) (1999) *Assessment Matters in Higher Education.* Buckingham: Society for Research into Higher Education/Open University Press.

Brown, S. and Knight, P. (1994) *Assessing Learners in Higher Education.* London: Kogan Page.

Carless, D., Joughin, G., Liu, N.F. and associates (2006) *How Assessment Supports Learning.* Hong Kong: Hong Kong University Press.

Frankland, S. (ed) (2007) *Enhancing Teaching Learning through Assessment.* Dordrecht, The Netherlands: Springer.

Gibbs, G., Habeshaw, S. and Habeshaw, T. (1984) *53 Interesting Ways to Assess Your Students.* Bristol: Technical and Educational Services.

Stephenson, J. and Laycock, M. (1993) *Using Contracts in Higher Education.* London: Kogan Page.

There are many books of practical suggestions on assessment; this list is a good sample. Brown and Glasner and Brown and Knight talk about the theory and practice of mainly CRA. Carless et al. is a collection of 'best practice' from university teachers across Hong Kong with 39 case studies, grouped under various headings of self- and peer-assessment, group assessment, building feedback into assessment tasks, addressing higher order thinking and the like. Frankland is a collection of 40 refereed papers given at the First International Conference 'Enhancing Teaching and Learning through Assessment' in 2005. Readers of Carless and Frankland are likely to find several ideas to improve their own teaching and assessment.

Examples of learning contracts

Nursing: http://www.health.qld.gov.au/northside/documents/contract_sample.pdf (accessed 2 February 2011).

Physiotherapy: http://www.latrobe.edu.au/physiotherapy/postgrad/profdoclearning contract.pdf (accessed 2 February 2011).

Websites

There are literally hundreds of websites advising on assessment. Here are a few accessed at the time of writing.

Polytechnic University of Hong Kong: www.assessment.edc.polyu.edu.hk/ (accessed 2 February 2011). Go to Assessment Resource Centre (ARC).

Queensland University of Technology: www.tedi.uq.edu.au/teaching/index.html (accessed 2 February 2011).

University of Melbourne, see especially the Assessment in Australian Universities project: www.cshe.unimelb.edu.au/assessinglearning (accessed 2 February 2011).

University of Sydney: www.itl.usyd.edu.au/ (accessed 2 February 2011).

E-assessment

Allen, M. (2009) Authentic assessment and the Internet: Contributions within Knowledge Networks. http://netcrit.net/content/aaceauthenticassessment 2009.pdf (accessed 2 February 2011).

www.educause.edu/ir/library/pdf/ELI3001.pdf e-portfolio portal: www.danwilton .com/eportfolios/ (accessed 2 February 2011). An overview of e-portfolio.

www.uwstout.edu/soe/profdev/eportfoliorubric.html (accessed 2 February 2011). Rubrics for electronic portfolio.

Assessing creativity

Jackson, N., Oliver, M., Shaw, M. and Wisdom, J. (eds) (2006) *Developing Creativity in Higher Education: An Imaginative Curriculum*. Abingdon: Routledge.

www.heacademy.ac.uk/2841.htm. See especially the chapters and papers by Lewis Elton, Norman Jackson and Tom Balchin.

Assessing workplace learning

The Journal of Workplace Learning. http://www.emeraldinsight.com/info/journals/ jwl/jwl.jsp (accessed 2 February 2011).

Peer-, self- and large class assessment

Boud, D. (1995) *Enhancing Learning through Self-assessment*. London: Kogan Page.
Carless, D., Joughin, G., Liu, N.F. and associates (2006) *How Assessment Supports Learning*. Hong Kong: Hong Kong University Press.
Gibbs, G., Jenkins, A. and Wisker, G. (1992) *Assessing More Students*. Oxford: PCFC/ Rewley Press.

Plagiarism

Turnitin home page: http://turnitin.com/

www.library.ualberta.ca/guides/plagiarism/ (accessed 2 February 2011). Excellent article on plagiarism and minimizing it.

Part 3

Constructive alignment in action

13

Implementing, supporting and enhancing constructive alignment

Now that we know how to put together all the components of constructive alignment – writing ILOs, designing TLAs and assessing and grading students' performance – we have the task of implementing constructive alignment in courses and programmes. Introducing educational change into the system is a procedure with its own pitfalls. We look at implementing constructive alignment at several levels: by the individual teacher, by a whole department or faculty, by a single institution, and on a wider front using the train-the-trainer model. In all cases, the strategy of implementation is similar, using transformative reflection and formative evaluation. Implementation isn't a one-off process but a continuing action learning cycle of reflection, application and evaluation that is basic to all quality enhancement. In fact, all procedures relating to implementing constructive alignment can be generalized to create quality enhancement procedures for the whole institution. The key is that all structures and procedures to do with teaching and learning, from classroom level to procedures and regulations that apply across the whole institution, are founded in the scholarship of teaching and learning to create an organic, reflective institution. We also point to common policies and procedures that may be counterproductive to aligned teaching.

A framework for implementing and supporting constructive alignment

So far, we have been presenting the framework of constructive alignment; the next step is the process of implementing it. As we argued in Chapter 3, considered professional change takes place through transformative reflection (p. 45). The intended outcome of this reflection is the successful implementation of constructively aligned teaching and learning, putting in place supportive infrastructure and continuing quality enhancement.

When used by individual teachers, transformative reflection shows the way forward under difficult or changing circumstances in the classroom: as for example in Box 3.1 (p. 48) where Stuart revised his TLAs. Transformative reflection may also be used by administrators and committees to address such questions as:

1 What is the espoused theory of teaching we are operating with here? Chapters 1–12 have hopefully provided the answer to that.
2 How can the theory provide answers to the problems and issues of implementation? What needs doing to support, facilitate and maintain implementation?
3 What is preventing effective implementation?

Transformative reflection can be used for implementing constructive alignment:

● at the classroom level by individual teachers in connection with the courses for which they are responsible;
● at the level of department, faculty, school or the whole institution by administrators and committees;
● at levels beyond the institution, such as regionally or nationally.

Implementing at any level requires some necessary conditions:

1 a felt need for change by all major participants;
2 a clear conception of what an aligned teaching system is;
3 the operational decisions made about writing ILOs, designing TLAs and ATs, and grading students' performances;
4 a willing climate in which all participants will be on side and institutional policies and procedures that support constructive alignment will be in place;
5 sufficient financial resources, time available for developing constructive alignment, any extra teaching space and equipment, educational technology and the like;
6 formative evaluation of progress, including evidence that the new system is working properly; and, if not, the means of finding out what to do to correct matters.

Implementation could start with a decision by state officials at a national level, or by the head of the institution, with implementation working top down through faculty, school and department, down to the classroom level. In our experience such top-down implementation is becoming quite common, but let us start instead at the classroom level, where the nitty-gritty decisions need to be made and be got right by individual teachers. Then we shall work upwards to define the sort of infrastructure that needs to be in place to support constructively aligned teaching. What that infrastructure amounts to, as we work through department and institution, is a quality enhancement system.

Implementing constructive alignment in the individual classroom

Let us start with you, an individual teacher who is willing to give constructive alignment a go. If you have persisted with this book so far, and have carried out the suggested tasks, then you will have met the first three necessary conditions: you are motivated, you have a clear idea of what you are trying to do and you have made all the main decisions.

Availability of the resources you think you need is limiting rather than lethal. You can always do something with what you have even if it is not what you'd most prefer to do. The first resource is time. You need time to prepare for the first run, for planning and writing the ILOs while teaching in the old way. If your head of department is sympathetic to what you are doing you might get some relief from other duties, which would make life easier. If not, then your commitment and enthusiasm will hopefully carry you through. But cheer up: once the course has run for a semester, it will demand much less time in maintaining and fine-tuning than the first run took.

Personnel and financial resources may present some problems: some ideal decisions may be expensive in terms of resources, but if the resources aren't available, it is usually possible to make less expensive, if less ideal, decisions. The selection of teaching/learning activities may be resource intensive. You might want to break down a large class into tutor-led groups or to utilize two separate classrooms, but if additional tutors or rooms are not available, those TLAs you had in mind may not be feasible. However, as we saw in Chapter 8, there is a range of TLAs available that you can use yourself in a large class.

Policies and regulations to do with assessment could be a major difficulty. If there is an iron-clad policy of grading on the curve, then a constructively aligned system is in real trouble. You could state your ILOs, align your TLAs and assess with aligned ATs – but then submit your grades according to the required proportions. That is possible, but it is an act of academic infidelity. You'll feel guilty afterwards; you'll have to look your students in the eye while you explain why they did not get the grades they had earned. They may never forgive you.

Other regulations may require a fixed percentage of the final grade to be by invigilated exam. The main problem here is that if the proportion is too high, it may severely limit the assessment of the more important, high order ILOs (see pp. 228–9). However, 'by examination' doesn't necessarily mean you have to use the assessment task of writing answers to questions but that you have to set your assessment tasks in a timed and supervised situation, which can allow some high-level assessment (pp. 243–9). Another regulation that is a nuisance rather than a critical impediment is being required to report assessment results in percentages or in other quantitative terms. It is important that the actual assessment is done qualitatively (see p. 239), but having done that it is simple to allocate numbers to grades (Table 11.2, p. 241) in order to give admin their precious numbers. They'll probably convert them back to grades anyway.

As to the willing climate, and the cooperation of colleagues, that may or may not be a problem. While Lee Shulman (quoted in D'Andrea and Gosling 2005: 67) complains that 'we close the classroom door and experience pedagogical solitude', that also means that you can get on with your teaching as you see fit. However, Shulman wrote that 15 years ago and today, when programmes are required to address graduate outcomes and to allow for credit transfer between universities and countries, cooperation between colleagues in programme planning is required. Shulman today might feel a twinge of loss of what was then quaintly known as the 'academic freedom' to teach as he saw fit but he would certainly feel less pedagogically lonely. Today, implementation is much more an institutional matter than used to be the case, as outlined later.

Right, you have designed your course or courses and taught for one semester. Did you, as an individual teacher, get it right? How would you know if you did, and how would you ensure that problems were rectified and ILOs, TLAs and ATs fine-tuned to keep doing it better?

The answer is action research, which we introduced in Chapter 3.

Quality enhancement through action research

We saw in Chapter 3 that action research is built on the 'action research spiral' – reflect–plan–apply–evaluate; reflect–plan–apply–evaluate, etc. – each such cycle building on the previous one (Kember and Kelly 1993). Applying this to implementing constructive alignment in your own classroom, you might take day one of implementation to present the ILOs to the students and explain that they are required to produce evidence as to how well they meet them. Box 6.1 (p. 96) explains what happened in John's first implementation: the students hadn't come across portfolio assessment before and many didn't like it. On reflection, John decided to introduce a trial run with the portfolio and to negotiate with them about some teaching/learning activities that would help them create the portfolio.

Thus, transformative reflection begins from day one. You first reflect on the situation or problem, plan what to do, do it, evaluate the effects it has, and after reflecting on those effects, plan the next step and so on. Even when the course is running for the first time, you will have your own gut feeling as to how well the students are taking it. Those feelings are the antennae that any teacher uses, but in action research you take deliberate steps to obtain harder evidence than your own intuitions, important though the latter are. More formally, the action research cycle goes like this:

1 obtain evidence of progress;
2 reflect on what seems to be working and what seems not to be working;
3 introduce changes at the points in the system that seem not to be working as well as you had hoped;

4 obtain evidence that enables you to evaluate how these changes seem to be working;

5 if they are not working, repeat (3) as appropriate;

6 use the offices of a 'critical friend' wherever possible.

It may sound rather bothersome, but much of the 'evidence' is there already, it's only a matter of systematically collecting what you think is relevant and sufficient for your purposes. Remember that much action research, well carried out, is publishable. If your institution supports publishing the teaching of your content area – as it should (see later) – you can kill three birds with one constructively aligned stone: you improve your teaching, you keep on improving it, and you add to your publication record (Kember and McKay 1996).

Evidence enabling you to evaluate your teaching and the changes you bring about comes largely from two perspectives: the students' and the teacher's.

Evidence from the students' perspective

The Learning Experience Inventory (LEI)

A questionnaire can tell you how the students see the TLAs and ATs are aligned to the ILOs. Were the ILOs clear? Did the TLAs help them achieve the ILOs? Which did not? Did the ATs address the ILOs? Were the grading rubrics understood? Did the ILOs help students plan for learning? Did they see the assessments tasks as fairly assessing what they had learned? A new instrument, tentatively named the Learning Experience Inventory (LEI), is being trialled at two Hong Kong universities to obtain students' reflections on their learning. It has five scales, with five items per scale:

1 What I am to learn. Are students clear about what they are to learn?

2 How did I go about learning it? Do students see that the teaching actively engaged them in appropriate learning?

3 How well did I learn it? Do students see the assessment as adequately addressing what they are supposed to have learned?

4 How I feel about my learning. Do students enjoy the course and feel satisfied with it?

5 Reflecting on my learning. Did the experience of constructively aligned teaching make students more reflective and more able to manage their own learning?

The wording is open, so that the LEI can be applied to traditional as well as to constructively aligned courses. Even in traditional courses alignment of teaching and assessment to what is intended students should learn is seen by quality assurance agencies as evidence of well designed teaching. The LEI could therefore be used generally as a quality assurance or quality enhancement measure. Initial results show a high degree of internal consistency and reliability. Trials are ongoing.

Students' approaches to learning: the study process questionnaire (SPQ)

Are the Roberts becoming more like the Susans after the introduction of constructive alignment? The shortened two-factor version of the study process questionnaire (SPQ) (Biggs et al. 2001), which has only 20 items and may be copied from the reference, will tell you. The SPQ is designed to reflect students' reactions to teaching in terms of their approaches to learning. We want to be able to say: 'Before I implemented constructive alignment, the students in the class were on average higher on the surface scale and lower on the deep, but after implementation they are higher on the deep and lower on the surface scale. It looks like I'm on the right track.'

Grade distributions

Grade distributions can be compared prior to the implementation of constructive alignment and after implementation, but *only if* the same grading criteria are used in assessing student performances. Has the *nature* of the grades changed? Is the 'A' grade after implementation the same kind as previous 'A' grades? But remember, you can't compare the distribution of norm-with criterion-referenced grades, as norm-referenced are artificially held constant year after year.

Samples of student performance

Pre- and post-implementation samples can be kept in a library of assessment tasks representing the worst grades, middle grades and best grades, to see if particular aspects or the general quality of performance has improved or not.

Student focus groups

Focus groups may be interviewed on how students reacted to aligned teaching and how their learning strategies might have changed, given that they have a clear idea of the ILOs.

Diaries and e-portfolios

Susan constantly reflects on how she is going about learning, on whether her learning and study strategies are fruitful, whereas Robert does not – which is Robert's main problem. Students can be encouraged to reflect on their learning by the use of diaries and e-portfolios (p. 61). Cheung et al. (2009) used e-portfolios specifically in the context of constructively aligned teaching, enabling the students to reflect on the clarity of their learning goals and the effectiveness of TLAs in helping them attain them and how they might become more independent in their ways of doing so.

Thus, requiring students to keep a learning diary, to bring them into the assessment with peer- and self-assessment and to assess by learning portfolio, are situations that encourage students too to carry out transformative reflection. This is not only helpful for them but is very important feedback in action research on constructive alignment.

Evidence from the teacher's perspective

Teaching portfolio

The best source of evidence is a teaching portfolio. This is a collection of evidence about your teaching and your students' learning, and a self-reflection on that evidence. It is your own quality enhancement process with the intended outcomes of helping you to:

1 keep a personal record of your teaching practice;
2 reflect on your teaching philosophy and practice;
3 identify your strengths and areas for improvement as a teacher;
4 plan your professional teaching development.

Box 13.1 suggests some contents of a teaching portfolio.

Box 13.1 Contents of a teaching portfolio

There is no standard list of contents of a teaching portfolio but it should include a statement of your theory of teaching on which all your teaching decisions are (or should be) based. The following is an indication of the types of evidence you could consider including.

1 Evidence provided by yourself:

- statement of your personal teaching philosophy underlying your own teaching;
- teaching qualifications and experience, focusing on your current teaching and other teaching-related responsibilities;
- achievements in teaching and other teaching scholarly activities, such as: teaching innovations, development of teaching materials and resources, curriculum development, postgraduate supervision, professional teaching development, action research and teaching-related publications, contributions to enhancement of teaching and learning within the institution, any official recognition of your teaching achievement, such as teaching awards or invitation to present in conferences, etc.;
- administrative duties enabling you to promote teaching and learning beyond your own, such as responsibilities as course or programme leader, member of teaching and learning committees, member of teaching innovation group, etc.

2 Evidence provided by colleagues, students and others:

- feedback from peer review from colleagues who have observed your teaching (see peer review below);

- evaluation and feedback from colleagues on your course materials and content;
- student evaluation of and feedback to your teaching, additional to the institution's quality assurance process: formal and informal student feedback provided by students during their learning with you, unsolicited emails, correspondence, 'thank you' cards from past and present students indicating their appreciation of your teaching. Evaluation of and feedback on any teaching development activities you have offered.

3 An overall self-reflection on:

- the strengths of your teaching;
- areas for further improvement;
- action plan for further professional development.

All your claims should be supported by concrete examples: your teaching materials, samples of student work, teaching development workshop materials, etc., and how your decision making is informed and based on your personal teaching philosophy.

Pages of raw evaluation data, no matter how positive, should not be included in the portfolio. Summary of the evaluation and your reflection on the results are more informative.

There is no fixed format to a teaching portfolio, just that it should be designed and structured to effectively reflect your teaching achievements and how your students' learning has been affected by your teaching, with reference to the context in which the portfolio is to be used. The portfolio is normally presented as a written document, either in hard or soft copy format, but the electronic format is becoming more common. Appropriate multimedia presentations could be considered such as a video or audio tape of your own teaching with accompanied self-reflection. The teaching portfolio should be a succinct documentation highlighting your strengths, accomplishment and reflection on your teaching, normally no more than three or four pages long. Detailed examples should be included in the appendices and an indication that further details could be available on request. A lengthy portfolio may hide the wood with all the trees – and bore your readers.

For quality enhancement at a particular course level, appropriate sections of the portfolio could focus on reflection on implementing constructive alignment. These reflections should be compiled while still teaching the course before constructive alignment was implemented, as a baseline. To provide evidence for evaluation of your teaching, the following would be addressed:

1 difficulties you have had in implementation: with ILOs, TLAs, assessment tasks, rubrics or with any other aspect;

2 insights into teaching and learning you have gained;
3 evidence of successful teaching incidents with constructive alignment;
4 comparisons with the 'old way';
5 suggestion for further improving implementing constructive alignment or your teaching in general.

Your reflection should focus on the alignment between the intended learning outcomes, teaching/learning activities, assessment tasks and grading, and how the alignment could be enhanced.

Role of 'critical friend'

Reflection is often not best carried out alone. So, as the fish is the last to discover water, it is helpful to have a 'critical friend' on dry land. The critical friend is part partner, part consultant, and a mirror to facilitate reflection (Stenhouse 1975). Your own reflections are sharpened if shared with someone who has a different perspective and some technical expertise. A colleague in the same department is particularly convenient as critical friend, because they know the context and at the right time can gently feed in suggestions to be reflected on; if they have educational expertise, so much the better. We look at peer review later as a normal part of quality enhancement; part of that process could well include the role of critical friend. Teaching developers are ideal as critical friends, especially in the early stages or where specific technical advice is required, but not the head of department, even if he or she is a friend.

Changes to your own teaching are more likely to be sustained and effective the more those changes are supported by departmental/institutional policy. Say, for example, that in your first run of constructive alignment, you get unusually high numbers of high distinctions and distinctions, say 37% and 40% respectively, whereas your colleagues usually turn in about 10% and 15%. At the examiners' meeting your results are queried, you explain what constructive alignment is all about, your results are passed.

The same happens next semester, but mutterings about 'slack standards of assessment' are louder. The students have given your course high evaluations, which proves to your more unkind colleagues that it is indeed a soft option – although when the students see what they have to do to get the high distinction, and at what standard, they may not see it as a soft option at all.

It would have been psychologically and politically easier if you and a colleague were critical friends for each other. Then two people would be implementing a course and if both obtained similarly improved grade distributions, remaining colleagues at the examiners' meeting might be more easily convinced. It is a short step from there for teachers within the department to act as critical friend for each other. Maybe the whole department becomes involved, not just in improving the skills of individuals, but the offerings and working of the department itself would then become the subject of collective reflection.

But before we move onto implementation at the departmental or other institutional level, Table 13.1 gives some stages or levels in the development

Table 13.1 Constructive Alignment Development Framework at classroom level

	Level 1	Level 2	Level 3	Level 4
Implementing CA	CA is at a declarative level of understanding: saying that CA is about aligning ILOs with teaching and assessment, but does not translate into practice.	CA is about defining ILOs, which are clearly defined, but TLAs and ATs only loosely aligned to the ILO.	ILOs, TLAs and ATs constructively aligned using verbs in the ILO. Evidence collected on the effectiveness of the implementation.	In addition to Level 3, ways of ongoing improvement to the system are in place through reflective practice and action research. CA is regarded as the norm for teaching.
Observable indicators: individual teachers at course level	Completion of necessary documentation but no clear alignment between ILOs and teaching and assessment ('lecture + tutorial', 'assignment'). Otherwise business as usual as far as CA is concerned. ILOs given to students but no consistent or clear explanation about alignment.	Completion of necessary documentation, with clearly defined ILOs and a list of TLAs and ATs relevant to ILOs, but alignment not always clear or consistent. Students given explanation of ILOs in class or in orientation activities but without ensuring they understand the alignment with TLAs and ATs.	Completion of necessary documentation with clear ILOs, TLAs and ATs constructively aligned in practice as well as in paperwork. Effective communication with students on CA. Ongoing collection and evaluation of feedback from students on effective implementation of CA and of more effective learning. Engage in ongoing teaching development.	In addition to Level 3, there is constant review of individual course for redesigning innovative and aligned TLAs, ATs. Teachers use transformative reflective practice e.g. through teaching portfolios and engagement in action research.

of implementing constructive alignment at the classroom level, and a self-assessing task (Task 13.1) enables you to see at what level you as an individual teacher might be in that process.

Task 13.1 What level are you at in implementing constructive alignment at the course level?

Using the 'Constructive Alignment Development Framework at classroom level' as a guide, reflect on what level you are at in implementing CA at the course level. Provide evidence to substantiate your claim.

What level are you at?

_____

What actions would you take to enable you to reach a high level in implementing CA in your course?

_____

_____

_____

_____

Implementing, supporting and enhancing constructive alignment in the department, faculty or school

Implementing constructive alignment across the whole department, faculty or school is obviously more complex than an individual teacher implementing one or more courses, in that infrastructure supporting constructive alignment also needs putting in place, with quality enhancement mechanisms. Such support involves leadership, strategies of implementation, formative evaluation for quality enhancement, and a developmental framework for implementing constructive alignment.

Leadership

The most important factor in department- or faculty-wide implementation is *leadership* (Toohey 2002; Taylor and Canfield 2007). Most of the conditions required for effective change – a felt need for change, a clear conception of an aligned teaching system, the operational decisions concerning ILOs,

TLAs and assessment and grading, and providing sufficient resources – are in the hands of the departmental or school leadership, whether that is an individual or various committees on which teachers are represented.

The formal leader, be it head of department, dean or subdean, has first of all to understand constructive alignment and the demands that proper implementation make on resources, and then, once the decision to implement it has been made, to emphasize with a smile: 'We *are* going ahead with this, you know!' However, leadership does not mean that implementation should be relentlessly top-down. Rather, the senior movers and shakers should be clear about what they want done, and engage and delegate in a way that brings in as many of the staff as possible. Thus, there will need to be a process leader who orchestrates the various phases of implementation, a content expert who can be relied upon for technical advice on implementation, and a political leader who understands how the committee system works and who knows whose elbows to grip in easing the implementation through various committees. There will be ruffled feathers to smooth of those who feel that their babies – the forms for courses and programmes, the teacher feedback and student feedback questionnaires, the software for collating and reporting student progress – have to be redesigned.

Strategies of implementation

Consciousness raising

Once the decision to implement constructive alignment has been taken, there will need to be widespread *consciousness raising*, addressing such questions as: what *is* constructive alignment, what are the advantages, how difficult is it to implement, why go to all that bother, and anything else the staff may want to know. This phase may well require the services of an outside consultant who can answer those questions, correct the misapprehensions and ease the anxieties that many are likely to hold.

The implementation itself

The actual implementation may well involve the services of someone who is an expert both in the content being taught and in constructive alignment. This person, who may be brought in from outside as a consultant or be a knowledgeable member of the department, works closely with teachers on writing intended learning outcomes. Writing ILOs is the first task and it must be done correctly, as all else, the teaching/learning activities and the assessment tasks, hinge on the ILOs. In our experience, one or a few teachers in the department 'get it' fairly quickly; their ILOs are well written and they have a flair for generating aligned and inventive TLAs and ATs. The courses of these teachers should become models for others, so these pioneers should be identified and become internal resources persons for others in the department – with a formal status, such as 'constructive alignment facilitator' – and their teaching loads adjusted accordingly. When this happens, the external subject consultant can take a much lower profile, to be called in only from time to time as need arises. A department needs to become self-sufficient as soon as possible, problems arising being solved by those who know and understand the workings of the department. As we emphasize later, the institution's staff developers should have an ongoing role here.

Do you start small with one or two courses or do you go for broke and implement across the board? Is it best to do so a course at a time, seeing how it goes, what the problems are, what works and what doesn't and learning from initial mistakes, introducing constructive alignment more broadly as colleagues become convinced? Or is it better to be more top-down, to announce ultimate deadlines that *must* be met, with rewards for the early birds and penalties for the slackers? Michael Fullan (cited in Toohey 2002: 196) supports the former strategy. Try pilot studies first and then, as it becomes apparent that the change is going to work, senior management will take it up and bring about the necessary policies and directives for the whole reform to work. But does this mean every faculty or institution has to run its own pilot studies? At what point is likely success assured? What do you do about those who still have doubts but whose cooperation is needed?

There will always be doubters. Many teachers understandably see themselves as committed researchers; they don't want to spend what could be time doing research in designing new courses that – as far as they are concerned – are working well enough already. Other teachers, frequently the more experienced, see themselves as inspirational lecturers with a wealth of teaching experience and a knowledge of all the Level 2 teaching tricks; they see no reason to change. If the conservative teachers are in the minority, a sound strategy is to leave them to it; they'll come to see that they'll be left behind. When a whole department requires courses to be written in a certain format, with ILOs, TLAs and ATs spelled out, with 'official' rubrics for different assessment tasks or outcomes, the conservative teacher would find it difficult not to fall into line. Or, as Toohey reports (2002), people will start to see that 'they don't have to feel bad about spending so much time on teaching because they're getting so much reward from it and enjoying their teaching time' (p. 196). Most younger teachers, who don't have so much confidence in their teaching, may indeed welcome a whole-department approach. After all, this is a safer environment for an inexperienced teacher.

The answer to the question of strategy – start small at first, or go for it across the board – would depend on the balance of pro- or anti-feeling among those who have to participate in one way or another. If change is to be effected, a majority needs to be positively committed. If the implementation was a collective decision by a department in which all or most cheerfully voted to implement constructive alignment, you have an excellent start as colleagues can mutually support each other in maintaining their commitment, keeping up motivation, solving problems and so on (Taylor and Canfield 2007: we summarize this account of a successful implementation in Chapter 14). But where the decision comes heavily top-down, a culture of compliance is a danger, in which a surface job is done on the paperwork and nothing else changes (Knight and Trowler 2000).

The implementation proceeds best when both troops and managers agree. They need each other if it is to work. If a department wants to go ahead and the middle managers are half-hearted, fearing perhaps the criticisms of more conservative colleagues; or if the managers are gung-ho but the teachers feel they are already doing a good job and see the direction to change as a criticism, trouble lies ahead. As we see in Table 13.1 at Level 1, once the new programmes or courses have been approved and the paperwork has been done, it can be business as usual with lecture plus tutorial and the greater part of the final grade by examination.

In such a case, where the majority of a department or faculty needs convincing, starting small with a few courses involving one or a few willing teachers is more likely to bring the majority around when they see how successful it is. As long as it is.

Formative evaluation for quality enhancement

The scholarship of teaching and learning (SoTL, see pp. 46–7) is the foundation of all institutional decisions, policies and structures to do with implementing and supporting constructive alignment, whether at departmental, faculty or institutional level. For example, SoTL transforms quality assurance (QA) to quality enhancement (QE). QA is concerned with maintaining the quality of the work institutions already do, and is retrospective, assuring that accountability and fire-fighting mechanisms have been working, that money has been well spent. Quality enhancement, however, is prospective, concerned with reviewing not only how well the whole institution works in achieving its mission, but also how it may keep improving in doing so. QE mechanisms look to the future, ensuring that through appropriate monitoring structures using transformative reflection, teaching and learning will be continually monitored and enhanced. An effective quality enhancement system pre-empts the need for quality assurance.

Implementing constructive alignment and setting up quality enhancement mechanisms means formative evaluation of teaching. Even before courses are implemented, plans for ongoing formative evaluation need to be established. As Toohey (2002) wisely puts it: 'Evaluation will always occur whether planned or not' (p. 197). Someone, usually the sceptics, will be only too willing to watch closely for any problems and gleefully pass on the good news that this new-fangled approach isn't working. Such judgements are anecdotal and most frequently made from a different perspective from that on which the course was designed. Critics of PBL point out for instance that PBL graduates don't know as much as traditional medical graduates – and can even produce evidence to prove that. Horror, PBL is a failure! Well, no, actually, because PBL graduates were *intended* to know less, and in the time they would otherwise spend knowing more, they would learn the skills to deploy what they do know more effectively and where they don't know, how to go about finding out what they need to know. On those criteria, PBL is more effective than traditional teaching (pp. 182–3).

The answer to such ill-informed criticism is to pre-empt it by planning a departmental or institutional evaluation. As with the individual teacher, the general plan is to employ action research (see pp. 284–5), but in the case of a whole department, faculty or institution, the design of the action research would need to be more comprehensive. In addition to the evidence taken from the students' and the teacher's perspectives, we have the departmental perspective to take into account.

The department, or its teaching quality committee (if it doesn't have one it should have, see later), could submit a reflective report on the experience in implementing constructive alignment at the end of the first year of implementation. The constructive alignment developmental framework at department/faculty level provides a useful framework for reflection (see Table 13.2, p. 301). Issues to be addressed in the report may include:

1 Impact on teaching: data from teachers' portfolios could be compiled, and course evaluations by students.
2 Impact on student learning: much the same data as gathered by teachers for individual course evaluations (p. 285 ff.).
3 Comparisons across different aligned courses: Which ones are working well? Which ones are experiencing difficulties? What were the difficulties and how were they dealt with?
4 What operational structures has the department or faculty with respect to implementing, supporting and enhancing the innovation?
5 Concerns regarding continuing implementation.
6 An action plan for future improvement.

Formative evaluation is an intrinsic part of implementation. It provides formative feedback and material on what is working and what is not, with transformative reflection suggesting how solutions to problems might be tried in the action research model to achieve ongoing quality enhancement.

It also pre-empts the nasty gibes of the doubters.

Change conceptions first or actions?
Teachers teach in a way consistent with their conceptions of teaching (Kember 1998). So before implementing constructive alignment, should we first try to change teachers' conceptions by getting them to *think* about teaching in terms of a Level 3 theory? Kember thinks that we should, as teachers would then understand more clearly what Level 3 teaching meant: otherwise, they will revert to their old ways.

Guskey (1986), on the other hand, says it is easier to change people's behaviour first, *then* to change their thinking. He sees improving teaching as like getting people to quit smoking. Education campaigns, which are aimed at what people think, are not as effective as 'No smoking' signs, or raising the tobacco tax. Then, when their behaviour is forced to change, people begin to think it might be a good idea to stop smoking anyway. In this view, teaching development should aim at changing teachers' behaviour first, then their beliefs will follow and the change will be maintained. Thus, the dean (or whoever) would issue a directive: 'From Semester 1, 2012, all departments will use constructive alignment. In the meantime, all staff are required to attend workshops in preparation.'

It works both ways. Some sort of official directive is necessary to get things moving. Thinking and doing reinforce each other, as in any reflective practice. Let us say you are not really convinced about constructive alignment but you are willing to give it a try. You find it works. You see that students are learning things you never anticipated; you begin to revise your ideas and conclude that good teaching is about what students do, not what teachers do. No longer sceptical, you ask: 'Why does it work?' This is a question that involves a transformation in thinking.

Ho (2001) confronted teachers with what they said they believed was good teaching with what they actually did. As a result, many changed their conceptions and their practices, with positive results for the students' approaches to learning. Prosser and Trigwell (1999) also emphasize that ways of teaching are interlinked with what teachers think teaching is. They need to:

1 become aware of the way they conceive learning and teaching, within the subjects they teach;
2 examine carefully the context in which they are teaching, so that they are aware of how that context affects the way they teach;
3 seek to understand the way their students perceive the learning and teaching situation;
4 continually revise, adjust and develop their teaching in light of this developing awareness.

To help teachers achieve this self-awareness, Prosser and Trigwell have developed the Approaches to Teaching Inventory (ATI), which addresses what they think and what they do. Levels 1 and 2 are combined in an information transmission/teacher-focused approach, which is contrasted with a conceptual change/student-focused approach (Level 3). This is a very useful instrument in teaching development, making teachers really think about the nature of teaching and learning.

Teachers always have some sort of theory of teaching, as we saw in connection with Figure 3.1 (p. 49), but it is usually implicit and unexamined. The possibility that there are different ways of looking at teaching does not occur to many teachers. Entwistle (1997: 19) points out that the systemic (Level 3) view 'offers a powerful insight to many staff in higher education who have not thought about teaching and learning in this way before . . . Indeed, that insight can bring about a totally new conception of teaching.'

And with that insight, the recognition that practice will need to change will follow.

Once constructive alignment is up and running successfully, conceptions will assuredly change. However, it might facilitate implementation by embarking first on conception changing using Prosser and Trigwell's ATI in a series of workshops, before proceeding with the actual implementation itself.

Departmental teaching and learning committee

A departmental teaching and learning committee, with student representation, should be established to make on-the-ground decisions relating to the setting up, design and administration of courses and programmes, to monitor teaching, define problems and benchmark with other similar departments locally and overseas. Such decisions should be made on the scholarship of teaching and learning, and to that end, a member of the university's teaching and learning development centre should be present to advise.

This committee might, for example, review deviations from expectations as to the annual grade distributions and remedies proposed. It is important to keep track with data that reflect change, such as student feedback, samples of student learning outcomes, staff reports, performance statistics and so on, which are kept in departmental archives. The work of this committee could give rise to action research projects within the department. Operating at the departmental level means that the problem of the reluctant underperforming teacher is drastically redefined. *Teaching* is the focus, not the problems that *individual teachers* might have.

Student representation on committees, especially committees dealing with teaching and learning at departmental or institutional level, is important for obtaining student input on how implementation is progressing: in fact, student representation should be part of normal quality enhancement procedures.

Regular departmental 'sharing sessions'

This is where staff tell each other what is working for them and what is not working. The experience of one teacher could easily provide the answer – or at least a point of reflection – for another who is experiencing problems. Alternatives that achieve better alignment may be explored, by pooling colleagues' ideas and by consulting the teaching and learning development centre and the departmental teaching and learning committee. A genuine sharing of problems and solutions through the lenses of constructive alignment can lift the game of the whole department.

A regular departmental retreat should be held at least annually, where teaching-related matters are top of the agenda.

Student inputs on teaching

Student feedback questionnaires should be organized through the unit responsible for teaching courses and programmes, be it department, faculty or school. Questionnaires should be worded to be supportive of constructive alignment, such as the suggested Learning Experience Inventory (p. 285), to ascertain whether students are clear about the ILOs, about the standards they have to reach to attain the various grades, and if they think that the TLAs really help them in achieving the ILOs.

A staff–student consultative committee can share views about the quality of their learning experiences. Focus groups might be organized and students might be asked to submit what they think are their best performances, to be placed in departmental archives as exemplars of good learning.

Many universities administer a graduate survey to students at the time of graduation or shortly after graduation when the graduates have been in the workforce. Apart from asking for information on career destination and development, these survey questionnaires could also provide useful feedback on graduates' reflections on how well the graduate outcomes have been met (see examples of graduate survey questionnaires provided in the Further Reading at the end of the chapter). The survey data should be substantiated, if possible, by focus group interviews of senior year students or graduates, asking them to reflect on the overall university learning experience with respect to achieving the graduate outcomes. Feedback from these sources provides valuable food for transformative reflection by the institution at all levels.

Apart from the general induction or orientation to university that students get, should there be any special induction with reference to constructively aligned teaching and learning? Or should this be left to when students turn up to classes on day one when they are given their course outlines, and get on with learning as required, just like they have done in any other course?

The answers to these questions probably depend on the stage of implementation. If students are used to traditional teaching and they are facing a large-scale changeover in the upcoming semester, it could well be good public relations, as well as saving multiple explanations, to have a meeting of students with presentations about the 'new' approach to teaching and assessment, how knowledge of outcomes will make things clearer for them, followed by a discussion panel with Q&A, with some input from senior students who have experienced constructively aligned courses. It would be very helpful for first-year students to hear this sort of experience of constructively aligned teaching from more senior students.

Teaching portfolios

We have discussed teaching portfolios as used by the individual teacher for transformative reflection on course implementation, but they may also serve two functions at departmental or faculty level: formatively, as a useful part of quality enhancement, and summatively, as teaching evaluation and other relevant decision making, including personnel decisions for promotion and contract renewal. The formative and summative uses of the teaching portfolio should be clearly differentiated. If used summatively, the aims and criteria for assessment of the portfolio should be clearly stated so that the portfolio could be appropriately structured and reflected on accordingly.

Peer review of teaching (PRT)

The primary purpose of peer review of teaching is to provide formative feedback for continuing professional development of individual teachers. A teacher invites a colleague, a critical friend, to observe his/her teaching and/

or teaching materials to provide feedback for reflection and improvement: in effect a QE process through action research of your own teaching. Peer review should form a major part of the overall teaching quality enhancement process, but only peers should be involved, not those in a position to make personnel decisions. Peer review has been used for summative evaluation as part of the institutional quality assurance process to satisfy external quality audit bodies, but as always, the formative and summative use of peer review must be clearly differentiated and agreed on by individual teachers. When used for summative purpose for personnel decision making, clear aims, procedures, guidelines and assessment criteria must be stated and agreed by all parties concerned.

Box 13.2 gives an example of some conditions for effective formative peer review of teaching.

Box 13.2 Some conditions for effective peer review of teaching (PRT) for quality enhancement

Following are some of the issues to be observed for effective PRT:

1 The purpose and the intended outcomes of the PRT exercise should be clearly defined.
2 It should involve all types of teaching staff (part time, full time, contract and tenure).
3 Participation must be voluntary.
4 The reviewee should be given the choice of:

   a his/her reviewer;
   b which classes to be observed or what teaching materials to be reviewed;
   c the focus of each review session;
   d use of review feedback for other purposes such as an application for promotion;
   e who should have access to the review report.

5 Staff development should be provided for both reviewer and reviewee.
6 All feedback should be returned to the reviewee and used for developmental purposes only.
7 Appropriate support provided to reviewee to enhance further improvement.

Peer review of teaching should include the following four stages:

1 Pre-review meeting between the reviewer and the reviewee to discuss purpose and intended outcomes of the review, type of feedback that would be helpful to the teacher and to make logistic arrangements. The focus of the review should also be clear: What specific aspects of teaching does the reviewee want to receive feedback on – for example, a teacher trying a TLA

to enhance student participation in a lecture situation would like to have feedback from the reviewer as to the effect, the teacher would like to have peer feedback on a new e-learning package that he or she has developed?

2 The actual review usually involves a real-time teaching session. Students should be informed why an extra person is present in the classroom. The reviewer should be non-intrusive to the teaching and learning process. It is useful for both parties together to review a video recording of the teaching session. A checklist or feedback proforma is useful for feedback purposes (see Further Reading). The review can also involve reviewing teaching materials or resources.

3 Post-review meeting. The teacher reflects on the teaching before the post-review meeting to identify any issues to be discussed. During the meeting, feedback is provided by the reviewer for further discussion and maybe clarification. Feedback should be specific, addressing the previously agreed intended outcomes and supported by evidence. It should be constructive providing suggestions for reflection and improvement. Further review could also be arranged if appropriate.

4 Post-review reflection by the teacher based on the feedback to identify areas for improvement and to develop an action plan for future changes. The review report should be kept in the teacher's teaching portfolio for record and future reference.

Table 13.2 presents the Constructive Alignment Development Framework for aiding reflection at the department/faculty/school level (see also Task 13.2).

Task 13.2 What level is your department/faculty/school at in implementing constructive alignment at the programme level?

Using the 'Constructive Alignment Development Framework at department/faculty/school level' (Table 13.2), reflect on what level your department/faculty/school is at in implementing CA at the programme level. Provide evidence to substantiate your claim.

What level is your department/faculty/school at?

_____

What actions would you take as either a programme leader or head of department or faculty dean to enable a higher level of implementation of constructive alignment in your department/faculty/school?

_____

_____

_____

_____

Table 13.2 Constructive Alignment Development Framework at department/faculty/school level

	Level 1	Level 2	Level 3	Level 4
Implementing CA	CA is worked on at a declarative level of understanding that CA is about aligning ILOs with teaching and assessment.	CA is about defining ILOs, but TLAs and ATs are only loosely aligned to the ILO.	ILOs, TLAs and ATs are constructively aligned using verbs in the ILO. Evidence collected on the effectiveness of the implementation.	In addition to Level 3, ways of ongoing improvement to the system are in place through reflective practice and action research. CA is regarded as the norm for teaching in the department/faculty/school.
Observable indicators – department/faculty/school at programme level	Completion of necessary documentation but no consistent or clear alignment between course and programme ILOs, little or no mention of graduate outcomes. No obvious staff support structures within the department/faculty/school.	Completion of necessary documentation, reasonable alignment between programme and course outcomes, but little attempt to align programme and graduate outcomes. Isolated supportive structures for departments, such as CA facilitators, but no clear or systematically defined roles; some staff development. Mechanism for systematic feedback and evaluation not implemented.	Mapping of course, programme and graduate outcomes done with thorough and wide consultation. Mechanism for systematic and reliable feedback and evaluation is properly implemented. Teaching is seen as a departmental, collegial activity, with systematic support structures and staff development. Encouragement and support of action research in CA in teaching and learning. CA facilitators, teaching and learning committee, course and programme committees etc. all interact systematically. CA effort rewarded.	In addition to Level 3, colleagues and departments generate new ideas, strategies, solutions, pedagogies and technologies for enhancing teaching and learning. Substantial evidence of success/effectiveness in implementing CA is collected, reflected and acted on. Quality enhancement is established as a culture. Scholarship of teaching is used reflectively as a source of innovation and development. Hard evidence of improved learning outcomes from departmental-based action research. Colleagues publish and/or present their research on teaching- and learning-related topics.

Implementing, supporting and enhancing constructive alignment at the institutional level

Many points made about implementation, support and quality enhancement at department, faculty or school level apply at the level of the whole institution. Just as transformative reflection by individuals is founded on a theory of teaching, quality enhancement in institutions is founded on a generally held philosophy of teaching: the scholarship of teaching and learning.

Courses in tertiary teaching

In most universities teaching is the major activity for most staff, and in the eyes of undergraduate students and of the general public the main reason for the existence of universities, yet even today people are allowed to enter this high-level profession without any formal qualification in teaching. Many universities require new staff to undergo induction courses, which would include teaching; many require staff to develop Professional Development Portfolios (PDPs), which would be a variant of the general teaching portfolio (see pp. 287–9); others again offer postgraduate certificates in tertiary teaching in which staff are strongly encouraged to enrol, such courses in the UK being accredited by the Higher Education Academy.

In other words, most universities are now regarding teaching as a professional activity and that some sort of exposure to the scholarship of teaching and learning is within a whisker of being compulsory, a matter that is currently being discussed by the Council of Australian Directors of Academic Development. So things have definitely moved from the days, not so long ago, when all teachers had to do was to know their subject and were presumed to be able to talk about it.

Kandlbinder and Peseta (2009) asked 147 course coordinators of postgraduate certificates in higher education in Australia, New Zealand and the UK what were the five most important ideas that they address in their courses. In order of frequency, these ideas were: reflective practice, constructive alignment, student approaches to learning, the scholarship of teaching and assessment-driven learning or assessing for learning. All these ideas are of course the very backbone of this book.

With significant numbers of teachers with a background in the scholarship of teaching and learning entering university, it seems very likely that the standards of teaching, and teaching culture of universities, will improve markedly in the years to come.

Teaching and learning development centres

Teaching and learning development centres (a generic name covering staff development units, educational development centres and so on) have previously been the poor country cousins in the establishment of universities: they have been underfunded, understaffed and frequently with the staff classified not as academics but as part of administration. What unaligned thinking! If the advisers on academic matters such as teaching are not even classified as academics, it's inviting academics not to take staff development seriously. In the past, too, the main job of the teaching and learning development centres was to provide one-off workshops for teachers on a voluntary attendance basis and to provide service courses on educational technology.

The teachers who attended voluntary workshops were mostly the already good teachers; those who didn't attend were frequently those who most needed to. The effect was to widen the gap between good and poor teachers. The basic problem was that the centres were perceived through Level 2 blame-the-teacher lenses, as places for providing tips for teachers or as remedial clinics for poor or beginning teachers. At worst, they were seen as inessential luxuries and when the hard times in Australia began in the 1990s, many were simply closed down to save money, an act as sensible as throwing all the doctors off an aircraft to lighten it while the pilot is having a heart attack.

This sorry state of affairs has now turned around. With the demands from fee-paying students for good teaching, the sudden emergence of SoTL as a Level 3 theoretical basis for teaching, and in the UK especially, the provision of compulsory courses for new academics and the establishment of the Higher Education Academy, the perception and role of teaching and learning development centres have changed hugely for the better.

It is also being recognized that these centres have a peripheral as well as a central role. In our experience, the best work in staff development is done from within the unit that provides the teaching, usually the department, when the staff developer is also an expert in the content taught in that department. This is partly a matter of credibility but perhaps more importantly, the staff developer can fully understand, for example, the significance of different wording of the ILOs. This is not such a hard call as may appear: after all, a staff developer always comes – or should always come – from a background in teaching a content area; it is simply a matter of allocating staff developers accordingly. Some faculties and schools have their own teaching and learning development centres, particularly in medicine and law.

There is also a central, generic role for teaching and learning development centres. Central decisions that bear on teaching and learning should involve the experts in teaching, learning and assessment. The design of course and programme approval forms, the architecture of teaching areas, software and hardware requirements of the platform used for teaching, regulations on assessment procedures and the reporting of assessment results are all areas that have direct effects on the effectiveness of teaching and learning. These and related decisions should therefore receive input from the teaching and learning experts.

Teaching developers should *not* be involved as 'teaching police', in assessing individual teachers and supplying information about individuals on their teaching competence to administration for personnel decisions, such as contract renewal. This utterly compromises their role. The argument is the same as that about revealing error in summative as opposed to formative assessment (pp. 195–7). The teaching and learning development centres' role is formative, not summative, and in order to teach better, teachers must feel free to expose their weaknesses in teaching and to express their doubts. There is also a question of professional ethics; the relationship between any professional person and client is based on confidentiality and on acting in the client's interests. It is deplorable that in some universities the directors of teaching development centres are required to gather such information on individuals for use in personnel decisions.

Teaching and research

Teaching should be accorded at least the same status and the same traction in personnel decision making as is research. Teaching and research may have the same status on paper, but it is still usually the case that the promotion goes to the individuals with most publications, even in universities where the most important function of the university in the public eye, and in its activities, is in fact teaching. This discrimination does not occur only in promotions. Some universities do not allow publications on the teaching of one's own discipline to 'count', either in an individual's CV or in the departmental publications list that is used for funding purposes. That sort of culture needs to be changed. An administration that is at all serious about the quality of teaching within the institution should provide adequate support, both in resources and in time for teachers to innovate, as discussed below, and in providing due recognition both for innovative and exemplary teaching and for publications on research on teaching.

Teaching development grants

Many universities provide teaching development grants to encourage and support innovative approaches to teaching and learning for individual or groups of teachers. The teaching development grants may come from the university's internal funding or from external sources such as the National Teaching Development Grants scheme in Australia, the Higher Education Academy in the UK, and the University Grants Committee in Hong Kong. Allocation of funding to individual projects is usually done via a peer review process of proposals submitted by individual or groups of teachers.

There are advantages and disadvantages to internal versus external funding. External funds are more lavish, but many teachers, not at all intimidated by applying for grants in their content research, are reluctant to apply for funds and go through all that form filling to research their own teaching, because they do not consider themselves to be educational researchers. Internal funding, with smaller amounts, is not nearly such a hassle. Many teachers, who later did significant research into their own teaching, started small. Universities should not therefore think that because external teaching development funding agencies are out there they needn't bother with an internal funding system. Indeed, many universities that are serious about their teaching take a thin slice from across the main budget and dedicate that to teaching development. It is vital that in encouraging teaching development projects, university-wide policy should be in place to ensure that scholarly publications on teaching should be recognized on the same level as publications in content area research. Topics might include curriculum development, constructive alignment, PBL, peer tutoring, clinical and applied learning, independent learning by students, innovative assessment tasks, web-based learning and assessment, and various teaching and learning resources.

Many teaching development projects are action research in nature, authentic to a real-life teaching and learning context, rather than tight research designs that attempt to be representative and generalizable. External consultants and/or internal departmental resource persons could work together to identify issues and develop project proposals. Teaching and learning development centres should also play an important role in coordinating teachers or groups of teachers in identifying and developing proposals on various teaching and assessment issues and to provide ongoing support during the implementation and dissemination of the teaching development projects.

As a general rule, teaching development projects are expected to disseminate their results to the wider teaching and learning community. Many projects have developed their own websites, and organized sharing seminars or thematic conferences to share their project results and insight both within and beyond their respective institution.

Implementing, supporting and enhancing constructive alignment beyond the institution

As pointed out in Chapter 1, some version or another of outcomes-based teaching and learning is being implemented on a wide scale, in the case of the Bologna Process across several countries. In Hong Kong, where eight universities are involved, each university is going at its own pace and in its own way, but in Malaysia, with over a thousand universities, this would not be possible. Instead the 'train-the-trainers' model is used, which is a methodology that has been around for some years and has been used for everything from running boot camps, through management training, to training gastroenterology experts – and now, to implementing constructive alignment (Biggs and Tang, in press).

In a train-the-trainers programme, staff developers attend workshops to acquire both declarative and functioning knowledge of constructive alignment to the point where (a) they would be able to teach others how to implement CA and (b) to be able to design a training programme that would fit the requirements in terms of the resources and teaching conditions of their target institution. Depending on circumstances, a train-the-trainers programme should not exceed about 40 participants. Where one is dealing with hundreds of institutions this may seem to make matters difficult, but there is an exponential effect: one person can train 40 trainers, who each in turn can train 40 more, so that in two cycles, 1,600 people can be reached (that is, if all participants learn adequately each time). The stages in a train-the-trainers programme we were involved in went like this:

1 The trainers need to understand constructive alignment to the point where they can apply the principles in the intended way. A seminar and discussion session, with pre-session reading material, should provide this conceptual foundation.
2 The trainers need to learn to write ILOs and design TLAs and ATs for themselves, before they can teach others to do these things. This can be accomplished through workshopping, using a course each brings along for the exercise.
3 The trainers need to design a staff development programme for their target institutions and work out strategies of implementation such that teachers and departments can become self-sufficient. The general nature of such a programme would follow the content of the present chapter, with resource backup with such things as a website, sharing sessions, workshops, peer review, teaching portfolios and so on.
4 The trainers, with senior administrators, need to review institutional policies so they are compatible with constructive alignment (see p. 309 –15). Quality enhancement procedure, such as reflective practice and action research, would need to be established.

This programme is still ongoing: a preliminary report is forthcoming (Biggs and Tang, in press).

Evaluation of constructive alignment

If we are going to all this trouble in implementing CA, will it be worth it? Will a constructively aligned teaching system deliver the goods? There are two ways of addressing this question: where people find constructive alignment useful as a framework or as a heuristic for designing courses or for quality assurance, and where hard data have shown that the quality of student learning has significantly improved.

There is no doubt that increasing numbers of people and institutions find CA useful as a framework for decision making and design, as a Google check will show. The principles of constructive alignment are used as descriptive frameworks for quality assurance agencies in the UK and Hong Kong, and constructive alignment itself is implemented in many universities in these and other countries. As Rust notes (2002: 148):

Although the term 'constructive alignment' is not used, this kind of systematic thinking is exactly what the QAA [UK's Quality Assurance Agency] are looking for when they refer to:

> effective and appropriate measurement of the achievement by students of the intended learning outcomes. (QAA, General principle 6)

Departments mindful of the QAA requirements, and seeking to follow Biggs' principles, would therefore be well advised to do two things:

1 To require all course modules or units to follow this design model, and to ensure that all assessment tasks, and assessment criteria, clearly and directly relate to the learning outcomes.
2 To audit all their modules' or units' learning outcomes and map them against the subject's programme specifications, to ensure that all the programme specifications will have been assessed for any student successfully completing the course programme.

The facts that CA is widely regarded as a key idea on postgraduate certificates in higher education (Kandlbinder and Peseta 2009), and that the principles of CA are used in quality assurance and quality enhancement of post-secondary teaching in several countries are encouraging. In similar vein, Entwistle and his colleagues in the large Enhancement of Teaching and Learning (ETL) Project (2001–2005) at Edinburgh University used constructive alignment as a general framework for assessing good teaching environments, while Edström (2008) writes: 'course evaluation should be regarded as a component of constructive alignment, together with the intended learning outcomes, learning activities and assessment' (p. 95).

Several other writers have mentioned the utility of constructive alignment: in designing e-learning (Lebrun 2007), in teacher education (Brook 2006), in overcoming the heavy reliance of exams in engineering education (Nightingale et al. 2007), in computing science (Colvin and Phelan 2006), and in teaching physiology (Ladyshewsky 2006). Cobham and Jacques (2006) found that reflective practice using constructive alignment achieved 'a philosophical shift in faculty assessment and delivery procedures'.

The above refer to the utility of CA as a heuristic. As to evidence relating directly to learning and related outcomes, Morris (2008) taught statistics in a constructively aligned design and found increases in mean marks in summative assessment, shifts to higher order cognitive demand in assessment tasks, and strong correlations between proportions of students reporting confidence in topic learning and exam performance: the students 'know what they know and know what they do not know' (p. iii). Moulding (2010), in social work, found that there was increased student satisfaction, but she notes that this seemed to be due more to the ILOs being related to the real world than to particular learning strategies per se.

McMahon and Thakore (2006), in a comprehensive review of higher order thinking and critical thinking in constructively aligned courses at University College Dublin, found:

- greater standardization leading to fairer and more reliable assessment: when assessment criteria follow from stated outcomes, decisions on how many marks are awarded are much easier to compare and defend.
- greater transparency leading to (a) easier and more accurate inter-university and international comparisons; (b) students being able to focus more effectively on the key learning goals.
- more effective evaluation of both modules and courses: given the outcomes, an evaluator can estimate how well teaching and learning strategies, content, materials, other resources and assessment procedures actually support students in achieving them.
- greater coherence in programmes of learning.
- an increase in the criticality and depth of student work.

(p. 17)

These writers concluded that these benefits are not inherent in the outcomes-based model itself, but when constructive alignment is the organizing principle.

Taylor and Canfield (2007) found that with increasing exposure to constructively aligned teaching, students' ratings along 'good teaching', 'clear goals and standards' and 'appropriate assessment' scales progressively increased. We have found the same thing in a Hong Kong university, where student focus groups reported that in constructively aligned courses they were much clearer about what they had to learn and that they found the TLAs helpful and the assessment 'fairer'. Some teachers complained of 'grade inflation' post implementation, and indeed in many cases grades were higher than previously, often at a statistically significant level. Putting this together with students' claims that the TLAs were helpful, we might conclude that students were indeed learning more effectively, but there were insufficient data to tie this down course by course in a systematic way. At least the grade increase shows that tying grades to stated and agreed standards post-implementation, assessment was too stringent pre-implementation. The issue was not grade inflation but grade *de*flation prior to implementing CA: that in following the bell curve previously, the grades had been selling students short.

Tynjala (1998) compared a course designed on constructivist lines using SOLO with traditional teaching and found the former produced higher level outcomes. Hoddinott (2000) also found that constructive alignment produced higher level outcomes, but it also increased the workload for both staff and students. Raeburn et al. (2009) report a study of online courses in health sciences that were redesigned along constructive alignment lines, with highly significant increases in student engagement and positive learning outcomes. Boyle (2007) used an annual reflection process to improve alignment between course aims in earth sciences and the delivery and assessment of the course with resulting improvement in student learning.

Jervis and Jervis (2005), on the other hand, claim that constructive alignment is simply a throwback to the bad old days of behaviourism and behavioural objectives because it articulates 'predetermined' outcomes. This criticism however misses the fact that while behaviourist outcomes are predetermined and quantitative in nature, higher level outcome statements in constructive alignment are not predetermined and are conceived qualitatively, for example ILOs using verbs such as 'design', 'create', 'hypothesize', 'reflect' and so on.

In sum, constructively aligned teaching seems to work as (a) a framework for assessing teaching quality on the assumption that alignment is indeed a characteristic of good teaching; and (b) as an approach to teaching that produces high quality learning outcomes and student satisfaction. What is now required are larger scale, properly controlled, studies that directly relate constructively aligned teaching over several subject areas to a range of outcomes, including lower and higher order ILOs, student metacognition and independent learning, student satisfaction, approaches to learning and to the attainment of graduate outcomes. Such studies might best be structured longitudinally, using pre-implementation measures as the baseline and relating any changes in these and other parameters to the progressive implementation of aligned teaching. Other aspects that need systematic investigation are the resource and other costs that are involved by teachers and institutions; what works well and what does not under what circumstances, with a view to a 'best practice' implementation strategy.

Policies and procedures that may be counterproductive

It is important to recognize that constructive alignment works as a system, which means that what goes on in the classroom is dependent too on the institution: Edström (2008) refers to 'system alignment', as a parallel to constructive alignment, at the system or whole institution level. For example, Jervis et al. (2006) aligned laboratory work with other aspects of the curriculum, but that did not work because of 'organizational aspects' in a complex modular degree scheme, which reinforces the view that alignment at the course level may not work in a non-aligned system.

We look first at policies and procedures that may be counterproductive to achieving alignment and then at policies and procedures that definitely are counter to good teaching.

Some marginal quality assurance procedures

Some mechanisms, in place in the name of quality assurance rather than of quality enhancement, can backfire, as they discourage risk taking and innovation.

External examiners

External examiners in the British system are a time-honoured means of ensuring that similar standards operate across institutions. It is important to bring outside perspectives and contacts to bear and to feel confident that one's own standards are comparable to those elsewhere.

Frequently, the role of external examiner is restricted to examining the setting and marking of final papers and to adjudicate the summative assessment of students. The person doing this needs to be completely aware of, and in sympathy with, the department's theory of teaching. We know of cases where the examiner required the examination questions to be changed well into the teaching of the course concerned – thereby putting alignment at risk. External examiners, selected for their content knowledge rather than for their educational expertise, may discourage innovative assessment practices and encourage decontextualized assessment. The pressure to comply with the external examiner is considerable in institutions where the examiner's comments are seen and discussed outside the department concerned. However, if the word 'examiner' is replaced with 'consultant', an outside adviser who can visit the department to advise on assessment and other matters to do with teaching and learning, the problem is solved.

External panels

External panels are often required to accredit and validate programmes and courses. This is a common quality assurance procedure that has obvious value, particularly where staff are required to deliver new courses in directions in which they may have had little experience, in which case course accreditation helps to ensure minimal standards. A similar argument applies to programmes that require approval by external professional bodies. Both procedures, however, discourage innovative teaching, although recently professional bodies increasingly require outcomes-based teaching for accreditation purposes.

External panels may well exert strong pressure to include more and more content. Each panel member thinks his or her own special interest must be given 'adequate' treatment – which is code for rather more treatment than is being proposed – a common result being an overloaded curriculum. Programme leaders and committees usually anticipate such pressures – they obviously design courses that they think are likely to be approved – and so the curriculum is overloaded from the start. Teaching subsequently becomes a frantic scramble to 'cover' all the listed topics – yet we know that coverage is 'the greatest enemy of understanding' (Gardner 1993: 24).

Panels may encourage conservatism in teaching, particularly when the panel has key figures from the profession whose knowledge of education is what they went through years ago in their own professional training. Muldoon and Lee (2007) say that 'the biggest obstacle in building constructive alignment in accountancy education is the compliance requirements of the accreditation bodies' (p. 106), which require inter alia that 50% of the summative assessment must be in the form of an invigilated examination.

Shepherd (2006) goes rather further, claiming that the requirements of the Institute of Actuaries of Australia refer to syllabus coverage and marking, grade distribution and exemption level at each university, and that this 'is consistent with level 1 thinking about learning and teaching. Has the syllabus been covered? Was the marking tough? Is the grade distribution consistent with what it has been in the past, and with that of other universities?' (Shepherd 2006: 6). Such requirements result, Shepherd continues, in content overload, narrow and inflexible assessment and they ignore student diversity. The Institute of Actuaries in Australia emphasizes 'high standards' but at the expense of good educational practice.

But it doesn't end there. Once a course has been approved, it tends to be set in concrete. Changing an already validated or accredited course or programme can be difficult. It may easily turn out that the curriculum is much too overloaded; that the student intake has changed; that recent research, post-validation, suggests that the curriculum should be changed. It may be possible to make minor modifications immediately, but any major changes are either not allowed, because they were not in the validated documents, or they have to go through yet another round of committees. Administrators usually discourage any attempt to do so. In one institution, a move to PBL was vetoed by a senior administrator: 'The course may have to be revalidated. What if it doesn't succeed? What then, eh?'

Teaching evaluation

Teaching evaluation seems an obvious part of quality enhancement but it needs to be carried out appropriately. There are two approaches, one that exactly parallels the measurement model and the other, the standards model (pp. 198–208). Evaluating teachers by a single instrument, such as a student feedback questionnaire, is operating according to the measurement model. Such instruments are worded to apply across all departments so that teachers can be compared along a quantitative scale, for promotion, awards, contract renewal and the like. This is a common approach to evaluating teaching, even in institutions that are otherwise quite innovative. It is an excellent example of misalignment. Such across-the-board measures assume a default method of teaching, almost always lecturing, so that the students rate the teacher on such items as 'speaks clearly', 'hands out clear lecture notes' and the like. This can be a serious impediment to reflective teaching. A teacher using a range of well-aligned TLAs that don't include much lecturing automatically gets a low score – and is passed over for promotion. Back to lecturing it is! We have seen this happen in several institutions. It should never happen in an institution running on the scholarship of teaching and learning. Teaching evaluation *à la* measurement model is an example of administrative convenience overriding educational sense (see Figure 13.1, p. 314).

Teaching should be evaluated using the standards model. That is, there are several criteria for good teaching and the teacher's task is to provide evidence that addresses those criteria, with evidence from a range of appropriate sources collected in a teaching portfolio (see earlier), where a teacher outlines his or her philosophy of teaching and then demonstrates how that is put into practice with samples of teaching and student evaluations specifically tuned to particular courses.

Distinguished teacher awards

Distinguished teacher awards frequently raise similar concerns if they are awarded on the basis of scores to such teaching evaluation questionnaires. But that aside, there are still worries. The message is: 'See? We reward good teaching in our institution!' – and it is indeed good to reward people for doing an outstanding job. However, it has to be done carefully, otherwise the message to the great majority of teachers – by definition the undistinguished ones – is that distinguished teachers are born, not made. The very names 'distinguished teacher' or 'outstanding teacher' suggest that here we have a bird of a rare species, whose exotic plumage ordinary teachers cannot hope to match. The sparrows and starlings therefore cannot be blamed if they follow what nature intended and teach on in their own undistinguished way. A generous distinguished teacher award system may also have the effect of absolving management from further support for teaching development.

Distinguished teacher awards encourage the perception that an outstanding teacher is one who does teacherly things better than other teachers do. Therefore, while distinguished teachers themselves tend to operate from Level 3, as reflective practitioners (Dunkin and Precians 1992), formal awards promulgate a Level 2 view of teacher as performer. Reward the excellent teachers by all means, but if we want quality teaching at an institutional level, the focus should not be on what the individual teacher does, but on the *teaching system* in the university. Recipients of awards may have nothing to do with all that crucial developmental teamwork – curriculum development, tutor mentoring, decisions as to delivery and assessment – that makes it possible for the star teacher to strut his or her stuff.

A revealing slant on this issue of individual versus collective responsibility for teaching comes from an international comparison of mathematics teaching carried out by Stigler and Hiebert (1999). They analysed videotapes of classroom teaching in three different countries and found that each culture developed its own 'script' for teaching. Japan had a script based on a Level 3 theory of teaching, while the US script was based on learning routines at Level 1. Not surprisingly, Japanese students achieved better results than did American students. But what determined the Japanese learning outcomes was the script, not the particular actor who delivered it. Awarding Oscars to the actors is not likely to improve their scripts. Just so in quality enhancement; we should be focusing on the script, not on the actor. Distinguished teacher awards, like quality assurance itself, are retrospective; they focus on what has been done; they do not make teaching across the board better in future.

By contrast, let us look briefly at awards in the Chinese school system, which might better be called distinguished teach*ing* awards:

> Good teachers may be honoured with titles (and salary bonuses). Such titles are awarded after they have been observed and have given demonstration lessons in a competitive situation, at one to three days' notice, in front of tens or hundreds of their peers. . . . The teachers . . . act as mentors to younger teachers and their mentoring role includes giving further demonstration lessons.
>
> (Cortazzi and Jin 2001: 121)

Good teaching is seen here as a collective responsibility that works prospectively to enhance future teaching in the institution or district.

Now why don't we in the West do that?

Student feedback questionnaires

Many institutions have mandatory student feedback questionnaires as summative evaluations at the end of each course, using standard questions across all courses. We have already discussed the difficulties with that. Additionally, student feedback questionnaires share with distinguished teacher awards the problem that they usually focus on the actor, not on the script. They tend to measure charisma, the Dr Fox Effect, not teaching effectiveness in terms of improved student learning (see p. 136). Used formatively, however, student feedback questionnaires make eminent sense where questions are tailored to specific courses on aspects on which feedback is required, as in the formative evaluation of implementing constructive alignment (pp. 294–5).

In short, some common quality assurance procedures have the opposite effect to that intended, conceived as they are within a retrospective framework. While the above procedures may be well meant, if two edged, other institutional aspects are unequivocally negative.

Policies and procedures that are definitely counterproductive

Distorted priorities

Distorted priorities are a major source of mis- or non-alignment. Probably all institutions would put educational considerations as their top priority in their list of graduate outcomes or mission statements. However, there is an institution to run, which generates a set of administrative priorities. Administrators want things to run on schedule; they want to ensure that plagiarism cannot occur, that public criticism about standards or fairness should be avoided, that awkward cases are anticipated and legislated for before they arise and cause trouble, that research is promoted over teaching because the university's prestige and income are based more on research output than on teaching.

For all this to happen (or not to happen), the safest working assumption is that students, and more recently teachers, are not to be trusted; the answer is to establish a Theory X climate. Unfortunately, as we saw in Chapter 3,

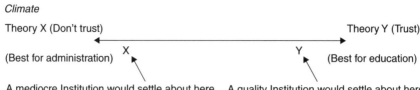

Climate

Theory X (Don't trust)   Theory Y (Trust)

(Best for administration)   X   Y   (Best for education)

A mediocre Institution would settle about here   A quality Institution would settle about here

Question: Where does your Institution lie – nearer to Point X or to Point Y?

Figure 13.1 Administrative and educational needs – striking the right balance

good learning thrives in a Theory Y climate. However, as a completely Theory X climate would be unbearable and a completely Theory Y climate unmanageable, we compromise (see Figure 13.1).

How the two sets of priorities are balanced is what separates a quality institution from a mediocre institution, in terms of teaching and learning. A quality institution is biased towards establishing the optimal conditions for learning (point Y), a mediocre one towards administrative convenience (point X). Where does your institution lie?

What sorts of things distort priorities?

A quantitative mindset

Quantitative assumptions reduce complex issues to units that can be handled independently, rather than as components in a larger interactive system. Thus, the curriculum becomes a collection of independent competencies, basic skills, facts, procedures and so on; passing becomes a matter of accruing sufficient independent correct answers.

A particular problem is the misapplication of the measurement model of assessment. Table 13.3 summarizes.

Table 13.3 Demands of the measurement model and those of good teaching

Measurement model	*Good teaching*
Performances need to be quantified, so they are reduced to correct/incorrect units of equivalent value that can be added	Students need to learn holistic structures that cannot meaningfully be reduced to units of equal importance
A good test creates 'a good spread' between students, preferably normally distributed	Good teaching produces reduced variance
The characteristic being measured is stable over time	Good teaching produces change: it is called 'learning'
Students need to be tested under standardized conditions	Students need to be tested under conditions that best reveal an individual's learning

The demands of the measurement model are simply incompatible with those of good teaching.

Norm-referenced assessment

A particular example of quantitative assessment is norm-referenced assessment, in particular grading on the curve. We might decree that the top 15% of graduates will achieve first class honours and then boast 'See here, all our departments are teaching to the same high standard!', but that is an illusion. We have no idea of the real standards reached by any department. Worse, grading on the curve makes aligned assessment impossible.

Invigilated examinations

These are hard to justify educationally, but are useful logistically and for assuring the public that plagiarism is under control.

Who teaches the first years?

Assigning the most junior teachers, who can't argue back, to teach those enormous first-year classes that the senior teachers don't want to teach is not a procedure that could be justified by the scholarship of teaching and learning.

Emphasize research at the expense of teaching

Although many universities officially place equal emphasis on teaching and research, research is almost invariably perceived as the activity of greater prestige and in promotions is rewarded more than is teaching. Some department heads do not even recognize publications on research into teaching the very subject the department is charged to teach as 'real' research.

Such impediments to quality teaching and learning result from poor alignment to the purpose of the institution, just as impediments to good student learning result from poor alignment of teaching/learning activities and assessment practices to ILOs. Quality teaching means trying to enact the aims of the institution by setting up a delivery system that is aligned to those aims. In practice, however, many institutions in their policies, practices and reward systems actually downgrade teaching. Some of this is externally imposed, ironically by some aspects imposed by quality assurance procedures. Other practices fall into the category of institutional habits; it's always been that way and it does not occur to question them.

Whatever the reasons for their existence, any adverse effects they might have on teaching and learning need to be identified and minimized. Task 13.3 is designed not for teachers but for administrators: heads of department, deans, DVCs.

Task 13.3   Do your quality assurance processes encourage or discourage aligned teaching?

Reflect on current quality assurance processes: are they encouraging or discouraging the implementation of constructively aligned teaching and learning?

You as head of department/dean of faculty:

QA processes encouraging aligned teaching and learning	*QA processes discouraging aligned teaching and learning*

On reflection, what changes would you make?

You as senior management (e.g. DVC, chairman of quality assurance committee) of the university:

QA processes encouraging aligned teaching and learning	*QA processes discouraging aligned teaching and learning*

On reflection, what changes would you make?

_____

_____

_____

_____

There was one task in Chapter 1 and two tasks in Chapter 3 that we should now revisit as Tasks 13.4, 13.5 and 13.6.

Task 13.4 The changing scene at your own institution

In Task 1.1 (p. 12), we asked you to reflect on your own institution, identify any changes that you are aware of which have affected your decision made or actions taken related to teaching and learning as a teacher/staff developer/administrator. Now that you have finished this book revisit these decision/actions and see if you would have acted differently.

Your previous decisions/actions related to teaching and learning based on the changes (at the beginning of this book):

_____

_____

_____

_____

Changes in your decisions/actions now that you have finished this book and why:

_____

_____

_____

_____

Task 13.5 Follow-up to Task 3.3

In Task 3.3 (p. 50), we asked you to reflect on a critical incident in your teaching/assessment and how you dealt with the problem then. Let us say you are faced with a similar incident now, after having read this book thus far. Consider it in terms of the following questions:

a What do you think is the problem? What has gone wrong? What is the evidence for a problem?

_____

_____

_____

b What is (are) the cause(s) of the problem?

_____

_____

_____

c How would you deal with the problem now?

_____

_____

_____

d What is the difference between your present answers here and your previous answers? Compared with Task 3.3, what change have you made in dealing with the problem? Why have you made such changes?

_____

_____

_____

Task 13.6 Follow-up to Task 3.4

In Task 3.4 (p. 54), we asked you to identify the *three most worrying* problems in teaching a semester- or year-long course; one that you would realistically hope to minimize by reading this book. What actions will you take to address these problems after reading this book so far?

1 _____

_____

_____

2 _____

_____

_____

3 _____

_____

_____

What is the theoretical basis for your actions?

_____

_____

_____

Summary and conclusions

A framework for implementing and supporting constructive alignment

So far we have been discussing the framework of constructive alignment as a means of rethinking familiar decisions about curriculum, teaching and assessment. We now need a framework for implementing and supporting it. Although ILOs, TLAs and ATs have been put in place, arrangements must be made for feedback from all parties to gauge how implementation is proceeding and what adjustments might need to be made. The mechanism underlying successful implementation is transformative reflection. This is a cyclical process, using theory to analyse problems and to derive solutions and test them. Such reflective practice is used by individual practitioners, but the same process applies to individuals on committees and in leadership roles.

Implementing constructive alignment in the individual classroom

Once a teacher is committed to trying constructive alignment in a course, the main problem of implementation is to mould its shape so that it fits the procedural and collegial requirements of the institution: assessment regulations are likely to be the most constraining. Action research, using transformative reflection, is a good paradigm for achieving the best fit. It is important to systematically collect evidence as to progress, both from the students' and from your own perspective, and to use a 'critical friend' to help in transformative reflection. It is short step from a critical friend to the peer review of teaching.

Implementing, supporting and enhancing constructive alignment in the department, faculty or school

Implementing constructive alignment over a range of courses across a department or faculty is obviously more problematic than in one course. Good leadership is essential to make the decision to go ahead, but it involves delegation to different individuals and committees. Equally important is to set up formative evaluation, as in the case of implementing courses. Students need to be represented on all committees dealing with teaching and learning and to provide feedback on department-wide implementation. Students are an essential source of feedback. Students would also find it helpful to have a suitable induction into constructive alignment, with inputs from students who have been there before.

Implementing, supporting and enhancing constructive alignment at the institutional level

The implementation of constructive alignment raises issues that apply to quality assurance and quality enhancement measures for the whole institution. Such measures should be founded in the scholarship of teaching and learning, involving staff development, continuing formative evaluation and policies and procedures for recognizing quality teaching and learning as an institutional priority. This way, teachers' conceptions will change and they are more likely to teach with conviction and a sense of priority.

Implementing, supporting and enhancing constructive alignment beyond the institution

With large numbers of institutions within a jurisdiction going over to OBTL and constructive alignment in particular, the train-the-trainers model is a good way of coping with the numbers of institutions involved. In this model, groups of staff developers are workshopped so that they may develop programmes for their target institutions; they in turn can workshop other staff developers so that the number of people equipped to train teachers increases manifold.

Evaluation of constructive alignment

Constructive alignment may be evaluated in two ways: as a framework or heuristic for course and programme design and quality assurance, and as actually improving learning and learning-related outcomes. There is much anecdotal evidence attesting to the value many people find in using constructive alignment as a scaffold for educational decision making. There is also a body of evidence where hard data have been used demonstrating the improvement of learning-related outcomes, but much of this work is isolated and at course level only. There is a need for large scale, institution-wide, studies investigating the effects of constructive alignment teaching on all ranges of ILOs, student metacognition, student approaches to learning and the attainment of graduate outcomes; and for research into the difficulties of implementation from the teacher's and institution's point of view.

Policies and procedures that may be counterproductive

Constructive alignment is systemic, which means that it affects, and is affected by, the policies and procedures of the institution as a whole. There are some policies that are meant as quality assurance but may be counterproductive, such as validation and accreditation panels, external examiners, even distinguished teacher awards. Other policies still are definitely counterproductive and many of these arise through misalignment arising from a clash between the priorities of good teaching and the priorities of smooth management.

Further reading

On reflective practice

Brockbank, A. and McGill, I. (1998) *Facilitating Reflective Learning in Higher Education.* Buckingham: Society for Research into Higher Education/Open University Press.
Cowan, J. (1998) *On Becoming an Innovative Teacher.* Buckingham: Open University Press.
Schön, D.A. (1983) *The Reflective Practitioner: How Professionals Think in Action.* London: Temple Smith.

Schön's book deals with the whole question of improving professional practice by reflection, using examples from several professions. The other two books refer specifically to university teaching. Brockbank and McGill provide detailed help in setting up situations (based mainly on the Schön model) to promote reflection with colleagues and on one's own teaching, with respect to promoting student learning and formal action learning projects. Cowan distinguishes several kinds of reflection, how teachers can best use reflection, how teachers can encourage their students to reflect and how to structure groups and reflective learning journals in ways that best promote the appropriate kind of reflection. The book is driven by a cycle of questions, examples, strategies and generalizations from the examples.

On action research

Gibbs, G. (1992) *Improving the Quality of Student Learning.* Bristol: Technical and Educational Services.

Kember, D. (2000) *Action Learning and Action Research: Improving the Quality of Teaching and Learning.* London: Kogan Page.

Kember, D. (2001) Transforming teaching through action research, in D. Watkins and J. Biggs (eds) *Teaching the Chinese Learner: Psychological and Pedagogical Perspectives.* Hong Kong: University of Hong Kong Comparative Education Research Centre/ Camberwell, Victoria: Australian Council for Educational Research.

Kember, D. and Kelly, M. (1993) *Improving Teaching through Action Research.* Green Guide No. 14. Campbelltown, NSW: Higher Education Research and Development Society of Australasia.

Norton, L. (2009) *Action Research in Teaching and Learning: A Practical Guide to Conducting Pedagogical Research in Universities.* London: Routledge.

Gibbs's book describes several strategies for deep learning and ten action research case studies in British tertiary institutions in which one or more of these strategies were used. Kember (2000) or Kember and Kelly (1993) describe how action research may be implemented and Kember (2001) describes a number of particular action research projects conducted in Hong Kong tertiary institutions. Norton's book emphasizes the practical: how to go about action research to address several common problems in teaching and learning, with illustrative case studies.

On graduate surveys

Australian Graduate Survey (AGS): http://strategic.curtin.edu.au/ags.html (accessed 2 February 2011).

University of Illinois: http://www.pb.uillinois.edu/dr/gs/ (accessed 2 February 2011).

University of Washington: www.washington.edu/oea/pdfs/reports/OEAReport9808q.pdf (accessed 2 February 2011).

On teaching portfolios

Seldin, P. (1997) *The Teaching Portfolio: A Practical Guide to Improved Performance and Promotion/Tenure Decisions.* Boston, MA: Anker.

Ohio State University: http://ucat.osu.edu/teaching_portfolio/teaching_port.html (accessed 2 February 2011).

Washington State University: www.wsu.edu/provost/teaching.htm (accessed 2 February 2011).

Electronic teaching portfolios:

http://electronicportfolios.com/portfolios/site2000.html (accessed 2 February 2011).

http://eduscapes.com/tap/topic82.htm (accessed 2 February 2011).

On peer review of teaching

www.edna.edu.au/edna/go/highered/hot_topics/cache/offonce/pid/960 (accessed 2 February 2011).

A comprehensive guide to peer review of teaching by Jackie Lublin: http://www.teaching-learning.utas.edu.au/__data/assets/pdf_file/0010/1054/Peer_review_of_teaching.pdf (accessed 2 February 2011).

14

Constructive alignment as implemented: some examples

In this chapter, we present examples of constructive alignment in action from several institutions. First, we present implementation at the university level, at faculty level, and at individual constructively aligned courses in several different areas: accounting, engineering, information systems, fashion marketing, language, management sciences, nursing, photography and veterinary science. These courses are recent implementations of constructive alignment, designed within institutional resourcing, policies and procedures and with ongoing quality enhancement. They are produced here with the permission of each course designer. The formatting and method and extent of implementation are quite varied: some, for example, use quantitative, and others qualitative, methods of assessment and grading; some specify quite precisely the alignment between ILOs and their associated teaching/learning activities and assessment tasks, while others use a more holistic alignment. This diversity is excellent, as it shows that there is no one way of implementing constructive alignment; transformative reflection is carried out realistically within each individual teacher's interpretation of the concept of alignment and according to his or her own zone of feasibility.

Implementation at institutional level

The present writers have been involved with implementing constructive alignment in several institutions, especially in Hong Kong. An important difference between Hong Kong and the tertiary sectors in other countries is that in Hong Kong the University Grants Committee (UGC) funds the institutions and provides guidelines and directions for institutions to follow. In May 2006, one such directive was that all universities should move towards outcomes-based approaches to student learning (OBASL) in the interests of the 'improvement and enhancement in student learning and teaching quality' (Letter to Hong Kong universities, May 15, 2006). A six year time-line was suggested, and universities could move towards OBASL at their own pace and in their own way.

There are advantages and disadvantages in a top-down approach, as explained in the previous chapter, but when the directive comes from the funding body, university administrations listen. Many universities started with consciousness-raising talks where experts, usually outsiders, would explain what OBASL (to use the UGC's current term) is all about; the authors were involved in this way in four institutions. From there, some universities used a bottom-up strategy, whereby a few departments voluntarily started with a few courses, with ongoing support mainly from the institutions' teaching and learning development centre (TLDC, to give it its generic name).The strategy here was to go gradually, see how it works, and when a few departments have got it right, it is easier for other departments to follow. At another university, one of the authors (CT) was then the head of the TLDC and obtained a large teaching development grant to implement constructive alignment in volunteer courses some years ahead of the UGC's directive. This gave that university a head start, and when she left, the TLDC continued this time to implement constructive alignment across the whole university.

We were involved as general consultants at another university that had decided to use a basically top-down strategy of implementation. Our role was to:

- explain OBASL to university-wide audiences;
- advise administration on policy implications, for example that the university switch from norm-referenced to criterion-referenced assessment, to set up OBASL coordinators in each department, to recognize time and effort spent by enthusiastic teachers (in fact a high proportion of teaching excellence awards went to those pioneers in OBASL);
- conduct workshops on writing ILOs, designing TLAs and ATs and grading procedures;
- be available for consultations with individual departments and key personnel.

The university recognized that it was also necessary to adopt a bottom-up approach by appointing subject-specific consultants who were experts both in outcomes-based teaching and learning and in a discipline. The latter was necessary so that they would understand more effectively how to write ILOs and also to have credibility within the department or faculty in which they were working that a generalist might find difficult to establish, particularly with traditional, hard-line teachers. These subject-specific consultants were essential for the success of the university-wide implementation as they could directly address the doubters in their own language.

In general this combination of top-down and bottom-up approaches proved to be successful in implementing OBASL across the whole institution. The top-down approach ensured endorsement and institutional support in establishing appropriate quality enhancement and quality assurance policies and procedures. The university also provided necessary resources and staff development opportunities; for example, 35 projects on OBASL had been funded from various sources, many of which led to publication or conference presentation. The bottom-up approach, for its part, helped establish collegial involvement and the personal engagement of individual teachers in their implementing constructively aligned teaching and assessment both inside and outside the classroom.

Since the implementation of the first constructively aligned courses in 2006, most faculties and departments are now developing their own quality enhancement and supportive structures. Some of these departments have become entirely self-sufficient, while others require occasional advice and support from external consultants.

By the end of 2010, constructive alignment was implemented in most courses in all faculties. With the changeover from the three-year to four-year undergraduate curriculum in 2012, it is envisaged that all undergraduate programmes and courses will be offered in outcomes-based format using constructive alignment. The university is currently working on the new elements of the four-year curriculum, such as general education, majors and minors which will strengthen the OBTL implementation.

Implementation at faculty level*

In 1997, the Faculty of Veterinary Science, University of Sydney, was in poor shape. It was suffering from a steady decline in government funding, the culture was disintegrating and lacked direction, students complained about teaching that was 'didactic and uninspiring'. There was a call for it to be amalgamated with two other small faculties.

That call for amalgamation was the wake-up – together with the internal appointment, in 1998, of a visionary dean who was determined to turn a bad situation around. He organized meetings with the then 55 (now approximately 70) academic staff members and a range of stakeholders – students, the veterinary profession, industry and key university personnel – who made clear their comments and criticisms of the faculty. It hurt, but putting all that together showed a way forward.

The first thing to be changed was the culture of the faculty. The plan was to make it more outwardly focused, receptive to the needs of students, the profession and funding/industry bodies and to place it on a sustainable basis. The leadership became distributed, with staff being given greater responsibility for teaching decisions; teaching was to be more student-centred, a move that coincided with a university-wide initiative in 2000 to support innovation and install quality enhancement systems. Staff agreed on

---

* We are indebted to Professor Rosanne Taylor for this account. See also Taylor and Canfield (2007).

a new goal: 'A shared culture of excellence and scholarship in teaching and learning'. There were three interacting principles to guide implementation of the new student-centred curriculum:

1 professionalism in education, involving the shared leadership in the newly restructured faculty, with rewards for teaching and support in staff development;
2 an innovative constructively aligned curriculum based on the scholarship of teaching;
3 quality enhancement, through a culture of continuous improvement based on evidence gained in particular from action research.

Supporting professionalism

The decision was made at the start to use an across-the-board approach, rather than focus on a few innovators and work out from them. This is not the usual approach (p. 292–4). However, the dean's change strategy was to build and articulate a new culture with shared values and a sense of a cohesive identity as a faculty, a strategy that the staff strongly supported. The dean spread responsibility personally among the staff. Departmental boundaries were removed so that teaching was organized by faculty teams not from the old departments, and cross-disciplinary units became easily feasible. External facilitators conducted workshops on leadership and teamwork to make the new structure work effectively and for colleagues to feel secure with collegial support yet free to think laterally and share ideas.

Professionalism was supported by rewards for good teaching, small teaching development grants to focus on innovative teaching, aligning the new curriculum to the university's graduate outcomes. Professionalism in teaching was progressively increased by staff development activities and numerous workshops and by recruitment. New staff were appointed on their interest in student-centred learning and their willingness to undertake formal training in education. By 2006, a third of the staff had qualified for the graduate certificate in educational studies (higher education).

Scholarly teaching

The curriculum was completely reconstructed. The old departmental subjects were replaced with integrated units drawing from several subject areas with a strong case-based emphasis. Timetabled teaching was reduced by 25% and all teaching was designed to be constructively aligned, using graduate outcomes to provide a framework for the whole curriculum. Large class teaching was held to a maximum of 50% of teaching time and was mostly less than this, thereby allowing a greater range of TLAs, including e-learning, case-based learning, placements and practical classes. The final year was lecture-free, using instead experiential learning in professional placements.

Pains were taken to create a Theory Y climate. As one student commented: 'You feel welcome and invited to contribute to all aspects of the faculty and they seem genuinely pleased about feedback.'

Quality enhancement through evidence-based teaching

Quality enhancement procedures involved action research by staff members with frequent, ongoing data collection and constructive reflection on evidence obtained that might throw light on the quality of teaching and learning and how it might be improved. Sources of evidence included: students, graduates, staff and the university. Agreed minimal levels of performance focused attention on struggling courses and additional resources used to improve performance. Staff development workshops and external consultants were used as needed. The teaching and learning quality enhancement exercise was overseen by the faculty learning and teaching committee and there were also quality enhancement initiatives in research and clinical practice.

What is the evidence for the success of the innovations? The *Student Course Experience Questionnaire* scale scores rose steadily from year 2000, and in 2005 the faculty obtained the highest or second highest score in the university in five out of the seven scales. In the years 2000 to 2006, 25 staff received teaching awards, whereas in the preceding seven years, none had. One of the spurs to this dramatic achievement was the decision to seek, and in 2005 to obtain, North American accreditation, which became a 'catalyst for transforming the local curriculum into one that had global acceptance and relevance'.

On a norm-referenced note, the faculty is today one of the leading veterinary and animal science schools in Australia, with a great increase in student demand and a correspondingly high admissions index. This was not, however, at the expense of research. On the contrary, in the warmer, task-oriented search for excellence in teaching, the indicators for research excellence – publications, research monies relative to the rest of the university, and numbers of successful research students – also increased, while the ratings by research students for supervision, infrastructure, research climate etc. rose from worst in the university to best during the period in question.

Taylor and Canfield (2007) saw the following factors as important in helping to establish and sustain the goal of scholarly teaching:

1 inspirational leaders and effective strategic planning;
2 commitment to shared leadership for student-centred learning;
3 agreed faculty culture inclusive of all staff and students;
4 engagement of external stakeholders in curriculum reform;
5 curriculum alignment with graduate attributes;
6 curriculum evaluation and accreditation for quality enhancement;
7 enabling and supportive structures in faculty and university;
8 innovation and research into student learning.

Comment

This astonishing success story shows what can be done with the leadership, the will and the commitment to the scholarship of teaching and learning. The overriding principle is *alignment*: every decision made has to conform to the culture established to implement constructive alignment. It is highly significant that the university as a whole was also committed to student-centred learning and was able to come up with the support structure needed in terms of staff developers, policies and procedures.

This is a textbook example, with one apparent exception, of the principles of implementation outlined in Chapter 13:

1 *Strong and committed leadership* and the thorough commitment of all staff (pp. 291–2). A few of the older academic staff did not share this commitment at first: some took early retirement, to be replaced by younger staff who did commit to the faculty goal; remaining doubters simply joined the teaching teams and were swept along with the general flow – and in due course became converts.

2 *Theoretical basis to the change* was there from the start: the scholarship of teaching in general and constructive alignment in particular when it came to course design. It was this SoTL theory that allowed the transformative reflection following the bad experience.

3 *Formative evaluation* was built in from the start and orchestrated by a teaching and learning committee. Staff contributed too with their own teaching development projects.

4 *Strategies for change:* the one apparent exception to the principles raised in Chapter 13 was Fullan's recommendation that one starts small and works outwards, based on successes (p. 293). The present decision to go full on across the whole faculty was a bold one, but given that the status quo was non-viable, and the faculty was totally restructured around the central goal to establish 'sustainable, scholarly teaching', this was in the event the right decision.

5 *Change teachers' conceptions first or make them teach differently first?* Here, teachers were required to teach differently, but the reasons, the theory underlying the change, were always upfront. The general answer to this point again lies in the climate created. Teachers weren't just ordered: 'You teach differently!' A rich context was provided in which the difference in teaching from what most were used to, to what was required, was fully supported by both physical resourcing and by a change in climate of thinking about teaching.

6 *The faculty climate* was thus a vital part of this context: a supportive Theory Y climate in which both staff and students felt mutual responsibility.

The fact of this transformation in the space of five years from one of the struggling to one of the best institutions for preparing veterinarians and animal scientists in Australia must allay any doubts that constructively aligned teaching is impractical.

Implementation at course level

Accounting

'Accounting 1' is a one-semester core course in the first year of a three-year bachelor of business administration (BBA) degree programme offered by the Department of Accountancy of the College of Business at the City University of Hong Kong. The number of students in each class is 200. The course was designed by Dr Olivia Leung of the Department of Accountancy.

Course aims

1 Provide students with technical knowledge in processing, preparing and reporting accounting information in accordance with GAAP (generally accepted accounting principles) for internal and external users in a modern economy.
2 Provide students with general knowledge about internal control procedures and financial statement analysis.
3 Encourage students to be responsible and active learners as well as complying with course policies.

Intended learning outcomes (ILOs)

On completion of this course, students will be able to:

ILO1 *Record* accounting transactions related to cash, receivables, inventories, fixed assets, payables, shareholders' equity, revenues, costs of merchandise sold and other expenses. *Complete* annual accounting cycle.
Prepare financial statements (balance sheets, income statements, statements of shareholders' equity, statements of retained earnings) for servicing and merchandising companies.
ILO2 *Identify* and *explain* fundamental GAAP (generally accepted accounting principles)
Select, justify and *apply* the appropriate GAAP to support accounting treatments in preparing financial reports.
ILO3 *Identify* and *develop* internal control procedures over cash.
Calculate and *interpret* fundamental financial ratios based on information collected from financial statements
ILO4 *Be a responsible learner*: *attend* classes and *submit* assignments on time, advance preparation for classes, attentive in classes.
Be an active learner: *actively participate* in various classes. *Comply* with course policies, *observe* course policy regarding absences in mid-term test and final examination; *comply* with any other course policies as stipulated.

Teaching and learning activities (TLAs)

TLA 1: Situation: interactive lecture
Concepts and general knowledge of financial accounting are presented with PowerPoint slides:

- Work-along exercise: students are given exercises and are encouraged to work along with the lecturer and their peers as the lecturer covers each topic. This exercise helps students follow the lecture closely and to visualize the applications of the concepts.
- Concept map: in the beginning or at the end of each lecture, the lecturer uses the concept maps to demonstrate links between various topics presented in the lecture.
- Incomplete PowerPoint slides: PowerPoint presentations provided the week before the lecture have had key words and figures on certain slides omitted. Students are encouraged to prepare before their classes and to participate during classes to complete the missing information.

Major focus: ILOs 1, 2 and 4; minor focus: ILO3.

TLA 2: Situation: tutorial
Technical procedures and practice questions are covered:

- Weekly tutorial assignments: assignments for each week are specifically assigned to give students opportunity to think through the concepts and to apply the concepts to various business transactions.
- Various in-class activities: students are given various activities such as work-along practice questions, group discussions, self-test multiple-choice questions, ideas sharing and presenting time etc.

Major focus: ILOs 1, 3 and 4; minor focus: ILO2.

TLA 3: Situation: outside classroom activities
Additional help is provided outside official class time:

- Tutor consultation: each tutor provides four consultation hours weekly to help his/her students with technical issues or issues with learning accounting in general.
- SI (Supplementary Instruction) scheme: performing second-year accounting major students are selected to be SI leaders. Each leader will head a group of FB2100 students and meet with them weekly to provide additional help on self-learning skills in accounting.
- Helpdesk: extra help is provided to students who have difficulties when they are preparing for mid-term test and final examination. Designated helpers provide help to students throughout the week before mid-term test and final examination to answer students' technical questions.

Major focus: ILOs 3 and 4; minor focus: ILOs 1 and 2.

Assessment tasks (ATs)

AT1: Tutorial assignments and participation (10%)
Weekly tutorial assignments are given to students to assess students' understanding and knowledge on topics listed in the weekly teaching schedule.
Major focus: ILOs 1 and 4; minor focus: ILOs 2 and 3.

AT2: Mid-term test (40%)
The test is designed to assess students' technical knowledge in analysing business transactions, journalizing and preparing financial statements for external reporting.
Major focus: ILOs 1 and 2.

AT3: Final examination (50%)
The examination is designed to assess students' technical knowledge in analysing business transactions, applying accounting principles to support accounting treatments, journalizing and preparing financial reports for external users.
Major focus: ILOs 1 and 2.

Grading criteria

Some examples of grading criteria are shown in Table 14.1.

Engineering

'Engineering Principles and Design' is a one-semester course in the first year of a three-year bachelor of manufacturing engineering programme in the College of Science and Engineering at the City University of Hong Kong. Usual enrolments are near 200 students. The course was designed by Dr Lawrence Li of City University Hong Kong, in consultation with Mark Endean, Open University, Milton Keynes, UK.

Course aims

Engineers plan, analyse, design and build anything that may move and sustain load – products range from toys to automobiles and aircraft. They employ an energy source and convert it into mechanical motions in machines such as robots or pumps. This is the second of two closely linked courses, 'Mechanics' and 'Engineering Principles and Design'. Both courses aim to lay down the foundations of mechanical engineering principles in such a way that the students can identify the appropriate concepts required in given engineering problems and apply them to formulate the suitable engineering solutions.

Table 14.1 Examples of grading criteria of different assessment tasks in accounting

Mid-term (AT2) and final examination (AT3)

ILO	Excellent A+ A A–	Good B+ B B–	Adequate C+ C C–	Marginal D
ILO1	Able to journalize accounting transactions in all areas covered with appropriate account titles and amounts; able to project the impacts of the journal entries to financial statements	Able to journalize accounting transactions in most areas covered; able to project the impacts of some journal entries to financial statements	Able to journalize some accounting transactions; able to carry some journal entries to financial statements	Able to journalize some accounting transactions
	Able to prepare all financial reports for both servicing and merchandising companies in an accurate and appropriate manner and format in reflecting a true and fair view of the financial reports	Able to prepare all financial reports for either servicing or merchandising companies in an accurate manner in reflecting a true and fair view of the financial reports	Able to prepare most financial reports for either servicing or merchandising companies	Able to prepare some financial reports for either servicing or merchandising companies
ILO2	Able to identify and clearly explain GAAP in writing; able to demonstrate application skills by selecting the appropriate GAAP in supporting various accounting treatments	Able to identify and describe GAAP in writing; able to discriminate between different principles under GAAP	Able to recall and describe some principles under GAAP	Able to recall some principles under GAAP

Intended learning outcomes (ILOs)

On successful completion of this course, students should be able to:

ILO1 *Apply* the principles of mechanical kinetics to single degree of freedom vibration systems.

ILO2 *Outline* the fundamental theory of friction and wear and its applications in engineering.

ILO3 *Describe* the basic theories of fluid mechanics and heat transfer.

ILO4 *Apply* the basic engineering mechanics principles to the design and implementation of a simple engineering system (such as a projectile machine) and the evaluation of its performance.

ILO5 *Work* effectively as a *team* member in a small-scale engineering project.

Teaching and learning activities (TLAs)

TLA 1: Situation: large class

Large class activities take place in the classroom setting and consist of lecturing and student activities in between. Office hours will be set aside during the semester to allow student/professor one-on-one consultation.
  Major focus: ILOs 1 and 2; minor focus: ILO3.

TLA 2: Situation: laboratory

The lab exercises are designed to supplement the taught materials such as friction, fluid mechanics and heat transfer.
  Major focus: ILOs 1 and 3.

TLA 3: Student-centred activity (SCA)

SCA is a project that utilizes the subject material of the courses 'Mechanics' and 'Engineering Principles and Design' to design a simple mechanism. The students are expected to work in teams to develop the schematic design, perform the kinematics/kinetic analysis, make an analysis of loading, investigate the behaviour of the components under elastic and dynamic loading and make appropriate design decisions. The students also investigate friction and lubrication aspects of the components and finalize their design.
  Major focus: ILOs 4 and 5.

Assessment tasks/activities (ATs)

There are three major assessment situations: final examination, laboratory report and the SCA (project) according to the weighting in Table 14.2.
  Examination and laboratory report are numerically marked and grades awarded accordingly.

Table 14.2 Weighting of the three assessment tasks in engineering with respect to the ILOs

ATs	Examination	Laboratory report	SCA	Total (%)
ILO 1	25		–	30
ILO 2	25	10	–	30
ILO 3			–	
ILO 4	–	–	36	36
ILO 5	–	–	4	4
Total (%)	50	10	40	100

The SCA (project) is graded using the following criteria.

Group assessment

a Prototype (40%): the working machine built to given specifications will be assessed based on its design, effectiveness, reliability and workmanship.

b Software (20%): a simple software programme will be written to determine the control parameter(s) for the machine to perform a given task (e.g. to propel the golf ball for a specified distance). The software can be implemented in any preferred computer languages or application software such as Excel.

c Report (40%): the typed report shall include:

- sketches of different design and related comments;
- calculations behind the final design;
- drawings with clear major dimensions;
- calibration data and graphs;
- reconciliation between theory and practice;
- software algorithm, description and also listing if available;
- anything that is useful to explain and promote the project work.

Peer-assessment

Assessment of others is an important skill for a professional engineer. Near the end of the project, each student will be asked to assess different members of the group objectively. This is used to differentiate the project contribution from each group member and their effectiveness as an engineering team player. The results are used to calculate the final project mark for each student.

Fashion marketing

Course: FdA **Fashion Marketing & Promotion**

The Integrated Group Project takes place in the final term of the first year of a two-year Foundation Arts Degree in Fashion Marketing and Promotion. This course is offered at the London College of Fashion, part of the University of the Arts London. The course was designed by Tim Williams, Course Director within the School of Management and Science.

Level 4 Unit: Integrated Group Project, 30 Credits

Intended learning outcomes (ILOs)

On completion of this course, students will be able to:

ILO1 *Investigate* and *evaluate* a range of marketing, advertising and PR issues relating to the fashion industry.

ILO2 *Use* marketing research methods to *identify* opportunities in the marketplace.

ILO3 *Apply* marketing, advertising and public relations theory to a practical task.

ILO4 *Design* a marketing and promotional plan for specific industry needs.

ILO5 *Evaluate* the effectiveness of your campaign.

ILO6 *Engage* with the PPD principles outlined in your course handbook and on Blackboard.

Teaching and learning activities (TLAs)

Students are organized into groups of five to six and given the brief at the start of the 10 week term.

The environment within which the students study is totally online; the activity and interaction is observed through the discussion boards plus live interactive online chat sessions. The essence of this unit is that it is self directed, with the students presenting their ideas and thoughts within the teams to each other. There is regular, critical, input from the tutor to ensure alignment to the learning outcomes with the feedback based on the students work in relation to the brief. The course is vocational so both the ILOs and TLAs are set in an industrial context.

Alignment towards the learning activities is achieved by the following.

ILO1 is achieved after the initial ideas have been proposed, through interactivity on the discussion boards and live interactive online chat; the students' ideas are further explored and undergo peer and tutor critique. The work and ideas that are discussed are initiated by the students within the framework of the brief that has been created by the tutor to expedite the ILOs.

ILO 2 is achieved by asking each team to research opportunities in a very competitive and crowded marketplace. Their proposals will be questioned on both a peer-to-peer and tutor-to-student basis. The principal intention is to facilitate the student to justify their ideas through third party research, to themselves, their peers and to third parties in industry.

ILO3 is achieved by the students referencing back to their previous two terms' work; the course is designed to give a flow in the first year to lead to this project. Elements within the first two projects, which are more closely directed, will have relevance to this unit. There is also the agenda of demonstrating the relevance in application of the theory learned in the first two terms of the course.

ILO4 is achieved by stipulating the content of the final report in terms of areas covered in the brief. The student teams offer their teamwork in week 7 for a formative assessment; they then receive formal feedback from the tutor as well as their peers. It is important that this process occurs with sufficient time before the summative deadline to enable the students to reiterate their work and amend as necessary subsequent to feedback and their own self-evaluation.

ILO5 is achieved by analysing the formative reports in an industrial context, and giving feedback as to whether this has been achieved; a principal aspect of this project, implied in the brief, is the sequential nature of the fashion business; one ILO builds on the next.

ILO6 is demonstrated by the students' self-reflection that is submitted individually at the end of the unit. PPD is integral to the FdA course.

Assessment tasks/activities (ATs)

A PowerPoint presentation (12–15 slides) of the group's plan posted on Blackboard for discussion in week 7, this is for formative feedback.

A written report per team 3,500 words, for formative feedback, deadline week 10.

A PPD reflection on the activity concerning the experience of team-working and links to professional contexts. This is summative and handed in individually and confidentially in week 10.

Assessment brief:

You are a team of marketing consultants brought in to advise a private label supplier on developing a new bra that will be sold through third party retailers. You are to choose what type of bra you believe shows the most opportunity and which retailer(s) will distribute this product with the greatest success.

You are to assume adequate funds for launching this product.

The report should cover all aspects of the marketing of the product from the identification of the type of bra that your team believes will have the greatest potential successes in the UK marketplace to how it will be distributed and marketed. Please pay special attention to the use of new media.

Information systems

'Management Information Systems I' is a one-semester core course in the first year of a three-year bachelor of business administration (BBA) degree programme offered by the Department of Information Systems of the College of Business at the City University of Hong Kong. The number of students is around 800, divided into small groups. The course was designed by Dr Ron Chi-Wai Kwok of the Department of Information Systems.

Course aims

1 Provide students with knowledge about the technological foundation of business information systems.
2 Equip students with the essential skills to work with common computer applications in today's business world.
3 Familiarize students with business information systems relevant to their professional career and applications in Hong Kong.

Intended learning outcomes (ILOs)

On completion of this course, students will be able to:

ILO1 *Describe* the basic concepts of information systems, their composition, configuration and architecture, including the Internet and web-based technologies in particular.
ILO2 *Explain* the social, economic, regulatory, political and mainly ethical aspects in the development, implementation and use of information systems in international business settings.
ILO3 *Apply* the general knowledge and methodologies of information systems, including the use of hardware and software, to *devise* and *evaluate* effective solutions to international business problems, given the information needs.
ILO4 *Design* and *develop* particular constructs and models to support various levels of international business activities using different tools such as Microsoft FrontPage, Microsoft Access and Microsoft Excel.
ILO5 *Work* productively as part of a team and, in particular, *communicate* and *present* information effectively in written and electronic formats in a collaborative environment.

Teaching and learning activities (TLAs)

TLA1: Situation: interactive lecture
Concepts and general knowledge of information systems are explained:

- Personal digital assistant (PDA) questions and answers: students respond to questions in lectures using their PDAs and the lecturer provides feedbacks based on students' response.
- Gobbets: showing videos about business cases and scenarios using the e-Organization (e-Org) cases.
- Concept map: the lecturer uses concept maps to conceptualize presented materials.
- Role play: students act as IT technicians and assemble a computer system.
- PDA one-minute note: at the end of the lecture, the lecturer reminds students to use their PDAs to write down the main topic that they find most difficult to understand in the session or the major question that they

want to raise. In the next lecture, the lecturer provides feedback based on students' concerns in their one-minute notes.

Major focus: ILOs 1 and 2; minor focus: ILO3.

TLA2: Situation: computer lab tutorial

Technical aspects of information systems design and development are covered:

- Computer lab exercises: hands-on activities on Microsoft FrontPage, Excel and Access.
- Group project discussion: discussion on various aspects of the group project (setting up a web page and a database for an online store, using Excel for decision support).

Major focus: ILO4; minor focus: ILOs 3 and 5.

TLA3: Situation: outside classroom activities

Additional help provided outside official class time:

- e-token: a PDA system in which students earn e-tokens by completing some learning-oriented activities such as crossword puzzles that are downloadable to their PDAs. Students can complete the downloaded PDA exercises at any time and anywhere (e.g. in MTR or on a bus).
- Online helpdesk: an online system to provide extra help to students having difficulties with the course outside the classroom. During the assigned periods, students can raise their questions about mid-term test or final examination in the online system. The tutors will answer their questions within four hours during office hours.

Major focus: ILOs 1 and 3; minor focus: ILO2.

Assessment tasks (ATs)

AT1: Tutorial assignments and participation (10%)

Two assignments (5% each) are given to assess the student's competence level working with Microsoft FrontPage, Microsoft Access and Microsoft Excel.
    Major focus: ILO4, minor focus: ILOs 3 and 5.

AT2: Group projects (35%)

The project is divided into three phases; each is designed to assess the student's ability in constructing interactive web pages, working with databases and devising decision support models in a business setting.
    Major focus: ILOs 3 and 4; minor focus: ILO5.

AT3: Mid-term test (15%)

The test is designed to gauge the student's grasp of information systems concepts and knowledge, as well as the ability to apply them to solve business problems in various situations.
    Major focus: ILOs 1 and 3; minor focus: ILO2.

AT4: Final examination (40%)

The examination is designed to gauge the student's grasp of information systems concepts and knowledge, as well as the ability to apply them to solve business problems in various situations.

Major focus: ILOs 1 and 3; minor focus: ILO2.

Grading criteria

Some examples of grading criteria are shown in Table 14.3.

Quality enhancement

To facilitate quality enhancement both for the course teachers and for individual students, Dr Kwok makes use of the assessment grade results for transformative reflection.

Table 14.3 Some examples of grading criteria for different assessment tasks in information systems

Group project phase 1 (AT2)

ILO	Content	Excellent A+ A A–	Good B+ B B–	Adequate C+ C C–	Marginal D
ILO3 **ILO4**	Overall design (sizing, grouping, alignment, colour, look and feel, etc.)	Designed in a professional way: fonts and graphics complement each other, text is in the appropriate size, making it easy to read, appropriate use of colour, easy navigation through the pages	The ability to design a professional web page is demonstrated in most pages with a few exceptions	The quality in most pages are average (e.g. inappropriate font size/ item grouping/ font colour/ background colour, etc.)	A merely acceptable design in general
ILO4	Creativity	Highly creative design: novel and original, clearly superior to templates or examples covered in class	Design with some creative idea on top of templates or examples covered in class	Average design with few creative ideas	Little creativity shown

(Continued overleaf)

Table 14.3 (*continued*)

ILO4	Practicability	Extremely practical design: can be considered a usable product even commercially, since it satisfies all the functional requirements set out	Quite a practical design: lacking a few minor components to be considered complete	Average design, but not very practical since a few major components are not implemented	Only satisfies a small number of practical needs

Mid-term (AT3) and final examination (AT4)

ILO	Excellent A+ A A−	Good B+ B B−	Adequate C+ C C−	Marginal D
ILO1	Demonstrate sound knowledge of most materials covered, able to describe all concepts of information systems and to identify relationship between difference concepts	Able to describe various major concepts of information systems with thorough comprehension of each and able to discriminate between different concepts	Able to recall and describe some important concepts of information systems and able to show some linkages between different concepts	Able to recall major concepts of information systems with simple description, with ability to grasp linkages between a small number of concepts
ILO2	Able to explain impact of information systems from various perspectives and how this determines the use of information systems in international business settings based on sound knowledge	Able to explain information systems' impacts in the various aspects, with well-rounded knowledge in international business settings	Able to explain some of the information systems' impacts in some aspects, with some knowledge in international business settings	Able to explain a few important impacts of information systems, with knowledge limited in local business settings

| **ILO3** | Able to make critical judgements by applying sound information systems knowledge, compare and discriminate between ideas and create unique solutions to business problems | Able to apply various components of information systems to solve open-ended as well as closed-ended business problems using skills and knowledge acquired | Able to apply some components of information systems to solve simple problems using skills and knowledge acquired | Able to apply some components of information systems to form partial solution to business problems using skills and knowledge acquired |

Course-level achievement

Table 14.4 shows the integrated (averaged) grades of all students in a given course, with respect to different ATs and different ILOs. The left-hand column lists the assessment tasks, the top row the ILOs. It also shows the overall grades of students in each AT and each ILO, as well as the final grade of students at the course level (cell entries are the mean grades obtained in the course). Looking at the bottom row of Table 14.4 it can be seen that, in general, students are good at the functioning ILOs 'design and develop' and 'work as part of a team' but the declarative ILOs 1 and 2, 'describe' and 'explain' are weaker. These results might suggest that the course leader focus more on tuning the TLAs for ILOs 1 and 2 in the next semester. The programme leader can think about the adjustment of the curriculum of the year 2 courses accordingly in order to help students strengthen their ILOs 1 and 2. The year 2 course leaders can also have a better understanding of their incoming students and better prepare the courses on these issues.

Individual student achievement

Table 14.5 corresponds to Table 14.4 but at student level, showing how the quality enhancement system works for an individual student's performance in the ATs and in each of the ILOs. This student is weak in ILO1 and ILO2, but strong in ILO4 and ILO5; weak in mid-term test and final examination, but good in group project. This provides feedback to the student about the sorts of areas represented by ILOs 1 and 2 and would help his/her decision making in years 2 and 3 to choose courses that would reinforce their learning in these areas if appropriate.

Table 14.4 A quality-enhancement measure focusing on the mean results for a given course

ATs	ILO1	ILO2	ILO3	ILO4	ILO5	Total
AT1				A–		**A–**
AT2				A–		**A–**
GP1			A	A	A–	**A–**
GP2			B+	A–	B+	**A–**
GP3			A–	A–	A–	**A–**
MTT	C+	C	B			**B–**
FEX	B–	B–	B			**B–**
PAT					A–	**A**
Total	**B–**	**B–**	**B+**	**A–**	**A–**	**B**

GP1 – group project 1
GP2 – group project 2
GP3 – group project 3
MTT – mid-term test
FEX – final examination
PAT – tutorial participation

Table 14.5 A quality-enhancement measure focusing on the results obtained by an individual student

ATs	ILO1	ILO2	ILO3	ILO4	ILO5	Total
AT1				A–		**A–**
AT2				B+		**B+**
GP1			A+	A+	B+	**A**
GP2			A–	A	B	**A–**
GP3			A	A–	A–	**A–**
MTT	C+	C–	C			**C**
FEX	C	C+	B			**C+**
PAT					A	**A**
Total	**C**	**C+**	**B**	**A–**	**A–**	**B**

Language

'Grammar of Modern English' is a three-unit course of MA in Language Studies Programme offered by the Language Centre at the Hong Kong Baptist University (HKBU). The course was designed by Professor Tony Hung of the Language Centre.

Course aims

The course aims to help students acquire a systematic and up-to-date knowledge of standard English grammar as used by educated speakers today, on the basis of corpus evidence. Through analysing English grammar from an *empirical, objective* and *descriptive* point of view, students will acquire a critical understanding of the nature of grammar and grammatical rules, and how they differ from traditional prescriptive 'rules'. There is an additional focus on the practical and pedagogic applications of grammar in language teaching.

By adopting a critical, enquiry-based approach to English grammar instead of the traditional prescriptive approach, the course aims also to foster most of HKBU's Graduate Attributes, particularly 1 (depth and breadth of knowledge), 2 (critical thinking), 3 (independent learning), 4 (language competence), and 5 (information literacy and management).

Intended learning outcomes (ILOs)

On completion of this course, students will be able to:

ILO1   *Use* an online English corpus (e.g. the Collins WordbanksOnline) to *search* for, *retrieve* and *tabulate* data on any given grammatical structure or lexical expression.

ILO2   *Critically analyse* and *interpret* data from a corpus, and use it as empirical evidence for the current state of the English language, and for *evaluating* the validity of traditional grammar rules.

ILO3   *Draw* well-supported *generalizations or hypotheses* from *analysing* corpus data, and *formulate* appropriate 'rules' to account for the grammatical patterns or structures analysed.

ILO4   *Apply* their knowledge of English grammar for pedagogic purposes, including the *identification* and *explanation* of grammatical errors.

Teaching and learning activities (TLAs)

TLAs will include the following:

ILOs 2 and 3
Students will investigate various aspects of English grammar by analysing data presented in class on selected grammatical structures, coming up with their own generalizations and hypotheses to account for the data, and checking them against the findings in corpus-based descriptive grammars (such as the *Longman Student Grammar*).

ILO 1
Students will learn how to use an online corpus (such as the Collins WordbanksOnline), including data search and retrieval and various

concordancing functions, through hands-on practice in tutorials in the computer lab, and independent exercises at home.

ILOs 1, 2 and 3

Students will search on their own for data on given lexical expressions and grammatical constructions, analyse the data for patterns and regularities, and draw well-supported generalizations on how these expressions or constructions are used today.

They will capture these generalizations in the form of descriptive grammar rules, contrast them with traditional prescriptive 'rules', and evaluate the accuracy and objectivity of the latter.

They will search the databank for evidence of *variation* in the form and usage of given grammatical constructions and lexical expressions, and compare the frequency and provenance of different variants.

ILO 4

Students will analyse data from samples of HK learners' English, and identify and explain the nature of the grammatical errors that they find; they will contrast these with the corresponding grammatical forms found in the corpus.

Assessment tasks (ATs)

Coursework: 60%

Term paper: 40%

AT1: Two written assignments (20% + 20%): addressing ILOs 1, 2 and 3

The questions include problem-solving tasks where students will analyse and evaluate given grammatical constructions and/or prescriptive 'rules', using data from a corpus as evidence, and construct their own grammatical rules or generalizations on that basis.

Students will be graded on their ability to:

(i)   retrieve and organize data from the corpus, using various concordancing functions efficiently;

(ii)   evaluate and analyse the data critically, selecting only relevant and valid tokens from the raw data, comparing the usage and frequency of different forms, and relating the forms to such variables as context, genre and provenance;

(iii) discover any patterns or regularities in the data on the grammatical structure in question, and formulate valid generalizations to account for them, supported by solid evidence;

(iv)   critically evaluate, and either support or reject, particular claims about English grammar, including traditional prescriptive rules and modern descriptive rules.

AT2: Oral presentation (15%): addressing ILOs 1, 2, 3 and 4

Students will make a 5–8 minute presentation in class, where they will analyse and evaluate a noteworthy grammatical structure or feature of their choice (including possible errors), either from local Hong Kong English or international English.

Students will be graded on their ability to:

(i)   select a structure or feature of potential interest from a grammatical point of view;
(ii) identify any noteworthy grammatical properties in the structure/feature in question;
(iii) marshal appropriate evidence and argue convincingly in support of their analysis and evaluation of the grammatical structure/feature in question.

AT3: Participation (5%)

This is a token recognition of the students' participation in class discussions, and their attendance.

AT4: Term paper (40%): addressing ILOs 1, 2, 3 and 4

A detailed, in-depth investigation of a given grammatical phenomenon in English, requiring a comprehensive process of data collection, analysis and argumentation.

Students will be graded on their ability to:

(i)   identify the grammatical issues involved in discussing the given phenomenon;
(ii) identify and explicate different points of view on the issues involved, including traditional prescriptive views, modern objective/descriptive approaches and modern pedagogic approaches, and compare their relative merits and shortcomings;
(iii) state their own analysis and evaluation of the grammatical phenomenon in question, citing pertinent data from the corpus as evidence and making convincing arguments in its support.

Grading criteria

For the assignments, student performance will be graded A–D according to the following criteria.

(i)   Retrieve and organize data from the corpus, using various concordancing functions efficiently:

   A The data are very comprehensive and clearly organized, and all necessary concordancing functions performed and the results clearly displayed.

B The data are fairly comprehensive and well organized, and most of the necessary concordancing functions performed.

C The data are barely adequate and loosely organized, and only some of the necessary concordancing functions performed.

D The data are clearly inadequate, and few if any concordancing functions performed.

(ii) Evaluate and analyse the data critically, selecting only relevant and valid tokens from the raw data, comparing the usage and frequency of different forms, and relating the forms to such variables as context, genre and provenance:

A The data are rigorously sifted to exclude irrelevant or invalid tokens; the valid data are thoroughly analysed to bring out all the salient features, and related to all the relevant contextual factors.

B The data are chosen with reasonable rigour, though a few invalid tokens still remain; the analysis brings out most of the salient features in the data, and relates them to most of the contextual factors.

C There is a mixture of valid and invalid data, which undermines the validity of the analysis; some salient features are noted, along with less pertinent features, with little attempt to relate them to contextual factors.

D The raw data are merely reproduced wholesale with little or no discrimination in the selection of valid and pertinent data; the analysis is thin and in any case invalidated by the unreliable data.

(iii) Discover any patterns or regularities in the data on the grammatical structure in question, and formulate valid generalizations to account for them, supported by solid evidence:

A All the patterns/regularities to be found in the data are exhaustively noted and thoughtfully presented, and accounted for with logical and valid generalizations based on solid evidence from the data.

B Most of the patterns/regularities in the data are duly noted, and reasonably well-supported generalizations are proposed to account for what is found.

C Some of the patterns/regularities in the data are noted, but some others are missed; the generalizations proposed are not strongly supported and only partially successful in capturing the regularities found.

D Few if any valid patterns/regularities are found, while some non-existent patterns are claimed; the generalizations drawn are therefore largely spurious.

(iv) Critically evaluate, and either support or reject, particular claims about English grammar, including traditional prescriptive rules and modern descriptive rules:

A The student subjects the claims to a thoroughly critical evaluation which exposes all the factual and theoretical fallacies, and confirms all the valid claims with qualifications where necessary; the argumentation is logical and effective, and supported by pertinent evidence.

B The student proves or disproves the claims with reasonable justification, using adequate data as evidence; the argumentation is fairly effective but not highly critical or rigorous.

C The student has an intuitive sense of which claims are valid or invalid, but is barely able to justify or support his viewpoint with adequate argumentation or evidence.

D The student shows little or no ability to discriminate between valid and invalid claims, and little evidence of critical thinking or basic knowledge of grammatical principles.

Management sciences

'SOM1: Design of Service Delivery Systems' is a one-semester course in the second year of the Service Operations Management degree programme offered by the Department of Management Sciences of the College of Business at the City University of Hong Kong. It is also offered as an elective or an out-of-discipline course to other students. The number of students is around 70. The course was designed by Ms Sandy Wong of the Department of Management Sciences.

Course aims

This course provides students with the knowledge of how to address the major issues involved in the design of the service package and the service delivery system. The strategic role of the supporting service facility and the challenges of delivering exceptional service quality are emphasized in the context of service organizations.

Intended learning outcomes (ILOs)

On successful completion of this course, students should be able to:

ILO1 *Describe* the service concept and the nature of services.
ILO2 *Discuss* the competitive service strategy and the role of information in services with examples.
ILO3 *Critically discuss* the service delivery including the service process and service encounter.
ILO4 *Identify* service quality problems and use the quality tools for *analysis* and *problem solving*.

ILO5 *Recommend* the facility design features to *identify* bottleneck operation and *remove* the anxiety of disorientation.

ILO6 *Evaluate* the service facility location to *minimize* total flow-distance of a service process layout and to *estimate* the expected revenues and market share.

Teaching and learning activities (TLAs)

TLA 1: Situation: interactive lecture

- Lectures: concepts and general knowledge of service operations management are explained.
- PDA questions and answers: students respond to questions in lectures using their PDAs and the lecturer provides feedback based on students' response.
- Peer learning: students will be asked to work in a group of two or three to recap and answer questions of the major topics that they learned in the previous lecture. They are required to share and present their answers to the class.
- Videos: videos about business cases and scenarios are shown and followed by class discussion.
- PDA one-minute note: at the end of the lecture, the lecturer reminds students to use their PDAs to write down the main topic that they find most difficult to understand in the session or the major question that they want to raise. In the next lecture, the lecturer provides feedback based on students' concerns in their one-minute notes.
- Learning log: students have to respond to each of the ILOs addressed in each lecture. Responses and reflection can vary from how they learned it, what activities reinforced the concepts learned, resources they used to learn the concept etc.

Major focus: ILOs 1, 2, 5 and 6; minor focus: ILOs 3 and 4.

TLA 2: Situation: tutorial

Students are required to team up with their classmates and participate in the following activities:

- Role play: students act as service providers and customers to simulate service encounters.
- Tutorial exercises and activities: students respond to and participate in in-class exercises and activities. They are required to apply real-life examples or their own service experiences to their learned subjects.
- Group discussion and case study: discussion on various aspects of the assigned major issues or questions as well as the assigned case studies.

Major focus: ILOs 3 and 6; minor focus: ILOs 1, 2, 4 and 5.

TLA3: Situation: outside classroom activities

Students are required to carry out some learning-oriented activities outside their classroom such as mystery shopping, walk-through audit, servicescape, process flow and layout improvement. Students present their findings and results of work to the class.

Major focus: ILOs 3, 4 and 5.

Assessment tasks/activities (ATs)

Group work (45% AT1, AT2, AT3)

The objective of group work is to equip students with the necessary knowledge, attitude and skills to become a deep learner by means of small group discussion and sharing. Students are required to form a group of 4–5 to work on the group course work, introduce themselves and exchange contact information; give a name to the group and appoint a group leader for coordination; let the teacher have the group name, student ID and names as well as the leader's contact number. Students are also asked to identify their learning expectations of the course.

AT1: Outside activities and presentation (15%)

Teams are asked to carry out some outside classroom activities to apply what they learned in lectures and to present the results of work during tutorial classes in weeks 9 and 10. Students may use other forms of presentation (e.g. role play, debate etc.). All team members have to show up but it's not necessary for all members to do the presentation.

Major focus: ILOs 3, 4 and 5.

AT2: Tutorial exercises and activities (20%)

Students can team up to a maximum of four to work on the assigned tutorial exercises and activities. Marks will be awarded to those students who demonstrate their familiarity with literature, their preparation and understanding of the topics and, more importantly, their contributions to the assigned activities.

Major focus: ILOs 1, 2, 3 and 5; minor focus: ILOs 4 and 6.

AT3: In-class participation and discussion (10%)

Students are required to critically discuss, share and present the assigned topics. Students can pair up or work individually to participate in the discussion topics and issues. They are expected to think and learn how to engage in an exchange of ideas to construct their understanding of knowledge and not just to memorize it. Students are expected to point out agreements or disagreements, to raise appropriate questions and to brainstorm solutions to problems. Extra marks are awarded to those who can draw relevant implications to apply to their daily life examples of service experiences. PDAs are required for the Q&A session.

Major focus: ILOs 1, 3, 5 and 6; minor focus: ILOs 2 and 4.

Individual work (55% AT4, AT5, AT6)

AT4: Learning log (5%)

The purposes of the learning log are to develop students' awareness of all the ILOs and learning processes; to develop their ability to reflect on learning activities; and to encourage instructors to inform students of weekly learning outcomes. Learning logs are submitted via Blackboard.

Major focus: all ILOs.

Self-reflection on outside activities (5%)

This is the individual work component of AT1. Each student is required to prepare and submit a one-page write-up to report their self-reflection on the assigned outside activities, focusing on (a) their reflection on the subjects/ topics they learned during the activities, (b) comments on their feelings about their learning experience and (c) give recommendations for further improvement.

Major focus: all ILOs.

AT5: Mid-term test (15%)

The mid-term test is scheduled during lecture session. It addresses only the first three ILOs for revision purpose and assesses the understanding of key concepts. The format is multiple-choice and/or closed-book short essays.

Major focus: ILOs 1 and 3; minor focus: ILO2.

AT6: Final exam (30%)

The final exam is a two-hour semi-closed-book in-class exam consisting of essay-type questions (both qualitative and quantitative). Students are allowed to bring in one A4-sized study aid prepared by themselves but no additional stickers or labels can be attached. Students are required to quote examples to support their arguments if appropriate.

Major focus: ILOs 5 and 6; minor focus: ILOs1 and 3.

Grading criteria

Some examples of grading criteria are shown in Table 14.6.

Nursing

'Philosophy and Science of Nursing' is a one-semester core course of a two-year part-time master of nursing degree programme in the Department of Nursing Studies of the Li Ka Shing Faculty of Medicine at the University of Hong Kong. The students are practising nurses, around 30 in number. The course was designed by Dr Agnes Tiwari of the Department of Nursing Studies.

Table 14.6 Some examples of grading criteria for different assessment tasks in management sciences

AT2: Tutorial exercises and activities

Excellent A+ A A− 4.3 4.0 3.7	Good B+ B B− 3.3 3.0 2.7	Adequate C+ C C− 2.3 2.0 1.7	Marginal D 1.0	Failure 0.0
Clearly and correctly state most critical points and important contributions of the assigned exercises and activities Discuss issues critically Draw significant and relevant implications to Hong Kong service sector Good presentation skills Strong evidence of familiarity with literature	Clearly and correctly state some critical points and important contributions of the assigned exercises and activities Discuss issues critically Draw some relevant implications to Hong Kong service sector Good presentation skills	Clearly and correctly state some critical points and contributions of the assigned exercises and activities	State a few critical points and contributions of the assigned exercises and activities	Little or no evidence of contributions to the assigned exercises and activities

AT4: Learning log

Excellent A+ A A− 4.3 4.0 3.7	Good B+ B B− 3.3 3.0 2.7	Adequate C+ C C− 2.3 2.0 1.7	Marginal D 1.0	Failure 0.0
Strong evidence of developing an awareness of learning expectations and processes as well as the ability to reflect on learning progress	Evidence of developing an awareness of learning expectations and processes as well as the ability to reflect on learning progress	Some evidence of developing an awareness of learning expectations and processes as well as the ability to reflect on learning progress	Sufficient organization of their learning that marginally enables the student to progress without repeating the assignment	Little or no evidence of ability to organize the learning and overall understanding of what the class is all about

(*Continued overleaf*)

Table 14.6 (*continued*)

AT6: Final examination

Excellent A+ A A– 4.3 4.0 3.7	Good B+ B B– 3.3 3.0 2.7	Adequate C+ C C– 2.3 2.0 1.7	Marginal D 1.0	Failure 0.0
Strong evidence of original thinking Good organization, capacity to analyse and synthesize Superior grasp of subject matter Evidence of extensive knowledge base	Evidence of grasp of subject, some evidence of critical capacity and analytic ability Reasonable understanding of issues Evidence of familiarity with literature	Student who is profiting from the university experience Understanding of the subject Ability to develop solutions to simple problems in the material	Sufficient familiarity with the subject matter to enable the student to progress without repeating the course	Little evidence of familiarity with the subject matter Weakness in critical and analytic skills Limited or irrelevant use of literature

Course aims

Although nursing is a practice discipline, it cannot solely rely on the accepted theories of practice. For nursing to evolve, it must continually expand its knowledge base, which should be disseminated and applied to practice. As the development of science entails the interpretation of phenomena and events, the context within which nursing science is located must be taken into account. Furthermore, the advancement of nursing science requires its practitioners to have the skills and inclination to reflect on the quality of one's thinking and to use one's critical thinking skills to engage in more thoughtful thinking and problem solving in work situations.

In this course, students will be able to develop and practise metacognitive self-correction (using one's own thinking to improve one's own thinking) while they interpret, analyse, explain and evaluate the philosophy and science of nursing within the western and Chinese context.

Intended learning outcomes (ILOs)

At the end of this course, students should be able to:

ILO1 *Explain* the nature of the philosophy of nursing and *relate* it to the western and Chinese philosophical context.

ILO2 *Describe* and *reflect* on the development of nursing knowledge.

ILO3 *Explain* the historical evolution of nursing science.

ILO4 *Analyse* the metaparadigm of nursing in terms of nursing, health, client and environment.

ILO5 *Reflect* on and *evaluate* the contemporary perspectives of nursing.

ILO6 *Analyse* and *theorize* the interrelationships among nursing theory, research, practice and education.

Teaching and learning activities (TLAs)

TLA1: Mini-lecture

A teacher-led mini-lecture precedes students' discussion activity. The purpose of the mini-lecture is to deliver key concepts and principles pertaining to the ensuing discussion.

TLA2: Small group discussion

Divided into small groups during the discussion activity, students develop and practise higher order cognitive skills as they *explain, analyse, reflect, evaluate* and *theorize* the philosophy and science underpinning nursing, with an aim to advance nursing practice and science from the past and present. Guidelines, framed in a series of critical thinking questions based on the ILOs of the particular class, are provided to help students conduct critical, interactive and dialectical discussion. Through the process of discussion, not only do students acquire disciplined-based knowledge, they also practise the habit of using their own thinking to improve their own thinking (metacognitive self-correction), which is an important nursing skill as nurses must be able to form good judgement in their professional work based on their own critical thinking. The teachers act as facilitators during student-led discussion by promoting meaningful discussion but not providing answers or solutions. In addition, one of the teachers records the thought processes demonstrated by the students in a selected group using the Holistic Critical Thinking Scoring Rubric (HCTSR) (Facione and Facione 1994) as an assessment of the students' ability to think critically about an authentic issue.

TLA3: Teacher-led think-aloud

After the discussion, a teacher-led think-aloud is used to provide feedback on students' responses to the critical thinking questions in the group selected. The teacher talks through the thought processes as demonstrated by the students during their discussion based on the HCTSR measures. Given the concentrated effort of using the HCTSR in the measurement of critical thinking, only one group can be assessed in each discussion session. The other groups of students are encouraged to listen to the feedback and learn from others' experience.

Assessment tasks (ATs)

Assessment is entirely by portfolio. The student:

1 submits two items of work, each item of which may cover one or more (whole or part) of the ILOs and is limited to 2000–2500 words;
2 justifies the selection of each of the items in relation to the ILOs;
3 ensures that the two portfolio items jointly cover *all five* of the ILOs specified for this module.

Students are given examples of items that may be submitted but are encouraged to go beyond the list. Examples include: an action plan, book or article review, a case study, a concept map, critical incidents, learning diaries, letter-to-a-friend, reflective diary, reflective report of a group discussion and the like.

Grading criteria

The criteria used to assess the quality of students' portfolio items are given in Table 14.7. Each item is graded holistically, but as the university requires a numerical grade, the grade for each item is converted to a percentage, as in Table 14.7, and the average of the two computed – which is then converted back to a letter grade.

Table 14.7 Holistic grading for the assessment portfolio in nursing

Grade	Description	Understanding demonstrated	Evidence provided (examples)
A ≥ 70	Excellent	Understanding at an extended abstract level	Theorize about a topic Generalize to new applications Reflect on experience
B 60–69	Good	Understanding at a relational and application level	Apply theory to practice Recognize good and bad applications
C 53–59	Fair	Understanding at a multistructural declarative level	Describe nursing knowledge Explain nursing philosophy Comprehend selected nursing theories
D 50–52	Pass	Understanding at the lowest nominal level	Name the concepts or theories Focus on one conceptual issue
F ≤ 49	Fail	Fail to achieve the stated learning objectives	Miss key issues Demonstrate erroneous understanding

Photography

This course 'RETHINK: Documentary Practice with Research Methods' is a 40 Credit course in an MA in Photojournalism and Documentary Photography. The Course Director is Paul Lowe, at the London College of Communication.

Course aims

This course is a transitional unit between the relatively structured practice unit in Phase 1 that has a series of prescriptive assignments, and the more open-ended and self-initiated final major project. This course challenges students to rethink their practice by experimenting with a new approach. The process and journey of exploration that is made is as important as the destination, i.e. the final product. In addition to the practice portfolio itself, students are required to evidence their explorations in a reflective way and to write a critical report as part of the final assessment.

The aim is to encourage students to become more critically reflective on their practice and to experiment and explore alternative ways of working. The process and journey that students take, evidenced in the critical report, is as important as the final product and that the whole submission can potentially gain high marks if there has been a transformative experience even if the final product itself in terms of the body of practice is not fully resolved. In practice, this has been very successful, with a significant number of students achieving a radical breakthrough in their work, producing entirely new approaches to their practice that perhaps would not have occurred without this encouragement to what we call 'glorious failure'.

Intended learning outcomes (ILOs)

ILO1 *Research, plan, produce, edit* and *present* an extended photo essay/documentary photography project.

ILO2 *Critically evaluate* your work and how it relates to the broader context of photographic practice through a process of *self-reflection* and *interaction* with peers.

ILO3 *Synthesize* theoretical and practical issues that have been addressed during the course.

ILO4 *Present* a well-researched, scholarly and contextualized report related to your practice.

Teaching and learning activities (TLAs)

The course content is delivered through lectures, workshops, seminars and group tutorials. In an iterative process throughout the unit the students work together in small teams to peer review their progress and to develop their ability to critically judge their own practice and that of others. Significant use is made of collaborative online tools such as Google Wave for brainstorming the individual project ideas. Indicative taught content includes:

- the principles/and methods of research for visual and journalistic practitioners;
- practical research planning;
- the execution and presentation of the extended photo essay;
- the marketplace for documentary photography;
- writing proposals and pitching them to clients;
- ethical, legal and copyright issues.

The student is expected to research, plan, produce, edit and present a body of practice, and to critically engage and reflect on this process during the entire project with their peers and tutors.

Assessment tasks (ATs)

- A portfolio of images related in subject or theme presented to a professional standard.
- The portfolio must be presented with an accompanying proposal of up to 500 words that explains the project to a potential client.
- A 1500 word critical report that evidences a reflective engagement with the process of producing the project.

Veterinary science

'Animal Structure and Functions 3A' (ASF3A) is a second-year course of a four-year degree programme of BAnVetBioSc at the University of Sydney. The number of students in the course in 2006 was 78. The course was designed by a team; the details supplied by Professor Rosanne Taylor and Dr Melanie Collier.

Course aims

The aims of this course are that students will integrate knowledge of structure (anatomy) and function (physiology) and draw on concepts introduced in Animal Science 2 to build their understanding of key systems that are integral to the maintenance of internal homeostasis. These concepts provide a basis for investigating the effect of genes, biotechnology, nutrition and reproductive changes on animal function and production in year 3 units.

Intended learning outcomes (ILOs)

On completion of this course students will be able to:

ILO1 *Analyse* the contribution of hormones to maintenance of internal homeostasis in animals.

ILO2 *Critically analyse* applied animal physiology research articles.

ILO3 *Advise* how the natural mechanisms animals use for defence from foreign molecules and organisms can be manipulated to confer immunity.

ILO4 *Advise* on animal management practices that meet the physiological needs of animals (considering the animals' sensory structures, central processing, autonomic and motor responses).

For purposes of illustration, we show alignment of the TLAs and ATs for ILOs 2 and 4 only.

Teaching and learning activities (TLAs)

TLA 1: Critical review

The students undertake a critical review of two recently published research papers on pain/welfare/research in animal husbandry/slaughter. They are encouraged to make their own choice as to topic. The specific ILOs of the critical review are that students will:

1 critically evaluate scientific literature;
2 relate the principles of neural processing to analysis of animals' responses to husbandry procedures;
3 use the structure and characteristics of good scientific writing;
4 provide constructive feedback on scientific writing of peers.

It is intended that undertaking this task will develop and demonstrate students' knowledge of central neural processing, sensory processing, pain and consciousness and provide an opportunity for students to integrate and apply these principles to assessment of humane animal husbandry and slaughter methods. As the task is completed, students will also develop key graduate attributes for animal and veterinary bioscientists in information retrieval, information management, critical analysis, written expression and animal welfare, attributes that will be further developed and assessed in their final-year honours/research project. The peer-assessment component provides an opportunity to reflect on their own scientific writing, to develop skills in editing and commenting on the work of peers and to improve on the quality of their own written work prior to final submission.

The students are prepared for the review with a tutorial on scientific writing to dissect and analyse a published paper and a class on how to critically review literature, which is supported by documents and a website showing students how to conduct their own critical review. A literature searching session with the librarians helps students learn how to find and to evaluate other sources of information that may be useful.

TLA2: Peer review

Students are required to review a critical review of their peers. The topic reviewed is completely different from the one they investigated in order to increase their appreciation of the other work in the field.

Students use grade descriptors and criteria to provide constructive feedback to their peers on a proforma by the following week. They frequently write several pages of useful suggestions and feedback on the hard copy (this is very popular with their peers) in accord with grade descriptors in the unit handbook:

1 purpose of research
2 selection and approach
3 quality of evidence
4 conclusions
5 general comments on format, word limit, grammar, spelling
6 suggested mark (/20).

One week later the students submit their revised critical review. The teacher sees the original, student comments, papers and the final submission. Only the final submission is marked; the earlier versions and comments give feedback to students on how they have improved their work to let the peer reviewers know that they have provided good constructive advice.

Assessment task (AT)

Critical review of research papers

This addresses ILOs 2 and 4. The critical review used in TLA1 forms part of the assessment of the course. The students are given a list of papers and are encouraged to make their own choice depending on their interest. This task encourages them to read more widely and to include some reviews and alternative perspectives. Feedback from the teachers is provided to students on how their works have improved. The critical review is worth 20% of the course, which is 6/24 credit points of one semester of the whole programme.

This assessment task is the only time where ILO2 is assessed in this unit. ILO4, as broader and encompassing several topics, is also assessed in other ways, including a written examination and project. The grading criteria are based on a combination of students' application of scientific knowledge in their evaluation of the work, as well as their ability to express their ideas effectively in the scientific critique.

Grading criteria for the critical reviews are provided to students in the handbook and are reproduced in Table 14.8.

Table 14.8 Grading criteria for the critical review of literature in veterinary science

Grade	Introduction/literature review

High distinction or mastery 85–100%

The report represents work of an exceptional standard:

- is a highly articulate and professional document;
- includes complex critical comments with extended justification (and appropriate referencing) in all sections that reflect an applied and transposable understanding of key issues;
- demonstrates initiative and originality in analysis or interpretation.

Comprehensive and highly professional:

- shows a high level of thought, knowledge and reflection;
- student is able to relate material to other knowledge domains;
- review critiques literature well, incorporating many sources to develop an argument with little to no summarizing of previous work;
- may resolve theoretical and/or empirical problems and show evidence of creative or innovative conceptualization;
- discussion is integrated into a logical, coherent whole: 'tells a story' and leads logically into research proposed;
- creates a sense of mastery of literature and relevant technical issues.

Distinction or high level of achievement 75–84%

The report is of a superior standard:

- is well written (as in credit) and free of errors;
- includes coherent critical comments with substantial justification (and appropriate referencing) in all sections that reflect an integrated understanding of key issues;
- provides evidence of broader appreciation of the relationships between key aspects of studies in this field;
- demonstrates complex, deep understanding of the subject matter.

Effective and comprehensive:

- evidence of thought and reflection;
- often relates material to other knowledge domains;
- includes critical appraisal, but may also summarize rather than evaluate some aspects of literature;
- review identifies and attempts to resolve theoretical puzzles;
- essential content within the domain is successfully integrated.

(*Continued overleaf*)

Table 14.8 (*continued*)

Grade	Introduction/literature review
Credit good level of achievement 65–74%	The report: • is complete, well structured and well presented; • is written in a clear style that communicates points effectively on first reading; • synthesizes and applies concepts appropriately to the problem; • includes coherent critical comments with justification based on evidence in all sections that reflect a sound understanding of key issues; • uses evidence/argument from the literature in the field in analysis. Review identifies and defines major issues: • clear and strong arguments are developed within some major issues; • some tendency to summarize literature rather than develop an integrative and logical argument; • technical issues treated competently.
Pass 50–64%	The report: • addresses all four major themes in the analysis but does not integrate or relate key ideas and issues effectively; • is presented in an organized manner but may contain irregularities in style, expression that do not interfere with meaning; • provides critical comments with justification in some sections that reflect a basic understanding of key issues; • demonstrates that the literature in the field has been consulted. Review identifies some major issues: • comments are essentially descriptive; • minimal critical analysis is attempted; • *or* analysis lacks depth; • *or* analysis is somewhat confused; • main focus is on concrete issues; • lack of integrating argument; • some technical expertise revealed; • may have non-major factual errors.
Fail < 50%	The report: • does not address the four major themes of the analysis; • evidence of plagiarism or academic dishonesty; • presented in a disorganized, incoherent manner; • contains no/little or inappropriate critical comments; • provides no/little justification for critical comments; • does not show any appreciation of the literature in the field.

Comments and conclusions

The examples in this chapter illustrate possible ways of implementing constructively aligned teaching, learning and assessment under differing conditions of class size, level of teaching, disciplinary areas, various contextual conditions such as faculty regulations as to assessment and personal philosophy of the teacher. Class sizes ranged from large (over 200 students), medium (70–80 students) to small (around 30 students); mode from full-time to part-time and levels from first-year undergraduate to postgraduate. Most courses were conceived in a qualitative framework for assessment, others in a quantitative; some assessed the ILO, others the assessment task.

What all examples have in common is that the TLAs and ATs were aligned to the clearly stated ILOs on the basis of the learning verbs in each ILO.

Intended learning outcomes

All the course ILOs are derived from the course aims and are articulated in a way that identifies what students are intended to achieve through attending the course. Verbs such as *identify, describe, explain, analyse, evaluate, apply, design, reflect, generalize, hypothesize* and *theorize* are used to indicate the levels of understanding or performance students are expected to achieve with respect to the content areas. These ILOs include both declarative and functioning knowledge, ranging from multistructural to extended abstract in terms of their SOLO levels. In several courses, the relative importance of the ILOs is reflected in the amount of teaching and learning support in the TLAs and by the weighting of the assessment tasks in deriving the final grade.

Most of these courses also include the more generic ILOs on teamwork and communication to address appropriate graduate outcomes.

Teaching and learning activities

Several different situations were used as contexts for TLAs:

1 *Large classes of hundreds of students in traditional lecture theatres:* examples from accounting, engineering and information systems show that even this unpromising situation can be made interactive by engaging students in student-centred learning activities such as peer discussion and learning, role play, developing concept maps, using PDA for Q&A and minute papers and working on work-along exercises.

2 *Small group situations:* TLAs such as small group discussions on case study and problem solving, working on tutorial exercises, while role play and think-aloud modelling were used in accounting, information systems, management sciences and nursing.

3 *Laboratory*: the laboratory context, supporting discipline-specific learning activities for functioning knowledge ILOs were used in engineering and information systems.

4 *Group projects* were used as TLAs in engineering and information systems: in both cases the TLA became the assessment task.

5 *Outside the classroom*: accounting, information systems, fashion marketing and management sciences all required students to engage in TLAs outside the classroom such as peer teaching, helpdesk, tutor consultation, individual work with PDAs, peer tutoring and field trips.

6 *Peer-review and peer-assessment*, authentic to much professional practice, is used formatively as a TLA in fashion marketing, photography and veterinary science.

7 *Online activities*: ET is used to provide aligned learning activities in most courses, especially fashion marketing, information systems, language and photography.

Assessment tasks

A variety of assessment tasks are used. Where departments had regulations requiring examinations, the latter were used strategically, as in point 1:

1 *Written tests and examinations*: these are used in many of these courses, but mainly to assess declarative knowledge as in such verbs as 'identify', 'describe', 'explain' and 'evaluate'. The danger, mostly avoided here, is that where regulations stipulate that x% of the final grade must be by examination, the functioning knowledge ILOs might be under-assessed.

2 *Project work* is used to assess functioning knowledge in engineering and information systems.

3 *TLA as assessment task*: alignment is maximized when the TLA becomes the AT: critical review of research papers in veterinary science; tutorial exercises and assignments in accounting, information systems and management sciences; and the student-centred activities (SCA) project in engineering.

4 *Portfolio assessment*: nursing used a portfolio of two items that students chose and that had to address all ILOs. Students in the photography course are assessed through presenting portfolios of images with accompanying proposal and a critical report.

5 *Peer-assessment* was used formatively and summatively in engineering.

Grading

Constructive alignment is achieved once TLAs and ATs are aligned to the ILOs. There are two remaining tasks: to turn the student's performance on a task into a grade or mark; and, after assessing individual ATs, to combine the results into a final grade. This may be done in various ways, according to the content area, the context including institutional policies, and personal decision:

1 *Assessing individual performances*: grades can be allocated by judging a students' performance top-down against established grading criteria or rubrics; or by quantitatively accruing marks bottom-up. Most courses here used judgement against grading criteria, so that the difference between grades reflected qualitative differences in performance.

2 *Deriving the final grade*: however an individual performance is assessed, it needs to be combined with other assessments to form a final grade for the student. Where marking the individual task has been done, combining results presents no problem: it is a matter of averaging the obtained results. Where the initial assessments have been made qualitatively, top-down, they can be converted into a number scale which can then be dealt with arithmetically, as in veterinary science, management sciences and nursing (see Tables 14.6, 14.7, and 14.8). Holistic assessment was used in nursing (Table 14.7). An example also appears in Table 12.1 (p. 259).

3 *Assessing the ILO or assessing the task*: we saw examples of both here. Assessing the task occurs in nearly all the courses. Some of these courses also provide rubrics for assessing and grading of their assessment tasks (language, management science, nursing and veterinary science). Assessing the ILO on the basis of a variety of sources occurs in accounting and information systems, with some examples of rubrics

Conclusions

We are extremely grateful to the designers of the faculty implementation of constructive alignment, and of the courses we have just visited, for allowing their inspirational work to be included here. They nicely demonstrate that, although so different in content and detail, constructively aligned teaching and learning can be implemented in so many different areas and institutional contexts: constructive alignment is a robust animal that can adapt to a variety of conditions. These courses are not here as models to be emulated in detail. Undoubtedly, they will change as a result of ongoing quality enhancement, as all good teaching does. Transformative reflection is by definition transforming. Our intention in presenting these examples is rather that they will provide ideas to fertilize your own transformative reflection about your teaching and assessment.

A final task (Task 14.1) asks you to revisit the intended outcomes that we have identified at the beginning of this edition (p. xxiv) and reflect on how well they have been achieved as far as you are concerned.

Task 14.1 Your achievement of the intended outcomes of this book

We have identified six intended outcomes for readers of this book (see p. xxiv).

We have discussed the theory and practice of designing and implementing constructively aligned teaching and learning and provided task activities for the different stages of designing and implementing constructive alignment. Now that you have finished reading the book, and hopefully have done the tasks, we would like to ask you to undergo some self-reflection and self-assessment of your achievement of these intended outcomes.

Your evaluation on achievement of intended outcome:

1 _____

   _____

2 _____

   _____

3 _____

   _____

4 _____

   _____

5 _____

   _____

6 _____

   _____

Your overall reflection:

1 Some of the most important things that you have gained from the book:

   _____

   _____

   _____

2 Questions that you still have regarding designing and implementing constructive alignment:

   _____

   _____

3 Actions that you will take to try to answer these questions:

_____

_____

_____

4 What is your intention to implement constructive alignment in your future teaching? Put a cross on the continuum to indicate your position:

_____

No intention   Definitely
to implement   intend to implement

References

Abercrombie, M.L.J. (1969) *The Anatomy of Judgement.* Harmondsworth: Penguin.

Abercrombie, M.L.J. (1980) *Aims and Techniques of Group Teaching.* London: Society for Research into Higher Education.

Airasian, P. and Madaus, G. (1972) Criterion-referenced testing in the classroom, *Measurement in Education.* Special Reports of the National Council on Measurement in Education 3, No. 4, East Lansing, MI.

Albanese, M. and Mitchell, S. (1993) Problem-based learning: a review of literature on its outcomes and implementation issues, *Academic Medicine*, 68: 52–81.

Allen, M. (2009) Authentic assessment and the Internet: contributions within Knowledge Networks. http://netcrit.net/content/aaceauthenticassessment2009. pdf (accessed 2 February 2011).

Altbach, P.G., Reisberg, L. and Rumbley, L.E. (2009) *Trends in Global Higher Education: Tracking an Academic Revolution.* Report for the UNESCO 2009 World Conference on Higher Education, 5–8 July.

Anderson, J.R. (1976) *Language, Memory, and Thought.* Hillsdale, NJ: Erlbaum.

Anderson, L.W. and Krathwohl, D.R. (2001) *A Taxonomy for Learning, Teaching, and Assessing: A Revision of Bloom's Taxonomy of Educational Objectives.* New York: Addison Wesley Longman.

Angelo, T.A. and Cross, K.P. (1993) *Classroom Assessment Techniques.* San Francisco, CA: Jossey-Bass.

Ashworth, P., Bannister, P. and Thorne, P. (1997) Guilty in whose eyes? University students' perceptions of cheating and plagiarism, *Studies in Higher Education*, 22: 187–203.

Atherton, J. (2010) Learning and teaching; SOLO Taxonomy. http://www. learningandteaching.info/learning/solo.htm (accessed 2 February 2011).

Ausubel, D.P. (1968) *Educational Psychology: A Cognitive View.* New York: Holt, Rinehart & Winston.

Baillie, C. and Toohey, S. (1997) The 'power test': its impact on student learning in a materials science course for engineering students, *Assessment and Evaluation in Higher Education*, 22: 33–48.

Bain, K. (2004) *What the Best College Teachers Do.* Cambridge, MA: Harvard University Press.

Balchin, T. (2006) Evaluating creativity through consensual assessment, in N. Jackson, M. Oliver, M. Shaw and J. Wisdom (eds) *Developing Creativity in Higher Education: An Imaginative Curriculum.* Abingdon: Routledge.

Ballard, B. and Clanchy, J. (1997) *Teaching International Students.* Deakin, ACT: IDP Education Australia.

Barrett, H.C. (2007) Researching electronic portfolios and learner engagement: the REFLECT Initiative, *Journal of Adolescent and Adult Literacy,* 50, 6: 436–49.

Barrie, S. (2004) A research-based approach to generic graduate attributes policy, *Higher Education Research and Development,* 23: 261–76.

Barrows, H.S. (1986) A taxonomy of problem-based learning methods, *Medical Education,* 20: 481–6.

Bath, D., Smith, C., Stein, S. and Swann, R. (2004) Beyond mapping and embedding graduate attributes: bringing together quality assurance and action learning to create a validated and living curriculum, *Higher Education Research and Development,* 23: 313–28.

Beasley, C. (1997) Students as teachers: the benefits of peer tutoring. http://lsn .curtin.edu.au/tlf/tlf1997/beasley.html (accessed 2 February 2011).

Beetham, H. and Sharpe, R. (2007) *Rethinking Pedagogy for a Digital Age: Designing and Delivering e-learning.* London: Routledge.

Bereiter, C. and Scardamalia, M. (1987) *The Psychology of Written Composition.* Hillsdale, NJ: Lawrence Erlbaum.

Biggs, J.B. (1973) Study behaviour and performance in objective and essay formats, *Australian Journal of Education,* 17: 157–67.

Biggs, J.B. (1979) Individual differences in study processes and the quality of learning outcomes, *Higher Education,* 8: 381–94.

Biggs, J.B. (1987a) *Student Approaches to Learning and Studying.* Hawthorn, Victoria: Australian Council for Educational Research.

Biggs, J.B. (1987b) Process and outcome in essay writing, *Research and Development in Higher Education,* 9: 114–25.

Biggs, J.B. (1993a) What do inventories of students' learning processes really measure? A theoretical review and clarification, *British Journal of Educational Psychology,* 63: 1–17.

Biggs, J.B. (1993b) From theory to practice: a cognitive systems approach, *Higher Education Research and Development,* 12: 73–86.

Biggs, J.B. (1996a) Western misperceptions of the Confucian-heritage learning culture, in D. Watkins and J. Biggs (eds) *The Chinese Learner: Cultural, Psychological, and Contextual Influences.* Hong Kong: Centre for Comparative Research in Education/Camberwell, Victoria: Australian Council for Educational Research.

Biggs, J.B. (1996b) Enhancing teaching through constructive alignment, *Higher Education,* 32: 1–18.

Biggs, J.B. and Collis, K.F. (1982) *Evaluating the Quality of Learning: The SOLO Taxonomy.* New York: Academic Press.

Biggs, J.B. and Moore, P.J. (1993) *The Process of Learning.* Sydney: Prentice-Hall Australia.

Biggs, J. and Tang, C. (in press) Train-the-trainers: implementing outcomes-based education in Malaysia, *Malaysian Journal of Learning and Instruction.*

Biggs, J.B., Kember, D. and Leung, D.Y.P. (2001) The Revised Two Factor Study Process Questionnaire: R-SPQ-2F, *British Journal of Educational Psychology,* 71: 133–49.

Billet, S. (2004) Workplace participatory practices – conceptualizing workplace as learning environments, *The Journal of Workplace Learning*, 16, 4: 312–24.

Blair, B and Millea, M. (2004) Quantifying the benefits of cooperative education, *Journal of Cooperative Education*, 38, 1: 67–72.

Bligh, D.A. (1972) *What's the Use of Lectures?* Harmondsworth: Penguin.

Bloom, B.S. (ed) (1956) *Taxonomy of Educational Objectives: Handbook I, Cognitive Domain*. New York: Longman.

Bloom, B.S., Hastings, J.T. and Madaus, G.F. (1971) *Handbook of Formative and Summative Education of Student Learning*. New York: McGraw-Hill.

Bok, D. (2006) *Our Underachieving Colleges: A Candid Look at How Much Students Learn and Why They Should be Learning More*. Princeton, NJ: Princeton University Press.

Bologna Process (2010) http://www.ond.vlaanderen.be/hogeronderwijs/bologna/ (accessed 2 February 2011).

Boud, D. (1985) *Problem-based Learning in Education for the Professions*. Sydney: Higher Education Research and Development Society of Australasia.

Boud, D. (1986) *Implementing Student Self-assessment*. Green Guide No. 5. Sydney: Higher Education Research and Development Society of Australasia.

Boud, D. (1995) *Enhancing Learning through Self-assessment*. London: Kogan Page.

Boud, D. and Feletti, G. (eds) (1997) *The Challenge of Problem-based Learning*. London: Kogan Page.

Boulton-Lewis, G.M. (1998) Applying the SOLO taxonomy to learning in higher education, in B. Dart and G. Boulton-Lewis (eds) *Teaching and Learning in Higher Education*. Camberwell, Victoria: Australian Council for Educational Research.

Boyer, E.L. (1990) *Scholarship Reconsidered: Priorities for the Professoriate*. Princeton, NJ: Carnegie Foundation for the Advancement of Teaching.

Boyle, A. (2007) Using alignment and reflection to improve student learning, *Elements*, 3, 2: 113–17.

Brabrand, C. and Dahl, B. (2009) Using the SOLO taxonomy to analyse competence progression of university science curricula, *High Education*, 58: 531–49.

Brandenburg, D. and Ellinger, A. (2003) The future: just-in-time learning expectations and potential implications for human resource development, *Advances in Developing Human Resources*, 5, 3: 308–20.

Brenton, S. (2009) E-learning – an introduction, in H. Fry, D. Ketteridge and S. Marshall (eds) *A Handbook for Teaching and Learning in Higher Education: Enhancing Academic Practice*, 3rd edn. London: Routledge.

Brew, A. (1999) Towards autonomous assessment: using self-assessment and peer-assessment, in S. Brown and A. Glasner (eds) *Assessment Matters in Higher Education*. Buckingham: Society for Research into Higher Education/Open University Press.

Brewer, G., Williams, A. and Sher, W. (2007) Utilizing learning contracts to stimulate ownership of learning. www.aaee.com.au/conferences/papers/2007/paper_88 .pdf (accessed 2 February 2011).

Brockbank, A. and McGill, I. (1998) *Facilitating Reflective Learning in Higher Education*. Buckingham: Society for Research into Higher Education/Open University Press.

Brook, V. (2006) Learning-focused curriculum development: the redesign of elements of a PGCE Science (Subject Year) Programme, *Investigations in University Teaching and Learning*, 3, 2: 27–35.

Brown, A., Carmichael, R. and Ryan, R. (2008) Supporting first year learning and teaching through academic mentoring and peer tutoring. Paper presented at the 11th Pacific Rim First Year Higher Education (FYHE) Conference, Hobart, Tasmania, 30 June – 2 July.

Brown, S. and Glasner, A. (eds) (1999) *Assessment Matters in Higher Education.* Buckingham: Society for Research into Higher Education/Open University Press.

Brown, S. and Knight, P. (1994) *Assessing Learners in Higher Education.* London: Kogan Page.

Buckridge, M. and Guest, R. (2007) A conversation about pedagogical responses to increased diversity in university classrooms, *Higher Education Research and Development,* 26: 133–46.

Burke, K. and Jopson, D. (2005) http://www.smh.com.au/news/National/Dark -plagiarism-cloud-hangs-over-lucrative-overseas-programs/2005/05/09/1115584 909943.html (accessed 2 February 2011).

Burns, G. and Chisholm, C. (2003) The role of work-based learning methodologies in the development of life-long engineering education in the 21st century, *Global Journal of Engineering Education,* 7, 2: 179–90.

Carless, D., Joughin, G., Liu, N.F. and associates (2006) *How Assessment Supports Learning.* Hong Kong: Hong Kong University Press.

Chalmers, D. and Fuller, R. (1996) *Teaching for Learning at University.* London: Kogan Page.

Chalmers, D. and Kelly, B. (1997) *Peer Assisted Study Sessions (PASS).* University of Queensland: Teaching and Educational Development Institute.

Chan, C.K.K. (2001) Promoting learning and understanding through constructivist approaches for Chinese learners, in D. Watkins and J. Biggs (eds) *Teaching the Chinese Learner: Psychological and Pedagogical Perspectives.* Hong Kong: Comparative Education Research Centre, University of Hong Kong/Camberwell, Victoria: Australian Council for Educational Research.

Chan, C.K.K., and van Aalst, J. (2008) Collaborative inquiry and knowledge building in networked multimedia environments, in J. Voogt and G. Knezek (eds) *International Handbook of Information Technology in Primary and Secondary Education.* Dordrecht, The Netherlands: Springer.

Cheung, H.L., Fisher, D.W., Pickard, V. and Chan, Y.F. (2009) Scaffolding student learning: integrating ePortfolios into the university experience, 34th International Conference on Improving University Teaching (IUT), Simon Fraser University, Vancouver, Canada, 14–17 July.

Cho, P. (2007) Enhancing teaching and learning in group projects through poster assessment, in S. Frankland (ed) *Enhancing Teaching and Learning through Assessment: Deriving an Appropriate Model.* Dordrecht, The Netherlands: Springer.

Cho, P. and Tang, C. (2007) Implementation and feedback on the use of reflective writing as a component of a clinical assessment, in S. Frankland (ed) *Enhancing Teaching and Learning through Assessment: Deriving an Appropriate Model.* Dordrecht, The Netherlands: Springer.

Cobham, D.C. and Jacques, K. (2006) Constructive alignment: reflections on implementation, *Proceedings of the 1st Annual Workshop on Constructive Alignment,* February 2006, Nottingham Trent University.

Cohen, S.A. (1987) Instructional alignment: searching for a magic bullet, *Educational Researcher,* 16, 8: 16–20.

Colbert, J., Trumble, K. and Desberg, P. (eds) (1996) *The Case for Education: Contemporary Approaches for using Case Methods.* Boston, MA: Allyn and Bacon.

Cole, N.S. (1990) Conceptions of educational achievement, *Educational Researcher*, 18, 3: 2–7.

Collier, K.G. (1983) *The Management of Peer-group Learning: Syndicate Methods in Higher Education*. Guildford: Society for Research into Higher Education.

Colvin, J. and Phelan, A. (2006) Evaluating student opinion of constructivist learning activities on computing undergraduate degrees. Paper presented to the 1st Annual Workshop on Constructive Alignment, Nottingham Trent University, February.

Cortazzi, M. and Jin, L. (2001) Large classes in China: 'good' teachers and interaction, in D. Watkins and J. Biggs (eds) *Teaching the Chinese Learner: Psychological and Pedagogical Perspectives*. Hong Kong: Comparative Education Research Centre, University of Hong Kong/Camberwell, Victoria: Australian Council for Educational Research.

Cowan, J. (1998) *On Becoming an Innovative Teacher*. Buckingham: Open University Press.

Cowan, J. (2002) *On Becoming an Innovative University Teacher*. Buckingham: Society for Research into Higher Education/Open University Press.

Cowan, J. (2004) Education for higher level capabilities. Beyond alignment to integration?, in V.M.S. Gil, I. Alarcão and J. Hooghof (eds) *Challenges in Teaching and Learning in Higher Education*. University of Aveiro and Netherlands Institute for Curriculum Development.

Cowan, J. (2006) How should I assess creativity?, in N. Jackson, M. Oliver, M. Shaw and J. Wisdom (eds) *Developing Creativity in Higher Education: An Imaginative Curriculum*. Abingdon: Routledge.

Cowdroy, R. and De Graaff, E. (2005) Assessment of high-level creativity, *Assessment and Evaluation in Higher Education*, 30, 5: 507–18.

Crooks, T.J. (1988) The impact of classroom evaluation practices on students, *Review of Educational Research*, 58: 438–81.

Cropley, A. and Cropley, D. (2009) *Fostering Creativity: A Diagnostic Approach for Higher Education and Organizations*. Cresskill, NJ: Hampton Press.

D'Andrea, V. and Gosling, D. (2005) *Improving Teaching and Learning in Higher Education: A Whole Institution Approach*. Maidenhead: Open University Press/McGraw-Hill Educational.

Dart, B. and Boulton-Lewis, G. (eds) (1998) *Teaching and Learning in Higher Education*. Camberwell, Victoria: Australian Council for Educational Research.

Davies, P. and Mangan, J. (2007) Threshold concepts and the integration of understanding in economics, *Studies in Higher Education*, 32, 4: 711–26.

Davis, B.G. (1993) *Tools for Teaching*. San Francisco, CA: Jossey-Bass.

Dearing, R. (1997) *Higher Education in the Learning Society*, Report of the National Committee of Inquiry into Higher Education (Dearing Report). Norwich: HMSO.

Diederich, P.B. (1974) *Measuring Growth in English*. Urbana, IL: National Council of Teachers of English.

Dienes, Z. (1997) *Student-led Tutorials: A Discussion Paper*. Falmer: School of Experimental Psychology, University of Sussex.

Dunkin, M. and Precians, R. (1992) Award-winning university teachers' concepts of teaching, *Higher Education*, 24: 483–502.

Edström, K. (2008) Doing course evaluation as if learning matters most, *Higher Education Research and Development*, 27, 2: 95–106.

Ellsworth, R., Duell, O.K. and Velotta, C. (1991) Length of wait-times used by college students given unlimited wait-time intervals, *Contemporary Educational Psychology*, 16: 265–71.

Elton, L. (1987) *Teaching in Higher Education: Appraisal and Training.* London: Kogan Page.

Elton, L. (2005) Designing assessment for creativity: an imaginative curriculum guide. http://www.heacademy.ac.uk/2841.htm (click 'Lewis Elton') (access 2 February 2011).

Elton, L. and Cryer, P. (1992) *Teaching Large Classes.* Sheffield: University of Sheffield Teaching Development Unit.

Enhancing Teaching-Learning Environments in Undergraduate Courses (ETL Project) (2001–2005). For publications: http://www.etl.tla.ed.ac.uk/publications.html (accessed 2 February 2011).

Entwistle, N. (2009) *Teaching for Understanding at University: Deep Approaches and Distinctive Ways of Thinking.* Basingstoke: Palgrave Macmillan.

Entwistle, N. and Entwistle, A. (1997) Revision and the experience of understanding, in F. Marton, D. Hounsell and N. Entwistle (eds) *The Experience of Learning.* Edinburgh: Scottish Universities Press.

Entwistle, N.J. and Entwistle, D.M. (2003) Preparing for examinations: the interplay of memorising and understanding, and the development of knowledge objects, *Higher Education Research and Development,* 22, 1: 19–42.

Entwistle, N., Kozeki, B. and Tait, H. (1989) Pupils' perceptions of school and teachers – II: relationships with motivation and approaches to learning, *British Journal of Educational Psychology,* 59: 340–50.

Entwistle, N. and Ramsden, P. (1983) *Understanding Student Learning.* London: Croom Helm.

Ewell, P.T. (1984) *The Self-regarding Institution: Information for Excellence.* Boulder, CO: National Center for Higher Education Management Systems.

Facione, P.A. and Facione, N.C. (1994) Holistic Critical Thinking Scoring Rubric (HCTSR). http://www.insightassessment.com/HCTSR.html (accessed 2 February 2011).

Falchikov, N. and Boud, D. (1989) Student self-assessment in higher education: a meta-analysis, *Review of Educational Research,* 59: 395–400.

Feather, N. (ed) (1982) *Expectations and Actions.* Hillsdale, NJ: Lawrence Erlbaum.

Feletti, G. (1997) The triple jump exercise: a case study in assessing problem solving, in G. Ryan (ed) *Learner Assessment and Program Evaluation in Problem-based Learning.* Newcastle, NSW: Australian Problem Based Learning Network.

Fox, D. (1989) Peer assessment of an essay assignment, *HERDSA News,* 11, 2: 6–7.

Frankland, S. (ed) 2007 *Enhancing Teaching and Learning through Assessment: Deriving an Appropriate Model.* Dordrecht, The Netherlands: Springer.

Frederiksen, J.R. and Collins, A. (1989) A systems approach to educational testing, *Educational Researcher,* 18, 9: 27–32.

Gabrenya, W.K., Wang, Y.E. and Latane, B. (1985) Cross-cultural differences in social loafing on an optimizing task: Chinese and Americans, *Journal of Cross-cultural Psychology,* 16: 223–64.

Galton, F. (1889) *Natural Inheritance.* New York: Macmillan.

Gardner, H.W. (1993) Educating for understanding, *The American School Board Journal,* July: 20–4.

Gardner, H. (1999) *Intelligence Reframed: Multiple Intelligences for the 21st Century.* New York: Basic Books.

Gelade, S. and Fursenko, F. (2007) Can intrinsic graduate qualities be developed through assessment? Mapping assessment practices in IT programs, in S. Frankland (ed) *Enhancing Teaching Learning through Assessment: Deriving an Appropriate Model.* Dordrecht, The Netherlands: Springer.

Gibbs, G. (1981) *Twenty Terrible Reasons for Lecturing.* Oxford: Oxford Polytechnic.

Gibbs, G. (1992) *Improving the Quality of Student Learning.* Bristol: Technical and Educational Services.

Gibbs, G. (1999) Using assessment strategically to change the way students learn, in S. Brown and A. Glasner (eds) *Assessment Matters in Higher Education: Choosing and Using Diverse Approaches.* Buckingham: Society for Research into Higher Education/Open University Press.

Gibbs, G., Habeshaw, S. and Habeshaw, T. (1984) *53 Interesting Ways to Teach Large Classes.* Bristol: Technical and Educational Services.

Gibbs, G. and Jenkins, A. (eds) (1992) *Teaching Large Classes in Higher Education.* London: Kogan Page.

Gibbs, G., Jenkins, A. and Wisker, G. (1992) *Assessing More Students.* Oxford: PCFC/ Rewley Press.

Gonzaels, J. and Wagenaar, R. (eds) (2008) *Universities' Contribution to the Bologna Process: An Introduction,* 2nd edn. Bilbao, Spain: Universidad Deusto. http://www. tuning.unideusto.org/tuningeu/index.php?option=com_frontpage&Itemid=1 (accessed 2 February 2011).

Goodlad, S. and Hirst, B. (eds) (1990) *Explorations in Peer Tutoring.* Oxford: Blackwell.

Goodnow, J.J. (1991) Cognitive values and educational practice, in J. Biggs (ed) *Teaching for Learning: The View from Cognitive Psychology.* Hawthorn, Victoria: Australian Council for Educational Research.

Gow, L. and Kember, D. (1990) Does higher education promote independent learning?, *Higher Education,* 19: 307–22.

Gow, L. and Kember, D. (1993) Conceptions of teaching and their relation to student learning, *British Journal of Educational Psychology,* 63: 20–33.

Gray, D. (2001) Work-based learning, action learning and the virtual paradigm, *Journal of Further and Higher Education,* 25, 3: 315–24.

Green, W., Hammer, S. and Stephens, R. (2006) Embedding graduate skills into a first year management course: theory, practice and reflection. http://eprints .usq.edu.au/2811/2/Green_Hammer_Stephens_2006_HERDSA.pdf (accessed 2 February 2011).

Guilford, J.P. (1967) *The Nature of Human Intelligence.* New York: McGraw-Hill.

Gunstone, R. and White, R. (1981) Understanding of gravity, *Science Education,* 65: 291–9.

Guskey, T. (1986) Staff development and the process of teacher change, *Educational Researcher,* 15, 5: 5–12.

Guttman, L. (1941) The quantification of a class of attributes: a theory and a method of scale construction, in P. Horst (ed) *The Prediction of Personal Adjustment.* New York: Social Science Research Council.

Hales, L.W. and Tokar, E. (1975) The effects of quality of preceding responses on the grades assigned to subsequent responses to an essay question, *Journal of Educational Measurement,* 12: 115–17.

Harris, D. and Bell, C. (1986) *Evaluating and Assessing for Learning.* London: Kogan Page.

Hattie, J.A.C. (2009a) *Visible Learning: A Synthesis of 800+ Meta-analyses on Achievement.* London: Routledge.

Hattie, J. (2009b) The Black Box of tertiary assessment: an impending revolution, in L.H. Meyer, S. Davidson, H. Anderson et al. (eds) *Tertiary Assessment and Higher Education Student Outcomes: Policy, Practice and Research*. Wellington, New Zealand: Ako Aotearoa.

Hattie, J. and Purdie, N. (1998) The SOLO model: addressing fundamental measurement issues, in B. Dart and G. Boulton-Lewis (eds) *Teaching and Learning in Higher Education*. Camberwell, Victoria: Australian Council for Educational Research.

Hattie, J. and Watkins, D. (1988) Preferred classroom environment and approach to learning, *British Journal of Educational Psychology*, 58: 345–9.

Hattie, J., Biggs, J. and Purdie, N. (1996) Effects of learning skills interventions on student learning: a meta-analysis, *Review of Educational Research*, 66: 99–136.

Hernandez, R. (2007) The impact of innovative assessment practices on students' learning, in S. Frankland (ed) *Enhancing Teaching Learning through Assessment: Deriving an Appropriate Model*. Dordrecht, The Netherlands: Springer.

Hess, R.D. and Azuma, M. (1991) Cultural support for schooling: contrasts between Japan and the United States, *Educational Researcher*, 20, 9: 2–8.

Higher Education Council (1992) *Higher Education: Achieving Quality*. Canberra: Australian Government Publishing Service.

Hmelo, C.E., Gotterer, G.S. and Bransford, J.D. (1997) A theory-driven approach to assessing the cognitive effects of PBL, *Instructional Science*, 25: 387–408.

Ho, A. (2001) A conceptual change approach to university staff development, in D. Watkins and J. Biggs (eds) *Teaching the Chinese Learner: Psychological and Pedagogical Perspectives*. Hong Kong: Comparative Education Research Centre, University of Hong Kong/Camberwell, Victoria: Australian Council for Educational Research.

Hoddinott, J. (2000) Biggs' constructive alignment: evaluation of a pedagogical model applied to a web course. *Proceedings of ED-MEDIA 2000, World Conference on Educational Multimedia, Hypermedia and Telecommunications*, Montreal.

Holbrook, J. (1996) Using ordered-outcome items in chemistry, in J. Biggs (ed) *Testing: To Educate or to Select?* Hong Kong: Hong Kong Educational Publishing Co.

Hu, X., Aberdeer, O. and Yusman, C. (2009) Evaluation of engineering work experience programmes I: Principles. The 20th Annual Conference for the Australiasain Association for Engineering Education, University of Adelaide 6–9 December.

Hudson, L. (1966) *Contrary Imaginations*. London: Methuen.

Huet, I., Oliveira, J., Costa, N. and de Oliveira, J. (2009) The effectiveness of curriculum maps of alignment in higher education, in C. Nygaard, C. Holtham and N. Courtney (eds) *Improving Students' Learning Outcomes*. Copenhagen: Copenhagen Business School Press.

Hughes, J. (2008) Letting in the Trojan mouse: using an e-portfolio to rethink pedagogy. http://www.ascilite.org.au/conferences/melbourne08/procs/hughes.pdf (accessed 2 February 2011).

Hussey, T. and Smith, P. (2002) The trouble with learning outcomes, *Active Learning in Higher Education*, 3, 3: 220–33.

Jackson, N. (2003) Nurturing creativity through an imaginative curriculum. *Imaginative Curriculum Project*. Learning and Teaching Support Network, Higher Education Academy.

Jackson, N. (2005) Our creative enterprise, *Imaginative Curriculum Network*, Newsletter, December.

Jackson, N. and Law, R. (eds) (2010) Enabling a More Complete Education: Encouraging, Recognising and Valuing Life-wide Learning in Higher Education.

Conference held 13–14 April, University of Surrey. http://life-widelearning conference.pbworks.com/ (accessed 2 February 2011).

Jackson, N., Oliver, M., Shaw, M. and Wisdom, J. (eds) (2006) *Developing Creativity in Higher Education: An Imaginative Curriculum*. Abingdon: Routledge.

James, W. (1899/1962) *Talks to Teachers on Psychology*, original edn New York: Henry Holt, reprinted New York: Dover.

Jervis, L. and Jervis, L. (2005) What is the constructivism in constructive alignment?, *BEE-j*, 6, November. http://www.bioscience.heacademyac.uk/journal/vol6/Beej-6-5.pdf

Jervis, L., Jervis, L. and Giovannelli, D. (2006) Aligning biochemistry to the interests of biology students using haloperoxidase to illustrate reactions of environmental and biomedical importance, *Biochemistry and Molecular Biology Education*, 33, 4: 293–301.

Johnson, D.W. and Johnson, R.T. (1990) *Learning Together and Alone: Cooperation, Competition and Individualization*. Englewood Cliffs, NJ: Prentice-Hall.

Johnston, D. (2002) Private communication.

Jones, J., Jones, A. and Ker, P. (1994) Peer tutoring for academic credit, *HERDSA News*, 16, 3: 3–5.

Jones, R.M. (1968) *Fantasy and Feeling in Education*. New York: New York University Press.

Kandlbinder, P. and Peseta, T. (2009) Key concepts in postgraduate certificates in higher education teaching and learning in Australasia and the United Kingdom, *International Journal for Academic Development*, 14, 1: 19–31.

Keller, F. (1968) 'Goodbye teacher . . .', *Journal of Applied Behavior Analysis*, 1: 79–89.

Kember, D. (1998) Teaching beliefs and their impact on students' approach to learning, in B. Dart and G. Boulton-Lewis (eds) *Teaching and Learning in Higher Education*. Camberwell, Victoria: Australian Council for Educational Research.

Kember, D. (2000) *Action Learning and Action Research: Improving the Quality of Teaching and Learning*. London: Kogan Page.

Kember, D. (2001) Transforming teaching through action research, in D. Watkins and J. Biggs (eds) *Teaching the Chinese Learner: Psychological and Pedagogical Perspectives*. Hong Kong: Comparative Education Research Centre, University of Hong Kong/Camberwell, Victoria: Australian Council for Educational Research.

Kember, D. and Kelly, M. (1993) *Improving Teaching through Action Research*. Green Guide No. 14. Campbelltown, NSW: Higher Education Research and Development Society of Australasia.

Kember, D. and McKay, J. (1996) Action research into the quality of student learning: a paradigm for faculty development, *Journal of Higher Education*, 67: 528–54.

King, A. (1990) Enhancing peer interaction and learning in the classroom through reciprocal questioning, *American Educational Research Journal*, 27: 664–87.

Kingsland, A. (1995) Integrated assessment: the rhetoric and the students' view, in P. Little, M. Ostwald and G. Ryan (eds) *Research and Development in Problem-based Learning. Volume 3: Assessment and Evaluation*. Newcastle, NSW: Australian Problem Based Learning Network.

Knapper, C. and Cropley, A. (2000) *Lifelong Learning in Higher Education*. London: Kogan Page.

Knight, P. (2006) The assessment of 'wicked' competences. http://kn.open.ac.uk/public/getfile.cfm?documentfileid=10242 (accessed 2 February 2011).

Knight, P. and Trowler, P.R. (2000) Departmental level cultures and the improvement of teaching and learning, *Studies in Higher Education*, 25: 69–83.

Knight, P. and Yorke, M. (2004) *Assessment, Learning and Employability*. Buckingham: SRHE/Open University Press.

Krathwohl, D.R., Bloom, B.S. and Masia, B.B. (1973) *Taxonomy of Educational Objectives, the Classification of Educational Goals. Handbook II: Affective Domain.* New York: David McKay.

Ladyshewsky, R. (2006) Aligning assessment, rewards, behaviours and outcomes in group learning tasks. Paper presented at Evaluation and Assessment Conference: Enhancing Student Learning, 30 November – 1 December, Curtin University, W.A.

Lai, P. and Biggs, J.B. (1994) Who benefits from mastery learning?, *Contemporary Educational Psychology*, 19: 13–23.

Lai, P. and Tang, C. (1999) Constraints affecting the implementation of a problem-based learning strategy in university courses. Implementing problem-based learning. *Proceedings from the 1st Asia-Pacific Conference on Problem-based Learning*, Hong Kong: The Problem-based Learning Project.

Lake, D. (1999) Helping students to go SOLO: teaching critical numeracy in the biological sciences, *Journal of Biological Education*, 33: 191–8.

Lane, B. (2006) Cheating study dismays dons, *The Australian: Higher Education*, 22 February.

Laurillard, D. (2002) *Rethinking University Teaching*. London: Routledge Falmer.

Leach, L., Neutze, G. and Zepke, N. (2001) Assessment and empowerment: some critical questions, *Assessment and Evaluation in Higher Education*, 26: 293–305.

Lebrun, M. (2007) Quality towards an expected harmony: pedagogy and technology speaking together about innovation, *Association for the Advancement of Computing in Education Journal*, 15, 2: 115–30.

Leinhardt, G., McCarthy Young, K. and Merriman, J. (1995) Integrating professional knowledge: the theory of practice and the practice of theory, *Learning and Instruction*, 5: 401–8.

Lejk, M. and Wyvill, M. (2001a) Peer assessment of contributions to a group project: a comparison of holistic and category based approaches, *Assessment and Evaluation in Higher Education*, 26: 61–72.

Lejk, M. and Wyvill, M. (2001b) The effect of inclusion of self-assessment with peer-assessment of contributions to a group project: a quantitative study of secret and agreed assessments, *Assessment and Evaluation in Higher Education*, 26: 551–62.

Lohman, D.F. (1993) Teaching and testing to develop fluid abilities, *Educational Researcher*, 22, 7: 12–23.

Lynn, L.E. (1996) *What is the Case Method? A Guide and Casebook.* Tokyo: The Foundation for Advanced Studies on International Development.

McCabe, P., Purcell, A., Baker, E., Madill, C. and Trembath, D. (2009) Case based learning: one route to evidence based practice, *Evidence-based Communication Assessment and Intervention*, 3, 4: 208–19.

McGregor, D. (1960) *The Human Side of Enterprise*. New York: McGraw-Hill.

McKay, J. and Kember, D. (1997) Spoon feeding leads to regurgitation: a better diet can result in more digestible learning outcomes, *Higher Education Research and Development*, 16: 55–68.

McKeachie, W., Pintrich, P., Lin, Y.G. and Smith, D. (1986) *Teaching and Learning in the College Classroom*. Lansing, MI: University of Michigan, Office of Educational Research and Improvement.

MacKenzie, A. and White, R. (1982) Fieldwork in geography and long-term memory structures, *American Educational Research Journal*, 19, 4: 623–32.

McMahon, T. and Thakore, H. (2006) Achieving constructive alignment: putting outcomes first, *The Quality of Higher Education (Aukštojo mokslo kokybė)*, 3: 10–19.

McNaught, C., Lam, P., Ong, D. and Lau L. (2007) Challenges in assessnments in a case-based science course, in S. Frankland (ed) *Enhancing Teaching Learning through Assessment: Deriving an Appropriate Model* Dordrecht, The Netherlands: Springer.

Magin, D. (2001) A novel technique for comparing the reliability of multiple peer assessments with that of single teacher assessments of group process work, *Assessment and Evaluation in Higher Education*, 26: 139–52.

Maier, P. and Warren, A. (2000) *Integrating Technology in Learning and Teaching*. London: Kogan Page.

Maier, P., Barnett, L., Warren, A. and Brunner, D. (1998) *Using Technology in Teaching and Learning*. London: Kogan Page.

Marton, F. (1981) Phenomenography – describing conceptions of the world around us, *Instructional Science*, 10: 177–200.

Marton, F. and Booth, S.A. (1997) *Learning and Awareness*. Hillsdale, NJ: Lawrence Erlbaum.

Marton, F. and Säljö, R. (1976a) On qualitative differences in learning – I: outcome and process, *British Journal of Educational Psychology*, 46: 4–11.

Marton, F. and Säljö, R. (1976b) On qualitative differences in learning – II: outcome as a function of the learner's conception of the task, *British Journal of Educational Psychology*, 46: 115–27.

Masters, G. (1987) *New Views of Student Learning: Implications for Educational Measurement*. Research working paper 87.11. Melbourne, Victoria: University of Melbourne, Centre for the Study of Higher Education.

Masters, G.N. (1988) Partial credit model, in J.P. Keeves (ed) *Handbook of Educational Research Methodology, Measurement and Evaluation*. London: Pergamon Press.

Mazur, E. (1998) *Peer Instruction: A User's Manual*. Englewood Cliffs, NJ: Prentice-Hall.

Messick, S.J. (1989) Meaning and values in test validation: the science and ethics of assessment, *Educational Researcher*, 18, 2: 5–11.

Meyer, J.H.F. and Land, R. (2003) Threshold concepts and troublesome knowledge (1): Linkages to ways of thinking and practising within the disciplines. http://www.utwente.nl/so/vop/nieuwsbrief_17/land_paper.pdf (accessed 2 February 2011).

Meyer, J.H.F and Land, R. (2006) *Overcoming Barriers to Student Understanding*. London: Routledge.

Morris, M.M. (2008) Evaluating university teaching and learning in an outcome-based model: replanting Bloom. Doctoral dissertation, University of Wollongong.

Morris, S. (2001) Too many minds miss the mark, *The Australian*, 5 September.

Moss, P.A. (1992) Shifting conceptions of validity in educational measurement: implications for performance assessment, *Review of Educational Research*, 62: 229–58.

Moss, P.A. (1994) Can there be validity without reliability? *Educational Researcher*, 23, 2: 5–12.

Moulding, N.T. (2010) Intelligent design: student perceptions of teaching and learning in large social work classes, *Higher Education Research and Development*, 29, 2: 151–65.

Muldoon, N. and Lee, C. (2007) Formative and summative assessment and the notion of constructive alignment, in S. Frankland (ed) *Enhancing Teaching Learning through Assessment: Deriving an Appropriate Model.* Dordrecht, The Netherlands: Springer.

National Center for Supplemental Instruction (1994) *Review of Research Concerning the Effectiveness of SI.* Kansas City, MO: NCSI, University of Missouri at Kansas City.

Nestel, D. and Kidd, J. (2005) Peer assisted learning in patient-centred interviewing: the impact on student tutors. *Medical Teacher,* 27, 5: 439–44.

Newble, D. and Clarke, R. (1986) The approaches to learning of students in a traditional and in an innovative problem-based medical school, *Medical Education,* 20: 267–73.

Nightingale, S., Carew, A. and Fung, J. (2007) Application of constructive alignment principles to engineering education: have we really changed? *Proceedings of the 2007 Australasian Association for Engineering Education Conference,* Melbourne.

Norton, L. (2004) Using assessment criteria as learning criteria: a case study in psychology, *Assessment and Evaluation in Higher Education,* 29, 6: 687–702.

Norton, L. (2009) *Action Research in Teaching and Learning: A Practical Guide to Conducting Pedagogical Research in Universities.* London: Routledge.

Novak, J.D. (1979) Applying psychology and philosophy to the improvement of laboratory teaching, *The American Biology Teacher,* 41: 466–70.

Perkins, D. (1999) The many faces of constructivism, *Educational Leadership,* 57, 3: 6–11.

Perkins, D. (2006) Constructivism and troublesome knowledge, in J.H.F. Meyer and R. Land (eds) *Overcoming Barriers to Student Understanding: Threshold Concepts and Troublesome Knowledge.* London: Routledge.

Petty, G. (2006) *Evidence-based Teaching.* Cheltenham: Nelson Thornes.

Piaget, J. (1950) *The Psychology of Intelligence.* London: Routledge & Kegan Paul.

Pintrich, P.R. and Schunk, D.H. (2002) *Motivation in Education: Theory, Research, and Applications.* Upper Saddle River, NJ: Merrill-Prentice Hall.

Pope, N. (2001) An examination of the use of peer rating for formative assessment in the context of the theory of consumption values, *Assessment and Evaluation in Higher Education,* 26: 235–46.

Prosser, M. and Trigwell, K. (1999) *Understanding Learning and Teaching: The Experience in Higher Education.* Buckingham: Open University Press.

Race, P. and Brown, S. (1993) *500 Tips for Tutors.* London: Kogan Page.

Raeburn, P., Muldoon, N. and Bookallil, C. (2009) Blended spaces, work-based learning and constructive alignment: impacts on student engagement, Proceedings ascilite Auckland 2009 *Same Places, Different Spaces,* 6–9 December. http://www.ascilite.org.au/conferences/auckland09/procs/ (accessed 7 February 2011).

Ramsden, P. (1984) The context of learning, in F. Marton, D. Hounsell and N. Entwistle (eds) *The Experience of Learning.* Edinburgh: Scottish Academic Press.

Ramsden, P. (1992) *Learning to Teach in Higher Education.* London: Routledge.

Ramsden, P. (2003) *Learning to Teach in Higher Education,* 2nd edn. London: Routledge.

Ramsden, P., Beswick, D. and Bowden, J. (1986) Effects of learning skills interventions on first year university students' learning, *Human Learning,* 5: 151–64.

Rosecoe, R. and Chi, M.T.H. (2007) Understanding tutor learning: knowledge-building and knowledge-telling in peer tutors' explanations and questions, *Review of Educational Research,* 77, 4: 534–74.

Rudner, L. and Gagne, P. (2001) An overview of three approaches to scoring written essays by computer, *Practical Assessment, Research and Evaluation*, 7, 26. http://pareonline.net/getvn.asp?v=7&n=26 (accessed 2 February 2011).

Rust, C. (2002) The impact of assessment on student learning: how can the research literature practically help to inform the development of departmental assessment strategies and learner-centred assessment practices?, *Active Learning in Higher Education*, 3: 145–58. http://alh.sagepub.com/cgi/content/abstract/3/2/145 (accessed 2 February 2011).

Ryan, G. (1997) Promoting educational integrity in PBL programs – choosing carefully and implementing wisely, in J. Conway, R. Fisher, L. Sheridan- Burns and G. Ryan (eds) *Research and Development in Problem-based Learning. Volume 4: Integrity, Innovation, Integration*. Newcastle, NSW: Australian Problem Based Learning Network.

Ryle, G. (1949) *The Concept of Mind*. Chicago: University of Chicago Press.

Saberton, S. (1985) Learning partnerships, *HERDSA News*, 7, 1: 3–5.

Salmon, G. (2003) *E-moderating: The Key to Online Teaching and Learning*. London: Kogan Page.

Santhanam, E., Leach, C. and Dawson, C. (1998) Concept mapping: how should it be introduced, and is there a long term benefit?, *Higher Education*, 35: 317–28.

Savin-Baden, M. (2000) *Problem-based Learning in Higher Education: Untold Stories*. Buckingham: Society for Research into Higher Education/Open University Press.

Scardamalia, M. and Bereiter, C. (1999) Schools as knowledge-building organizations, in D. Keating and C. Hertzman (eds) *Today's Children, Tomorrow's Society: The Developmental Health and Wealth of Nations*. New York: Guilford.

Scardamalia, M. and Bereiter, C. (2006) Knowledge building: theory, pedagogy, and technology, in R.K. Sawyer (ed) *The Cambridge Handbook of the Learning Sciences*. New York: Cambridge University Press.

Scardamalia, M., Bereiter, C. and Lamon, M. (1994) The CSILE Project: trying to bring the classroom into World 3, in K. McGilley (ed) *Classroom Lessons: Integrating Cognitive Theory and Classroom Practice*. Cambridge, MA: MIT Press.

Schmeck, R. (ed) (1988) *Learning Strategies and Learning Styles*. New York: Plenum.

Schön, D.A. (1983) *The Reflective Practitioner: How Professionals Think in Action*. London: Temple Smith.

Schwartz, S. (2010) Restoring wisdom to universities, 2010 Annual Lecture, Macquarie University. http://www.vc.mq.edu.au/speeches.php (accessed 2 February 2011).

Scouller, K.M. (1996) Influence of assessment methods on students' learning approaches, perceptions, and preferences: assignment essay versus short answer questions, *Research and Development in Higher Education*, 19, 3: 776–81.

Scouller, K. (1997) Students' perceptions of three assessment methods: assignment essay, multiple choice question examination, short answer examination. Paper presented to the Higher Education Research and Development Society of Australasia, Adelaide, 9–12 July.

Scouller, K. (1998) The influence of assessment method on students' learning approaches: multiple choice question examination vs. essay assignment, *Higher Education*, 35: 453–72.

Seldin, P. (1997) *The Teaching Portfolio: A Practical Guide to Improved Performance and Promotion/Tenure Decisions*. Bolton, MA: Anker.

Shaw, G. (ed.) (2005) *Tertiary Teaching: Dealing with Diversity*. Darwin: Charles Darwin University Press Centre for Learning Research.

Shepard, L.A. (1993) Evaluating test validity, *Review of Research in Education*, 19: 405–50.

Shepherd, J. (2006) Mistakes? We've seen a few. http://www.soa.org/library/research/actuarial-research-clearing-house/2006/january/arch06v40n1-iv.pdf (accessed 2 February 2011).

Shermis, M. and Burstein, J. (eds) (2003) *Automated Essay Scoring: A Cross-disciplinary Perspective*. Mahwah, NJ: Lawrence Erlbaum Associates.

Shuell, T.J. (1986) Cognitive conceptions of learning, *Review of Educational Research*, 56: 411–36.

Simpson, E. J. (1972) *The Classification of Educational Objectives in the Psychomotor Domain*. Washington, DC: Gryphon House.

Skinner, B.F. (1968) *The Technology of Teaching*. New York: Appleton-Century-Crofts.

Smythe, D. (2006) Research paper assignments that prevent plagiarism, in D. Carless, G. Joughin, N.F. Liu and associates (eds) *How Assessment Supports Learning*. Hong Kong: Hong Kong University Press.

Sonnemann, U. (1954) *Existence and Therapy*. New York: Grune & Stratton.

Starch, D. (1913a) Reliability of grading work in mathematics, *School Review*, 21: 254–9.

Starch, D. (1913b) Reliability of grading work in history, *School Review*, 21: 676–81.

Starch, D. and Elliott, E.C. (1912) Reliability of the grading of high school work in English, *School Review*, 20: 442–57.

Stedman, L.C. (1997) International achievement differences: an assessment of a new perspective, *Educational Researcher*, 26, 3: 4–15.

Steffe, L. and Gale, J. (eds) (1995) *Constructivism in Education*. Hillsdale, NJ: Lawrence Erlbaum.

Stenhouse, L. (1975) *Introduction to Curriculum Research and Development*. London: Heinemann Educational.

Stephenson, J. and Laycock, M. (1993) *Using Contracts in Higher Education*. London: Kogan Page.

Sternberg, R.J. (ed) (1988) *Handbook of Human Intelligence*. New York: Cambridge University Press.

Sternberg, R.J. and Zhang, L.F. (eds) (2001) *Perspectives on Thinking, Learning, and Cognitive Styles*. Mahwah, NJ: Lawrence Erlbaum.

Stigler, J. and Hiebert, J. (1999) *The Teaching Gap*. New York: Free Press.

Sumsion, J. and Goodfellow, J. (2004) Identifying generic skills through curriculum mapping: a critical evaluation, *Higher Education Research and Development*, 23: 329–46.

Susskind, A. (2006) Cheat wave, *The Bulletin*, 18 October.

Tait, H., Entwistle, N.J. and McCune, V. (1998) ASSIST: a reconceptualisation of the Approaches to Study Inventory, in C. Rust (ed) *Improving Students as Learners*. Oxford: Oxford Brookes University/Oxford Centre for Staff and Learning Development.

Tang, C. (1991) Effects of two different assessment procedures on tertiary students' approaches to learning. Doctoral dissertation, University of Hong Kong. http://sunzi1.lib.hku.hk/hkuto/record/B31232413 (accessed 2 February 2011).

Tang, C. (1993) Spontaneous collaborative learning: a new dimension in student learning experience?, *Higher Education Research and Development*, 12: 115–30.

Tang, C. (1996) Collaborative learning: the latent dimension in Chinese students' learning, in D. Watkins and J. Biggs (eds) *The Chinese Learner: Cultural, Psychological and Contextual Influences*. Hong Kong: Centre for Comparative Research in Education/Camberwell, Victoria: Australian Council for Educational Research.

Tang, C. (1998) Effects of collaborative learning on the quality of assessments, in B. Dart and G. Boulton-Lewis (eds) (1998) *Teaching and Learning in Higher Education*. Camberwell, Victoria: Australian Council for Educational Research.

Tang, C. (2000) Reflective diaries as a means of facilitating and assessing reflection. Paper presented to the Pacific Rim Conference on Higher Education Planning and Assessment, Hilo, Hawaii, 3–7 June. www.ecu.edu.au/conferences/herdsa/main/papers/nonref/pdf/CatherineTang (accessed 2 February 2011).

Tang, C., Lai, P., Tang, W. et al. (1997) Developing a context-based PBL model, in J. Conway, R. Fisher, L. Sheridan- Burns and G. Ryan (eds) *Research and Development in Problem-based Learning. Volume 4: Integrity, Innovation, Integration.* Newcastle, NSW: Australian Problem Based Learning Network.

Taylor, C. (1994) Assessment for measurement or standards: the peril and promise of large-scale assessment reform, *American Educational Research Journal*, 31: 231–62.

Taylor, R. and Canfield, P. (2007) Learning to be a scholarly teaching faculty: cultural change through shared leadership, in A. Brew and J. Sachs (eds) *The Transformed University: Scholarship of Teaching and Learning in Action*. Sydney: Sydney University Press.

Thomas, E.L. and Robinson, H.A. (1982) *Improving Reading in Every Class: A Source Book for Teachers.* Boston, MA: Allyn & Bacon.

Tiwari, A., Chan, S., Sullivan, P.L., Dixon, A.S. and Tang, C. (1999) Enhancing students' critical thinking through problem-based learning. Paper presented to the 1st Asia-Pacific Conference on Problem-Based Learning, Hong Kong, 9–11 December.

Tomporowski, P.D. and Ellis, N.R. (1986) Effects of exercise on cognitive processes: a review, *Psychological Bulletin*, 99: 338–46.

Toohey, S. (2002) *Designing Courses for Universities.* Buckingham: Open University Press.

Topping, K.J. (1996) The effectiveness of peer tutoring in further and higher education: a typology and review of the literature, *Higher Education*, 32: 321–45.

Topping, K.J. (2005) Trends in peer learning, *Educational Psychology*, 25, 6: 631–45.

Torrance, H. (ed) (1994) *Evaluating Authentic Assessment: Problems and Possibilities in New Approaches to Assessment.* Buckingham: Open University Press.

Trigwell, K. and Prosser, M. (1990) Using student learning outcome measures in the evaluation of teaching, *Research and Development in Higher Education*, 13: 390–7.

Trigwell, K. and Prosser, M. (1991) Changing approaches to teaching: a relational perspective, *Studies in Higher Education*, 22: 251–66.

Trigwell, K., Martin, E., Benjamin, J. and Prosser, M. (2000) Scholarship of teaching: a model, *Higher Education Research and Development*, 19, 2: 155–68.

Trueman, M. and Hartley, J. (1996) A comparison between the time-management skills and academic performance of mature and traditional-entry university students, *Higher Education*, 32: 199–215.

Tulving, E. (1985) How many memory systems are there? *American Psychologist*, 40: 385–98.

Tyler, R.W. (1949) *Basic Principles of Curriculum and Instruction.* Chicago: University of Chicago Press.

Tyler, S. (2001) The perfect teaching tool? Paper presented to Learning Matters Symposium 2001, Victoria University, Melbourne, 6–7 December.

Tynjala, P. (1998) Writing as a tool for constructive learning – students' learning experiences during an experiment, *Higher Education*, 36: 209–30.

von Glasersfeld, E. (1995) *Radical Constructivism: A Way of Knowing and Learning.* Washington, DC: The Falmer Press.

Walker, J. (1998) Student plagiarism in universities: what are we doing about it?, *Higher Education Research and Development*, 17: 89–106.

Walsh, A. (2007) An exploration of Biggs' constructive alignment in the context of work-based learning, *Assessment and Evaluation in Higher Education*, 32, 1: 79–87.

Ware, J. and Williams, R.G. (1975) The Dr Fox effect: a study of lecturer effectiveness and ratings of instruction, *Journal of Medical Education*, 50: 149–56.

Waters, L. and Johnston, C. (2004) Web-delivered, problem-based learning in organization behaviour: a new form of CAOS, *Higher Education Research and Development*, 23, 4: 413–31.

Watkins, D. and Biggs, J. (eds) (1996) *The Chinese Learner: Cultural, Psychological and Contextual Influences.* Hong Kong: Centre for Comparative Research in Education/ Camberwell, Victoria: Australian Council for Educational Research.

Watkins, D. and Hattie, J. (1985) A longitudinal study of the approach to learning of Australian tertiary students, *Human Learning*, 4: 127–42.

Watson, J. (1996) Peer assisted learning in economics at the University of NSW. Paper presented to the 4th Annual Teaching Economics Conference, Northern Territory University, Darwin, 28 June.

Watson, J. (1997) A peer support scheme in quantitative methods. Paper presented to the Biennial Conference, Professional Development Centre, University of NSW, 20 November.

Webb, G. (1997) Deconstructing deep and surface: towards a critique of phenomenography, *Higher Education*, 33: 195–212.

Weller, M. (2002) Assessment issues in a web-based course, *Assessment and Evaluation in Higher Education*, 27: 109–16.

Wiggins, G. (1989) Teaching to the (authentic) test, *Educational Leadership*, 46: 41–7.

Wilson, K. (1997) Wording it up: plagiarism and the interdiscourse of international students. Paper presented to the Annual Conference, Higher Education Research and Development Society of Australasia, Adelaide, 8–11 July.

Wiske, M.S. (ed) (1998) *Teaching for Understanding: Linking Research and Practice.* San Francisco, CA: Jossey-Bass.

Wittrock, M.C. (1977) The generative processes of memory, in M.C. Wittrock (ed.) *The Human Brain.* Englewood Cliffs, NJ: Prentice-Hall.

Wong, C.S. (1994) Using a cognitive approach to assess achievement in secondary school mathematics. Unpublished MEd dissertation, University of Hong Kong.

Yamane, D. (2006) Concept preparation assignments: a strategy for creating discussion-based courses, *Teaching Sociology*, 34: 236–48.

Yuen-Heung, J., To, D. and Ney, C. (2005) Measuring qualitative attributes: using a multidimensional approach to measure university learning goals. The 1st International Conference on Enhancing Teaching and Learning through Assessment, Hong Kong Polytechnic University, 13–15 June.

Zeng, K. (1999) *Dragon Gate: Competitive Examinations and Their Consequences.* London: Cassell.

Index

Note: Only the first author of multi-authored work is listed. *References* are not included in this Index. Terms that recur constantly, such as ILO, TLA, assessment, outcomes and so on, are indexed only when the reference is significant.

The Society for Research into Higher Education

The Society for Research into Higher Education (SRHE), an international body, exists to stimulate and coordinate research into all aspects of higher education. It aims to improve the quality of higher education through the encouragement of debate and publication on issues of policy, on the organization and management of higher education institutions, and on the curriculum, teaching and learning methods.

The Society is entirely independent and receives no subsidies, although individual events often receive sponsorship from business or industry. The Society is financed through corporate and individual subscriptions and has members from many parts of the world. It is an NGO of UNESCO.

Under the imprint *SRHE & Open University Press*, the Society is a specialist publisher of research, having over 80 titles in print. In addition to *SRHE News*, the Society's newsletter, the Society publishes three journals: *Studies in Higher Education* (three issues a year), *Higher Education Quarterly* and *Research into Higher Education Abstracts* (three issues a year).

The Society runs frequent conferences, consultations, seminars and other events. The annual conference in December is organized at and with a higher education institution. There are a growing number of networks which focus on particular areas of interest, including:

Access	FE/HE
Assessment	Graduate Employment
Consultants	New Technology for Learning
Curriculum Development	Postgraduate Issues
Eastern European	Quantitative Studies
Educational Development Research	Student Development

Benefits to members

Individual

- The opportunity to participate in the Society's networks
- Reduced rates for the annual conferences
- Free copies of *Research into Higher Education Abstracts*
- Reduced rates for *Studies in Higher Education*

- Reduced rates for *Higher Education Quarterly*
- Free online access to *Register of Members' Research Interests* – includes valuable reference material on research being pursued by the Society's members
- Free copy of occasional in-house publications, e.g. *The Thirtieth Anniversary Seminars Presented by the Vice-Presidents*
- Free copies of *SRHE News* and *International News* which inform members of the Society's activities and provides a calendar of events, with additional material provided in regular mailings
- A 35 per cent discount on all SRHE/Open University Press books
- The opportunity for you to apply for the annual research grants
- Inclusion of your research in the *Register of Members' Research Interests*

Corporate

- Reduced rates for the annual conference
- The opportunity for members of the Institution to attend SRHE's network events at reduced rates
- Free copies of *Research into Higher Education Abstracts*
- Free copies of *Studies in Higher Education*
- Free online access to *Register of Members' Research Interests* – includes valuable reference material on research being pursued by the Society's members
- Free copy of occasional in-house publications
- Free copies of *SRHE News* and *International News*
- A 35 per cent discount on all SRHE/Open University Press books
- The opportunity for members of the Institution to submit applications for the Society's research grants
- The opportunity to work with the Society and co-host conferences
- The opportunity to include in the *Register of Members' Research Interests* your Institution's research into aspects of higher education

Membership details: SRHE, 76 Portland Place, London W1B 1NT, UK Tel: 020 7637 2766. Fax: 020 7637 2781. email: srheoffice@srhe.ac.uk
world wide web: http://www.srhe.ac.uk./srhe/
Catalogue: SRHE & Open University Press, McGraw-Hill Education, McGraw-Hill House, Shoppenhangers Road, Maidenhead, Berkshire SL6 2QL. Tel: 01628 502500. Fax: 01628 770224. email: enquiries@openup.co.uk – web: www.openup.co.uk